The Official Book of
The Labrador Retriever

Distributed in the UNITED STATES to the Pet Trade by T.F.H. Publications, Inc., One T.F.H. Plaza, Neptune City, NJ 07753; distributed in the UNITED STATES to the Bookstore and Library Trade by National Book Network, Inc. 4720 Boston Way, Lanham MD 20706; in CANADA to the Pet Trade by H & L Pet Supplies Inc., 27 Kingston Crescent, Kitchener, Ontario N2B 2T6; Rolf C. Hagen Ltd., 3225 Sartelon Street, Montreal 382 Quebec; in CANADA to the Book Trade by Vanwell Publishing Ltd., 1 Northrup Crescent, St. Catharines, Ontario L2M 6P5 ; in ENGLAND by T.F.H. Publications, PO Box 15, Waterlooville PO7 6BQ; in AUSTRALIA AND THE SOUTH PACIFIC by T.F.H. (Australia), Pty. Ltd., Box 149, Brookvale 2100 N.S.W., Australia; in NEW ZEALAND by Brooklands Aquarium Ltd. 5 McGiven Drive, New Plymouth, RD1 New Zealand; in Japan by T.F.H. Publications, Japan—Jiro Tsuda, 10-12-3 Ohjidai, Sakura, Chiba 285, Japan; in SOUTH AFRICA by Multipet Pty. Ltd., P.O. Box 35347, Northway, 4065, South Africa. Published by T.F.H. Publications, Inc.

MANUFACTURED IN THE UNITED STATES OF AMERICA
BY T.F.H. PUBLICATIONS, INC.

The Official Book of
The Labrador Retriever

The Labrador Retriever Club, Inc.
Bernard W. Ziessow, PhD, Editor

Sandringham Chive, bred by H.M. The Queen of England, owned by Lady Jacqueline Barlow. Drawing by John Weiss.

Acknowledgments

The Official Book of the Labrador Retriever is unique. It represents the work, not of a single author, but many contributors, each sharing his or her expertise and years of experience in a given field of endeavor related to the Labrador Retriever breed. All contributors or co-authors are members of the Labrador Retriever Club, Inc., or closely associated with retriever gun dogs. Their names read like a "Who's Who" in the Labrador world. Each has devoted many hours to assure that the book is informative, authoritative and interesting; a book that will not grow old or become obsolete with the passage of time.

Following is a listing of co-authors, in alphabetical order:

Lady Jacqueline Barlow
18 Winter Avenue
St. Johns, Newfoundland AIA-IT3

Mrs. Juxi Burr
4401 Yale NE
Albuquerque, NM 87107

Mr. John V. Carroll, Jr.
The American Kennel Club
51 Madison Ave.
New York, NY 10010

Mr. Jack Chojnacki
7523 Brigham Road
Gates Mills, OH 44040

Autumn Davidson, DVM
18 Snow Court
Orindo, CA 94563

Mrs. Mary Feazell
512 Linda Lane
Arlington, TX 96010

Mrs. Marianne Foote
531 Old Horseshoe Pike
Downingstown, PA 19335

Mrs. Judith M. Hunt
38 Hayes Dr., SW
Calgary, Ab. Cda. T2V-3C3

Ann Huntington, DVM
577 East Street South
Suffield, CT 0607

Mr. Fred Kampo, Jr.
5880 Murmuring Water
Oshkosh, WI 54901

Miss Mary Knapp
Black Watch N88 W22936 N. List
Sussex, WI 53089

Miss Karen Marcus
304 Stratford
Ferndale, MI 48220

Mr. John McAssey
121 Main Street
Boise, ID 83702

Mr. Robert H. McKowen
The American Kennel Club
51 Madison Ave.
New York, NY 10010

Miss Jane Russenberger
Route 164 Box 228A
Patterson, NY 12563

Mr. A. Nelson Sills
RD1 Box 122D
Houston, DE 19954

Francis Smith-Walton, DVM, PhD
5162 Union Lake Trail
Lonsdale, MN 55046-4314

Christopher Wincek, Esq.
9690 Wilson Mills Road
Chardon, OH 44024

Mr. Robert Wolfe
3 Duck Pass Road North
St. Paul, MN 55127

Mrs. B. W. (Madge) Zicssow
32695 Redfern
Franklin, MI 48025

Dr. B. W. Ziessow, Editor

The Labrador Retriever Club, Inc.

Officers and Directors

President and AKC Delegate
A. Nelson Sills

Vice President
John Morgan, DVM

Treasurer
Bernard W. Ziessow, PhD

Secretary
Christopher Wincek, Esq.

Newsletter Editor
Ralph Mickelson

Board of Directors

Sally Bell	Richard Greenleaf, MD	Joan Shoemaker
Jane Borders	Fred Kampo	A. Nelson Sills
William Bowen	Robert Kennon, Esq.	Marshall Simonds, Esq.
Juxi Burr	John McAssey	Frances Smith, DVM
Cal Cadmus, DVM	Ralph Mickelson	Jerry Wickliffe
William Daley	John Morgan, DVM	Christopher Wincek, Esq.
Marianne Foote	Sally Munson	Bernard W. Ziessow, PhD

Contents

Ch. Tabatha's Dodena of Franklin CD, TD, WC. Photograph by Carol A. Heidl, owner.

Introduction

by Dr. Bernard W. Ziessow

The Labrador Retriever Club, Inc., published its first yearbook in 1945. This rare and coveted volume covers the period 1931 to 1945, the formative years of the Club. The names of the lady and gentlemen sportsfolk that comprised its Officers, Directors and Members read like a combination of "Who's Who" and the New York Social Registry.

These were the people that imported the first Labrador Retrievers into this country, organized the first field trials and held the first conformation events for the breed. The Certificate of Incorporation of the Labrador Retriever Club, Inc., dated October 7, 1931, states the particular objects for which the organization was formed, as follows:

(a) To maintain, foster and encourage a spirit of cooperation in the breeding, owning and exhibiting of pure-bred Labrador Retriever dogs by individuals, organizations, kennel clubs, show clubs and specialty clubs.

(b) To formulate, define, ascertain and publish the standard type of Labrador Retriever dogs and to procure said standard type and to induce the adoption of said standard type by breeders, judges, dog owners, dog-show committees and others and to endeavor to have said standard type recognized by all, so that the Labrador Retriever breed shall be judged by said standard.

(c) To encourage, foster, help, aid and assist to protect, advance and increase the interest of people in the Labrador Retriever dog breed.

Failure to comply with these objectives does a disservice to the Labrador Retriever Club and to the Labrador breed.

In April 1992, TFH Publications, Inc., indicated a strong interest in publishing a new literary work on the Labrador Retriever and sought to engage the parent club to cooperate with them to produce an authoritative and reliable book on the breed. At the publisher's suggestion we solicited the assistance of L.R.C. members and others closely associated with the breed (some nineteen in all) to contribute chapters about topics which related to their particular areas of expertise.

Hopefully, this work will, at the very least, "advance and increase the interest of people in the Labrador Retriever dog breed."

Foxhanger Merlyn, known as Hawke, looking over the tiny harbor of Quidi Vidi, Newfoundland in 1966. Photograph courtesy of Lady Jacqueline Barlow.

The Origin and Purpose of the Labrador Retriever

by Dr. Bernard W. Ziessow

The recent proliferation of books written about the Labrador Retriever is consistent with the breed's growth in popularity. All seem to have at least one thing in common: if not the first, one early chapter pertains to the origins and/or history of the Labrador Retriever. Where did he come from?

To understand the origin of the Labrador Retriever almost requires a study of the history of Newfoundland—the island whence he came. According to Dick Wolters, the first people to settle Newfoundland were the Dorset Eskimos. However, they didn't have any dogs, nor is there any evidence that any dogs inhabited the island when they arrived.

The so-called "new world" was known by whalers and fishermen as early as the 15th century. Traders from the Bristol Company (England) "discovered" Newfoundland in 1494 and attempted to establish its first settlement in 1504; however, it was not until over 100 years later that Newfoundland was finally settled, almost entirely by fishermen that jumped ship. It is said that for almost two centuries afterward, the island had no law— courts, police, schools and churches were non-existent.

Notwithstanding its harsh life, Newfoundland's fishing industry grew and prospered. Each year fleets of fishing boats from England and other European nations were sent to fish its waters. The dried salted fish was shipped to European countries, principally the Catholic countries of the south.

The rugged life in Newfoundland give us some idea of the environment in which the Labrador Retriever originated and was developed. Yet, where the dog originally came from is open to question. There are many theories pertaining to the origin of the Labrador. One states that it was a descendant of the Newfoundland dog; hence the name Lesser Newfoundland was used to describe the smaller dog. There is still no evidence, however, that any dogs existed in Newfoundland before the fishermen arrived, and it is generally agreed that the ancestors of the Newfoundland dog were also brought to the island by fishermen from European countries.

Since game was abundant on the island and a good hunting dog could provide food to supplement their fish diet, it is believed that the early settlers brought or imported dogs of good hunting stock from home. Accordingly, both the larger and smaller Newfoundland dogs were likely introduced to the island.

Because utility was an important factor, the dogs also had to be good strong swimmers and be small enough for the fisherman to take in his dory. A good friend and business associate (W. Wallace Anderson), who was born and raised in Newfoundland, reports that as late as the 1920s, Newfoundland fishermen carried a Labrador Retriever in the dory to retrieve fish that came off the trawl. He also stated that, while the larger and smaller dogs (Newfoundlands and Labradors) slept together under the house, they did not interbreed.

The Labrador's hunting and swimming ability, as well as his good disposition, did not go unnoticed by the English sportsmen. When the organized shooting of pheasant, grouse and partridges became popular among the landed gentry in the late 18th and early 19th centuries, it became the custom to replace pointers and setters with retrievers. In the early days, a retriever was simply known as a "Retriever" and the owners

FTCh. Ming, whelped July 9, 1933, became the first English and American field trial champion. Owner, Frederick T. Bedford.

The late Jay F. Carlisle, the owner of Wingan kennels and president of the Labrador Retriever Club from 1935 to 1938, is largely credited for the breed's rise in popularity in the United States.

freely interbred short-coated, long-coated and curly-coated retrievers. Many dogs were imported from Newfoundland and their owners considered them vastly superior as retrievers to any other working dogs.

Colonel Hawker, in 1830, referred to the St. John's breed of water dogs as, "by far the best for any kind of shooting. He is generally black and no bigger than a pointer, very fine in legs with short smooth hair and does not carry his tail so much curled; is extremely quick retrieving, swimming and fighting."

The Second Earl of Malmsbury is credited to have imported some of the first St. John's or Labrador dogs about or before 1830. His son, the Third Earl (1807–1889) imported many and bred them. Among others who imported dogs from Newfoundland about 1835 were the Fifth Duke of Buccleuch, his brother Lord John Scott and the Tenth Earl of Home.

The Third Earl of Malmsbury in a letter written to the Sixth Duke of Buccleuch said: "We always call mine Labrador dogs and I have kept the breed as pure as I could from the first I had—the real breed may be known by their having a close coat which turns water off like oil, and, above all, a tail like an otter." However, all breeders did not always "keep the breed pure." Many breeders, realizing the excellent qualities, crossed Labradors with other retrievers. Still, if a Labrador is crossed with some other strain, the Labrador type nearly always predominated and their descendants were most always called Labradors.

Stonehenge, writing in 1873, included the following in his description and scale of points of the Labrador Retriever:

In 1923 the Hon. A. Holland Hibbert (later Lord Knutsford) wrote an article which enumerates various points of the breed conformation: "Having been asked to write something of description and characteristics of the Labrador

National retriever trial in Barrington, IL in December 1944.

"Symmetry and temperament—the symmetry and elegance of this dog are considerable and should be valued highly. The evidences of a good temper must be regarded with great care since his utility depends on his disposition."

The Labrador Retriever was first recognized as a special breed by the Kennel Club (England) on July 7, 1903, at which time it was decided to give classes at the Kennel Club Show for Labradors as a separate breed. On November 3, 1903, Labradors were definitely recognized as a separate breed and on January 3, 1905, they were separately classified as a sub-variety of retrievers.

Retriever for those taking an interest in the breed, let me first give recognized description:

Shoulder Height

21 to 23 inches
Bitches 2 or 3 inches less

Average Weight

About 60 lbs.

Coat

Straight, neither wave nor curl, the thicker and closer the better. Dogs have a harder and coarser coat than bitches.

Head

Skull broad and well-domed leaving plenty of 'brain pan.' Ears rather far back and set fairly high (but not cocked up like a collie's) and rather small. Avoid mastiff-like head with its heavy hang and shape of ears. The 'stop' is not very pronounced. Muzzle on the square side as opposed to the snipey shape, which is much to be avoided.

Colour of Eye

Brown—the colour of burnt sugar, a generous affectionate aspect is characteristic of the breed.

Shoulders and Body

Rather laid back, chest on the broad side—ribs really well sprung. Body compact—back straight and good loins.

Feet and Legs

Forelegs straight and the more cat-like the feet the better. Splay feet are much to be avoided.

Tail

The nearer the level carriage and the closer resemblance to an otter tail the better, i.e., short and thick at stump with the hair underneath divided almost as if parted.

General Appearance

The general appearance should be that of a strong-built, short coupled, very active dog. Wider in the head than a flat coat and wider through the chest. Ribs well sprung. Coat close and dense, free from curl and wave. Skull wide giving plenty of brain room. Tail short and straight. Eyes colour of burnt sugar. Feet small and upright."

Labrador Retriever Club meeting in Peapack, NJ in November 1935.

THE LABRADOR IN AMERICA

It was not until 1917 that the first Labrador was registered by the American Kennel Club. In 1927, there were only 23 retrievers of all kinds (Labradors, Goldens, Flat Coat, Curly Coat and Chesapeake) registered with the AKC. During the 1920s, American sportsmen, attempting to emulate the Scottish sport of pass shooting, brought in young Scottish gamekeepers, bought guns from the finest London gunsmiths and imported dogs from British kennels. Some wealthy families virtually turned their estates into shooting preserves. It wasn't long before the "shoots" developed into field trials. The first trial licensed by the AKC was held December 21, 1931. According to James Cowie, early licensed Labrador Retriever trials were the result of the work of Franklin B. Lord, the moving force behind the small group of sportsmen that organized the Labrador Retriever Club.

The Labrador Retriever Club was incorporated under the laws of the state of New York on October 7, 1931. The club's first annual specialty show was held on May 18, 1933 in New York City. The judge was Mrs. Marshal Field, and best in show was awarded to Mr. F.B. Lord's Boli of Blake, who was the first Labrador to earn his American championship on November 1, 1933.

The first best in show Labrador in this country, Ch. Earlsmoor Moor of Arden, ran and placed in field trials. When Labradors were a relatively rare breed, his show record would,

Ch. Shamrock Acres Light Brigade.

even today, be considered remarkable: times shown 42, best of breed 40, placed in Sporting Group 27 times, won Sporting Group 12 times, awarded best in show five times, and won the national specialty five times. Based on the number of the Labradors shown today, perhaps

ice cold water in Minnesota to retrieve a shot bird; he'll work all day hunting doves in the heat of the southwest. His only reward is a pat for a job well done.

As a judge of the breed for over 35 years and a breeder since 1951, my personal description of the breed is

FTCh. Blind of Arden, whelped March 20, 1933, was America's first Labrador field trial champion.

this proves proliferation sometimes works in reverse.

It is important for any Labrador fancier or judge to recognize and appreciate that the Labrador imported into England and introduced into this country by gentlemen and lady sportsfolk for one, and only one, purpose—to retrieve upland game and water fowl.

The American sportsmen adopted the breed from England and subsequently developed and trained the dog to fulfill the hunting needs of this country. Today, as in the past, the Labrador will eagerly enter

that of a strongly built, medium-size, short-coupled, active dog possessing an athletic, well-balanced conformation that enables it to function as a retrieving gundog; the substance and soundness to hunt waterfowl or upland game for long hours under difficult conditions; the character and quality to win in the show ring; and the temperament to be a family companion. Physical features and mental characteristics should denote a dog bred to perform as an efficient retriever of game with a stable temperament suitable for a variety of pursuits beyond the hunting environment.

Above all the Labrador Retriever must be well balanced: the components of his anatomy in proper correlation, enabling him to move in the show ring or run in the field with little or no effort. The true Labrador possesses elegance without over-refinement and substance without lumber or cloddiness.

The officers and directors of the Labrador Retriever Club, as well as the majority of the other sportsmen involved in the breed, are disturbed with a recent trend towards the two so-called "types" of Labrador Retrievers: field dogs and show dogs. We are concerned if the trend persists that the breed may be divided into two separate and distinct kinds of dogs, as have so many other breeds in the Sporting Group.

It is our opinion that the show dog and field dog should have exactly the same conformation and condition. Additionally, we believe the first question that should come to mind in judging the Labrador Retriever is "Can the dog do the job he was originally intended to do?"

Dual Ch.-NFTCh. Shed of Arden owned by Paul Bakewell III.

The Labrador Dog

by Franklin B. Lord

Bramshaw Bob owned by Lorna Countess Howe.

"If you look to its antiquity, it is most ancient.

If to its dignity, it is most honorable."

The above, extracted from fly leaf of "A History of the Schuylkill Fishing Company" (The Fish House) 1732-1888, now the oldest club in the world, seems a fitting description of the Labrador breed.

Those who really want to get a thorough knowledge of the Labrador dog and its history should study *The Labrador Dog, Its Home and History* by Lord George Scott and Sir John Middleton, London, 1936, and *The Labrador Retriever* by Leslie Sprake (London, 1933). We have Lord George Scott's permission to quote from his book, but as our space is limited we state that all the information and the following quotations come from his book unless otherwise indicated by the context.

The Labrador dog did not come from Labrador but from Newfoundland, mostly from the vicinity of St. James and White Bay. There were two kinds of dogs on Newfoundland, the big, long-haired, black dog known as the Newfoundland and the small short-haired dog known as the Labrador or St. John's breed. Colonel Peter Hawker in his "Advice to Young Sportsmen" (1814) describes the two breeds. (See *The Labrador Dog*, p. 17.) We quote the following from the first American edition, 1846,

p. 108, under the heading "New-foundland Dogs":

"Here we are a little in the dark. Every canine brute, that is nearly as big as a jackass and as hairy as a bear, is denominated a fine New-foundland dog. Very different,

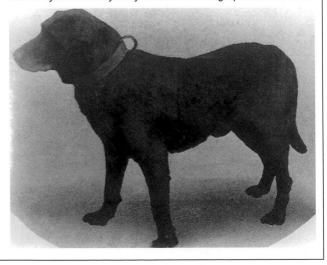

Avon bred by the Third Earl of Malmesbury and owned by the Sixth Duke of Buccleuch. Photograph taken in 1885.

however, are both the proper Labra-dor and St. John's breed of these animals. . ."

We do not believe that Hawker meant to distin-guish between the proper Labrador and the St. Johns breed, but suggest that the "and" be read as "or." He continues to describe the Labrador as distinguished from the Newfoundland:

"The other, by far the best for every kind of shooting, is more often black than any other color and scarcely big-ger than a pointer. He is made rather long in the head and nose; pretty deep in the chest; very fine in the legs;

has short or smooth hair; does not carry his tail so much curled as the other; and is extremely quick and active in running, swimming, or fighting.

"Their sense of smelling is scarcely to be credited. Their dis-crimination of scent, in following a wounded pheasant through a whole co-vert full of game, or pinioned wild fowl through a furze brake or warren of rabbits, appears almost im-possible."

The dogs were used by the fishermen of Newfoundland to haul in the winter's wood and to retrieve fish that had become unhooked near the surface and the dogs were sent overboard to retrieve them. The esteem with which these dogs were held by their

Ben of Hyde owned by Lady Radcliffe. Photograph taken in 1899.

owners is indicated by a letter in *The Field*, March 3, 1870, written from Halifax, a part of which we quote:

"I have always thought that this smooth breed of Labrador dogs cannot be surpassed for sagacity by any of the canine race. I have offered as high as ten sovereigns to very poor men for their dogs, which has been refused, having been told many times that no sum of money would tempt them to part with their chief support, their faithful ally."

Neither Lord George Scott or Sprake seem to be able to state definitely when the first Labrador was brought to England but both agree that it was in the last decade of the 18th century or the first decade of the 19th. The former quotes from the "Shooting Journals of the Second Earl of Malmesbury" (1778-1841) which proves that he had what he called a Newfoundland dog in December 1809. Scott seems to think that these were the small dogs described by Hawker at about the same period and there is further corroborative evidence to support this fact because the Third Earl of Malmesbury (1807-1889) who in-

Buccleuch Daniel in 1926.

herited the kennel is quoted as saying, "we always called mine Labrador dogs and I have kept the breed as pure as I could from the first I had from Poole."

That the dogs from Newfoundland were being exported to Poole in 1807 is shown by the fact that in the fall of that year two Newfoundland puppies were taken off a sinking English brig which had been bound for Poole. They were taken to Baltimore and became the founders of the Chesapeake Bay dog. (See *The Labrador Dog*, p. 21.)

Skinner's *The Dog and Sportsman* (Philadelphia, 1845), from which Scott quotes and which we have before us, has an illustration of a large hairy dog entitled "The Newfoundland" and prints a letter written in January 1845 describing the rescue of the dogs in 1807 in which they are called Newfoundlands but described as follows:

"The dog was a dingy red color and the slut black. They were not large; their hair was short, but very thick coated; they had dew claws."

Looking through our own library to find what we could on this question, we found in *Researches into the History of the British Dog*, by G.R. Jesse (London, 1866) Lord Byron's tribute to his dog "Boatswain." The tombstone describes the dog as born at Newfoundland May 1803 and died at Newsread Abbey November 18, 1808. Whether this was a Labrador or a Newfoundland we do not know, but it corroborates the other dates because it reveals importations from Newfoundland at that time.

Obviously there is no reason why every dog that was brought from Newfoundland should have been the big dog instead of the little one.

A large part of *The Labrador Dog, Its Home and History* is devoted to a description of the antecedents of the Labrador dog in Labrador. It appears that the aboriginal inhabitants of the island, the Beothucks, did not have any dogs. The English began to fish in Newfoundland in 1498; the Portuguese came in 1501; and the French in 1504. The English were the only fishermen who engaged in shore fishery and made certain settlements about 1522. Most of the settlers came from Devon and were hunters. They wanted dogs for hunting and to retrieve their fish so they probably took the dogs that were then common in England over with them. There are references to a greyhound and a mastiff on the island as far back as 1611. These dogs brought by the men of Devon were the only canine population of Newfoundland and were bred and trained to meet the needs of their owners. From these various breeds of dogs bred for over a period of 280 years under rigorous conditions, there were evolved the Newfoundland dog and the Labrador. They were the product of environment and survival and perhaps selection.

Lord George Scott goes into great detail about their evolution. Chapter 7 of *The Labrador Dog* opens with the following statement:

"The modifications in the dogs brought to Newfoundland by the early settlers, which can be attributed to long and continuous exposure to changed conditions of life, the effects of climate and food, and the intercrossing of breeds already formed, would form an interesting subject of investigation. The early settlers were scattered along the coast in small groups of ten, 20, and in no case more than 100 souls. They would not all be likely to take with them as companions the same breed of dogs."

The remainder of the chapter contains a very scholarly discussion with quotations from scientists including Darwin.

The Labrador dog that was imported to England was of very ancient lineage, was rugged, had been trained to hunt and work, and was therefore probably docile despite what Hawker says about his fighting qualities.

will leap from the summit of the highest cliff into the water in obedience to the commands of their master. To man they are ever gentle and good-natured; so much so, indeed, that it has been customary of late years to cross their breed with an English bulldog, whereby they are rendered more fierce and surly towards strangers. It is pretended that a

Dual Ch. Banchory Bolo and some of his famous progeny in 1928. All owned by Lorna Countess Howe. Left to right: Ch. Beningboro Tangle; Ch. Banchory Bolo's Trust; Ch. Banchory Danilo; ΓTCh. Kirkmaker Rover; Ch. Banchory Kelpie; Banchory Corbie; and Dual Ch. Banchory Bolo.

Lt. Edward Chappell who spent the summer of 1818 in the Straits of Belle Isle, describes what he calls a Newfoundland dog as follows:

"Most of the fisheries are plentifully supplied with these dogs, and they prove of great utility in dragging home the winter fuel. Their docility is so remarkable that they

thorough-bred Newfoundland dog may be known by certain black marks on the roof of its mouth; but this is by no means a positive proof, as many other kinds of dogs have the same mark."

It is very difficult to ascertain whether the early writers are referring to a Labrador or a

Newfoundland, but whether the dog was a Labrador or a Newfoundland they were all used for the same purpose and probably had the same characteristics.

In 1822, W.E. Cormack, an accomplished naturalist, made his journey on foot across Newfoundland. After pointing out that wild fowl constituted a large part of the provisions of the inhabitants, he writes:

"The dogs here are admirably trained as retrievers in fowling and are otherwise useful. The smooth or short-haired is preferred because in winter the long-haired kind become encumbered with ice on coming out of the water."

Thus there appeared in southern England about the beginning of the 19th century a well-trained retriever. The main trading point for the fishermen at that time was Poole.

Lord Malmesbury had a shoot at Hurn Court which was not far from Poole. The First Earl of Cairns lived at Bournemouth. Lord Dalkeith and Lord Home spent several winters at Bournemouth and used to shoot in the vicinity as did Hawker and the Duke of Buccleuch. Lord Malmesbury gave some of these dogs to the Duke of Hamilton and Lord Ruthven living in the south of Scotland. Doubtless the dogs were crossed with pointers and setters from time to time and later with Flat Coats and Goldens, but because of their ancient lineage they were prepotent. In the late 1880s the Third Earl of Malmesbury, who had said he always kept his breed as pure as he could, gave Ned (1882), Avon (1885), and Nell (1886) to Lord Dalkeith, afterwards the Sixth Duke of Buccleuch; Dinah (1885) to Lord Home; and Juno (1885) and Smut (1885) to the Hon. Herbert Cairns, afterwards the Third Earl of Cairns. These are the foundation of the pedigrees of the Labrador dogs found in Lord George Scott's book plus the Duke of Hamilton's Sam (1884) by Preston Hall Diver out of the Duke of

The famous Avon is regarded as the ancestor of all British Labradors. In this photograph he is 11 years old.

Important gun-dog trials were held at the Countess Howe's Idsworth, Horndean, Hants estate. These gentlemen partook in the Labrador Retriever Club's 25th field trial.

Hamilton's Fan. Ned was by Lord Malmesbury's Sweep (1887) ex his Juno (1878); Avon by Lord Malmesbury's Tramp ex his Juno; Nell by Lord Winborne's dog (1882) out of Lord Malmesbury's Juno (1882); Dinah by Lord Malmesbury's Nelson out of his Nell. Juno and Smut's pedigrees are not given. Preston Hall Diver was by a dog of Lord Malmesbury's out of Lord Ruthven's Jet.

The Labrador Dog contains a pedigree of Mrs. Hill Wood's Hiwood Chance. The earliest date in the pedigree is 1872 and there is one break in the seventh generation, and one part goes back 15 generations. There are also pedigrees of Lady Howe's Dual Ch. Bramshaw Bob and Buccleuch Daniel.

The Labrador dog was not known to the English public generally during the 19th century because they were mostly used at shoots and were largely keepers' dogs. Lord Vivian told the story of how he happened to get his great dog, Scandal of Glynn, who sired Lady Howe's Dual Champion Banchory Bolo. It seems that he had had a Springer which he used as a retriever. The Springer died and he sent his servant on to see the dog dealer who had sold him the Springer. His servant returned with Scandal of Glynn explaining that the man said he did not have any Springers but thought this dog, which was a Labrador dog, would probably do very well for him! Labradors were first recognized by the Kennel Club as a breed on July 7, 1903, and in 1905 they were separately classified as a sub-variety of retrievers.

Mr. Lord was a vice-president of the Labrador Retriever Club, Inc. during the years 1931–1934 and a member of the Club's Board of Directors from 1931–1944.

Ch. Boli of Blake, whelped June 24, 1932, was America's first bench champion. Owner, Franklin B. Lord.

Ch. Boli of Blake
A. K. C. 861200

Sire: Ch. Ingleston Ben	Ch. Duke of Kirkmahoe	Withington Banter Kirkmahoe Dina
	Ingleston Nancy	Banchory Roger Brocklehirst Nell
Dam: Banchory Trace	Self Starter	Ch. Banchory Corbie Sable Snake
	Jetter	Withington Sweeper Banchory Kelpie

Labrador Successes through the Years

by Dorothy Howe, Rupert Kennels, Manchester Depot, Vermont
[Reprinted from Popular Dogs, *March 1962]*

Leading Dual Ch. breeding has resulted over the years from Dr. Milbanks' Ch. Raffles of Earlsmoor, born in 1931. This dog sired very few litters, but through him have come nine of the 20 Dual Chs. in this country. Raffles not only sired the immortal three-time Natl and Dual Ch. Shed of Arden, owned and handled during his field career by Paul Bakewell III, but the same breeding as Shed produced two other Dual Chs. in Mrs. Morgan Belmont's Gorse of Arden and Mrs. McManus' bitch, Braes of Arden.

When Shed was bred to Huron Lady, he produced Thomas Merritt's Dual Ch. Grangemead Precocious which, in turn, when bred to Grangemead Sharon, sired Dual Chs. Cherokee Medicine Man and Cherokee Buck (Buck also won BOB at Westminster one year, and late in life became a house pet for Miss Floback). Now we have the '61 Dual Ch. from this line in Mr. Cook's Alpine Cherokee Rocket x Nelgard's Madam Queen which, this year, completed all series of the Natl. Shed also was the

Above: *Dual Ch. Shed of Arden winning the 1946 National Retriever Championship. Thomas Merritt presenting trophy to Paul Bakewell III.* **Below:** *Ch. Rupert Dahomey with Dorothy Howe. This dog was a homebred grandson of Dual Ch. Shed of Arden and FTCh. Timber Town Clansman.*

grandsire of two Dual Chs., Bakewell's Hello Jo of Rocheltree and Romadka's Kingswere Black

FTCh. Braeroy Roe.

Ch. Earlsmoor Moor of Arden.

Am-Can. Ch. Dark Star of Franklin.

Ebony. What a record for 30 years of U.S. breeding of good-looking working dogs! And, we hope more to come!

Other Dual Chs. are Paul Bakewell's Little Pierre of Deer Creek ('41 Natl Ch.) which sired Matchmaker for Deer Creek for Bakewell. Mrs. Loening's Bengal of Arden, Mr. Angle's Michael of Glenmere, Mr. Bartlett's Yodel of Morexpense, Little Miss Timer (bitch), Mrs. McCue's Beau Brummell of Wyndale, Mr. Grunwald's Boley's Tar Baby, Mr. Pomeroy's Bracken's Sweep ('47 Natl Ch.) Mr. Kavanaugh's Problem Big Duke of Wake, and Mr. Spaulding's British dog Treveilyr Swift.

The list of English Dual Chs. should be headed by Lorna Countess Howe's Banchory Bolo, as this dog is behind almost all of our show dogs today as well as many trial dogs. Through our FTCh. Timber Town Clansman, '49 Natl Ch. and Dual Ch. Bracken's Sweep, and that great bitch, '41 Natl Ch. Tar of Arden and many others, Bolo's influence will be felt for many more years to come. Lady Howe also owned three other Dual Chs. in Banchory Sunspeck, Branchory Painter and Bramshaw Bob (also responsible for some of today's show dogs and FT Ch. Major VI).

Another Dual Ch. was Titus of Whitmore, owned by Mr. Twyford, which was the sire of another Dual Ch., Lord Joicey's Flute of Flodden (also the grandsire of Dr. Milbank's Ch. Raffles of Earlsmoor). Mr. MacDonald's Rockstead Footspark is another. Mr. Winter's Staindrop Saighdear's name comes in the pedigrees of many of our best yellows and, with Mrs. Wormald's Knaith Banjo, are the only two British Dual Ch. yellows (in this country we have none). The only English bitch to make the list is Mrs. Morris' Lochar Nessie. This makes a total of 10—hope I have not missed any!

You all must know by now that the top-winning show dog during the last two years has been Grace Lambert's Eng.–Am. Ch. Sam of Blaircourt. However, so far he has not beaten the record of the Ziessows' Am.–Can. Ch. Dark Star of Franklin (now retired) with 8 BIS, 93 Sporting Group wins (including 40 GR1) and a Labrador specialty included in his 117 BOB.

Perhaps the most successful stud dog today is the '55 Natl Ch. Cork of Oakwood Lane, owned by Bill Rook. (I asked Mr. Rook for his record but have not heard.) I understand he sired a tremendous number of puppies—many of them yet to be heard from and we hope for some Dual Chs. However, in field trials his influence is being felt in a big way by siring seven of the 52 dogs qualified for the National this year, as well as '61 winner—Mr. Snoeyenbo's FTCh. Del Tone Colvin.

The outstanding show breeding kennel in recent years seems to me to be Whygin Kennels, owned by Helen Ginnel of Bedford Hills, NY. The kennels' foundation litter, born in '51 out of their Cedar Hill Whygin, by my Ch. Rupert Dahomey, went

Dual Ch. Banchory Bolo.

Dual Ch. Staindrop Saighdear.

King George VI was a patron of the Labrador Club and the Yellow Labrador Club. He won the open in 1948 with his Windsor Bob and placed fourth in '49 in the Labrador Club open all-age. The dog pictured here is Sandringham Glen, bred and worked by the King himself, by Dual Ch. Staindrop Saighdear x FTCh. Braeroy Fudge, by Graeroy Jack; later in Lady Howe's kennel and renamed Banchory Jack x Braeroy Chips.

Rupert Sam Howe by Eng-Am. Ch. Sam of Blaircourt x Rupert Aurora Borealis, yellow daughter of Eng-Am. Ch. Kingley Comet of Harham. Bred by Dorothy Howe, this excellent male was owned and handled by Mary G. Swan.

on to produce in succeeding generations 15 champions and six others listing either a Whygin sire or dam. Here's the record of wins at some of the shows: At the '56 Labrador specialty BOB, Whygin Skia of Southdown (Mrs. Godsol) owner, Tuttle; WD, Whygin Rob Roy, owner, Ginnel. The '59 specialty, BOS, Whygin Prunella Duck (Cowie), owner, Mrs. Kelley. The '60 specialty, Best Puppy, Whygin Campaign Promise (Wilson), owner, McCarthy. The '61 specialty, BOB, Whygin Campaign Promise (Rich), owner, McCarthy; BOW, Whygin Gentle Julia, owner, McCarthy.

At Chicago '52, BOS, Whygin Dark Magic (Riddle), owner, Ginnel; in '56, BOS, Whygin John Duck (Rich) owner, Ginnel; in '61 BOB, Ch. Whygin Gold Bullion (Van Court),

owner, Ginnel; BOS, Whygin Campaign Promise, owner, McCarthy; WB, Whygin Gentle Julia, owner, McCarthy.

At Westminster, in '54, BOB, Whygin Poppitt (Heckmann), owner, Ginnel. In '56 BOB, Ch. Whygin John Duck (Van Court), owner, Ginnel; BOS, Whygin Skia of Southdown, owner, Tuttle. In '57, BOB, Whygin Rob Roy (Howes Burton), owner, Ginnel; WB, Rupert Mt. Mist of Whygin, owner, Howe. In '61, BOB, Ch. Whygin Gold Bullion (Kenderick), owner, Ginnel; BOS, Whygin Campaign Promise, owner, McCarthy.

At Westchester in '55, WD, Whygin John Duck (Philips), owner, Ginnel. In '56, BOB, Whygin John Duck (Mrs. Mangrum), owner, Ginnel; BOS, Whygin Skia of Southdown, owner, Tuttle; BOW, Whygin Rob Roy, owner, Ginnel.

At Eastern in '59, BOB, Ch. Whygin Eager Nerissa (Schoeneck), owner, Williams; BOS, Ch. Whygin Poppitt, owner, Ginnel.

At Morris & Essex '57, BOB, Ch. Whygin Poppitt (Bloomquist), owner, Ginnel; WB, Whygin Tarry, owner, Bierman.

FTCh. Del-Tone Colvin, owned by L.J. Snoeyenbos of Baldwin, WI, won the National Retriever Field Trial Club Stake in Smyrna, DE.

Ch. Bolo and his winning line of descendants at the famous kennels of Lorna Countess Howe.

THE "GOOD OLD DAYS"

Dr. Milbank needs no introduction. But perhaps, since he has become famous with his handling and winning field trials with his Springers, some of you may have forgotten that he is a great Labrador judge, with Morris & Essex and the Labrador specialty among his assignments. I believe he might like to be called a "Dual Champion dog man," with his influence being felt not only through his dogs but through his work in the AKC and as secretary of the Westminster Kennel Club. His letter follows:

"In answer to your letter of July 1st, you have asked a number of questions that I will try to answer.

"Many years ago, about 1925, the famous Ferguson family of Fishers Island started using English Springer Spaniels, a breed that was so well qualified for the cover on Fishers Island. They imported one English judge each year to come over and show us how trials should be run. Henry L. Ferguson, secretary of the English Springer Spaniel Field Trial Assn., invited Dr. James Wilson, Redhurst, Irvine, N.B., Scotland, to come over to judge. He was the outstanding lung surgeon of his time in Scotland, being the first to operate on tubular lungs successfully. He agreed to accept the invitation to judge provided, that while he was here, he would be taken to all tubular clinics and sanitoria in the vicinity. Mr.

Ch. Ballyduff Candy, imported to the States in 1952, became the foundation of Lockerbie retrievers. Candy's get were exported to Mexico, North Africa, the Dominican Republic and France. She was the first imported yellow female to gain an American bench title and was sired by Eng. Dual Ch. Staindrop Saighdear. Owners, James and Helen Warwick.

States who would look after the dog en route. I suggested he send the dog to Scotland where a friend of mine would be grouse shooting on August. He sent me a cable saying that the dog had never been handled by anyone except his trainer and himself, and he did not want it to be ruined by the Ghillies.

Ferguson turned him over to me, for at that time I was senior visiting physician at St. Joseph's Hospital for Tuberculosis in New York City.

"Dr. Wilson was a most interesting man. After having seen all that I could show him from the professional standpoint, I was taking him down to the boat on which he planned to return to his home. This was in November. At that time, he asked me where I kept my Labrador Retrievers. I told him I had never had one. He said that a retriever was a 'must,' and the next time he found a good one, he said he was going to send it over.

"The following July, he wrote me that he had found the dog. It belonged to one of his patients and he said he would send it over if I had any friend returning to the

"The friend of mine who was returning in October agreed to bring the dog. They were having a very big Labrador specialty at the Westbury, L.I. show. I got the necessary particulars by cable and entered the dog, whose name, when I received him, was 'Raffles.' I was allowed to add my kennel name of Earlsmoor. The first time out, Raffles of Earlsmoor beat all the champions and went Best of Breed. Later he placed second in the Sporting Group. In the three subsequent shows he won his American bench show Ch. title. He was a most biddable dog to handle and I ran him in a few field trials. I never got any higher than second in a championship trial but I was usually in the money or with a Certificate of Merit.

"William Averhill Harriman, later

Governor of our State and at the present moment, Roving Ambassador for the President of the United States, had a wonderful kennel with his brother at Arden, NY, of Labradors and English-type Cocker Spaniels. The famous Tom Briggs was his trainer and head kennel man. He asked if I would allow Mr. Harriman to breed his famous field trial champion, Decoy of Arden, to Raffles.

Eng. Ch. Lockerbie Blackfella produced a record number of winners, bench champions as well as gun dogs. He was known to pass on his strong head, good angulation and coat texture. His offspring made an impact in the U.S. as well as Canada. Owners, James and Helen Warwick.

"The mating resulted in seven puppies, born Feb. 1, '37, all named after shooting places in Scotland. They included Moor, whom I chose, Heather, Grouse, Banks, Braes and Gorse. Gorse belonged to Mrs. Morgan Belmont and was a dual champion, both in the field and on the bench.

"It was such a successful mating that again Decoy bred to Raffles. This time I picked a bitch. All in this litter were named after fish, for some reason or other. I took one named Marlin which became a bench show champion. She was nicknamed 'Marlene' because she had such beautiful legs and feet. Another was named Bass; a third was supposed to be called Shad but, in being registered, the name was misspelled and came out Shed. This was the great dog which won the national championship two years running. All of Raffles' get had wonderful coats.

"As a matter of interest, at the time this litter was born, the King and Queen of England, King George VI and Queen Elizabeth, came to this country on a visit and, since one of Raffles's ancestors had belonged to the King's father, it was known as the 'Royal' litter, and was so called in the newspapers.

"I have a very vivid memory of Marlin. Years ago, when Mrs. Walton Ferguson, who was a wonderful judge both on the bench and in the field, was judging a bench show, she came to Marlin which went right on to win under her. She said later, 'It is like a drink of cold water to a thirsty man to have such a beautiful and perfect specimen appear.'

"Moor was used in the field and was fairly successful. However, he went best of breed at Morris & Essex and BIS at Greenwich, beating the famous My Own Brucie in the group. His record was 40 times BOB, 12 GR1, 27 GR placings, and five BIS. Ch. Earlsmoor Moor of Arden won bench show challenge cup outright—three times each year for three years. He retired the cup, and later went on to win another challenge cup under the same conditions again, so he has two bench show challenge cups to his credit. In all his career, he was handled only by Jim Cowie.

"You asked about the 'good old days.' When I handled Raffles of Earlsmoor in the field, he was a remarkable dog, but about that time, or shortly after, the late Jay Carlisle brought a young English handler over to handle his dogs in the field. He instituted a brand new method of handling and was eminently successful.

"It was patterned after sheep dog trials where the handler could stand and send his dog for any distance by whistle and hand signals. It was a grand and glorious feeling to have a dog trained so well that you were absolutely his master in every particular. The only criticism was that you took away some of the natural initiative of the dog to hunt and, to my mind, that is too bad. Carlisle was very successful for a long time—until some of our bright American boys got on to the method of handling and soon out did him. However, that same method is still in use."—Samuel Milbank, M.D.

Mrs. Macpherson has been an outstanding breeder of yellow Labradors for many years and is a field trial judge of note. "Her name will assuredly rank among the immortals of the yellow working history" (British Labrador book, '49). The picture she sent show Glencoe Mac 1923 (grandson of Hyde Ben), FTCh. Braeroy Roe 1927 and, her latest hopes for '62, Braeroy Pola 1953. We all know how difficult it is to produce outstanding bitches and Mrs. Macpherson has produced two which have had tremendous influence on the yellow color. Her FTCh. Braeroy Roe (granddaughter of Clyde) produced the outstanding sire, Braeroy Rab, which in turn produced the famous bitch FTCh. Braeroy Ruddy 1932. It is also interesting to note that Mrs. Macpherson bred her FTCh. Braeroy Roe to two brothers of Dr. Milbank's Ch. Raffles of Earlsmoor. Mrs. Macpherson's letter follows:

"I am sending you a few photographs (sorry, some not very good) of several dogs directly descended from Glencoe Mac and Western Reiver. The former came from the old strain of Red Labradors from Lord Faversham's kennel in Yorkshire. The latter, a son of Clyde (a Chesapeake Bay) and Dunskey Jean, a little bitch imported into this country from Labrador.

"The dam of FTCh. Braeroy Roe was a daughter of Glencoe Mac and her sire was Western Reiver. All my dogs are still of this old line. About once every 10 years or so I

The King's brace was exhibited at Crufts Dog Show in 1932. Like his father and mother before him, H.M. King George V maintained the large kennel of Labrador Retrievers at Sandringham.

have had to find an outcross. Sometimes this has been very successful, but once or twice results have not been so satisfactory.

"I have always aimed to keep really good temperament and natural working ability with reasonable standard of looks. Glencoe Mac went to India where he had a very successful career and lived to a grand old age. Western Reiver went to your country. He was purchased by a shooting tenant we had one season who admired him and his work so much.

"Owing to domestic conditions I had to curtail breeding considerably in recent years but I still have good foundation stock. I am especially interested in two six-month-old bitches I have at present—granddaughters of Ch. Whatstandwell Coronet (BOB, Crufts '56-215 Labradors) on dam's side; sire is Braeroy Polar. A black dog I bred has become a FTCh, this season—Rivington Braeroy Swift.

"In my opinion, some of our winning show dogs are inclined to be too 'stocky'. I prefer the lively active dog which can last for many years but I agree so heartily with you that good temperaments in our Labs should be preserved at all costs. I fear this desirable quality is being lost in some of our present-day show dogs but this is being penalized severely by many of our show judges, a good thing." *Thank you, Mrs. Macpherson.*

Above: Rupert Admiral Duckworth retrieving in Middle Cove, Newfoundland. Photograph courtesy of Lady Jacqueline Barlow. **Below:** Two of Lady Barlow's blacks cavorting near Cape Spear, Newfoundland. Photograph courtesy of Lady Jacqueline Barlow.

The Labrador Retriever in Newfoundland

by Lady Jacqueline Barlow

Throughout their history, Newfoundlanders were busy surviving on a barren island of rock, gaining their living from the unforgiving North Atlantic. They kept no records of their dogs, as survival was a full-time battle, and so it is frustrating for those of us who want to go back in the history of our dogs to be able to get only a glimpse here and there.

One thing is very obvious when you are in Newfoundland with your dogs—why the Labrador standard is so particular as to strength of chest, waterproof coat, etc. My Drake would swim and inspect a grounded iceberg and return neither cold nor wet. We made a film for the CBC shown across the country on the Labrador in Newfoundland. Now nobody in their right mind would be shooting white domestic ducks off a rocky beach into six-foot waves, but I was fascinated to see my dogs wait for the enormous wave to curl, ready to break, dive into and through it, and be carried out to the duck. (In passing I will add that I allowed my dogs to do it exactly twice.)

When I first came to Newfoundland with my four Labradors

Ch. Knaith Beatty was the first Newfoundland champion of the breed in history. Photograph courtesy of Lady Jacqueline Barlow.

(champions and gundogs all), I chose a bank with a splendid view of St. John's Harbour since I knew that one of my dogs was fascinated with boats in the bath and would more than appreciate this view of an enormous bath with ships and boats bustling about. I was right —he did. Next to the bank's parking lot was a house belonging to Jacob, a merchant dealing exclusively in the hairdressing concoction known as Bay Rum, which, purged of its perfume, was sold to the down-and-out population of the waterfront. "Jakey's Gin" was a cheap and potent drink. On returning to my car one day I saw a chap several sheets to the wind, swaying on the balls of his feet looking at the dogs, his Bay Rum bottle handy for a swalley (Newfoundland for a drink).

"Wot's them dogs?" he asked with a sneer. "Labrador Retrievers, but,"—I got no further! "Wot do ye call 'em that for?" he asked belligerently. "Thems nothing but water dogs!" and he staggered off. If he had let me finish, I was going to say just that, having been in Newfoundland long enough (about two weeks), and having been told 20 times a day that the Labrador dog was a Husky and against the law in Newfoundland.

In passing it is interesting to note that in other countries, children who are afraid of dogs are afraid of black ones and embrace a yellow; in Newfoundland it is the reverse: children expect dogs to be black.

The name Labrador is misleading to the uninitiated, and it is surprising how many people who ought to know better think the dogs came from Labrador, which they did not.

Captain Cartright, trading and hunting, spent about 20 years in Labrador during the first half of the 19th century, leaving three large diaries in which he lists every single detail of what he did and saw and he did not once mention the small black water dogs found in Newfoundland, nor could the dogs he took with him from England, which he listed, have been the ancestors of the Labrador.

Whereas in 1822, W.E. Cormack, of St. John's,

The last Water Dog in Newfoundland photographed in 1974 with Harold Melbourn. Photograph courtesy of Lady Jacqueline Barlow.

Above: A feast for British eyes: Ch. Valleyview Seymour, Ch. Castlemore Martin CD, WC, and Sandringham Chive photographed in St. John's, Newfoundland in 1987. Photograph courtesy of Lady Jacqueline Barlow.
Below: Sandringham Chive poses at the Queen's Battery at the entrance to St. John's Harbour. Photograph courtesy of Lady Jacqueline Barlow.

Above: Newfoundland historically has been a fishing community. The Grand Bruit, the south coast of Newfoundland in 1974. Photograph courtesy of Lady Jacqueline Barlow. *Below:* Three fishermen on the wharf on the Grand Bruit. Photograph courtesy of Lady Jacqueline Barlow.

journeyed across Newfoundland and along the western coast, and he writes of "Small water dogs, admirably trained as retrievers. The smooth and short haired dog is preferred because in frosty weather the long haired kind becomes encumbered with ice on coming out of the water." Presumably these dogs were established long before they were seen by Cormack.

I have seen an account, dated early in the 17th century, of a black dog in a Newfoundland outport, amusing himself on a rocky beach by diving into the sea and returning with a fish which then no longer interested him, and he would add it to his pile of fish already caught. A tantalizing tidbit with no other details.

I have seen references to the Yellow Dogs of Petty Harbor, but there again there are no details. They are obviously the ancestors of our yellow Labradors.

When I asked in Petty Harbor, the only

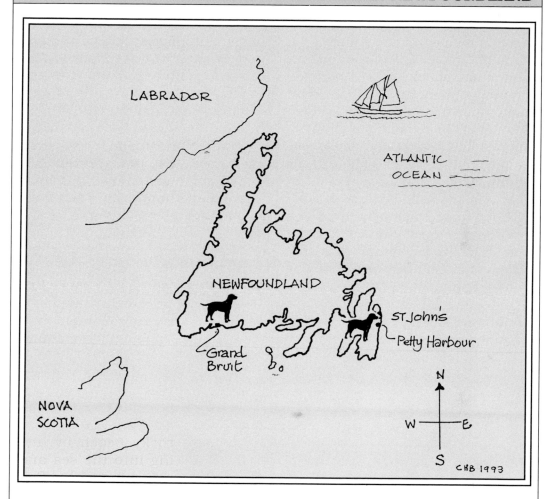

man who could remember (but I think Newfoundland dogs) remembered his horror as a boy, seeing two dogs hauling a load of wood that was too heavy for them, and which they were unable to pull uphill, so the enraged owner went and got an axe and cut off their heads. "What price the yellow dog?" I know on the southern coast they ate dogs. Survival, with nothing going in their favour, on a barren rocky island, they saw nothing wrong with their treatment of animals, which shows a strange state of mind where dogs were concerned. They kept no records —the dog that got to the bitch first sired the litter.

There has been endless and fruitless speculation as to the origin of the Newfoundland Water Dog. The indications are only that it is a very old breed indeed. It has some similarity to a working dog of northern Portugal (now rare), which is the most likely possibility, according to the well-known American all-breed judge and historian of the early Portuguese in the New World, Max

Riddle. The Portuguese fished along the coast of the Americas a century before Columbus, but on being annexed by Spain destroyed all their charts and navigational instruments. This Portuguese theory makes sense too —the Portuguese have long been dog lovers as many a dog owner in St. John's knows to his cost. Each fishing boat has all sorts of dogs aboard, with a sod of grass placed on the deck for the dogs to do their business. But there is no provable connection with any breed of dog from anywhere!

My own theory is that God on the Seventh Day sat down and put his feet up, but was uneasy that He had forgotten something! "Aha," He thought, and sprinkled a few water dogs on Newfoundland, and then sat back and was satisfied!

During the 19th century there was a great deal of trade between Newfoundland and Poole in Dorset, England and frequently water dogs accompanied the schooner or fishing boat back to England. Around 1823 or 24 they came to the attention of the second Earl of Malmesbury, whose estate of

A three-week-old Water Dog puppy in Grand Bruit in 1974. Photograph courtesy of Lady Jacqueline Barlow.

Above: Ch. Rupert Admiral Drake and Rupert Admiral Duckworth waiting to retrieve in Middle Cove, Newfoundland. Photograph courtesy of Lady Jacqueline Barlow. *Right:* A Water Dog in Newfoundland and his young master. Photograph courtesy of Lady Jacqueline Barlow.

43

Lady Jacqueline Barlow with Sandringham Chive, bred by H.M. The Queen in 1979. Photograph courtesy of Lady Jacqueline Barlow.

The Earl and Countess of Malmesbury with Sandringham Chive in 1992. Photograph courtesy of Lady Jacqueline Barlow.

Heron Court was next to Poole. He was so impressed with the two dogs he saw retrieving sticks and abandoned fish for small boys that he acquired the dogs as likely to make good retrievers for wildfowling. Finding them excellent, he procured two couples and set up kennels, naming the dogs The Little Newfoundler.

It was the third Earl of Malmesbury (1807-1889) who seriously started importing and breeding Newfoundland water dogs, and it was he who changed the name from the Little Newfoundler to the Labrador Retriever. Gradually his friends followed suit and the Labrador Retriever it became. (Labrador is part of Newfoundland.)

What of the water dogs in Newfoundland itself? They were used by fishermen to retrieve any cod that escaped the hook on the surface.

We were walking my black Labrador Drake along a rocky beach on the north coast some years ago when a fisherman mending his nets came over to us and said, "It does me good to see that dog —that's the true Newfoundland dog that we took to sea." "What about the large hairy fellow?" I asked.

"Oh no, he was used for hauling wood and that, the ice stuck to his coat, *that's* the dog we took to sea!"

The Sheep Act of 1885 and later 1927 virtually wiped out the dog population of Newfoundland. The majority of electors in a district could prohibit the owning of dogs and 130 districts did just that. A pity as sheep never really flourished in Newfoundland; the men were fishermen. Also, a licensing fee was introduced and the fee for

bloodlines in his kennels. The six-month quarantine laws in England were now in force and importation of water dogs had ceased, owing to the difficulties.

The Newfoundland Governor, Sir John Middleton, gave the job to

The rugged landscape of Newfoundland gives the dogs a hearty workout. Photograph courtesy of Lady Jacqueline Barlow.

a female was considerably more than for a male so people drowned the bitches in their litters. Thus, water dogs became scarce, and only very few survived in small, cut-off outports.

In the 1930s a Noble Duke in Scotland asked the Governor of Newfoundland to find him a water dog of the following description, to be shipped over to him, to renew the

one of his Aide de Camps, Sir Leonard Outerbridge, who some months later found just the dog of the Duke's description on board a fishing boat in St. John's Harbour. He asked to buy the dog for two pounds sterling, if the Governor approved. The fishing skipper readily agreed, but when Sir Leonard returned, the wily skipper, figuring there was evidently something he had not noticed about this particular dog, demanded *five* pounds. This princely sum was complained about by the Noble Duke to his dying day. That night, amid jollification amongst the younger staff of Government House, a suitable pedigree was invented for this unknown dog. For all the sires, they put the leading Newfoundland politicians of the day, and for the dams, the ladies of the waterfront.

In 1972 I persuaded a friend of my husband's to take me in his trading schooner along the south coast of Newfoundland to look for what must be the only water dogs left, reported to be in Grand Bruit.

I found two ancient and pure water dogs, indistinguishable from many of the Labradors of 25 to 50 years ago. Sadly they are both now gone and I suspect with them the last pure water dogs in Newfoundland.

It gave me pleasure to bring Labradors back to the land of their origin in 1966 (Come Home Year in Newfoundland). Now there are quite a few. With the arrival of several more dogs of top quality, we began the Labrador Retriever Club of Newfoundland, hoping to advise people and maintain the high standard of the dogs brought in. My (gun-trained) Scots dog Knaith Beatty went Best in Show

Ch. Castlemore Martin CD, WC and Ch. Rupert Admiral Drake at Cape Spear, Newfoundland. Photograph courtesy of Lady Jacqueline Barlow.

at the first show given by the New-foundland Kennel Club in 1967. Three shows later he gained his championship, thus making him the first Labrador Retriever to do so in the land of the Labrador's origin, Newfoundland.

For years we managed to insist on a high standard of Labradors, but unfortunately outsiders sold a few lemons to people who didn't know enough and then bred from them, so sadly the standard of Labradors in Newfoundland is now varied.

In July 1992 the Sixth Earl and Countess of Malmesbury came to Newfoundland: she to fish, he to visit the land of the origin of the dogs he loves so much. Four generations and 159 years later a man who knows and understands Labradors more than anybody I have ever met came and saw the countryside that shaped his family's dogs and was very happy.

The family of Lady Barlow's dogs at Christmas 1979. Photograph courtesy of Lady Jacqueline Barlow.

A glorious moment for Ch. Knaith Beatty, the first champion Labrador in Newfoundland. Benbow was bred in Scotland by Mrs. Arthus Wormald. Photograph courtesy of Lady Jacqueline Barlow.

The six-year-old Ch. Charisma's Lone Star Rick enjoys staying home overlooking his lake.

Pets and Great Pets

by Mary Feazell

Perpetual **E**go **T**ransformers lick tears, lower blood pressure, dance at laughter, and always, all ways love you. Pets can be everything from your own cherished family member to the top winning, top producing dogs of all time.

Is the Labrador Retriever the right breed for you? Are you fooled by great-aunt Nellie's ten-year-old bitch or a neighbor's seven-year-old trained gundog standing quietly with tails gently waving? Labradors are happy, fun-creating, energetic, slow-maturing dogs with a great need for time with their family. Given the time and training to meet their needs, Labradors can become almost human, having a vocabulary of hundreds of words. Ninety-five percent of what a Labrador becomes is up to the new owners; five percent depends upon the dog. This need for human contact has made the Labrador one of the leading breeds for guide dogs, disabled helpers, search and rescue workers and drug or bomb detectors. Being realistic, Labs swim well, but they cannot walk on water. There are indeed a very few things they do not do well. If you want a guard dog, kennel or back-yard dog, object to hair showing in the carpet or butter, and/or have no time or interest in obedience classes, then perhaps another breed deserves your study.

To find the right Labrador it is a great help to dispense with preconceived notions of age, sex and color. It is the personality, temperament and soundness with which you will live for the next 11 to 15 years. When choosing a Labrador, have no fear of picking an older puppy, adult or rescued dog. The "49th-day tale," referred to in some books as the ideal day to take a puppy, was not written for nor does it apply to Labradors. This breed does adapt well and love at all ages.

Are you ready for a Labrador? One of the first questions following "Why did you decide on a Lab?" that a breeder will ask is "Do you have a fenced yard and what type of fencing?" A Labrador is a hunting breed and that essence affects everything including its tendency to wander, to jump out of the back of pick-up trucks (no matter how well trained), or to have no fear of moving vehicles. Fencing is absolutely mandatory for the safety of the dog.

Charisma's Joy of Franklin.

You will need to identify the plants in your backyard removing the poisonous ones; know if your outdoor furniture or deck has been treated with phenol; puppies and bored, lonesome adults will chew on anything. If you are choosing a special dog area, check it through the day to be sure the shade is constant as the sun moves; have a shaded low tub or child's wading pool available for body cooling as Labs are prone to heatstroke. If you have a swimming pool, a puppy or adult must not only be gently taught to swim (please no throwing it in the pool) but also taught how to find the steps from any angle in the pool. Labradors of any age find pools irresistible. The results may be dire as they panic because they cannot find or claw their way out.

As children are not born knowing table manners nor how to read and write, neither are Labradors born knowing the house rules. Do you know where you will be four months from the date of purchasing a puppy? Unless attending a good puppy kindergarten class, puppies should be started in obedience classes no later than six months, as Labradors have most of their height and strength by nine months. Decide which member of the family will be responsible for taking the puppy or adult to weekly obedience classes and spending a little time each day practicing those lessons. Without any training they can often be unmanageable. For some owners it is easier to blame the dog than train the dog. Start out the way you wish to end. What is cute or funny at 12 pounds may be neither at 85 pounds. Obedience training is as important as fencing to their longevity both in lifespan and as a family member. In addition to being fun, the education and bonding formed during training will have a wonderful life-long effect on the owner as well as the dog.

Finding a reputable breeder is quite easy; contact the American Kennel Club for the address of the current secretary of the Labrador Retriever Club, Inc. Our national club will send a packet of complete information on the breed and breeders for a small fee. Veterinarians in most metropolitan areas have lists of local breed clubs. Have your goals and expectations for this puppy or adult well in mind, such as family member, hunting companion, ring competition, field trialing, therapy dog or possible breeding. Recognizing your own interests will help the various contact people guide you in the correct direction quickly.

There are responsibilities and etiquette for both buyers and breeders. The breeders are expected to have healthy, socialized puppies from sound parents and all paperwork in order. Be aware of where the puppies were born and raised; good hygiene, though a slight doggy smell is normal; puppy toys and evidence of long-term interest in the breed, i.e., books, magazines, awards or photos. When you visit the breeder, ask how long they have been in Labradors; how many litters have they produced; what they hoped to achieve in this particular breeding; how they assess the structure and temperament of the ancestors in the pedigree. The following paperwork should be examined before visiting with the puppies. The breeder should provide AKC individual registration forms, orthopedic certifications and current (within 12 months) CERF or ACVO eye clearances on both parents, a three- to four-generation pedigree, feeding instructions and accurate health records for each puppy in the litter. Possible additions could be a reading list, recommendations for veterinary care, obedience facilities, trustworthy field trainers, reputable boarding kennels, canine products and a sales contract which may include a statement that the breeder is willing to take the dog back at any time in the future.

A typical serious breeder/competitor is a super parent, most hold full-time jobs, have family plus dog responsibilities and travel many weekends to competitive events. They are not a "one-stop-dog-shop" open to buyers 24 hours a day. If you make an appointment, keep it, be on time or call to cancel. Treating a breeder with the same courtesy given to friends and clients will give this new relationship a good start.

Plan to visit only one kennel per day. To do more may seem convenient to you, however, it is not only confusing but can spread germs and virus. Parvo is a lethal airborne virus which is carried on shoes, hair, hands and clothes. It will rampage through a kennel killing young and old, costing thousands of dollars and even more heartbreak. The breeder will not allow very young puppies to be handled as their immunities are not yet in full effect. Wear clean old clothes, changing between kennel visits and be prepared to sit on the floor to play. Never step into a whelping box without permission or with your shoes on: it is a baby bed! In fact, do not be surprised if you are asked to leave your shoes outside. Keep in mind these rules may be protecting *your* puppy. Visit the litter more than once to better observe the differing personalities. Limit your stay to an hour or less. Do see the adult dogs, remembering puppyhood is endearing, but very brief. Ask as many questions as you wish; there is no such thing as a dumb question. It may have been 35 years ago, but the breeder asked the same questions of someone. When your questions have been answered, be prepared. A responsible breeder will want to know your goals, that you can love, care and train their Labrador for its natural life; not just that you have available funds to satisfy your immediate desire. As you expect

Wyndcall's Gulliver Travelin' proves how great Labs are with children. Owner, Shae Beck. Breeder, Mary Feazell.

Ch. Beautawn's Instant Replay CDX, WC is the dam of this new whelp who became Beautawn's Extra Trace of Gold. Beautawn kennels is located in Calgary, Alberta, Canada and is owned by Bill Gugin.

honesty from the breeder, be honest about your goals.

All too frequent occurrences are buyers who request "pet quality" when in actuality they hope some day to compete or breed. With the exception of "show quality," puppies in each litter are usually priced alike, so no money is saved by this request. There will be a seismographic reaction if you buy the cheapest puppy on the market, then call back to another breeder you have previously visited for advice. At best you may be told to call the breeder of your puppy. The worst is not printable. A buyer offering extra cash to be moved to the head of the waiting list or attempting to bargain down the price may quickly find other sources being recommended. Many times a breeder will hold two puppies from a litter for a few months to perhaps as long as two years before making the final decision as to which dog to keep. The best quality can be had by taking the breeder's second choice, to say nothing of the training, maturity, and veterinarian savings. When a family decides to obtain a Labrador, emotionally they want it yesterday, not tomorrow. It is far better, particularly considering the longevity of Labs, for a buyer to be on a good breeder's waiting list for several months. Utilize the time to read Labrador books and training manuals, visit obedience classes, check your dog area and in general prepare for a new family member. The careful breeder's goals are excellence and generational improvement rather than livelihood. They as reputable breeders do not make use of quick-stop shop tactics, hard sells, "bait and switch" or bargain-basement prices. Most breeders have bred the litter to keep one or more puppies, therefore they have "first pick." After several visits with the litter, be prepared to make a non-refundable deposit, if you are a serious buyer. It is non-refundable because if you change your mind the breeder must continue to feed, vaccinate and perhaps pay for advertising. A waiting list is on a first-come, first-served basis with some restrictions against obvious mismatches between families and individual Labradors. Unfortunately, many books recommend choosing the most active puppy in the litter. With the normal Labrador level of energy, this can be wonderful for some families and disastrous for others. If you have chosen an experienced breeder, allow that breeder to help in the choice. That person is not trying to foist off a lesser puppy. What a breeder wants most is the puppy or adult to be happily in the correct home for all of its 11 to 15 years.

Ch. Springfield's Native Fancy CD, WC was the first bitch owned by Bill Gugin of Beautawn kennels.

Above: Six-week-old puppies by FTCh.-AFTCh.-FC-AFC Ironwood Tarnation x Ch.-FTCh.-OTCh. (Triple Ch.) Kenosee Jim Dandy, WCX photographed in 1989 at WhistInwings kennels of Canada. *Below:* Can. Ch. Windanna's Snow Queen CD instructing daughter Ch. Windanna's Petruchio's Kate CD. Owners, Windanna kennels of Canada.

Why do breeders feel as negatively as they do about surprise or Christmas puppies? As much as any adult may talk about wanting a dog, there may be unspoken reasons of which you are unaware as to why he has not purchased one himself. The dog you choose for someone may well not be the one he would choose. Breeders develop an uncanny ability to recognize matches and mismatches, but only if they have met the people and observed the interaction between dog and human. In some circumstances, a breeder will sell to a family in which they have not personally met all members, but only after the telephone and postal services have shown a profit.

Isn't that Christmas card with the puppy in the stocking or box adorable? Who is thinking about the puppy's feelings? He or she has been taken from its mother, littermates, familiar surroundings and brought alone into the unfamiliar and the bedlam of Christmas Day. Young puppies have developed enzymes to digest only puppy food. Anything else will make it sick if it does not become ill just from over handling and excitement. Most homes are abounding in dangerous or poisonous materials at Christmas time: poinsettias, holly, mistletoe, chocolate, tinsel, electrical cords, glass decorations, angel hair, flocked trees, dyes in wrapping paper, ribbons, candles and turkey bones. Buy a food pan, collar and leash and cut out a picture of a Labrador to put under the tree. Collect your new addition at a later date. The whole family will be able to separate the inanimate toys from a live sensitive puppy. Before a Labrador is purchased is the time to develop the habit of considering its physical and emotional well being.

There are two types of registration, the first regular having been in existence since the beginning. More recently the American Kennel Club has provided breeders with a wonderful protection for each breed titled "Limited Registration." Many breeders will register most of the litter on this basis. "Limited" means that the dog has or will be fully registered with AKC. However, if bred as an adult, no puppy from this dog may be registered with AKC. These are not junk-bond puppies; this is a careful, thoughtful breeder who knows that however much an owner loves a dog or no matter how smart the dog is, it simply should not be bred. Limited Registration can only be reversed by the breeder. If after two years or more, the dog has cleared the orthopedic x-rays, one or more eye examinations, is a very good representative of the breed physically and in temperament, the breeder may decide to change the type of registration. However, no breeder is ever under any obligation to do so. On rare occasions an unsuspected defective gene may be expressed in one or more of the littermates. Depending upon the problem perhaps none of the dogs from that litter should be bred. Some breeders use a spay/neuter contract. It is certainly legitimate and may increase the dog's health and longevity. Given today's overpopulation problem, there are published statistics showing the staggering mathematics of one bitch and her first litter in six years can produce 67,000 offspring.

To crate or not to crate. They are crates, not cages. As much as we like to humanize our pets, they are still dogs and as such are den animals who need a snug, secure place of their own. Crates are great for security, housebreaking, safety in auto travel, and a "must" for air travel. These wonderful dens can be innocently abused by having the puppy or adult spend too much cumulative time in them. Other than at night, for an extended length of time a sheltered outdoor environment would be more appropriate for any active growing puppy or young adult. Plastic airline crates are required by the FAA for air travel, good for the house and in winter, but heat can build up too quickly if used outside in the warm seasons.

Labradors shed hair a little all year with a fairly massive shed in the spring to eliminate their winter coats. Although they may jump in the bathtub with you, Labs rarely need a bath, unless a confrontation with a skunk has occurred. Bathing may cause skin and coat problems. Their coats are meant to be weather resistant; a swim in moderately clean water or hosing is sufficient. Because of the natural light oil and sharp point on each hair shaft, mud will slide off in a matter of hours. Labradors are as close to self-cleaning as you will find. They do enjoy

Rick and Ricky playing Labrador games.

being brushed with a soft natural bristle brush. At that time check ears, teeth, toe nails and general body condition. Drop-eared dogs have a proclivity for ear infections, mites and fungus due to a lack of air circulation in the ear canal.

A BREEDER'S DOZEN OF COMMONSENSE TIPS

1. Go to the place the dog made its mistake for a correction. If you call a dog to you to correct it, you are then correcting the dog for obeying the "come" command.

2. Teach "sit" by putting one hand across under the dog's tail, the other under its chin and tip it into the sit position.

3. Train barefooted on hard surfaces in warm weather.

4. If you choose an "invisible fence," it will not keep other dogs out as they do not wear electronic collars.

5. For reasons unknown to mankind, Labradors prefer to take liquid refreshment in the bathroom. Keep in mind that some continuous clean toilet-tank tablets are highly suspect as carcinogens.

6. Water in a hose can heat to over 130 degrees; tissue damage can be done at 120 degrees. Always check, letting the water run until cool.

7. If you give a puppy an old tennis shoe, remember it smells the same as your designer loafer. How is it to know the difference?

8. To discover which dog has diarrhea, put different colored cake dye in each dog's food. Remember which dog ate which color! You will know the next morning.

9. If you paper train a puppy, you are teaching it that it is permissible to relieve itself in the house. If you also put papers in its crate, guess what the puppy will do.

10. It is cruel to let a Lab run loose even if you own acreage; its lifespan will be exceedingly shorter.

11. Alcohol and chocolate are highly toxic to dogs. Chocolate contains theobromine which their livers cannot clear. Seizures or death may occur.

12. To stop Labrador excavation, fill in the hole, scatter its own feces across, finish with another inch of soil. No odor, no flies, no more digging in that location for at least one month.

13. Labradors were bred to break ice with their chests. They are extremely prone to heatstrokes. Learn to read your dog's tongue. As the dog overheats, the mouth will open wider, the tongue will extend perhaps hanging from the side of its mouth and will begin to darken from light pink towards purple. Get the dog's whole body wet and place it in a shaded area with good air circulation.

Part of the price of a Labrador is having a guardian angel available for help, even when puppy whiskers have become a gray beard. Between breeder and buyer should be an attitude of concern as to what is best for that particular Labrador.

FTCh.-AFC-CFC Franklin's Tall Timber bred by Mrs. Bernard W. Ziessow. Owners, Roger and Pat Magnusson.

'68 NFC '67 & '68 NAFC Super Chief (Paha Sapa Chief II x Ironwood Cherokee Chica) owned and handled by August Belmont.

Some Pet Labradors that Became Famous

by Marianne Foote and Mary Feazell

Mary Feazell wishes to express her deepest appreciation to Marianne Foote for her contribution to make this chapter possible.

The majority of people acquire a Labrador Retriever as a companion for the family or for a hunting buddy. However, the characteristics of the breed, and the interest and dedication of individual owners, have led to some loftier accomplishments. The following vignettes offer insights into the temperament and unique attributes of some very famous Labradors:

'68 NFC '67 & '68 NAFC Super Chief (Paha Sapa Chief II x Ironwood Cherokee Chica) owned by August Belmont.

The Belmonts acquired "Soupy" from Wilbur Goode as a replacement for an earlier dog. Soupy remained an untrained puppy until he went to Rex Carr at six months. "Augie" Belmont recalls the circumstances: "It so happened that Louise and I had worked with Rex Carr previously during the year. At one point he had told us that he wished someday to have a pup that was completely untrained, so he would not have to undo a lot of previously acquired bad habits. Louise and I remembered this and decided to take the pup when he was six weeks old; bring him up in the house and keep him untrained until he would reach six months of age, before sending him to Rex. Louise didn't look forward to having an untrained pup in the house without being able to train him. As a result of this, I really got the pup by default.

Soupy lived an untrained life in the house with several other dogs. He was housebroken very early and endeared himself to us by his sensible and affectionate nature. We didn't even allow anyone to throw a ball for him, or drill him in obedience in any way. He slept by our bed and went everywhere with us. He did have one habit that presented some difficulty. We had a fireplace in the living room, unused, but replete with kindling wood and logs in a bed of sifted ashes. This was Soupy's playhouse where he would rest, as well as distribute the wood and ashes all over the house.

We kept him till he became six months old in December, and sent him to Rex as planned. We tried to persuade Rex to let him sleep by his bed, but Rex rightly maintained that he couldn't do that without all his clients wanting their dogs to have the same privilege.

Soupy immediately took to the training routine, and after Rex had worked on him for four weeks, he wrote us, saying that the pup was making his days. He said the sun shone brighter because of Soupy. He ended his letter by saying, "Send me more Soupys."

Soupy stayed with Rex until the following fall when Augie came to take him to Maine to run him in competition for the first time. He won the Amateur and took fourth in the Open. The rest is history. Soupy would be taken to a trial by Louise and she would run him on Friday and then Augie would motor or fly on Friday after work to the trial and handle him on the weekend. Soupy continued to sleep by the Belmont's bed at home or on the road, and, despite the often grueling schedule, he never lost his trust in his handlers. He would go back to Rex after each of the Nationals for training and then return to the Belmonts. After Soupy won his first National, Rex allowed him to sleep by his bed. His other clients understood.

Soupy won the National Amateur Championship in 1967 and the National Open and Amateur Championship in 1968; accumulating 242 Open points and 112 $1/2$ Amateur points during his career; and he became an outstanding producing sire whose influence is still evident in today's pedigrees.

Ch. Broad Reach's English Muffin UDT, WC (Springfields Chauncey x Springfields Kimberly) owned by Martha Lee and Buddy Voshell.

In 1976 at the age of three years, Muffin became the first champion Labrador Retriever bitch in the history of the breed to earn a Utility degree, a Tracking degree and an LRC, Inc. Working Certificate, and was only the fourth Labrador at that time to accomplish this.

Muffin's official name became Ch. Broad Reach's English Muffin UDT. Muffin came to the Voshells at the age of three months as a hopeful for the breed ring. She finished her show title in August 1974 and completed her obedience Companion Dog degree shortly after that. In the spring of 1975 Muffin was ready for Open work and completed her CDX degree in three straight shows.

Martha Lee describes Muffin "... as one of the happiest working Labs I have ever known, and her 'trademark' has always been a finish by jumping up in the air while turning—having learned this completely on her own. Often she would let out a 'woof' while taking the broad jump, and occasionally the high or bar jump. Muffin was a real show-off, usually putting in little twists of her own, which did not help the point system! But she was always happy, eager and willing."

Muffin finished her Utility title in the fall of 1975, earned her Working Certificate and then ran a Gundog trial where she received a JAM. Her tracking training was stepped up and she was certified in December. After missing a turn during her first tracking test in

Ch. Broad Reach's English Muffin UDT, WC (Springfield's Chauncey x Springfields Kimberly) owned by Martha Lee and Bud Voshell.

'76 NFC AFC San Joaquin Honcho, (FC AFC Trumarc's Raider x Doxie Gypsy Taurus) owned and handled by Judith S. (Weikel) Aycock.

Florida in February, Muffin was entered for a second test in April. Martha Lee recalls the circumstances, "... The location was lovely with beautiful fields—some open and some hilly with a variety of cover. Muffin and I drew the next to the last track as we were on the standby list until the week prior to the trial. The weather was warm, quite windy with a rainstorm brewing. Fortunately, we finished a great track minutes before a cloudburst. This was an experience I shall never forget, as it was the first dog I completely trained myself. That TD was probably our most difficult achievement."

The Voshells had Muffin for 15 years and commented ... "there was a no more friendly, outgoing and smart pet!"

'76 NFC AFC San Joaquin Honcho (FC AFC Trumarc's Raider x Doxie Gypsy Taurus) owned by Judith (Weikel) Aycock. Judy Weikel recognized San Joaquin Honcho's potential and purchased him just before the end of his Derby career. Judy, together with Rex Carr, the California trainer, developed Honcho's unique capabilities that culminated in a National Championship at the age of three. Ed Aycock, Judy's husband, highlighted the events of Honcho's career during an acceptance speech on Honcho's behalf for an award for outstanding contributions to field trials: "Judy purchased Honcho at 20 months of age from John Folsom, who had owned him since he was a puppy. John gave Honcho away when he was a young dog because he consistently overran marks—even on repeats. Honcho lived on a ranch in California for several months, where he was allowed to run free, hunting everything from rabbits to deer....When John Folsom learned that Honcho was not being properly cared for, he reclaimed him and started to train him. When Judy purchased Honcho, his field-trial record consisted of one JAM in the Derby. Honcho and Judy became a formidable team. He and she were at their best when things were most difficult. He had a brief, but very successful field-trial career. He was a National finalist four times; a double-header winner; and was forced to retire at six years, three months of age with 74 Open points and 68 Amateur points."

In early 1979 Honcho began coughing and running a slight fever. Ed prescribed antibiotics, and Judy left on a field-trial circuit with Honcho, however a lethargy set in that began to worry Judy and he was sent home to Ed for further treatment. By the time pulmonary blastomycosis was diagnosed, Honcho's weight had dropped 25 pounds and he was skin and bones. Judy immediately returned home and began around-the-clock care, forcefeeding balls of hamburger and butter, and an experimental drug, Ketoconazole.

Honcho recovered in six months, but severe lung damage prevented his return to competition. Ed characterizes the next part of Honcho's life as Chapter II, The King (Chapter I he titled The Competitor). As the King, Honcho conducted himself with grace and dignity. Ed recalls, "He possessed a regal presence that let you know who he was and how important he was. He was friendly to all creatures great and small, and, like Will Rogers, 'he never met a man or woman he didn't like.' "

However, sometimes the 'regal presence' required a break in routine or a holiday celebration and one of those incidents sticks in Ed's memory: "One Thanksgiving, while Judy and I were rushing to get ready to go to my mother's for Thanksgiving dinner, Honcho wandered off. No amount of calling or whistling brought him home. We live at the end of a dead-end road. Certain that he could not have gone far, we searched neighbor farms and houses, stopped people on the road and asked if they had seen a wayward old black dog with a white muzzle. After hours of searching we were in tears and despair, knowing that our friend had either been picked up by someone, or worse, killed on a distant farm road. In desperation I drove to a secluded neighbor's farm. The farmer had just arrived home to find a wayward old black dog in his chicken yard. Score–Honcho 6, Chickens 0. I profusely apologized for his behavior and bailed Honcho out of trouble for $30. Having had his Thanksgiving dinner, we hurried off to ours and gave thanks for having our friend back."

Honcho's remaining years were enjoyed as a hunting dog and constant companion. He recorded an unparalleled record as a sire: the leading producer of All-Age point earners from 1982-1990; sire of three National Amateur Champions; sire of one National Derby Champion; and sire of 68 dogs with FC or AFC titles. Hail the King!

FC '84 NAFC Trumarc's Zip Code (NFC AFC San Joaquin Honcho x Seymour's Windjammer Mist) owned by Judith and Ed Aycock.

"Cody" was given to Judy as a puppy by Jerry Patopea, however he did not give much of an indication of his potential during his early training. Like his sire, Honcho, Cody was entirely trained by Judy under the tutelage of Rex Carr. However, it was not until Judy began to run him in trials that Cody's inherent capabilities

became apparent. He placed in a major stake at the age of 17 months and went on to win the National Amateur Championship in 1984. His record included: qualifying for 20 U.S. Nationals (Open and Amateur); becoming a National finalist seven times; winning five double-headers; earning the honor of being the number two High Point Retriever with 444 All-Age points; and earning the Ralston Purina "Outstanding Field Trial Retriever Award" twice–in 1984 and 1987.

According to Judy and Ed, "Cody is a spoiled house pet who shares his home with his father and his two half-brothers."

Katie (Ch. Sunnybrook Acres Black Blaze x Ch Pinetree's SmoothSailin' CD, JH, WC) owned by Curtis Leming.

Katie, a black Labrador Retriever, handled by Oklahoma Highway Patrol Trooper Curtis Leming, was awarded the Big T Multi-purpose Dog of the Year Award in 1992. This award was first given in 1986, however, it is not an annual award. It is presented only to those dogs who show outstanding achievements in the fields of law enforcement and search and rescue.

Trooper Leming works with Katie on a regular basis on several kinds of training, including tracking. He had been training with Katie only a year when the incident occurred that earned her citation. Leming related the following: "Katie earned her award by tracking a trail that was 91 hours old. She tracked a doctor from Fort Worth, Texas who

NAFC-FC Trumarc's Zip Code (NFC-AFC San Joaquin Honcho x Seymour's Windjammer Mist) owned by Ed and Judith Aycock.

had fallen down a chimney in the Wichita Game Preserve. The doctor had been repelling and fell into the chimney. I happened to be at the game preserve on a training exercise with Katie when the guy was reported missing. Katie tracked the scent on a four- to five-mile trail." The last reported case of a dog successfully tracking a person on such a trail was only 24 hours old. According to Leming, "This is the first time a Labrador Retriever has been documented in such an instance."

The canine-training program is a fairly new one for the Oklahoma department. The dogs, as well as the training time for dogs like Katie, are donated.

Ch. Shamrock Acres Light Brigade (Ch. Shamrock Acres Casey Jones CD x Ch. Whygin Busy Belinda) owned by Sally McCarthy and Mrs. James Getz.

Ch. Shamrock Acres Light Brigade completed his championship with three majors by the time he was 13 months old, however, his owners decided to keep him home for two more years to grow up. It was not until the spring of 1967 that he came out to be campaigned. "Briggs" was co-owned by Sally McCarthy and John McAssey for one year, and then John sold his

Ch. Shamrock Acres Light Brigade (Ch. Shamrock Acres Casey Jones CD x Ch. Whygin Busy Belinda) owned by Sally McCarthy and Mrs. James Getz.

interest in the dog to Mrs. James Getz, who co-owned him with Sally for the rest of his life. Briggs was handled by Dick Cooper to all of his wins as a champion. He was beautifully trained and a very cooperative dog to show, however, Dick confessed that occasionally Briggs would doze off in his show stance if the Group went on too long and he'd have to remind him that the show was still in progress. During his show career Briggs earned 12 bests in show (including BIS at the International Kennel Club in 1968), 45 Group firsts, 12

FC-AFC-CFC-CAFC Franklin's Tall Timber (FC Del-Tone Buck x Franklin's Golden Charm owned by Roger and Pat Magnusson. Breeder, Mrs. B.W. Ziessow. Drawing by Judi Hardin.

Group seconds, nine Group thirds and seven Group fourths, and all of these placings were gained during a period of 14 months in 1967–68. He also became the sire of 94 champion get including two BIS winners.

Briggs died at 14 in 1978, still a handsome dog at that advanced age. Sally describes him as "... above all a gentleman—well-mannered, polite, and sensitive. He could be kenneled with any dog I owned, male or female. He loved children (was always finding his training dummy for them to throw) and enjoyed everyone. He was a very easy dog to live with and an easy dog to condition... Briggs was known not only for his record-setting wins but for his smile. He was quite a smiler, and would do so on request." Briggs lived all of his life with Sally except for the 14 months he was with Dick Cooper.

FC AFC CFC CAFC Franklin's Tall Timber (FC Del-Tone Buck x Franklin's Golden Charm) owned by Roger and Pat Magnusson.

The following highlights from this talented dog's career were written by his owner:

"Timber was Michigan-bred by Mrs. B.W. Ziessow and our first Lab. Pat and I went to our first field trial at Wolverine in 1965. That's all it took!

1967 was our Derby year. We ran five trials and received one first, two fourths, one JAM and broke once.

In 1968 we ran three Qualifiers and received one first, one second and one thrown out for fighting. Also ran one Amateur and received our first JAM–'lined all blinds.'

Billy Voigt told us, 'If we could make that dog stop on a whistle, I guarantee he will be one of the best in the country because I have never seen a dog line like him. There is something to be desired in his marking ability, but the way he lines I wouldn't worry about it.'

In 1969 Billy and I went to work and tried everything, including Ben Franklin's method and several others. Last resort, Mr. John Olin's AA method seemed to take effect at the end of the year.

In 1970 at the age of four, 'here we come.' Timber Dog was still an outlaw, but he was ready. He made his CFC in back-to-back weekends. Turned around and did the same to get his FC. To finish things up, he completed his AFC. Doing this, Timber became Michigan's first FC and AFC.

Timber competed in one Open, three Amateur and three Canadian Nationals. He had now fulfilled all our dreams and then some. He was retired from active competition in his prime, at six years of age, to remain a Super Duck Dog and Companion until the ripe age of 14. He was then called to Valhalla to wait for us.

He was a thrill to us. We still, and always will, talk about how he loved to lay down the blind retrieve his own way."

Am-Can. Ch. Dark Star of Franklin (Ch. Labcroft Mr. Chips x Am-Can. Ch. Pitch of Franklin) owned by Fred Martin.

Dianne Ziessow relays: "This poem was written about International Champion Dark Star of Franklin who was one of the greatest American-bred Labrador Retrievers. He died at the age of nine years with eight bests in show, 40 Sporting Group wins, and over 100 bests of breed. His memory lies not only in the hearts of the family that owned him but in the hearts of those who followed his records and watched him climb to his glory at the many shows that he was in. I presented this poem to my mother in May 1965, as a Mother's Day present."

The Black One
Where has my dog gone?
He lies in a grave outside my window.
Black... Black he was... Black as night
And so beautiful
He was a champion, you know
Broke records for this breed
So many acclaimed him as the greatest Lab to step foot in the show ring.
As a pup he was a fat roly-poly ball
Called freak for he was the only one out of the bitch
No one would buy him . . . now they all wish they had
Stupid people!
Named after a Derby winner who was as black as he

Am-Can. Ch. Dark Star of Franklin (Ch. Labcroft Mr. Chips x Am-Can. Ch. Pitch of Franklin) owned by Fred Martin.

The horse only won the run for the roses... but this black dog won much more

So many trophies line the shelves... so many ribbons fill the boxes.

"Ahda" was so proud of this black knight

He didn't think the black one was different

He only knew that the animal had greatness

He bought him ... took him in ... raised him ... "Ahda" and I together

I was so young then... yet I loved him and had faith in him

Then one sad Monday, "Ahda" died

The black dog that we both loved became mine.

Such a great animal... all mine

I was so proud

But he didn't seem like a celebrity... He was my friend ... in fact, one of my best

He pulled my brother on my sled with this custom-made harness.

A showman... Yes

But not a conceited star

A dark star in vainness... a bright star in truth.

All memories of a great dog

So many years have passed.

His picture is on my desk

They... my scholar friends... ask who he is

I say he was the greatest of them all... A Man O'War... only one of them.

Yes... even here in college after all those many years since his passing... he is with me

My strength to face my problems comes from his great head that is in front of me now

So many years... and now where is he?

He sleeps outside my window... protecting me from all evil

My great black friend.

'90 and '91 NFC Candlewoods Tanks a Lot ('92 NFC '90 NAFC Candlewood's Super Tanker x Candlewood's Tiz Too) owned by Randy Kuehl and Mary Howley.

'90 and '91 NFC Candlewoods Tanks a Lot is owned by Mary Howley of Madison, Wisconsin and Randy Kuehl of Springville, Iowa. "Lottie" is part of a two-generation team that has dominated the national retriever scene for the past two years. Between Lottie and her sire, '92 NFC '90 NAFC Candlewood's Super Tanker owned by Joyce Williams, they have accounted for four out of seven Nationals championships. Mary sold Lottie as a seven-week-old puppy to Andy Atar who started her "learning-to-learn" program right away. Credit for Lottie's successful foundation work goes to Andy and his boss, Mike Lardy, a Wisconsin professional retriever trainer. However, at eleven months, Mary learned that Andy was going to sell Lottie and she and Randy Kuehl bought her back. In turn, they hired Mike Lardy to continue her training. Lottie won her first Derby at eleven months, earning 108 Derby points and the National Derby Championship. She was 14 months old when she won both the Derby and the Qualifying Stakes on the same day, becoming the youngest dog known to have achieved such an accomplishment. Lottie completed her field championship

'90 & '91 NFC Candlewood's Tanks A Lot (NFC-NAFC Candlewood's Super Tanker x Candlewood's Tiz Too) owned by Randy Kuehl and Mary Howley. Breeder, Mary Howley.

with her first Open win at 27 months and earned her Amateur title three weeks later.

In November 1990 Lottie became the youngest dog in field–trial history to win the National Retriever Championship Stake. She was just three years and four months of age and had taken time off in February to whelp her first litter of puppies. She repeated that achievement in 1991—a phenomenal feat—becoming the first bitch and only the second retriever to ever accomplish such a distinction. She was also a finalist at the '93 National Amateur Championship.

Lottie has been bred three times and the puppies show great promise. The first litter has already produced one FC AFC, two more with Open wins, and three more All-Age qualified. In August Lottie won an Open and her daughter was second—hints of things to come!

Lottie lives with Mary when she is not with Mike Lardy and she is a wonderful house dog. Low key, she may jump on the bed or couch for a few minutes, but prefers the floor. She loves to climb in your lap when you sit down on the floor with her. However, she is obsessed with tennis balls and loves to roll one of them on the floor to Mary and have it rolled back to her. If Mary is reading and not paying attention, Lottie will flip the ball in her lap. Lottie shares the home with two other dogs, and Mary walks them at least one-half to one and one-half hours everyday. Lottie goes everywhere with Mary—the front seat in the Dodge van is only used by Lottie (the license plate on the van reads 2XNFC). In addition to winning the National, Lottie helped Mary's father get eight geese during hunting season.

Heatherhill's Blitz (Brazos Brookhurst x Wyndcall's Morgan) owned by Vanessa Lepard.

For hunters there may be one good reason not to "de-snake" dogs. Blitz, an 11-month-old yellow puppy, went hunting for the first time with his owner's father, Randy Lepard, and grandfather, E. M. Spraberry. Although untrained, Blitz did very well retrieving dove all day. The next day Mr. Spraberry, whose long-standing heart condition greatly restricted his speed and movement, decided to take Blitz hunting again while his son-in-law worked in an adjoining pasture. The puppy and grandfather set off together at a slow pace. Some time later Randy heard his father-in-law yell out, an emergency signal on Texas ranches. Randy raced to find Mr. Spraberry had almost stepped on a four-foot coiled rattlesnake. The elderly gentleman could not have moved quickly enough to avoid the deadly strikes. Had it not been for the puppy throwing himself in front of the grandfather's legs and attacking the snake, Mr. Spraberry undoubtedly would have died. Nicked on the leg while dispatching the rattler, Blitz was rushed to the veterinarian and very luckily recovered without the usual tissue sluffing. Vanessa Lepard, Blitz's owner, believes those nine rattles to be the finest trophy the puppy will ever earn.

Breeding Your Own

by Madge Martin Ziessow and Karen Marcus

When we were asked to write a chapter on breeding Labrador Retrievers, we agreed with one provision: we wanted it to reflect our personal experience as breeders rather than follow the usual prototype. There are many excel- lent books on breeding and rais- ing puppies as well as pamphlets from dog-food manufacturers and your veterinarian that explain the biological and technical aspects of dog breeding. We first want to show how we became involved with this

Presented to Mrs. B.W. Ziessow by Mrs. Grace Lambert, this painting represents Ch. Sam of Blaircourt and Ch. Golden Chance of Franklin with their son, Ch. Harrowby Luke.

breed, and then we will touch on some of the important considerations in becoming a responsible breeder of Labrador Retrievers.

Madge's unique initial exposure to Labrador Retrievers awakened her interest in breeding them. It began as a result of her love of horses. She and her husband Berney were members of Bloomfield Open Hunt, and were active in showing horses and in fox hunting. In 1950 at a local horse show, their good friend Cary Rogers, from the Mill Creek Hunt, offered to give them a Labrador Retriever from good stock. He knew Madge wanted to give Berney either a skeet gun or a Labrador Retriever for his birthday. After several weeks passed, she returned home from an errand to see a station wagon with Illinois plates and a black dog looking out the back window: the promised Labrador Retriever!

However, Cary wasn't so sure they would want her, this lovely two-year-old bitch was either in whelp to a Foxhound or was in the state of false pregnancy. Madge assured Cary that they wanted Mickey (her call name) and that they would have little trouble finding homes for Labrador/Foxhound puppies among their sporting friends. One day Mickey didn't act quite right so they took her to their veterinarian, Dr. Hodder. He examined Mickey and said, "Madge, you had better take her right home, she is going to whelp in an hour." Shortly thereafter, Mickey presented them with five

Mother with her puppies at age of one week.

healthy black puppies with white spots or patches.

Being real neophytes to puppy rearing, they turned to their veterinarian for advice and help to care for the bitch and puppies properly. With proper nutrition, vaccination and lots of attention and love, all five went to new homes. Their owners still claim they were the best dogs they ever had. Certainly the most important lesson they learned was that their veterinarian was their best friend as he guided them by providing the basic knowledge about whelping and raising a litter of puppies.

Uniformity is achieved through selective breeding. These puppies are now two weeks old.

Mickey had a very impressive pedigree, she was sired by FC Pickpocket for Deer Creek, a son of three-time National Field Champion and Dual Ch. Shed of Arden. Her dam Wardwyn Warbler was sired by Best in Show Ch. Earlsmoor Moor of Arden and out of Ch. Buddha of Arden. Both of these dogs had also run in field trials. They registered Mickey as Pitch of Franklin, and she became the foundation bitch of their breeding program and is behind all Franklin Labradors.

When they decided to show her, they contacted one of the best sporting dog handlers in the country, Dick Cooper. This was at the suggestion of their friend Julia Gasow. Dick said he would consider showing her provided he could see her before taking her into the ring. He liked what he saw and handled her at the Detroit Kennel Club Show where she took the points and was on her way, finishing in less than two months with an occasional placing in the Sporting Group.

At the urging of their friends in the Wolverine Retriever Club, they decided to breed Mickey. The stud they chose was Ch. Labecoft Mr. Chips for two reasons: one he was a grandson of Shed of Arden and two he was within easy driving distance. This breeding produced a litter of five puppies, two of whom became champions. One pup, Ch. Troublemaker of Franklin, finished easily, placing in groups all along the way.

BREEDING YOUR OWN

He later sired Ch. Golden Chance of Franklin, the only female to win two National Specialty shows and also place Best of Opposite Sex twice.

Mickey was bred again to Ch. Labecoft Mr. Chips and produced one large black male puppy, Am-Can. Ch. Dark Star of Franklin. He was the top Sporting dog in the country in 1955, breaking the breed record for bests in show. He held this for ten years before Ch. Sam of Blaircourt broke it. However, Dark Star did defeat Ch. Sam of Blaircourt in 1960 at the National Specialty at the age of seven-and-a-half years.

Madge and Berney always followed the practice of breeding Mickey to the finest dogs available in both bench and field. They had been taught that the first lesson in breeding is to breed the best to the best and hope for the best. An excellent example of this was her litter by FC Freehaven Muscles that produced two bench champions and a dog and bitch that both qualified for Open All-Age Stakes.

To their knowledge, the Ziessows were the first Labrador people in Michigan to x-ray hips. This was at the suggestion of their dear friend Dorothy Howe. In those days, before the existence of OFA, they submitted hip x-rays taken by their veterinarian to Dr. Schnele at Angel Veterinarian Hospital in Boston for examination and grading. Mrs. Howe also made them aware of hereditary eye problems that caused her much loved Brookhaven Angel to lose its eyesight. Dorothy was a perfectionist, and Madge is very grateful that she was able to learn from her.

She taught them never to breed to unsound animals regardless of their show record. It could only result in producing other unsound animals and breaking people's hearts.

Karen Marcus became involved in Labradors in a much more conventional way. Being a veterinary technician, she was exposed to all kinds of breeds of dogs, but she fell in love with the Labrador. One of the local all-breed clubs in the area, the Ann Arbor Kennel Club has a booklet listing local breeders, that have passed the club's requirement in honesty and breeding ethics. She used this as her source in finding her first Labrador. Franklin Kennel was listed and close to her home. So she called Madge and was invited out to the house to meet her. Madge was very nice to her but she also wanted to make sure that she was good enough for one of her puppies. Madge wanted to know how she would care for a pup and why she wanted this puppy. To make a long story short, I did get a male puppy from Madge that she showed in obedience in both the States and Canada. He also obtained his WC in both countries.

After 15 years in Labradors learning from the experts, I started my own breeding program. Breeding dogs is not for everyone, especially beginners. You must be dedicated to the breed and if you cannot make this commitment, maybe you should plan to purchase rather than breed. When you do decide that you want to involve yourself in Labradors seriously and start a breeding

80

As puppies continue to grow, the litter is moved out of the original whelping room. At around three weeks of age, they now reside in two pens.

program, education should be your first priority. Read everything you can find, go and meet the experts at shows, trials and hunt tests. Decide what kind of Labrador you want, and go to a successful well-established breeder to obtain the best dog or bitch you can. A good adult or pick-of-the-litter puppy is hard to find and many breeders are reluctant to part with them, but this is what you should strive for to start a responsible breeding program. As a novice to the dog game, it is very important to find someone you can trust and who can answer your questions. You need to find a mentor and teacher to show you the ropes. Breeding is much more complicated today than it was 20 or 30 years ago. There are many more factors to consider besides just obtaining a decent bitch and having puppies. There are many questions you have to research before you start your breeding program. One often overlooked problem is city or county zoning laws that must be observed. You do not want to make painful decisions about what dogs you can keep if you are caught over the limit.

If you think that breeding and selling puppies is a good way to supplement your income, think again. It is possible that you could have over four digits invested in the litter before a single puppy is sold. A responsible breeder spends a great deal of time and money to produce the best quality puppies he or she can.

Chow time for these puppies at four weeks of age.

Labradors are very popular today, therefore, it is very important that when you decide to raise a litter it is for the best possible motive: to improve on your stock and to improve the breed in general. It is important always to strive toward that almost impossible goal of perfection. Once you have found what you hope is your foundation bitch, you should have her examined and certified to be free of various controllable genetic defects found in dogs. The eyes need to be examined by a veterinary ophthalmic specialist to be certified by the Canine Eye Registration Foundation (CERF). Progressive retinal atrophy or PRA is unfortunately a very serious problem in Labradors today. The Orthopedic Foundation for Animals (OFA) will certify two-year-old dogs to be free of certain orthopedic problems, most notably hip dysplasia. It is also a good idea to have the dog's elbows, hocks and shoulders checked by a confident veterinarian.

It is very important to study your Labrador's pedigree and the pedigrees of its relatives for these congenital problems such as seizures or von Willebrands (bleeding disorders). You should also obtain this information on your chosen stud dog and his relatives. It is very important to try to reduce the incidence of congenital disorders and the only method we know presently is to abstain from breeding affected dogs and their close relatives, especially with well-documented genetic disorders like PRA.

Carefully research your bitch's and stud dog's pedigree to see how they compliment each other; consider the animal's conformation and temperament. A Labrador must have the sweet disposition the breed is known for or it's not a quality Labrador. Labradors are also working dogs—it is important that you strive to retain the strong retrieving drive even if you personally don't hunt and the only thing your Labrador will retrieve is a worn-out tennis ball.

Now that you have the perfect bitch and have found the perfect stud, it is time to get down to the serious act of actually producing a litter. Both the bitch and stud should be CERF- and OFA-certified and should be free of congenital problems to the best of your knowledge. Before breeding it is a good idea to have both animals tested for brucellosis, a form of canine VD that can lead to sterility in males and abortions in females. The bitch should be up to date on all vaccinations and have a heartworm test. She should also be free of intestinal parasites before breeding so as to reduce the incidence of worms in the puppies. It is advantageous to test the female for her optimal breeding time. This procedure is usually performed by a veterinarian and involves checking blood–hormone levels and vaginal cytology.

If you choose to use a non-local stud, there will be shipping costs for your female to send her to the dog or costs for shipping fresh or frozen semen from the male to your bitch and having her artificially inseminated. Sometimes even with a local stud, artificial insemination may be required.

It is a very good idea to establish a good relationship with your veterinarian if you plan to breed your female. He or she can be invaluable to you to answer questions about nutrition for pregnant and lactating bitches, as well as to help you through the actual whelping process. It is very important to understand this process before the bitch is actually in labor. There are many very well-written books on this subject and hopefully your mentor and your veterinarian will also be available to help you.

It is vital to know what to expect so that you can spot potential problems before they can become life-threatening to both the bitch and the puppies. Sometimes a bitch may need a Caesarean section. Know how your veterinarian handles after-hour emergencies and make arrangements to be prepared for this possibility. Even if the female whelps without problem, it is always a good idea to have her checked by your veterinarian for any potential post-partum problems.

It is a very good idea to have a whelping pen for your bitch. These can be as simple as a baby swimming pool to elaborate home-made ones with movable walls that can expand outward as the puppies mature. The whelping pen should be in a quiet but easily excisable part of the house. Madge has converted a walk-in closet into a small tiled room with an access door that permits the dam to go in or out her own private run. It also has a Dutch door so she can watch the litter

New experiences...eating outdoors.

without her other dogs bothering the litter and mother. I have converted an unused bedroom into a whelping area so that I can stay close to the new mother and her litter.

Puppies need to be exposed to many different stimuli as they mature. Once they are weaned, they need to leave the whelping area and move to a more active part of the house. Get them used to being handled and played with by different people from all age groups. Expose them to household noises such as the vacuum, the loud T.V., and kitchen pots and pans and appliances. Having puppies also involves a lot of cleaning time—the more they eat (at least three times a day), the dirtier they can get. The puppies will also need their first vaccination before they leave your care. You should also have them checked for intestinal parasites at the time of their first vaccination. Your veterinarian should be able to consult with you on the optimum time to do all this. Many breeders now test their litters to help with placing the puppies into the right environment. You also have to find responsible people to take your puppies. Remember these puppies are a very large responsibility and they are depending on you to find them a family that will keep and love them for the rest of their lives.

This hungry litter is five weeks old.

When you find the perfect new owners, you need to educate them on the care of their new puppy. They need to take the pup to see their veterinarian within 48 hours to have it checked and to set up a complete vaccination schedule. Always send information on nutrition, housebreaking, crate training and socialization.

Breeding Labradors is a very costly and time-consuming undertaking, but for those hardy souls who truly want to improve the breed, it is worth every second and cent. There is a lot of satisfaction in knowing that you have bred a new champion, obedience winner, field–trial contender, hunt test winner or loving family pet. We do not mean to discourage new breeders but rather to open their eyes to the commitments that all responsible breeders must willingly undertake.

Dual Ch. Michael of Glenmere, whelped March 24, 1935, was the first dual champion of the breed. Owner, Jerry Angle of York, NE.

Dual Ch. Michael of Glenmere
A. K. C. A150354

Sire:
Ace of Whitmore

- Tad of Whitmore
  - Toi of Whitmore
  - Ch. Throne of Whitmore
- Lily of Harwood
  - Colonel of Harwood
  - Dinah of Harwood

Dam:
Vixen of Glenmere

- Decco of Glenmere
  - Sab of Tulliallan
  - Neegla
- Vamp of Glenmere
  - Glenmere Joe
  - Niths Double

Famous American Show Labradors

by Dr. Bernard W. Ziessow

The title of this chapter raises the question, "What makes any show dog famous, a Labrador Retriever or any other breed?" I believe the answer lies in the quality and extent of his competition, plus the knowledge and background of the person or persons that made the evaluation. In this latter regard, I'm reminded of a truly famous Labrador that was virtually ignored by a so-called "breeder judge" at a specialty show, only to win the Sporting Group on the following two days at all-breed shows and go on to win best in show on the final day. While it is not my intention to question the ability of "breeder judges" or to belittle the importance of a specialty show win (after all we all started as breeder judges), it is significant that dogs are normally evaluated by only one person at a specialty show, but must win under three different judges, two of whom are approved for at least one entire group, to win best in show at an all-breed show. Accordingly, the famous dogs I have selected are multiple-best-in-show winners, though collectively they won ten national specialties.

Last week, browsing through our library, I happened upon a book entitled *Modern Dogs (Sporting)*, written over 100 years ago by a Mr. Rowdan B. Lee, and published by Horace Cox in London in 1893. The section on retrievers is most interesting.

On judging retrievers, Mr. Lee relates: "At the last Birmingham show, Mr. Lloyd Price had an unusually fine class of dogs before him, which included one called Rightaway, which his owner, Mr. Shirley, considered to be one of the best dogs he ever saw. The judge thought otherwise, and gave the chief award to another from the same kennel. The winner was a much more active-looking dog than Rightaway, equally good in coat, head and expression, and in legs and feet; but he stood a little higher on the legs, and was not so heavy in bone as the favorite of the Kennel Club's President, who should know a good dog if any man does. Still, on this occasion we endorse the judge's decision in giving first prize to the more active and workman-like animal, and it is to be hoped that judges will be consistent and award the leading honours to those dogs that from appearance seem most likely to be useful in the field."

In his "Thoughts on the Borzoi" written by the late Louis Muir for the 1979 Borzoi Club of American yearbook, he relates a similar story:

"In 1925, the author first judged Borzoi at Westminster where there was an entry of 50 or so dogs. When, strange as it seems, into the ring walked a cowboy with hat, spurs and so forth, with a Borzoi on a chain who went best of breed from the classes. The cowboy brought two other Borzoi almost as good. These were O'Valley Farm dogs raised in Wyoming on a ranch by the cowboys and used to hunt coyotes." Mr. Muir goes on to say "proper conformation is basic to survival of the breed and is equally important to a pet, show dog or a hunter." Ignorance of this fact is a clear indication that such a person does not or refuses to understand what has always been required of the Borzoi or any other breed.

The first question that must come to mind when judging the Labrador (or any breed) is "Can this dog do the job it was originally intended to do?" In the case of the Labrador Retriever, the dog must be capable of retrieving waterfowl and upland game; any animal unable to perform these tasks is not a Labrador.

The Labrador Retriever Club held its first annual specialty show on May 19, 1933 in the garage of Marshall Field's townhouse in New York City. Mrs. Marshall Field, president of the club, judged the 33 dogs entered in the show and best of breed was awarded to Mr. Franklin B. Lord's Boli of Blake. The dog went on to become the first Labrador American bench champion.

It is interesting to note that the participants were the same as those entered in the first field trials—they were owned by F.B. Lord, W.A. Harriman, Kathleen Start and Wilber Lloyd Smith, to name a few. These 33 dogs were their owner's shooting dogs, and the show was held to determine the dogs that were the best looking (conform most closely to the breed standard).

The first dual champion in America was Michael of Glenmere, owned by Jerry Angel of York, Nebraska. His field trial championship certificate was awarded May 20, 1941; he finished his bench championship on December 10 of that year.

If I were asked to name the five top winning Labrador show dogs of all time, the list would have to include Ch. Earlsmoor Moor of Arden, Ch. Dark Star of Franklin, Ch. Sam of Blaircourt, Ch. Shamrock Acres Light Brigade and Ch. Charisma's Lone Star Rick. While their show careers encompassed almost six decades, they all possessed a singular quality: elegance. All except one were American bred and traced their ancestry to great field-trial dogs.

All of the top best-in-show Labradors I have named were shown across the board, "taking on all comers." They were not flown across the country in search of favorable

Ch. Earlsmoor Moor of Arden, whelped February 1, 1937, was the first Labrador to win a best in show. Moor was shown 42 times and went best of breed 40 times and five times best in show. He was sired by Ch. Raffles of Earlsmoor x FTCh. Decoy of Arden. Owners, Dr. and Mrs. Samuel Milbank of New York.

Ch. Earlsmoor Moor of Arden

A. K. C. A159966

Sire: Ch. Raffles of Earlsmoor	Thatch of Whitmore	Titus of Whitmore Tee of Whitmore
	Task of Whitmore	Toi of Whitmore Teazle of Whitmore
Dam: FTCh. Decoy of Arden	Odds On	The Favourite Jest
	Peggy of Shipton	Ronald of Candahar Gehta

Am-Can. Ch. Dark Star of Franklin at eight years old winning the 1960 Labrador Retriever Club National Specialty. The judge was Mr. Hollis Wilson; handled by breeder, Mrs. B. W. Ziessow.

situations or judges for the sole purpose of setting a record or winning an award; and expensive advertising campaigns were unheard of. Moreover, they were shown under experienced, well-respected breed, all-breed and multi-group judges.

If I had to name the one dog that had the greatest influence on the Labrador breed as a show dog it would have to be Earlsmoor Moor of Arden. He was the first Labrador to win a best-in-show award in the United States. He was the "bell weather": he set the course for the others to follow. Moor was shown only 42 times with the following record.

40 times best of breed

12 times Sporting Group first

27 times placed in the Sporting Group

5 times best in show

5 times best in a national specialty (twice from the field dog class)

Moor's best-in-show record remained in tact for 12 years, when in 1955, it was broken by Am-Can. Ch. Dark Star of Franklin, owned by Mr. Fred T. Martin and bred by Mrs. B.W. Ziessow. He was shown throughout his career by Mr. Richard Cooper, except for his last show. In 1960 he was taken out of retirement and won the Labrador Retriever Club's national specialty show under the respected judge Mr. Hollis Wilson. He was shown by Mrs. Madge Ziessow (Mr. Martin's daughter) and owned at that time by Mr. Ziessow.

During his show career, which extended over only 18 months, his record included eight bests in show, 40 Groups wins, 93 Group placements, 116 Best of Breeds, one national specialty win and an LRC Working Certificate. He was awarded top sporting dog of 1955.

Eng-Am. Ch. Sam of Blaircourt was imported by Mrs. Grace Lambert in 1959 at two years of age. He was shown throughout his career by the late Mr. Ken Golden. His enviable record includes 61 bests of breed, 53 Sporting Group firsts, nine bests in show and three times winner of the national specialty. He was retired in 1965.

Sam's record remained intact until 1968 when it was broken by Ch. Shamrock Acres Light Brigade, bred by Mrs. Sally McCarthy Munson and owned by Mrs. McCarthy and Mrs. James R. (Betsy) Getz. He was shown throughout his enviable career by Mr. Richard Cooper. His record which covered only nine months includes 12 bests in show, 45 Sporting Group wins, 75 Group placements and 95 bests of breed. He won top Sporting dog of 1968 and ranked number five all-breed that year. "Briggs" sired 93 champions and one Canadian champion.

There is an old adage that states

Ch. Shamrock Acres Light Brigade winning the Sporting Group under judge Bernard W. Ziessow at the Saginaw Valley Kennel Club. Handler, Dick Cooper.

"all records are made to be broken." The top winning Labrador in the history of the breed is Ch. Charisma Lone Star Rick. This most renowned son of 1978 world champion Ch. Franklin's Golden Mandigo CD won 13 bests in show, under 12 different judges; one specialty show win, 64 Group firsts, 146 Group placements and 221 bests of breed. He was the number one Labrador Retriever in 1985, 1986 and 1987. He was bred by Renee Loyless and owned by Joyce and Roy Loyless. His handler throughout his career was John "Buddy" Downey.

Rick's elegance, ability to move and disposition are stamped in his offspring; unfortunately he died at an early age and his influence on the breed is limited.

Will these records be broken? Will the legacy passed on by Moor, Dice, Sam, Briggs and Rick continue? The answer lies in the devotion to the breed, the will to maintain the integrity of the Labrador as a true sporting dog and the determination on the part of the breeders to strive for excellence. The emphasis must be on quality not on numbers.

Ch. Charisma's Lone Star Rick winning Best in Show at the Illinois Valley Kennel Club under Dr. B. W. Ziessow. Handler, Buddy Downey.

Judging the Labrador Retriever

by Dr. Bernard W. Ziessow

One of the questions most frequently asked of judges is "What do you look for in judging the Labrador Retriever (or any breed)?"

In my particular case, one thing that helped me was the fact that I judged horses (hunters and jumpers) long before I ever considered judging dogs and learned that a knowledge of anatomy and soundness is essential of one who considers entering the show ring as a judge. Accordingly, "What do I look for when judging Labrador Retrievers?" I consider the following points:

Conformation
Quality
Substance
Soundness and
Movement.

The word *Conformation* has two connotations: 1.) The individual must conform to a specific pattern or standard and 2.) it must possess the physical attributes necessary to perform its intended purpose or functions. In her "Analysis of the Labrador Retriever and the Standards," Janet Churchill writes: "The Lab has been developed as a hunting dog (called a shooting dog in England). This fact should be taken into consideration by both show and field trial groups, as the physical features of the dog should allow it to do its job most effectively."

Quality, when applied to dogs, relates to the manner in which the various parts of the animal are put together to present a pleasing picture. Are the points well distributed, do they bear good relation one to another, and are they in proportion so the animal appears well balanced?

Substance pertains to the bone structure and muscular development. However, too much substance or lumbar causing the animal to appear cloddy is as bad or worse than too little. Countess Howe, the renowned English sportslady, Labrador breeder and authority on the breed, compares the Labrador to an Irish hunter or thoroughbred horse capable of standing up to a day's work in the hunt field.

Soundness is important to any breed but especially to a Labrador because he is first and foremost a retrieving gundog and must be physically able to perform his intended purpose. Accordingly,

Kerrybrook Knight Hawk, SH owned by Robert and Judith Meyer.

animals with such defects as bad feet, straight shoulders, long, sway or roached back, cowhocks, long or let down pasterns, or weak quarters must be severely penalized. They just will not be able to stand up to a day's work.

Movement or way of going is the crucial test of conformation. Many defects which are difficult to detect when the dog is stationary become apparent when he moves. The movement of the Labrador should be sound, free and effortless.

The Labrador Retriever standard speaks of a strongly built, short-coupled, very active dog; fairly wide over the loins and strong and muscular in the hind quarters. Short coupled means short from the withers to hipbone. Emphasis is placed upon this particular point because long-backed dogs cannot perform their intended functions.

There are three points described in the standard as distinctive to the breed: head, coat and tail. The *head* is described as wide in skull, clean cut and free from fleshy cheeks; there should be a slight stop and the jaws long and powerful. Importantly, the head should be in balance with the animal. The head and expression should reflect quality, intelligence and good temperament. The head is described in a "blueprint" of the Labrador standard written by Mr. Richard Anderson, a prominent English judge, as: "moderate in all respects...The skull should be fairly wide but not coarse....Heads that are wedge-shaped or thick through the cheek bones or behind the ears are definitely wrong."

The description of the Labrador's *coat* in the standard has not changed in 60 years –"short, very dense and without wave, and should give a fairly hard feeling to the hand." While the Labrador has an undercoat, he is not a "double-coated" dog as are most northern breeds, e.g., Siberian Husky, Alaskan Malamute, Norwegian Elkhound. Heavy "stand-offish" coats are incorrect.

The *tail* is the third distinctive feature of the breed. It is described in the standard as very thick towards the base, gradually tapering towards the tip and of medium length. It should be free from any feathering and clothed all around with the Labrador's thick, dense coat giving that rounded appearance described as the "otter" tail. The tail may be carried gaily but it should not curl over the back. Teapot curve or tails inclined forward from the root are serious defects.

While the head, coat and tail are distinctive features of the breed, it is important to remember in judging the Labrador not to place undue emphasis on any feature or characteristics so as to ignore their

Ch. Franklin's Mandigo owned by Laurel Jenny.

relationship to the overall dog; all points should bear a good relationship to one another—none should be awarded such prominence as to ignore the others.

Another hallmark of the breed, although not emphasized in earlier standards, is *temperament*. While he has no peers as a retrieving gundog, the Labrador is equally tibly overweight not only are incorrect but are unable to perform in the manner intended of the breed. The late Helen Warwick, in her book *The Complete Labrador Retriever* also talks about condition: "Nobody will tell me why retrievers are sent into the ring in such conditions that, if they worked, they would be useless within minutes." She continues: "All

Ch. Franklin's Hickory Grove at 11 years old with Ch. Franklin's Balliwick Rally at age nine placing in the Brace class at the LRC Specialty 1981.

admired as a faithful family friend and companion. Aggressiveness towards humans or other animals is not characteristic of the breed.

Dogs over or under the prescribed size limits, which also have not changed in over 60 years, or percep- dogs should be fit when shown. A retriever must be fit when worked....Class by class, they (Labradors) come in too fat. Many are gross in jowl and dewlap, flabby, thickly underlined in frame and sloppy in foot."

The Labrador Retriever, like most other breeds, was bred and developed to serve a purpose. To better acquaint prospective judges of the breed of this purpose, it is recommended they attend a licensed field trial or hunting test to observe the dogs at work. The experience will be educational and entertaining.

CONFORMATION REQUIREMENTS: WORKING VS. SHOW DOGS

The question is frequently asked, "Are the conformation requirements the same for a working dog and a show dog?"

Many years ago someone asked my long-time friend and respected all-breed judge, the late Louis Muir, the same question. He responded that both the field dog and show dog should have exactly the same conformation and condition.

If one were to examine the history of the Labrador Retriever, he would find the dog was bred with one purpose in mind—to be a working retriever. This was true in Newfoundland, where the fishermen carried a Labrador Retriever in the dory to retrieve fish that came off the trawl. Their hunting and retrieving ability was the reason the breed was imported to England by sportsmen in the early 19th century. It is also the reason why gentlemen and lady sportsfolk brought the dog into this country.

By definition, conformation in any breed is the symmetrical formation and arrangement of (body) parts; conforming to a model or a plan (i.e., the breed standard). The first question that must come to mind in judging any breed or evaluating an individual specimen is "Can the dog do the job he was originally intended to do." It is axiomatic that proper conformation is basic to the survival of any breed and is equally important to both the show dog and the hunter. It is ludicrous, therefore, to think of "type" as something extra to breed conformation and/or soundness (which is tantamount to proper movement). Without them you can't have true breed type. Accordingly, there is one (and only one) correct "type" of Labrador Retriever.

The ideal Labrador, and I say ideal because the perfect specimen hasn't been born, should, in my opinion, possess the conformation of a retrieving gun dog able to excel in field work, the quality to win in the show ring, the substance and soundness to hunt upland game and water fowl for long hours under difficult conditions, and the disposition to be a faithful companion and family friend. In all, the physical features and mental characteristics should denote the work the dog was bred to perform.

It is important to remember conformation is not a quality which is either entirely present or entirely absent. There are many degrees of conformation. The problem that faces the Labrador Retriever (and many other breeds) today is to define what degree of variation from the standard of perfection is acceptable for ourselves and, therefore, for the breed. It is most unfortunate, but true, there are many people in the dog fancy today that have the mistaken idea that the ideal specimen of the breed is what is winning at dog shows or successfully competing in field trials, as opposed to the characteristics that were essential in the development of the breed. This false notion has led to the demise of many sporting breeds as working dogs—while capable of winning ribbons at dog shows, they are unable physically to do the job the breed was originally intended to perform. They are lacking in those features which formed the basis for breed conformation and standard. Equally disturbing are the number of dogs being run in field trials (and used for breeding) that do not come up to the breed standards of conformation and soundness.

THE LABRADOR RETRIEVER STANDARD

Hopefully, most breed standards describe an animal that will, indeed, be able to perform its intended purpose. The Labrador standard speaks of a dog "well balanced in all its parts," well laid back or angulated shoulders, well turned stifles and free and effortless movement.

Balance, angulation and movement—these qualities or characteristics are contained in the standard to describe a dog that was bred for water fowling and retrieving upland game. I have already suggested that anyone that aspires to judge the breed or is seriously interested in breeding should attend a licensed retriever field trial or hunting test and learn firsthand what is expected from the animal, at least from the standpoint of physical characteristics.

Before we examine the standard in detail, perhaps we should consider the aforementioned attributes:

Balance This factor considers the relationship of the anatomical parts one to another. To better understand the term, I measured photographs of many of the top winning American and English Labradors past and present. The standard speaks of a short coupled dog—my measurements disclosed that the distance from the fore chest to the rump was about the same as the dog's height at the withers and the distance from the brisket to the ground is one-half the height at the withers. Other important measurements disclosed that the head appears to be one-half for the muzzle and one-half for the skull, and the distance from the occiput to the withers is about one-half the distance from the withers to the tail set, accordingly, cloddy short-legged individuals do not conform to the breed standard (either here or in England); neither do specimens that are lacking in substance.

Angulation This dichotomy is closely related to balance— one cannot exist without the other. The most common connotations of the term refer to the relationship of the shoulder blade or scapula in the upper arm and of the pelvis to the upper thigh or femur. The ideal relationship, both

Sunspots Wish Upon A Star winning the breed under Dr. Ziessow at the Northwestern Connecticut Dog Club in 1992. Owners, Lisa Keplar, John Schumer and Frances S. Doris.

front and rear, is a 90 degree angle. I emphasize the word *both;* a dog that is straight in front but with good rear angulation is not in balance, and this defect will be manifested in the dog's movement (hackney action, crabbing or side winding, pacing and, possibly of greater importance, the dog's reach is restricted and his ability to

Ch. Charisma's Lone Star Rick was the number one Labrador from '85 through '87.

ferred to as "snatch of the hocks," an attribute required of swimming dogs. This quality is lacking in dogs that are straight in stifle; moreover, it may be indicative of a structural weakness or, in extreme cases, slipped stifle.

Movement I am told that a great Chinese poet and philosopher once said that a picture is worth a thousand words. This also may be said about movement—movement tells more about a dog than can be learned from any other method of examination and discloses otherwise hidden faults. What is the judge looking for when he asks the handler to "go down across and back" or to "make an L"? He wants to view the dog's movement: going forward, coming back and from the side. What does he see? All of the results or effects of conformation or structural defects: straight shoulders, weak pasterns, straight stifles, cow hocks and, oh yes, that sway back that was so cleverly hidden by expert "stacking" and maintained by a well–appointed thumb to the ribs.

We will now consider what we should look for and what should be avoided regarding the various parts of the Labrador's anatomy as set forth in the standard. But first, I would like to relate a story:

"cover ground" is impaired). Another structural weakness related to angulation and balance is the comparative length of the shoulder blade to the upper arm. If they are not of equal length, the dog's front legs will not "stand under" the withers. This fault will result in too much or too little fore chest and also restrict the dog's movement.

Well-turned stifles (or rear angulation) provides the needed propelling power necessary for good movement. This is sometimes re-

Many years ago, a respected Labrador breeder (Lorna Countess Howe) compared the breed to a "cleverly made Irish hunter that could take the rough ground and jump in stride, measuring the last fence as eagerly and as well as he did the first." Accordingly, the ideal Labrador should not resemble a draft animal, neither should he be like a sprint horse; rather he should possess the physical qualities to perform his intended purpose—retrieving water fowl in open water or in heavy marsh and/or spending a long day afield in search of upland game.

I am sure many of you have read the breed standard over many times and are probably as familiar with the wording as I am; however, I would like to share my interpretation:

Interpretation of the Labrador Retriever Standard

GENERAL APPEARANCE

COMMENTS AND EXPLANATION: The Labrador Retriever should be a medium-sized well-balanced retriever gun dog. Physical features and mental characteristics should denote a dog bred to perform as an efficient retriever of game with a stable temperament suitable for a variety of pursuits beyond the hunting environment. The most distinguishing characteristics of the Labrador Retriever are his short, dense, weather resistant coat; his "otter" tail; his clean cut head with broad back-skull and moderate stop; and his kind dark eyes, expressing character, intelligence and good temperament. Above all the Labrador Retriever must be well balanced—the components of his anatomy in proper correlation. A dog well-balanced in all points is preferable to one with outstanding good qualities and defects. A typical Labrador possesses quality without over-refinement and substance without lumber or cloddiness.

FAULTS: Any deviation from the ideal described in the standard should be penalized to the extent of the deviation. Because the Labrador is bred primarily as a working gun dog, structural faults or any unsoundness common to all breeds are especially undesirable, even though such faults may not be specifically mentioned in the standard.

SIZE, PROPORTION AND SUBSTANCE

Approximate weight of dogs and bitches in working condition:

Dogs: 65–80 lbs. Bitches: 55–70 lbs.

Height at shoulders:

Dogs: 22½ inches to 24½ inches Bitches: 21½ inches to 23½ inches

COMMENTS AND EXPLANATION: Length from the point of the shoulder to the point of the rump is equal to or slightly longer than the height from withers to ground. Distance from elbow to the ground is one-half the height at the withers. The brisket extends to elbows, not perceptibly deeper. Substance and bone are proportionate to the overall dog.

FAULTS: Light, weedy individuals are definitely incorrect; equally objectionable are cloddy, lumbering specimens. Labrador Retrievers should be shown in working condition well muscled and without fat. Dogs or bitches more than one-half inch over or under the prescribed heights should be penalized.

HEAD

COMMENTS AND EXPLANATION: The skull should be wide and well developed but without exaggeration. The muzzle is neither long and narrow nor short and stubby. The correct foreface is nearly as long as and parallel to the plane of the back skull. The nose should be wide and nostrils well developed, black on black or yellow dogs, brown on chocolates. Fading to a lighter shade in cold weather is not a serious fault in yellows and chocolates. The teeth should be strong and regular with a scissors bite. The lower teeth just behind but touching the inside of the upper incisors. The ears are rather short, reaching to the inside corner of the eye when pulled forward, hanging moderately close to the head; set somewhat far back and even or slightly above eye level. Kind dark brown eyes imparting good temperament and intelligence are a hallmark of the breed. They should be of medium size, set wide apart and neither full nor deep set. The eye color should be brown in black and yellow Labradors and brown or hazel in chocolates. Eye rims are black in black or yellow Labradors; brown in chocolates.

FAULTS: A wedge-shaped head is faulty; as are massive heads. Undershot or overshot and misaligned or missing teeth are serious faults. Large heavy ears are incorrect; equally faulty are low-set houndy ears. A round, prominent eye is faulty; small eyes set close together are not typical of the breed. Black- or yellow-colored "bird of prey" eyes give harsh expressions and are equally undesirable.

NECK, TOPLINE AND BODY

COMMENTS AND EXPLANATION: The neck should be of proper length to allow the head to reach to ground for game to be retrieved. The neck rises strongly from the shoulders and arches moderately as it joins the head. The shoulders are well laid back, long and sloping, forming an angle with the upper arm of approximately 90 degrees. The length of the shoulder blade should equal the length of the upper arm. Correct chest conformation will effect a tapering sternum between the front legs that allows unrestricted forelimb movement. The back is strong and the topline is level from the withers to the croup, when standing still or in motion. The ideal Labrador is close-coupled with good spring of ribs tapering to a moderately wide chest that extends to, but is never above and not perceptively below, the elbows. The underline is almost straight with little or no tuck-up in mature individuals. Loins are short, wide and strong, extending to well-developed, powerful hindquarters. When viewed from the side, the

Ch. Franklin's Affirmed is the sire of two leader dogs for the blind.

Labrador should show a well-developed, but not prominent, forechest.

FAULTS: A short thick neck or a "ewe" neck, both of which are found with straight shoulders, are incorrect. A straight shoulder blade, short upper arm or heavy muscled or loaded shoulder should be severely penalized. The Labrador should not be narrow-chested giving the appearance of hollowness between the front legs; equally incorrect are wide-spread fronts. Slab-sided individuals are incorrect; equally objectionable are rotund or barrel-chested specimens. Long-backed, short-legged individuals are not typical of the breed.

LEGS AND FEET

COMMENTS AND EXPLANATION: When viewed from the front, the legs are straight and good strong bone; however, never to the point of coarseness. Viewed from the side, the elbows are directly under the withers and the front legs are perpendicular to the ground well under the body. The elbows should be close to the ribs without looseness. Pasterns are strong and short and slope slightly from the perpendicular. The Labrador's hindquarters are broad, strong and well developed with well-turned stifles and strong short hocks. Viewed from the rear, the hind legs are straight and parallel. Viewed from the side, the angulation of the rear legs is in balance with the front, the femur joins the pelvis at a 90 degree angle. When standing, the rear toes are only slightly behind the point of the rump.

FAULTS: Short-legged, heavy-boned individuals are to be severely penalized. Tied-in elbows or out in the elbows, splayed feet, knuckling over, pigeon toes, or feet turning in or out are serious faults. Cowhocks, spread hocks or sickle hocks are serious structural defects; over-angulation produces a sloping topline, not typical of the breed.

TAIL

COMMENTS AND EXPLANATION: The tail is a distinctive feature of the breed; it should be very thick toward the base, gradually tapering towards the tip, of medium length, should be free from any feathering and should be clothed thickly all round with the Labrador's short, thick, dense coat, thus giving that particular "rounded" appearance which has been described as the "otter" tail.

The tail is well set-on, following the natural line of the croup in repose or on the move. It may be carried gaily but should never curl over the back.

FAULTS: Docking or otherwise altering the length of the tail is cause for dismissal from the show ring. Since the tail acts as a rudder when the dog is swimming, either short stubby tails or long, thin tails are serious faults.

COAT

COMMENTS AND EXPLANATION: The coat should be short, straight and very dense, giving a fairly hard feeling to the hand. The Labrador's weather resisting undercoat provides protection from water, cold and all types of ground cover. A slight wave down the back is permissible but a straight coat is preferred; heavy thick coats or soft silky coats are equally objectionable.

FAULTS: Heavy, thick, "wooly bear" or soft silky coats are not typical of the breed. Any color combination or colors other than black, yellow or chocolate as described in the standard is cause for dismissal.

MOVEMENT

Movement or action is the crucial test of conformation. The Labrador legs should be carried

Ch. Shirlyn's Double Trouble going Best of Breed at the Ann Arbor Kennel Club, April, 1987. Owner-handler, Mrs. Shirley Rauch.

straight forward while traveling, the forelegs hanging perpendicular and swinging parallel with the sides, like the pendulum of a clock. The principal propulsive power is furnished by the hind legs, perfection of action being found in the Labrador possessing long thighs and muscular second thighs well bent at the stifles, which admit of a strong forward thrust or "snatch" of the hocks. When approaching, the forelegs should form a continuation of the straight line of the front, the feet being the same distance apart as the elbows.

FAULTS: When stationary, it is often difficult to determine whether a dog is slightly out at the shoulder, but directly he moves, the defect—if it exists—becomes more apparent, the forefeet having a tendency to cross or "weave." When, on the contrary, the dog is tied at the shoulder, the tendency of the feet is to move wider apart, with a sort of paddling action. When the hocks are turned in— cowhocked—the stifles and feet are turned outwards, resulting in a serious loss of propulsive power. When the hocks are turned out-wards, the tendency of the hind feet is to cross, resulting in an ungainly waddle.

TEMPERAMENT

True Labrador Retriever temperament is as much a hallmark of the breed as the "otter" tail. The ideal disposition is one of a kindly, outgoing, tractable nature; anxious to please and nonaggressive towards man or animal. The Labrador has much that appeals to people, his gentle quiet ways and his fidelity and adaptability make him an ideal dog, either as a field-trial competitor, shooting companion, show dog or household pet. Aggressiveness towards humans or other animals and any evidence of shyness in an adult are serious faults and should be severely penalized.

Ch. Franklin's Corbi of Limerick and his daughter Ch. Healani Alii O'Koolau.

Influential Kennels 1930–1970
"Records live—Opinions die."

by Marianne Foote

AUTHOR'S NOTE: To keep this section within the constraints of a single chapter the following criteria for kennel selection were used:

Established before or within the 40–year timeframe;

Bred successive generations of producers that can be traced in today's pedigrees;

Made significant contributions that affected both conformation and field pedigrees;

Produced dogs or bitches that made Labrador Retriever history;

Have focused on dual champion progeny.

The dogs and the people who make up the kennel profiles in this chapter have had a lasting influence on the development of the Labrador Retriever in the United States. Some of the kennels are no longer breeding, but a number are currently active. The contributions of each are unquestioned, and their legacies remain within the pedigrees of our present and future Labradors. Despite their competition and individuality, common principles link these Labrador Retriever breeders. Each had or has an absorbing interest or participation in field trials and conformation events. Although many current Labrador Retriever pedigrees are focused toward either performance or conformation accomplishments, the lineage from the majority of these kennels exhibits a cross-section of field-trial and conformation titles, establishing and keeping a profound foundation for the breed. Outstanding producing bitches are a shared theme, and thoughtful use of imported stock as well as evaluations for conformation and soundness are a part of each pedigree chain.

Many of the early kennels imported trainers and gamekeepers to maintain their kennels and shooting facilities. You will find the names of several Scottish trainers within the following kennel profiles. These trainers deserve credit for the development of the breed as a sporting dog in the United States and introducing Americans to retriever training. Helen Warwick in her book *The New Complete Labrador Retriever* included this list: Dave Elliott for Wingan; Colin McFarland for Glenmere; Tom and Jasper Briggs for Arden; Douglas Marshall for Caumsett; Jim Cowie, Arden, and later on his own under the kennel name, Fonab; Jock Munro; Lionel Bond; and in the West, the Hogan family—father, Martin and sons, Francis and James. This fortuitous union of people and dogs launched the American Labrador Retriever and established the breed in its present successful position at the top of the performance roster for retrievers. For a number of affluent New York and Long Island sportsmen, pheasant drives and duck shoots patterned after the Scottish hunting style were a popular pastime in the early 1920s. The Eastern Flyway with its migrating waterfowl, and the resultant need for a water-retrieving dog, became an appropriate place for the Labrador Retriever. Although full recognition for the Labrador as a separate breed did not come until the end of the 1920s in the United States, the importation of Labradors from England by American sportsmen began around the turn of the century. By the early 1930s there were a number of kennels with significant breeding stock toward establishing the breed in the U.S.: Black Point, Daniel E. Pomeroy (owned and campaigned '47 NFC and Dual Ch. Bracken's Sweep); Barrington, T.M. Howell; Blake, Franklin B. Lord; Caumsett, Marshall Field; Catawba, Mrs. James M. Austin; Dunotter, Mr. & Mrs. Henry S. Morgan; Glenmere (breeder of the first American Dual Ch. Michael of Glenmere), Robert Goelet; How Hi, Mrs. Howes Burton; Invail, Mr. & Mrs. Clifford

V. Brokaw, Jr.; Kenjockey, Wilton Lloyd-Smith; Kilsyth, Gerald Livingston; Ledgelands, Mr. & Mrs. David Wagstaff; Marvadel, Mr. & Mrs. J. Gould Remick; Meadow Farm, Charles L. Lawrence; Squirrel Run, Mrs. S. Hallock du Pont; Timber Town, Kathleen Starr Frederick; Wardwyn, Mrs. David Poor; West Island, Mrs. Junius Morgan. All contributed to the development of the breed, but the kennel profiles that follow had truly exceptional accomplishments.

EARLY 1920s—ARDEN, Arden, New York

The Arden prefix still stands as a precedent for quality that has never been equaled by any other Labrador kennel in America. Owned by the Hon. William Averill Harriman, the former Governor of New York and Ambassador to Russia and Great Britain, this was a kennel that consistently produced prominent individuals that competed and won equally in conformation and field-trial events.

Arden was the country home of the Harrimans. Situated along the Hudson River in New York, Arden became the natural site of numerous shoots and retriever events. Tom Briggs was the trainer, head gamekeeper and catalyst. An import from Scotland, he was known as a man of few words, however he was liked and respected by all for his dog handling and game-management ability. James Cowie (who was later to become known as "Mr. Retriever") was his assistant. The real Labrador Retriever breeding program at

Dual Ch.-NFTCh. Shed of Arden (Ch. Raffles of Earlsmoor x FC Decoy of Arden) with his progeny at the 1949 Labrador Retriever Specialty Show. Bred by the Hon. W. Averill Harriman, owned and handled by Paul Bakewell III in the field as well as in conformation, Shed became the premier stud dog of the day. Practically all field-trial dogs and many bench champions of today go back to him. In this photo Shed is on the right, handled by Paul Bakewell III.

Arden did not begin until a black Labrador bitch, Peggy of Shipton (Ronald of Candahar x Gehta), was imported from England in 1924. From her first litter (sired by Duke of Kirkmahoe), whelped in 1929, Governor Harriman kept a dog, Sam of Arden, a good working Labrador who acquired a few trial placements. However, it was a later mating to Mrs. Marshall Field's imported dog, Odds On (The Favorite x Jest), that "Peggy" began to show her worth. The 1933 whelping produced Decoy of Arden and Blind of Arden, later to become the first American field champions in each sex. These outstanding offspring precipitated a repeat breeding and Joy of Arden, who was to win several field-trial awards, was sold to Mrs. Morgan Belmont. Peggy was then bred to an import from the Hon. Lady Hill-Wood's English kennel, Hiwood Risk (Hiwood D'Arcy x Hiwood Chance), and Paul Bakewell III (Deer Creek) acquired Tar of Arden as a young puppy. FC Tar of Arden and her half-sister, Decoy, became brood matrons of lasting fame.

The late 1930s and early 1940s saw the breeder's dream come true with the whelping of four Labradors that later became dual champions. FC Decoy of Arden was bred to Dr. Samuel Milbank's Ch. Raffles of Earlsmoor. The 1937 "Scottish" litter produced Dual Champion Braes of Arden, owned by Mrs. J. R. McManus, and Dual Champion Gorse of Arden, owned by Mrs. Morgan Belmont. Dr. Milbank selected

"Moor" (Ch. Earlsmoor Moor of Arden) as a stud–fee puppy. Moor became an outstanding specimen and carries the distinction of being the first American Labrador to win best in show. Decoy's second litter to "Raffles" was whelped in 1939 and the puppies in that litter were named after fish—two became bench champions and a third, Paul Bakewell's peerless three-time National Retriever Champion and Am. Dual Champion, Can. Ch. Shed of Arden, made breed history.

In 1944 Burma of Arden (Fife of Kennoway x Pitch of Arden) was bred to Good Hope Angus and Mrs. A.P. Loening acquired Bengal of Arden who became a precedent-setting fourth dual champion for this kennel. In all, Arden produced four dual champions, a three-time National Retriever Champion, five field-trial champions, and eight bench champions (four that placed in open stakes and two of those were National qualifiers). A record that has never been surpassed.

1935—EARLSMOOR, Long Island, New York

During its early years, the Earlsmoor prefix was associated with the best of terriers, and Dr. Samuel Milbank was famous for his handling and winning in the field with English Springer Spaniels. He did not acquire a Labrador Retriever until a visitor from Scotland, Dr. James Wilson, came to the United States to judge for the English Springer Spaniel Field Trial Association. Because of their common medical interests, Dr. Milbank spent a good deal of time with Dr. Wilson during his visit. Before he left, Dr. Wilson told Dr. Milbank that he should have a Labrador, and that he would try to find him a good one. The following year Raffles arrived. Dr. Milbank's comments from Dorothy Howe's column, *Popular Dogs,* March 1962, follow: "They were having a very big Labrador Specialty at the Westbury, L.I. show. I got the necessary particulars by cable, and entered the dog, whose name, when I received him, was Raffles. I was allowed to add my kennel name of Earlsmoor. The first time out, Raffles of Earlsmoor beat all the champions and went best of breed. Later he placed second in the Sporting Group. In three subsequent shows he won his American bench show championship title. He was a most biddable dog to handle and I ran him in a few field trials. I never got any higher than second in a trial but I was usually in the money or with a Certificate of Merit."

Helen Warwick in her book *The New Complete Labrador Retriever* stated, "What Banchory Bolo was to England, certainly Raffles became to America; a beautiful dog in his own right, superbly bred, an excellent worker as well as a bench winner, he was soon to exert influence as a gifted stud force. The old saying that 'good ones rarely come from anything but good ones' was never more clearly demonstrated than with Ch. Raffles of Earlsmoor." Raffles and his son, Moor, were to become foundations of the breed in the United States.

Mr. Averill Harriman (Arden) asked to breed FC Decoy of Arden (Odds On x Peggy of Shipton) to Ch. Raffles of Earlsmoor (Thatch of Whitmore x Task of Whitmore). This collaboration between Arden and Earlsmoor proved to be an auspicious beginning for the breed. A litter of seven puppies was whelped in February 1937 and they were named after shooting places in Scotland—Banks, Braes, Burn, Gorse, Heather, Loch, and Moor. Two of the puppies died young and, of the remaining five, two became dual champions—the first of each sex to do so, and three were bench champions. Dr. Milbank selected a dog puppy in lieu of a stud fee— Earlsmoor Moor of Arden. Dr. Milbank remarks about Moor from Nancy Martin's *Legends in Labradors:* "Moor was used in the field and was fairly successful. However he went Best of Breed at Morris & Essex and BIS at Greenwich, beating the famous My Own Brucie [Editor's note: a renowned American Cocker Spaniel who won

Ch. Earlsmoor Moor of Arden (Ch. Raffles of Earlsmoor x FC Decoy of Arden), Dr. Samuel Milbank's pick from the famous Scottish litter.

Westminster twice] in the Group. His record was 40 times bests of breed, 12 Group firsts, 27 Group placings and five bests in show. Ch. Earlsmoor Moor of Arden won the bench show challenge cup outright—three times each year for three years. He retired the cup, and later went on to win another challenge cup under the same conditions again, so he has two bench show challenge cups to his credit. In all his career, he was handled only by Jim Cowie." Moor was shown only 42 times.

Unlike the specialists of today, many of the Labradors being shown were the same ones running in field trials, and retriever trainers frequently handled clients' dogs in conformation events as well as trials. James Cowie was Dr. Milbank's trainer and show handler. The following comments are also from Nancy Martin's interview with "Mr. Retriever" in *Legends in Labradors,* "My best dog was Dr. Milbank's Earlsmoor Moor of Arden who won Best of Breed at the Labrador specialty shows in 1938, '39, '40, '41 and '43 (he was not shown in '42). Moor also won about ten groups and I think two bests in show [Editor's note: Moor won five BIS— see Dr. Milbank's quote], which was something for a Labrador to do in those days. I was sorry that I could not make Moor a dual champion. I could place him and win at unlicensed trials but just couldn't make that first in Open. Moor also was runner-up to Best in Show at Westminster."

The top winners at the Labrador Retriever Club Specialty Show in 1948. Left to right: BOB Jim Cowie handling Mrs. Kathleen Poor's Ch. Stowaway at Deer Creek; LRC Club President J. Gould Remick presenting trophies; judge Dr. Samuel Milbank; Joan Redmond Read with WB and BOS Ch. Chidley Spook. Photo by Evelyn Shafer, courtesy of Mrs. Curtis Read.

1933—WINGAN, Long Island, New York

Jay F. Carlisle had maintained a kennel of pointers and retrievers. After the death of his wife, he turned to the retriever activities of his Wingan Kennels to help cope with his loss. With the help of Scotsman David Elliott as manager and trainer, this kennel developed to its full potential. When he arrived in the early '30s to act as kennel manager for Wingan, Dave brought his own Labrador, Whitecarin Wendy (Ranger of Kentford x Lochar Kate) with him. "Wendy" had competed successfully in trials on her home turf and she soon took up the Wingan banner. Several Labrador Retrievers were already in residence at Wingan. Orchardton Doris (Ingleston Ben x Orchardton Dawn) was Mr. Carlisle's personal favorite. Banchory Night Light of Wingan (Blackworth Midnight x Dinah of Wongalee) had been purchased earlier from Lady Howe's famous kennel in England and he soon earned his American field champion title under Dave's tutelage. Banchory Varnish of Wingan (Dual Ch. Banchory Painter x Hawkesworth Glimmer) also became a field trial champion. Varnish was later acquired by Mrs. Kathleen Starr Frederick. Drinkstone Mars, Ch. Drinkstone Span and Ch. Drinkstone Pons of Wingan (Ch.

Banchory Danilo x Ch. Drinkstone Peg) were obtained from Dr. G.H. Monro-Home. Their dam, Ch. Drinkstone Peg (Toi of Whitmore x Pride of Somersby) arrived in whelp to Lady Howe's great Dual Champion Bramshaw Bob. Wingan regularly supported the Labrador entries at conformation shows and five of "Peg's" litter of seven became champions: Ch. Bancstone Ben of Wingan, Ch. Bancstone Countess of Wingan, Ch. Bancstone Lorna of Wingan, Ch. Bancstone Peggy of Wingan and Ch. Bancstone Bob of Wingan (who was acquired by Joan Redmond Nee: Joan Read/Chidley). Several other imports, Banchory Jetsam, Banchory

Ch. Drinkstone Pons of Wingan (Ch. Banchory Danilo x Ch. Drinkstone Peg) earned field-trial awards.

Trump of Wingan (Blenheim Scamp x Lady Daphne), Ch. Liddly Bulfinch of Wingan (Tar of Hamyax x Delyn of Liphook) also became American bench champions. Mr. Carlisle generously offered his dogs at stud to new Labrador breeders and his outstanding group of imports helped build foundation stock for many in the breed.

Dave Elliott wrote the following for the "Foreword" in the book *The Labrador Retriever,* published by Wingan Kennels in 1936: "Labradors have at last invaded this country and they are here to stay for they are proving to the American sportsman their high value in the field. It is not only their working abilities which endear them to the hearts of all who come in contact with them. They possess a most kindly disposition, are very rarely aggressive or quarrelsome and are patient and reliable with children. In fact, from every aspect—that of a show dog, worker or companion—Labradors seem to grasp instinctively what is required of them."

Ch. Drinkstone Peg (Toi of Whitmore x Pride of Somersby) imported from England in whelp to Lady Howe's great Dual Ch. Bramshaw Bob.

Dave Elliott must also be credited with introducing "handing" to the American retriever-training fraternity. In Scotland, he had been fascinated by whistle and hand signals used by handlers to direct sheepdogs. In trials, retrievers were frequently called upon to execute a "blind" retrieve—to search out a bird they had not seen fall without assistance from the handler. Dave began to use whistle and hand signals to direct his dogs to the birds—eliminating undue disturbance of ground. Criticism for this unorthodox training soon gave way to acceptance and respect, and the blind retrieve is now defined as giving and taking direction to an unmarked fall by hand and whistle signal without undue disturbance of ground. It also altered our field trial concepts forever, a fact that greatly disturbed Dave Elliott for the rest of his life.

1930—CHIDLEY, Oyster Bay, New York

Joan Redmond (Mrs. Curtis Read) began exhibiting and breeding Labrador Retrievers at a very young age. She was just a girl when she received her first Labrador as a gift from her uncle, Geraldyn Redmond—a six-month-

Orchardton Doris of Wingan (Ingleston Ben x Orchardton Dawn) and Jay Carlisle.

Drinkstone Peg). Bob became her first champion. Cinders took advantage of the circumstances—she picked her own mate, Bob! From that 1935 litter came "Bender," sire of Ch. Star Lea Sunspect, forerunner of the Whygin Kennels.

Joan trained her own dogs as shooting companions with help from Higgins at Wilton Lloyd-Smith's Kenjockety Kennel, Dolly Marshall at Marshall Field's Caumsett Kennel and Jim Cowie in Commack, New York, running them in some of the early trials.

old black bitch puppy that was to become a constant and devoted companion. "Cinders" was sired by the imported Scottish gundog Diver of Liphook and was out of Ridgeland Black Diamond. Joan then purchased Wingans Maid of the Mist (Ch. Liddly Bulfinch of Wingan x Ch. Drinkstone Span) from Jay Carlisle with money she had saved from prizes won at horse shows. Some time after that, Mr. Carlisle gave Joan a dog puppy, Bancstone Bob of Wingan (Eng. Dual Ch. Bramshaw Bob x Ch.

In 1939 "Mist" was bred to Ch. Earlsmoor Moor of Arden and whelped Marsh who was then bred to Ch. Bancstone Bob of Wingan and whelped Hugger Mugger in 1944. Ch. Hugger Mugger became an exceptional producer, as well as an outstanding shooting dog. He was the sire of the good field trialer and specialty-show winner Ch. Wildfield Mickcy Finn. His daughter Ch. Chidley Spook was a top winner and the dam of Ch. Chidley Hocus Pocus (by Ch. Zelstone Duke), Jim and Helen

Warwick's first champion. "Mugger" provided foundation stock for the Unklebach's Walden Kennel, Mrs. Johnson Smith's Ashur Labradors, Barbara Barty-King's Aldenholm Kennel, Barbara Barfield's Scrimshaw Kennel, the Wolcott's Blacmor Kennel, Mary Swan's Chebacco Labradors, and Sally Munson's Shamrock Acres Kennel through Ch. Whygin Campaign Promise.

Joan also bred and finished the first American-bred yellow Labrador Retriever bitch champion, Ch. Chidley Almond Crisp (Loki of Clarendon x Ch. Chidley Marsh-mallow) in 1950. "Crisp" was a great-granddaughter of Marsh/Bob breeding. However, Joan's Labrador Retriever activities were curtailed with a growing family and a bout with polio in 1952. In 1958 she began to judge Labradors, adding the four other retriever breeds, and then the Norwich and Norfolk Terriers. Little breeding was attempted, but she did import a yellow dog, Castlemore Mask (Eng. Sh. Ch. Kingsbury Nokeener Moonstar x Castlemore Linnet), from Irish bloodlines in 1970, searching out the lineage that followed from her

An early influential sire, Ch. Hugger Mugger (Ch. Bancstone Bob of Wingan x Marsh) owned and bred by Joan Redmond Read.

Ch. Polywog Comic of Chidley (Castlemore Mask x Yarrow's Polywog Sabrina) was Winners Dog at the 1977 LRC National Specialty Show and Obedience Trial.

original bitches. Polywog Comic of Chidley, a black dog sired by that import (and out of Yarrow's Polywog Sabrina) owned and shown by Beth Sweigert, was Winners Dog from the Novice Class at the 1977 Labrador Retriever Club, Inc., National Specialty and completed his title soon afterward. Mrs. Read still maintains strong ties with the breed and has a Labrador Retriever bitch belonging to her daughter, Barbara Ege, that shares her household—Chidley Night Music (Quissex Sebastian x Chebacco Chidley Jenny Lind)— along with several Norwich and Norfolk Terriers. Although the terriers are the prime focus of her breeding program, Joan's guidance and help in evaluating Labrador Retriever breeding stock is highly respected. She is an avid collector of historical data on the Norwich and Norfolk Terriers, and the author of the book *The Norfolk Terrier*, earning the added respect of owners around the world in both those breeds.

1937—DEER CREEK, St. Louis, Missouri

Retriever owners did not handle their own dogs in the Open Stakes at early retriever trials. During the '30s it was a professional's game, but Paul Bakewell III changed that. He was a talented and dedicated trainer and the first amateur to compete successfully against the professionals. In 1939 Paul Bakewell won his first national championship,

Chidley Night Music (Quissex Sebastian x Chebacco Chidley Jenny Lind), whelped February 1992, is owned by Joan Redmond Read's daughter, Barbara Ege. Photo courtesy of Barbara Ege.

the Field and Stream trophy, with a dog that he purchased for $35.00—Rip, a Golden Retriever. The Field and Stream trophy was offered by the sporting dog magazine of the same name to the Outstanding Retriever of the Year (the dog accumulating the most points in Open All-Age Stakes during year) and was a precursor to the National Retriever Championship Stake. Bakewell's owner-trained dogs accomplished this feat seven times, six times with Paul as handler and the one time with Clifford H. Wallace as handler (Paul was away during World War II). Paul Bakewell III became the first owner-handler to win the National Championship Stake—the first time in 1942 with Dual Ch. Shed of Arden and again in 1943. He repeated the accomplishment two more times—with Shed again in 1946 and with FC Marvadel Black Gum (Mint of Barrington x Marvadel Cinders) in 1949. In addition, Marvadel Black Gum had some other exceptional accomplishments. He finished his field trial title at 18 months, the youngest retriever to accomplish that distinction, and won the Country Life trophy for the Top Derby Dog the same year. For a decade—1939 to 1949—Paul Bakewell and his dogs dominated the National competition.

Amazing as Bakewell's accomplishments were with the Golden Retriever, Rip, it was two Arden-bred Labradors that brought this kennel to the forefront. FC Tar of Arden's brilliant work earned her the Field and Stream trophy in 1941. She also became an outstanding producer. "Tar" bred to Mrs. John Williams' Eng-Am. FC Hiwood Mike (Pettistree Dan x Pettistree Poppet) produced Mr. and Mrs. Mahlon Wallace's '45 NFC Black Magic of Audlon, the first Labrador bitch to win the National Championship; Confusion at Deer Creek; and the incomparable Dual Ch. Little Pierre of Deer Creek. When bred to FC Banchory Varnish of Wingan (Banchory Painter x Hawkesworth Glimmer) she produced FC Firelei of Deer Creek. Mated to her son, Little Pierre, she produced D.E. Pomroy's FC Mary-Go-Round at Deer Creek.

Shed of Arden (Ch. Raffles of Earlsmoor x FC Decoy of Arden) was purchased as an adolescent for $250.00 on approval for 30 days from the Harriman's kennel. He was faulted for refusing to enter the water for a second retrieve, but Bakewell had no trouble overcoming that shortcoming. Shed was considered a nice prospect, but nothing out of the ordinary. Bakewell's comments on Shed are recorded in his interview in Richard Wolter's book *The Labrador Retriever . . . the History . . . the People*: "He took to training very nicely with just a little affection and appreciation along with the necessary discipline. He made his field trial championship quickly and, when I realized he was so good-looking, I had Hollis Wilson take him around to a few shows in this country. This took very little time as I don't think he was ever defeated." Three-time National

Champion and Can-Am. Dual Ch. Shed of Arden became the epitome of every retriever owner's or breeder's desires. Shed and his kennelmate, Little Pierre, developed into a strong stud force for Deer Creek with major influences in conformation, as well as field-trial pedigrees.

Performance events were not Paul Bakewell's only expertise as almost all of his dogs he considered worthy were exhibited on the bench, showing them himself or using a handler. He also judged a few conformation shows as well as trials. However, Bakewell normally did not show his dogs in conformation until they had completed their field title, with one exception—Dual Ch. Hello Joe of Rocheltree (Snikebs Ding Ding Ding x Billy Black Babe). An example of his determination to maintain the dual-purpose qualities can be shown in the following story from his reminiscences in Richard Wolter's *The Labrador Retriever . . . the History . . . the People Revisited:* "He needed only a couple of points on the bench and a point or two in the field to complete his championships back in the '40s. When the Midwest trial was held in Chicago and a bench show nearby in Skokie, Illinois, 'Hello Joe' competed in both. When a certain water test came along, he was one of the first to complete his work. I drove him over to the show where Labradors were being judged while the rest of the field-trial test was still going on. He completed his bench championship and I took him back to the trial where he won the Open Stake, making him a field trial

and a bench champion on the same day, which I think was a very unique accomplishment."

Deer Creek also proved to be a learning ground for an outstanding trainer. T.W. "Cotton" Pershall came to work as a groomer for Bakewell from his native Arkansas. However, his aptitude with dogs was soon discovered and Bakewell tutored him in the new sport of retriever trials. Cotton trained both Tar and Shed of Arden until he left for a stint with the K-9 Corps during World War II. Cotton acknowledges fully the dog-training expertise he acquired from Paul Bakewell. He was able to take that aptitude to its zenith as the trainer for Nilo Farms.

1940—GRANGEMEAD, St. Charles, Illinois

The Grangemead prefix belonged to Mr. and Mrs. Thomas W. Merritt. Grangemead had a small breeding program based on high quality and the dual-purpose principle. Tom Merritt was a serious student of pedigrees and his friend, John McAssey, recalled that the wall of his den held a 4' x 8' board with an extended pedigree reflecting the background of dogs at Grangemead. One of the first puppies bred at Grangemead was Grangemead Angel, a daughter of FC Freehaven Jay. She in turn was bred to Eng-Am. FC Hiwood Mike and produced Grangemead Sharon. Sharon's one and only breeding was to seven-month-old "Precocious" and what a legacy it produced—FC Freehaven Muscles (sire of multiple FC offspring including Paha Sapa Chief II, sire of NFC NAFC Super Chief), FC Cherokee Medicine Man and Dual Ch. Cherokee Buck (sire of Dual Ch. Alpine Cherokee Rocket)—continuing a descending line of four dual champions from Shed of Arden. This exceptional start was only the beginning for this dog that became Dual Ch. Grangemead Precocious. His name still appears in the pedigrees of many of today's top dogs. He was whelped in 1946 and sired by NFC and Dual Ch. Shed of Arden and out of a Wingan-bred bitch, Huron Lady (Ch. Banchory Trump of Wingan x Ch. Bancstone Lorna of Wingan). Tom Merritt's comments on Grangemead and Precocious from Helen Warwick's book *The New Complete Labrador Retriever* bear quoting: "We first ran in trials in 1940. At the start I did the training and running, but after we acquired several young dogs, it took more time than I could give. We never had yellows—only blacks. . . . Precocious was a bigger dog than Shed. He was a good marking dog, especially in

'49 NFC Marvadel Black Gum, winner of the Field and Stream trophy and the National Championship Stake, owned by Mr. and Mrs. Paul Bakewell III and trained and handled to National Championship by Paul Bakewell III.

water and especially strong in water triples."

Tom Merritt was a quiet and unassuming man. However, his contributions to the retriever community more than equaled the excellent dogs produced at Grangemead. He was president of the Labrador Retriever Club, Inc., from 1946 to 1950 and initiated the concept of the Labrador Retriever Club record books. This project required a tremendous amount of research and hard work, and Tom

Merritt, along with John McAssey and Richard Hecker, left retriever breeders an invaluable source of information in the five volumes subsidized by the LRC, Inc. Mr. Merritt was also president and editor-in-chief of *Retriever Field Trial News* from 1954 until his death in 1971. He judged the first National Amateur Stake in 1957 and was a National Open judge four times. He was also very involved with the development of retriever trials. The following is from his obituary in the *Retriever Field Trial News:* "...through the years Tom guided the Retriever Advisory Committee, developing the principles and language by which trials should be conducted. During his many years as a director of the American Kennel Club, retrievers enjoyed a strong and respected voice in Kennel Club affairs."

1941—RUPERT, Manchester Depot, Vermont

Rupert Kennels began at a dairy farm near Rupert, Vermont and then moved outside the small village of Manchester Depot. Dorothy Howe started animal husbandry with a variety of farm animals, but Labrador Retrievers became her preoccupation. Her foundation bitch, Lena, was whelped in 1941. Lena was a black bitch by FT Timbertown Clansman x Wingan's Primrose, and went back to Dual Champion Banchory Bolo on both

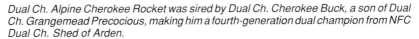

Dual Ch. Alpine Cherokee Rocket was sired by Dual Ch. Cherokee Buck, a son of Dual Ch. Grangemead Precocious, making him a fourth-generation dual champion from NFC Dual Ch. Shed of Arden.

Ch. Rupert Dahomey (Dauntless of Deer Creek x Lena) whelped in 1947, bred, owned and handled by Dorothy Howe.

sides of her pedigree. Bred to a son of Dual Champion Shed of Arden, Dauntless of Deer Creek, she produced working ability as well as good Labrador type. From the first breeding, whelped in 1947, came: Ch. Rupert Dahomey, who was BOB and placed fourth in the Sporting Group at his first dog show at six months of age; Rupert Daphne, who was rarely shown, but to whom all Rupert bitches are related; and Ch. Rupert Desdemona. During those early years almost all retriever events took place on Long Island. Dorothy drove hours to attend training sessions with Dave Elliott and to visit with Labrador owners to learn more about the breed. Through her effort and handling Dahomey had a chance to prove his retrieving ability by placing second in the Novice Dog Stake at the Long Island Retriever Trial in 1949.

Dorothy imported several stud dogs to add to her line. Breedings with the yellow dog, Ch. Glenarvey Barrister, and the handsome black, Ch. Nokeener Pinchbeck Seafarer, figured in her pedigrees. However,

123

she did not hesitate to use stud dogs such as Eng-Am-Can. Ch. Sam of Blaircourt and Ch. Killingworth Thunderson from outside the kennel.

start x-raying for hip dysplasia, and after 1957 she eliminated all stock from her breeding program that was not x-rayed and found sound. She would not breed to dogs or use stud

Ch. Rupert Marleigh Bingham (Rupert Comet x Ch. Rupert Foster of Spruce Brook), owned and bred by Dorothy Howe, was the dam of five champions.

The strength of any kennel lies in its bitches, and Rupert bitches showed their worth. Ch. Rupert Marleigh Bingham (Rupert Comet x Ch. Rupert Foster of Spruce Brooks) was the dam of five champions. Her dam had four champion offspring. Ch. Rupert Aurora Borealis was the dam of five champions. All together Rupert bitches produced 33 champions, seven with Working Certificates, and one obedience champion. Although Rupert foundation stock was black, many of Dorothy Howe's most famous dogs carried the yellow coat color.

Dorothy Howe was a pioneer in establishing soundness criteria for her breeding stock. She was the first Labrador Retriever breeder to

dogs with bitches that were not x-rayed normal. Whygin and Shamrock Acres both traced their foundation stock to Dorothy Howe's Ch. Rupert Dahomey and Lena through a breeding with Helen Ginnel's Cedarhill Whygin.

Dorothy wrote the Labrador Retriever column for *Popular Dogs* magazine from 1958 to 1974 and through that column she was able to educate readers about x-raying for hip dysplasia and examining breeding stock for hereditary eye disease. *This Is the Labrador Retriever,* Dorothy Howe's book on the breed was published in 1972 by T.F.H. Publications, Inc., and again in 1984, after her death, with additional chapters by Anna Katherine Nicholas.

The yellow dog Ch. Glenarvey Barrister (Eng. Ch. Glenarvey Brand x Sandylands Goldie) was imported by Dorothy Howe.

1944—BIGSTONE, Beardsley, Minnesota

Bigstone Kennels traced its beginnings to Arden and Wingan through its bitch line. Two of the top winners produced by this kennel were Bing Grunwald's 1962 National Retriever Champion, FC Bigstone Hope (NFC Cork of Oakwood Lane x Bigstone Ricky), and Mr. and Mrs. Paul Bakewell III's Dual Ch. Matchmaker for Deer Creek (Dual Ch. Little Pierre of Deer Creek x Tops of Bigstone). The kennel name belonged to Bill and Louise Rook, and the one dual champion and eight homebred field champions were the result of a strong bitch line through Tops (FC Banchory Night Light of Wingan x Scarborough Shenka) and Little Tops of Bigstone (Dual Ch. Little Pierre of Deer Creek x Tops of Bigstone). Following are the names of the other field champions produced by Bigstone—they include a large percentage of bitches: William K. Lauglin's FC Bigstone Bandit (Dual Ch. Shed of Arden x Little Tops of Bigstone); a bitch, AFC Bigstone Shady Lile (FC Crowder x Bigstone Bang, a Little Tops daughter); a bitch, FC Ladies Day At Deer Creek (Dual Ch. Little Pierre of Deer Creek x Tops of Bigstone); a bitch, FC Jibodad Gypsy (Dual Ch. Little Pierre of Deer Creek x Tops of Bigstone); FC Webway's Crusader (FC The Spider of Kingswere x Little Tops of Bigstone); a bitch, FC Howie's Happy Hunter (Bigstone Tar Gum x Bigstone Jumper); and a bitch, FC Bay City Lady Jane (NFC Cork of Oakwood Lane x Bigstone Breeze).

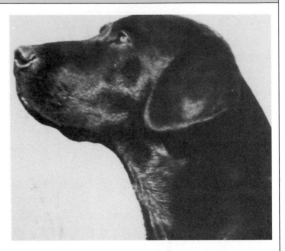

(Eng. Ch. Sandylands Tweed of Blaircourt x Sandylands Shadow) and his sister Lockerbie Sandylands Tidy. Tarquin and Tidy proved to be important acquisitions. Tarquin was widely used and sired a long list of champions that included Janet Churchill's famous bitch Can-Am-Ber. Ch. Spenrock's Banner. One of Tidy's four champion offspring was the yellow dog, Ch. Lockerbie Kismet (sired by

*Above: Ch. Lockerbie Blackfella (Ballyduff Treesholm Terryboy x Ch. Ballyduff Candy) was the first homebred of the Warwicks' Lockerbie kennels and a dog of great influence on the breed in America. **Below:** Ch. Lockerbie Brian Boru (Ch. Lockerbie Kismet x Lockerbie Tackety Boots) was bred by the Warwicks and owned by Marjorie and Cy Brainard (Briary), Alderwood Manor, WA. Brian and his kennel mate, Ch. Lockerbie Shillelagh, were influential foundation stock for Briary. Brian sired more than 60 champions to a wide number of dams. Photo by Marianne Foote.*

large number of champion offspring bred to a variety of dams and those offspring, in turn, continued to produce winning get. Kismet was included on a list of top producers with 17 champions out of ten dams. His most famous son, Ch. Lockerbie Brian Boru (out of a Tarquin daughter), outdid his sire with more than 60 champions out of a wide cross-section of bitches. Ch. Lockerbie Brian Boru, (Ch. Lockerbie Kismet x Lockerbie Tackety Boots) and

Lockerbie Panda, a Ch. Lockerbie Blackafella son). It has been said that a dog is not a producer until his sons produce and in that case both Ch. Lockerbie Kismet and Ch. Lockerbie Sandylands Tarquin have priority. Both produced a Ch. Lockerbie Shillelagh (Ch. Lockerbie Sandylands Tarquin x Princess of Marlow) became the foundation stock for the Briary Kennel of Cy and Marjorie Brainard, Alderwood Manor, Washington.

The Warwicks continued to make use of imports throughout their breeding program. Some of the other Labradors they acquired were: Ch. Lockerbie Goldentone Jensen, Ch. Lockerbie Pebblestreet Dinah, Ch. Lockerbie Scwarlodge Brigadier, Ch. Lockerbie Stanwood Granada and Ch. Lockerbie Lown Neptune. The last imports the Warwicks purchased were Ch. Sandylands Markwell of Lockerbie (Eng. Ch. Sandylands Mark x Eng. Ch. Sandylands Waghorn Honesty) and his sister Sandylands Margie of Lockerbie. Both were co-owned and lived with Diane Jones of Jollymuff Kennels during the Warwicks' later years.

The Warwicks both began judging in 1959. Jim became the Labrador Retriever Club, Inc., delegate to the AKC. Helen Warwick wrote the breed column for the LRC, Inc., in the AKC *Gazette* for many years and her first book on the breed in 1964, *The Complete Labrador Retriever*. The third edition, *The New Complete Labrador Retriever*, was published in 1986.

Ch. Lockerbie Sandylands Tarquin (Eng. Ch. Sandylands Tweed of Blaircourt x Sandylands Shadow) here at almost 12 years old. Photo by Marianne Foote.

1948—WHYGIN, Bedford Hills, New York

Helen Ginnel's life encompassed more than 57 years of involvement in dog activities and dog breeding. Her first paying job was with a herding-dog trainer, her first sporting dog was an English Setter. She registered her first litter in 1932 and by 1948, when she acquired her first Labrador Retriever, Cedar Hill Whygin ("Dinah"), she had produced six generations of field-trial setters. Her first field-trial winner was a setter bitch called Whygin Martini, a descendent of that first litter of setters.

Helen Ginnel with two of her favorites, Ch. Whygin John Duck (black) and Bully, Ch. Whygin Gold Bullion (yellow).

Her most fulfilling field-trial winner was the Labrador Retriever, two-time National Champion Whygin Cork's Coot ('55 NFC Cork of Oakwood Lane x Whygin Dark Ace). Her only interest was to promote the dual-purpose dog.

Helen began using the Whygin prefix in 1946—a combination of her maiden name Whyte, and her married name Ginnel. Her initial steps in establishing a Labrador Retriever line began with Cedar Hill Whygin's (Tar Rock Pluto x Cedar Hill's Kate) second litter sired by Dorothy Howe's Ch. Rupert Dahomey, a grandson of Dual Ch. Shed of Arden. Helen kept two puppies, Whygin Poppitt and Whygin Dark Magic. She used the knowledge of tight linebreeding and inbreeding acquired in her setter breeding program to establish the foundation for her Labrador Retrievers. Helen wrote:

"Every dog carrying the Whygin prefix that I have bred is a descendent of Cedar Hill Whygin and Whygin Poppitt." Her success is exemplified in the many outstanding dogs she produced: Ch. Whygin Gold Bullion (Ch. Kinley Comet of Harham x Whygin Popsicle), a sire of multiple conformation champions and a grandsire of BIS-winner Ch. Shamrock Aces Light Brigade; Ch. Whygin John Duck (Ch. Whygin Poppitt x Ch. Rupert Desdemona); Ch. Whygin Rob Roy; Ch. Whygin Royal Rocket; '66 & '69 NFC Whygin Cork's Coot; as well as the three famous bitches that became foundation stock for the Shamrock Acres kennel—Ch. Whygin Campaign Promise (Ch. Wildfield Mickey Finn x Ch. Whygin The Bedford Brat), Ch. Whygin Busy Belinda (Ch. Whygin Poppet x Bengali Sari, an Australian import)), and Ch. Whygin Gentle Julia of Avec (Ch. Whygin Gold Bullion x Ch. Whygin Black Gambit of Avec). When Helen was asked by Nancy Martin during an interview for her book *Legends in Labradors* how it feels to be the breeder of a National winner, Helen said: "The best thing about it was that it proved a line could compete in both areas with a Best-in-Show dog, Ch. Shamrock Acres Light Brigade, and a two-time National FTC, Whygin Cork's Coot. They were both Ch. Poppitt grandsons."

Ch. Westwind Winchester CD, JH, Can. CD (Shamrock Acres Robin Hood x Whygin West Wind Maja) was co-owned by Helen Ginnel. Chester was one of the last champions of her breeding finished before her untimely death in 1990.

Guiding Eyes for the Blind in Yorktown Heights, New York was a recipient of intense interest and effort on Helen Ginnel's part. In the late '60s they began using her stock and developed their own line of guide dogs going back to Ch. Whygin Gold Bullion, Ch. Whygin John Duck, Ch. Whygin Poppitt and, of course, to Cedar Hill Whygin.

The gap that separated the performance and conformation pedigrees of Labrador Retrievers was slowly widening as specialist breeders began to dominate during the late '40s. However, several kennels emerged in the '50s that sought to keep the interests favoring the dual-bred dog.

1951—NILO FARMS, Brighton, Illinois

John Olin, of Winchester-Western fame, was a prominent pioneer for conservation and wild game preserves, so the

Ch. Whygin Gold Bullion (Ch. Kinley Comet of Harham x Whygin Popsicle) at ten years of age.

'52 & '53 NFC King Buck (Timothy of Arden x Alta of Banchory) was a great favorite of John Olin.

Grangemead Precocious x Grangemead Sharon), FC Ace of Garfield, FC Ace's Shed of Ardyn II, FC AFC Discovery of Franklin, FC Ardee's Smorgasbord, FC Nodak Boots, FC Country Club's Jet Pilot, FC Pomme De Terre Pete, FC Marten's Stormy, FC Cinderfella of Stonesthrow, FC Carity's Smudge, FC Stonegate's Ace of Spades, FC Truly Yours of Garfield (bitch), and FC Ace of Southwood.

Several imports were also acquired from English performance and conformation lines and earned American titles—the yellow FC AFC Staindrop Ringleader

Mallardhurn Countess of Keithray (Eng. Ch. Sandylands Tandy x Ch. Hollybank Beauty) a yellow bitch imported by Nilo kennels.

establishment of his own retriever kennel was a natural offshoot. Nilo ("Olin" spelled backward) became the kennel name and numerous dogs with good working bloodlines were acquired. When T.W. "Cotton" Pershall became available, Mr. Olin quickly installed him as the trainer at Nilo Farms in 1951. The list of Labradors completing field championships by this kennel is impressive—27 under Cotton's tutelage—however, the following stand out: two National Champions—'52 and '53 NFC King Buck (Timothy of Arden x Alta of Banchory) and '65 NFC Marten's Little Smoky (FC Crowder x Marten's Little Bullet)—Cotton's fourth National win. A partial list of field champions at Nilo includes: FC Freehaven Muscles (Dual Ch.

'58 NFC Dual Ch.-AFC Nilo Possibility, Jinks as he was called, was bred at Nilo, but trained and handled to his national title by Billy Wunderlich. His owners selected his call name when the puppy first arrived because several people had questioned his prospects as a trial dog. Jinks proved to be a big winner for Mr. and Mrs. Kenneth Williams of Wisconsin. Photo courtesy of Rhoda Williams.

(Shavington Ted x Brackenbank Jessie) and FC Staindrop Murton Marksman (Shavington Ben x Adderly Thought) from Mrs. Wormald's kennel. From Lady Hill Wood came FC Hiwood Larry (Creedypark Gleaner x Hiwood Lucky Lass) and FC Hiwood Storm (Greatsford Pettistree Shadow x Mackland Peggy). A lovely yellow bitch, Mallardhurn Countess of Keithray (Eng. Ch. Sandylands Tandy x Ch. Hollybank Beauty) was imported as breeding stock. This list is by no means complete, but it is intended to show the scope of involvement this kennel brought to the retriever scene.

Nilo Farm's two National champions were not bred at Nilo, however, the kennel name does appear on a National titled dog— '58 NFC Dual Ch. and AFC Nilo Possibility (FC Black Prince of Sag Harbor x Kingswere Black Widow). Nilo Possibility was sold at eight months to Mr. and Mrs. Kenneth K. Williams when he did not show much potential as a competitive retriever. The Williams settled on the callname "Jinks" after they were told the circumstances of the sale, but Mr. Williams liked the dog and his faith was certainly justified. Jinks's early training was done by Rollie Madecky, but the dog was placed with William Wunderlich at the Mahlon Wallace's Casa Audlon Kennel in St. Louis after he completed the Derby, and Billy handled him to his National win. Jinks finished his bench championship for his dual title the year after he won the National.

Without a doubt, John Olin's favorite Labrador was NFC King Buck. His comments from Richard Wolter's book *The Labrador Retriever...the History...the People:* "Cotton and I never once had a sour note all the time we were together. We disagreed sometimes, like when I bought King Buck. He bought Freehaven Muscles the same week . . . King Buck was the greatest Labrador I've seen anywhere. The dog seemed to have almost human brains. When the going got tough, he got tougher, it was just unbelievable. That dog was really part of me before we parted company with his death."

King Buck qualified for seven consecutive National Championship Stakes during his field-trial career, fail-ing to complete only two series in all—the eleventh in 1951 and the twelfth in 1957. In 1959 the painting that Maynard Reece did of King Buck was issued as a federal duck stamp, the earliest United States stamp to feature a dog.

We have all benefited from the health and soundness programs for retrievers that were conducted by Nilo Farms. Mr. Olin was a prime backer for Cornell University's Veterinary Virus Research Institute for Animal Health headed by Dr. Baker, the Morris Animal Foundation, and the Orthopedic Foundation for Animals (OFA). In the book *Training Retrievers: The Cotton Pershall Method,* Cotton Pershall recalls

This life-sized statue of King Buck stands on a hillside at Nilo kennels. Of all the dogs that John Olin owned—hundreds representing many different breeds—there was only one King!

Drawing of King Buck—the National Champion for 1952 and 1953.

Olin's efforts to come up with a formula for breeding clean hips: "We experimented on that hip dysplasia for quite a few years. Mr. Olin put a lot of money into it—millions I guess. He had a specialist from Sweden over here. He spent a fortune.

"Mr. Olin spent so much time and money on trying to get rid of dysplasia and here you got people out there that just don't care. There were some great dogs that were dysplastic and people just bred 'em and bred 'em. Don't misunderstand me, you're going to get sound ones, good sound ones. But you're going to get a lot of dysplastic, too.

"We worked a lot through Cornell University on other diseases in dogs, too. Cornell had the only, I guess the only, disease-free kennel. When you went in this building, well, you had to take bath and put on their clothes and when you left, you took their clothes off, put your own clothes back on. We eventually had that up at Nilo."

1950—HARROWBY, Princeton, New Jersey

Mrs. Grace Lambert's first Labrador was a black male who was given to her by a friend because he kept running away. However, the yellows became a great favorite after seeing a yellow Labrador owned by Dorothy Howe, and Mrs. Lambert arranged for the purchase of Inga of Nascopie (from Mr. William Copeland's Canadian kennel). Kenneth Golden became her show handler. Ch. Rupert Eight Ball and Ch. Harrowby Rupert Channel Point from Dorothy Howe soon followed. Ch. Golden Chance of Franklin (Ch. Troublemaker of Franklin x Pretty Iris), a lovely show bitch, was purchased from the Ziessows in 1955. "Lassie" was twice BOB at the National Specialty. More Labradors in black and yellow followed: Ch. Northholt Timothy came from Canada, as well as Labradors from Nilo and

The lovely show bitch, Ch. Golden Chance of Franklin (Ch. Troublemaker of Franklin x Pretty Iris).

Eng-Am. Ch. Sam of Blaircourt (Dusk of Luscander x Olivia of Blaircourt) at his last show, the 1965 Labrador Retriever Club Specialty.

Lockerbie—Ch. Nilo Timothy Buck, Ch. Lockerbie Biffy, Ch. Lockerbie Blackfoot, Ch. Lockerbie Minnie.

This kennel imported two famous English stud dogs that were to leave a strong legacy with the breed in the U.S. In 1959 Mrs. Lambert purchased the handsome black, Eng. Ch. Sam of Blaircourt (Hawk of Luscander x Olivia of Blaircourt). "Sam" was bred by Mr. and Mrs. Grant Cairns of Scotland and owned by Mrs. Gwen Broadley of Sandylands fame. He was less than two years old when he came to the U.S. and quickly gained his American and Canadian title within the year handled by Kenneth Golden, as well as going WD and BW at the National Specialty. In total Sam won nine bests in show, 53 Sporting Group firsts and 261 bests of breed.

The yellow Irish-bred Loughderg Labradors of Mrs. Pamela Sims were acquired in 1962. Loughderg Erc, Ket, Brogue, Bangor, Hiawatha, Cunard, Niamh, Mary, Minnehaha, Cadbury, along with Sandylands Tar and Loughderg Strokestown Blackguard Boy were imported. Only two, Mary and Cadbury, did not become champions. These dogs became part of a successful breeding program for Harrowby. Ch. Loughderg Niamh was a top producer with seven champions, all sired by Eng-Am. Ch. Sam of Blaircourt. Three of these were top-ten winners: Ch. Harrowby Punch, Ch. Scipio and Ch. Prince II.

The second dog, Eng-Am. Ch. Sandylands Midas (Eng. Ch. Reanacre Mallardhurn Thunder x

Eng-Am. Ch. Sandylands Midas (Eng. Ch. Reanacre Mallardhurn Thunder x Eng. Ch. Sandylands Truth).

Am-Can. Dual Ch. Happy Playboy (Irish-Am-Can. Ch. Castlemore Shamus x Suzie), one of the three dual champions owned by Harrowby kennel. Photo courtesy of the Retriever Field Trial News.

Eng. Ch. Sandylands Truth) was imported in the late '60s from Mrs. Gwen Broadley's renowned kennel. Midas proved to be a very good stud dog and became a top producer with 48 champions out of 32 dams.

Nancy Martin in her book *Legends in Labradors* included the following from her interview with Mrs. Lambert: "I'm sure my greatest show dog was International Ch. Sam of Blaircourt. He certainly had the best record, and was a real showman. In the beginning my interest was strictly in show dogs. Then in 1957 I got my first field-trial dog, Ace Hi Scamp of Windsweep, who was later to become an American and Canadian field trial champion. He was a super dog and we called him 'Rum.'"

Some of the other field-trial dogs campaigned for Harrowby were: Am-Can. FC Duxbak Scooter; FC Bel-Aire Lucky Boy; FC Flints Nifty Arrow; FC Lord Beaver of Cork; FC Nassau's Nar of Minnewaska; and FC Nethercroft Nemo of Nascopie. William "Billy" Wunderlich became the field trainer for Mrs. Lambert. Both felt that "a Labrador should look like a Labrador" and all the Harrowby dogs were good representatives of the breed. During the 13 years that Billy Wunderlich trained for Mrs. Lambert, the kennel finished three dual champions—Am-Can. Dual Champion Happy Playboy (Irish-Am-Can. Ch. Castlemore Shamus x Suzie); Dual Ch. Markwell's Rambling Rebel (FC AFC Yankee Clipper of Reo Raj x Rushmore's Calamity Jane); and Dual Ch. Danny's Cole Black Slate (Blake's Cole Black Banner x Wondawhere You Are)—and ten field

Grace Lambert and William Wunderlich at a field trial. Photo courtesy of William Wunderlich.

Left to right: FC Lord Beaver of Cork, FC Ace High Scamp of Windsweep, FC Duxbak Scooter, Am-Can. Dual Ch. Happy Playboy and FC Nethercroft Nemo of Nascopie all qualified for the 1966 National. Photo courtesy of the Retriever Field Trial News.

FC Ace High Scamp of Windsweep with trainer William Wunderlich. "Rum" was one of Mrs. Lambert's favorites. Photo courtesy of William Wunderlich.

championships. None of the dogs acquired by the kennel had titles at the time of their purchase. All three dual champions continued to be campaigned and earned multiple All-Age points after completing their titles. For two years in a row, this kennel had six dogs qualified for the National Championship. Those accomplishments, along with the conformation championships finished, represent a remarkable record for an individual kennel owner.

Billy's comments on two of the Harrowby dogs: "Scooter was probably the best of all the dogs. He won six straight Open All-Age stakes, but was really a one-man dog. Happy Playboy was a very good dual champion—a beautiful dog with lots of style, especially in cold water. None of the dogs were bred much." Billy Wunderlich also has some very warm memories of Mrs. Lambert. After she acquired her field dogs, she liked to attend trials and frequently accompanied Billy in the dog truck. The Labrador Club was holding its trial on Long Island and a cocktail party followed the trial at the A.P. Loening's. It was a rather formal affair, but Mrs. Lambert insisted upon Billy taking her to the cocktail party in the dog truck. They pulled up in front of the house surrounded by distinguished vehicles and the butler arrived at the door and announced, "Deliveries in the back." Billy ignored him and got out of the truck and walked around to the passenger side. The butler repeated the announcement. Billy opened one of the dog boxes and removed a small step-stool that he had made to assist Mrs. Lambert in getting in and out of the truck because of its height. Mrs. Lambert emerged very elegantly dressed, asked Billy to pick her up in a couple of hours and went into the cocktail party. When Billy returned and Mrs. Lambert came out of the house, the butler preceded her, and, without a word, walked to the truck, opened the dog box and put the step-stool in front of the truck door.

1951—FRANKLIN LABRADORS, Franklin, Michigan

Franklin Labradors was established in 1951 by Mr. and Mrs. Bernard Ziessow. Madge Ziessow wrote, "To say that good fortune had not played an important part in our success would not be telling the truth. Our first Labrador, Am-Can. Ch. Pitch of Franklin, was given to us as a pet and hunting companion by Cary Rogers, Huntsman at Milcreek Hunt in Illinois. Her call name was 'Mickey.' She was the daughter of FC Pickpocket for Deer Creek and a granddaughter of National and Dual Champion Shed of Arden, BIS Ch. Earlsmoor Moor of Arden and Ch. Budah of Arden. She finished her conformation championship easily in less than two months, winning bests of breed and Group placements on the way, at a time when a Labrador was almost a 'rare breed.' While she was one of the few dogs that was able to pass on her excellence and brilliance to her offspring (producing ten champions, including FC AFC Discovery of Franklin), she was bred selectively to only bench champions, field

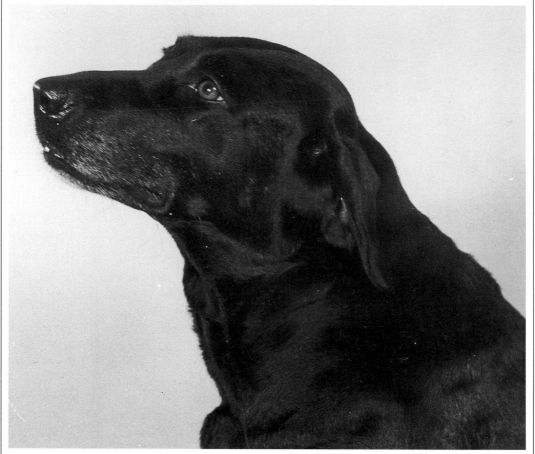

Am-Can. Ch. Pitch of Franklin (FC Pickpocket for Deer Creek x Wardwyn Warbler) is the foundation bitch of Franklin kennels.

champions and dual champions. An old friend once told us the only way to get the best was to breed to the best."

Mickey was bred to Ch. Labcroft Mister Chips and produced Am-Can. Ch. Troublemaker of Franklin, sire of seven champions. In her next litter she produced Franklin's most famous bench champion, BIS Ch. Dark Star of Franklin, the top winner in the breed for over ten years. In 18 months of active competition he won 116 bests of breed, 93 Group placings including 40 Group firsts and eight bests in show. In 1960, at eight years of age, he was taken out of retirement and won the National Specialty over the top competition of the day. On the same day, one of Mickey's other sons, Am-Can. Ch. Troublemaker of Franklin, won the veteran's class and the stud dog class. Mickey's great-granddaughter, the lovely yellow Ch. Golden Chance of Franklin, owned by Grace Lambert, was best of opposite sex. Mickey is also the granddam of the yellow dual champion bitch, Dual Ch. Sherwood's Maid Marion (Sun Beau of Franklin x Sandy of Danville).

Franklin produced two field trial champions. CFC CAFC FC AFC Franklin's Tall Timber (FC Deltone Buck x Ch. Franklin's Golden Charm) became the first Michigan owned and bred retriever to finish a field championship. He was trained and handled to his title by owner Roger Magnusson. FC AFC Discovery of Franklin (FC Timberstone Trigger x Ch. Pitch of Franklin) was owned by John Olin and campaigned to his title by Cotton Pershall.

Ch. Franklin's Tally of Burywood (Ch. Franklin's Sun Star x Ch. Franklin's Spring Dawn) was a top producer with 16 champion off-spring. One of her most famous sons was the 1978 World Champion Am-Can-Mex. and Int. Ch. Franklin's Golden Mandigo CD (Ch. Shamrock Acres Light Brigade x Ch. Franklin's Tally of Burywood) owned by John and Laurell Jenny. "Mandigo" was a multiple-group placer in three countries. His son Ch. Charisma's Lone Star Rick broke the record for BIS by a Labrador Retriever by winning 13 top awards.

Mr. and Mrs. Ziessow both became respected conformation judges, however Mrs. Ziessow has now retired from judging and Mr. Ziessow accepts only ten or twelve assignments a year. A limited breeding program is still underway. During the 40-plus years of its existence Franklin has pro-duced 65 champions, two Field and Amateur Field Trial Champions, two

Am-Can. Ch. Dark Star of Franklin, owned by Mr. Fred Martin and bred by his daughter Mrs. B.W. Ziessow.

National Specialty winners, a best-in-show dog, dogs for the blind, one Master Hunter, and numerous wonderful pets and hunting companions.

1958—SHAMROCK ACRES, Waunakee, Wisconsin

Sally McCarthy Munson's first purebred dogs were Smooth Dachshunds. However, the McCarthy family realized that their outdoor and hunting interests required a retriever and in 1955 they purchased their first Labrador for $35.00 from Martin Julseth. Marlab Gypsy CD was to have a real impact on Sally's life and, in turn, the Labrador Retriever breed. Members of

CFC-CAFC-FC-AFC Franklin's Tall Timber (FC Del-Tone Buck x Ch. Franklin's Golden Charm) and his owner and trainer, Roger Magnusson, became the first Michigan-owned and bred retriever to finish a field trial championship.

Wisconsin's Madison Retriever Club provided the McCarthys with helpful assistance in training their new retriever for hunting and eventually encouraged them to enter some sanctioned field trials. Gypsy was ultimately bred to the Wisconsin Open Stake Field Champion, Nemec's Jeff and the McCarthys selected a bitch puppy—Shamrock Acres Domino Queen CDX, who later qualified for the National Amateur Retriever Trial and won a high in trial at an AKC-licensed obedience trial. The kennel name Shamrock Acres was an obvious choice given Sally's last name and the Irish influence.

Sally decided that she wanted to expand her kennel and turned to Helen Ginnel's Whygin Kennels for additional breeding stock. The link to Whygin and Shamrock Acres was forged through strong bitch lines. In 1959 Sally purchased two unrelated seven-week-old black puppies from Helen Ginnel of Whygin kennels, a dog and a bitch. The dog puppy became Am-Can. Ch. Whygin Royal Rocket CD and the bitch, Am-Can. Ch. Whygin Campaign Promise (Ch. Wildfield Mickey Finn x Ch. Whygin the Bedford Brat). Campaign Promise still holds the record for top producing Labrador dam, with 17 champion offspring. Her BOB win at the National Specialty in 1961 was the first time a bitch had won that honor.

Sally first saw the black bitch, Whygin Gentle Julia of Avec (Ch.

GROUP
SECOND

MARQUETTE
KENNEL CLUB
AUG.
1991 BOOTH PHOTO
BY RITTER

SPORTING GROUP

Ch. Franklin's Champagne (Ch. Franklin's Affirmed x Charisma's Joy of Franklin, a Ch. Charisma's Lone Star Rick daughter) is presently being shown by the Ziessows.

Whygin Gold Bullion x Ch. Whygin Black Gambit of Avec) at the 1960 National Specialty. She belonged to an east-coast owner, but that owner died and "Julie" passed from family member to family member until she ended up with a nephew in Ohio. He could not tolerate her behavior (she opened doors, letting herself out at will, and frequently visited a neighboring turkey farm where she dutifully returned home with "samples") and sought out Helen Ginnel for assistance in placing her. Helen immediately thought of Sally. Despite her long list of "bad deeds," Sally decided to have Julie sent to her. She arrived in excellent condition and within three weeks of her arrival, Julie was entered in a show at Debuque, Iowa, where she went BOB over specials for five points and then finished off with a second in the Sporting Group. The following weekend she was WB at the International in Chicago for three points. Julie was bred to the Wisconsin Open Stake Field Champion Brodhead's Bar Booze and was not shown for five months. From that litter came Ch. Shamrock Acres Jim Dandy, Ch. Shamrock Acres Sugar, and Ch. and AFC Shamrock Acres Simmer Down. ("Simmer" lacked only a half point to become a field trial champion and earn her dual champion title.) When she was back in coat, Julie went to two shows in

Ch. Whygin Campaign Promise (Ch. Wildfield Mickey Finn x Ch. Whygin the Bedford Brat) is the all-time top-producing Labrador bitch with 17 champion offspring. Here she is winning at Westminster Kennel Club.

Ch. Whygin Busy Belinda (Ch. Whygin Poppitt x Bengali Sari) was the dam of 11 champion offspring, including BIS Ch. Shamrock Acres Light Brigade.

New York and Connecticut. She was WB for four points under James Warwick and the following day BW for five points at the LRC National Specialty under Judge Jerome Rich, completing her championship with four majors. Sally credits Julie "with probably being the key to my most successful breedings, and most everything I have in my show lines goes back to her."

Despite fortuitous outcrossings, and with considerable study of pedigree and offspring, Helen Ginnel and Sally decided to breed Julie back to her sire Ch. Whygin Gold Bullion. From the litter of nine, six blacks and three yellows, five champions were finished— Am–Can Ch. Shamrock Acres Sonic Boom, Ch. Shamrock Acres Casey Jones CD, (sire of 12-time BIS winner Ch. Shamrock Acres Light Brigade), Ch. Shamrock Acres Whygin Snow, Ch. Whygin Luck of Shamrock Acres and Ch. Shamrock Acres Twenty Carat. This breeding was repeated twice more, but only one other puppy finished a title, Ch. Shamrock Acres Sparkle Plenty CD. In 1963 a third bitch was acquired from Helen Ginnel, Whygin Busy Belinda (Ch. Whygin Poppitt x Bengali Sari). She completed her championship in 1965 and produced 11 champions including two BIS winners, Ch. Shamrock Acres

Ch. Whygin Gentle Julia of Avec (Ch. Whygin Gold Bullion x Ch. Whygin Black Gambit of Avec) produced 13 champions, including AFC-Ch. Shamrock Acres Simmer Down.

Dapper Dan and Ch. Shamrock Acres Light Brigade. Sally's acquisitions of the three bitches from Helen Ginnel, all top producers—Campaign Promise, "Julie" and Busy Belinda formed the foundation for Shamrock Acres breeding, along with progeny from the first Labrador, Marlab Gypsy CD. Use of the two Whygin stud dogs, Ch. Whygin Poppitt and Ch. Whygin Gold Bullion strengthened the Whygin influence. Three Shamrock Acres-bred stud dogs became top producers—the yellows, Ch. Shamrock Acres Light Brigade and Ch. Shamrock Acres Benjamin; and the beautiful black dog, Ch. Shamrock Acres Sonic Boom. Several other Shamrock Acres-bred dams are also top producers—among them: Ch. Shamrock Acres Cotton Candy, Ch. Shamrock Acres Yellow Ribbon and Ch. Shamrock Acres One Way Ticket.

Shamrock Acres breeding stock is divided between dogs and bitches with conformation backgrounds and those with field backgrounds, and some with combinations of both. The show lines are based on line-breeding with an occasional

Above: Ch. Shamrock Acres Light Brigade (Ch. Shamrock Acres Casey Jones CD x Ch. Whygin Busy Belinda) 12 times BIS and a top-producing sire with 93 U.S. champion get. Here he is winning the Sporting Group on his way to BIS at the 1968 Greater Miami Kennel Club. **Below:** Ch. Shamrock Acres Yellow Ribbon (Ch. Shamrock Acres Royal Oaks R.F.D. x Hollidaze Could Be A Classic) co-owned and bred with Barbara J. Holl, is a group winner and the dam of 11 champions.

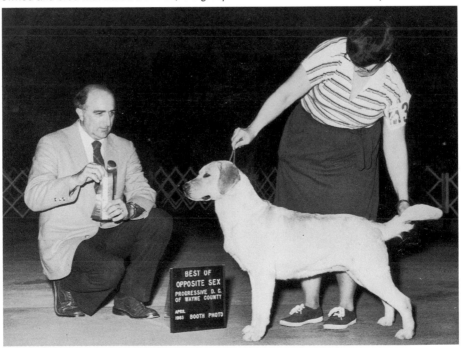

Triple Threat (FC Air Express x Ch. Sunburst Blackfoot Nell—Air Express is a son of Super Chief and Nell a daughter of Shamrock Acres Sonic Boom), breeder, Judy Weikel Aycock. This kennel has also produced a National Champion, the 1979 NFC AFC McGuffy (FC NAFC Ray's Rascal ex Candlewood's Southern Deal). Unfortunately, the novice owner inadvertently omitted the Shamrock Acres kennel name when registering the puppy. It is a sad quirk of fate to have achieved this goal and then not have the dog carry your kennel name.

In October 1980 Sally began a collaboration with Barbara Holl (Hollidaze Kennel in Indiana) and the conformation stock is now managed and shown by Barbara. Some of the dogs are registered with the Shamrock Acres kennel name and some with the Hollidaze prefix. However, Barbara is not associated with the field-trial breedings, nor does she whelp and raise the puppies. As of April 1993 Shamrock Acres has produced 505 conformation champions, two dual champions, one NFC, 25 FC, 37 AFC, two OTCh. and 535 Labrador Retrievers with obedience titles.

1957—CANDLEWOOD, Madison, Wisconsin

Mary Howley's breeding program at her Candlewood Kennels has concentrated on performance pedigrees with uncanny success. Mary acquired her first Labrador Retriever in 1957. She was a junior in high school and her father wanted a Labrador to train for hunting. After answering an ad in a local newspaper, father and daughter came home with two males and joined the Madison Retriever Club to get help training. One of the dogs turned out very well and Mary eventually sold him to the well-known trainer Charles Morgan. She then bought another puppy, a bitch, from a club member and this dog also turned out well, placing in Derby and Qualifying Stakes, and Mary sold her for what was considered a large sum of money at that time. Mary developed an interest in coat color, particularly the yellows (although she did acquire some chocolate breeding stock) and in 1964 she began her own breeding program using the outstanding black field trial champion sires that threw color—NFC NAFC Super Chief and NFC AFC River Oaks Corky. With a careful study of pedigrees for intelligence and conformation, and using titled dams when possible, she has made tremendous progress in the last decade and produced some of the finest field-trial yellows in the country. Her own dog, Candlewoods Nifty Nick ('72 and '74 NAFC '71, '73 and '74 CNFC River Oaks Corky x FC AFC Candlewood's Nellie-B-Good) was a very handsome specimen. Mary ran him until the rigors of the Open competition proved to be too much pressure for "Nick," but he set a precedent for Mary's conformation requirements and became the sire of several successful trial competitors. Titled bitches are the backbone of Mary's breeding program and FC AFC Candlewoods

'90 & '91 NFC-AFC Candlewood's Tanks A Lot (NFC-NAFC Candlewood's Super Tanker x Candlewood's Tiz-Too) and her handler Mike Lardy on the line in the tenth series at the 1991 National Championship.

Nellie-B-Good (NFC NAFC Super Chief x Gahonks Rebel Queen) and her daughter, AFC Blackgold's Candlewood Kate (sired by FC NAFC River Oaks Corky) have made invaluable contributions. In addition, Candlewood's Delta Dash, a "Nellie" daughter and full-sister to AFC Blackgold's Candlewood Kate, although untitled, has produced four FC and AFCs and one National Champion, duplicating her sister Kate's production record.

Candlewood's first well-known yellow field trial champion was FC AFC Candlewood's Mad Mouse (FC River Oaks Rascal x Shamrock Acres Duck Soup) owned by Charles and Yvonne Hayes. Mary's yellow field-trial lines have proven themselves in successive generations. The '93 NAFC FC MD's Cotton Pick'N Cropper through his sire, FC AFC Candlewood's MD Houston is a direct descendent of FC AFC Candlewood's Nellie-B-Good. However, it is through two of her black field trial champions that she has

153

Candlewood's Nifty Nick (NAFC-CNFC River Oaks Corky x FC-AFC Candlewood's Nellie-B-Good), a handsome yellow who proved to be a valuable stud dog.

achieved the most memorable accomplishments—two generations of National Champions! "Lottie," '90 and '91 NFC AFC Candlewoods Tanks A Lot ('92 NFC '91 NAFC Candlewoods Super Tanker x Candlewood's Tiz Too) is a two-time National Champion and her sire, '92 NFC '91 NAFC Candlewoods Super Tanker (NFC AFC San Joaquin Honcho x Candlewood's Delta Dash) won the National Amateur and the National Open. Many very successful field-trial bitches are not bred. This has not been so for Lottie, who has whelped three litters. Her first litter has already produced an FC AFC and several others have Open All-Age wins.

The kennel names Candlewood and Shamrock Acres are often intertwined. Sally Munson (Shamrock Acres) and Mary Howley are closely situated geographically (within two miles) and have an excellent relationship, sharing information, breedings and puppy evaluations.

1959—WINROC®, Livermore, California

Lynn Foote was introduced to Labradors in 1953 when his college fraternity required pledges to care for the house mascot—a male

Sally McCarthy Munson, Shamrock Acres kennel, with two yellow FC sired puppies and Mary Howley, Candlewood kennel and FC-AFC Candlewood's Nellie-B-Good.

black Labrador Retriever named "Guy," a stud dog for Guide Dogs for the Blind, Inc. When the time was right to acquire a dog, a Labrador was the obvious choice (although Lynn's wife, Marianne, admits to having had a preference for a Keeshond puppy). That first Labrador had to be destroyed be- cause of a congenital heart defect, however, a second puppy became Gypsy Nikki CDX and won seven bench points, including one major. "Nikki" traced her lineage to Ch. Earlsmoor Moor of Arden through Ch. Port Fortune Knight Star and FC Black Panther. When bred, she produced the Foote's

155

FC-AFC Candlewood's Nellie-B-Good and Mary Howley after Nellie won the open and completed her field trial championship.

AFC Winroc's Ripper (Crook's El Toro x Shamrock Acres P.D.Q.) owned by William K. Laughlin.

first qualified Open All-Age dog, Boatswain of Bitter Hill, and a bench-winning litterbrother.

Miss Fiddlesticks (AFC Black Mike of Lakewood x Kempers Sassy Sue) was from a repeat breeding of the lines that produced the great FC Michelle, but she did not work out for her original owners, Budgie and Maria Mack, so she was given to the Footes. "Georgie" was bred to the Mack's Canadian import, Carnmoney Spud (Can. FC Bandit of Carnmoney x Carnmoney Boots)—lacking only a win to complete his FC. She produced a litter of exceptional field-trial competi- tors that included the '69 National Derby Ch. and '74 NAFC FC Ray's Rascal owned by Mr. and Mrs. Ray Goodrich and trained by Ray. "Rascal" became an important sire of more than 40 progeny with Open or Amateur placements. One son became a National Champion—'79 NFC AFC McGuffy owned and trained by T. J. Lindbloom and bred by Sally McCarthy. Another son, Rascal's First Edition, was the 1972 National Derby Champion. In 1978 Rascal was awarded the Thomas W. Merritt Memorial Trophy, an annual award to the Outstanding Sire of Field Trial Retrievers. [Editor's

157

note: Rascal was acquired before the Foote s registered their kennel name in 1968. Winroc is a combination of the words—wine and rocks—common elements in the Livermore Valley.]

Shamrock Acres P.D.Q. (NFC Marten's Little Smoky x Ch. Whygin Gentle Julia of Avec) arrived as a birthday gift for Marianne. Using the formula so successfully proven by Sally McCarthy, "Shu-Shu" was bred to her grandsire, Ch. Whygin Gold Bullion, and she produced Ch. Whygin Taurus of Winroc and one trial dog with a win. Bred to Crook's El Toro (FC AFC Crook's Tahoe Pat x Black Rapids of Baranof, a NFC Cork of Oakwood Lane daughter), Shu-Shu produced two winners, AFC Winroc the Ripper owned by William K. Laughlin, and Winroc Chaos (Open win). A littersister, Winroc Wily Witch, was sold to Mr. and Mrs. Elmer Rose in Modesto, California and, in turn, provided

Boatswain of Bitter Hill (Stormy of Arbordale x Gypsy Nikki CDX),a qualified open all-age dog, with handler Lynn Foote.

Ch. Winroc Picaro (Ch. Lockerbie Sandylands Tarquin x Ch. Winroc's Nada Bear), co-owned by Merlyn Foote and Barbara Nowak, sired two national-specialty-show winners. Photo courtesy of Barbara Nowak.

foundation stock for Beth Davis's Sailin' Kennel.

A search to acquire another bitch ended in two disappointing purchases. Instead, a black male from the field-trial trainer Wayne Crook joined the kennel. The puppy became Ch. Mach Zero CD (Crook's El Toro x Lewisfield Contessa). He finished his title owner-handled in only a few shows (five-point major his first time out); his obedience title in three shows on a three-day weekend and a first place at the final show; and his LRC Working Certificate by completing a licensed field trial with a JAM. "Macho" also passed on his quality characteris-

tics in limited breeding by producing seven conformation titled offspring, three HIT dogs, and numerous handsome obedience title holders and hunting dogs.

The Footes were so taken with the characteristics in this dog with his "cross-over" pedigree that they sought out his breeder and arranged to "lease" his sister, Sara's Dixianna, for a breeding to a Ch. Lockerbie Kismet son, Ch. Lewisfield Beret. From that mating they acquired their first quality yellow, Ch. Winroc's Nada Bear. "Nada" was a charming and lovely puppy that earned her conformation title at ten months of age in five shows from

Ch. Winroc Western Edition CD (Ch. Mach Zero CD x Surprising's Extra Edition) co-owned with Bea Asbury won the veteran bitch class at the 1982 National Specialty.

the puppy classes. She developed into a beautiful bitch with a wonderful temperament, a "nanny" to all—puppies, children, and baby goats—and continued to be shown very successfully as an adult winning several bests of breed. Nada was sent east to Dave Elliott for a breeding to the Warwick's Ch. Lockerbie Sandylands Tarquin and whelped the "P" litter. The eight black puppies included Ch. Winroc Picaro, Winroc Pandora (dam of two-time specialty winner Ch. Winroc Thunderstruck CD by Ch. Killingworth Thunderson) and Winroc Phylyra UD. Ch. Winroc Picaro was co-owned by Merlyn Foote (Somersett) and Barbara Nowak (Broyhill). "Rogue" became the sire of multiple champions and the WB at the 1976 National Specialty (Judy Heim's yellow, Broyhill Baroque Inspiration) and the 1983 National Specialty (Mrs. Thomas's black, Weklyn's Markflite Corey). Winroc has seven generations of this line.

After a trip to England and Scandinavia in 1974, the Footes

imported a bitch puppy from Surprisings Kennel in Norway. Surprising's Extra Edition (Nor. Ch. Surprising's Charlie x Nor. Ch. Jayncourt Star Sound) produced only one litter of four blacks (the "W" litter) to Ch. Mach Zero CD before she was spayed because of a uterine infection. "Molly" was an excellent worker with very good conformation. The Macho/Molly combination produced good-looking, talented offspring. Two bitches from the litter became champions and multiple specialty winners. Ch. Winroc Winter Edition won major points at two specialties and was the dam of the WD at the 1983 National Specialty, Ch. Winroc the

Jester (sired by Ch. Sandylands Flash Harry CD) owned by Juxi Burr of Juste B Labradors. Ch. Winroc Western Edition CD earned majors under Helen Warwick and Ann Wynyard, and won the veteran bitch class at the 1982 National Specialty judged by Joan Macan.

In 1979 Marianne, together with a good friend, Lin Tobin, began a retriever magazine—*Retriever International*. Using their retriever experiences and editing skills, the magazine became an award-winning publication that provided valuable educational material and communications for retriever owners around the world until it was sold in 1989.

FC '74 NAFC Ray's Rascal and his owner-handler-trainer Ray Goodrich. Rascal's daughter, FC-AFC Nakai Anny, with her owner-handler-trainer Tom Quinn.

Non-regular class: brace heel free. Photography by Booth.

The Labrador Retriever and Obedience

by Mrs. Juxi Burr and Karen Marcus

HISTORY AND INTRODUCTION

Obedience exercises were introduced in the United States by Mrs. Helene Whitehouse Walker in October 1933. She set out to prove to others that her Standard Poodles, far from being "sissy dogs," were quite intelligent. It was her intent to pattern the tests after the ones given by the Associated Sheep, Police, Army Dog Society in Great Britain. These tests had recently been modified to be held at both indoor and outdoor shows, and for the first time were open to all breeds in England.

The first obedience test in the United States took place on Mrs. Walker's father's estate at Mt. Kisco, New York. Held in conjunction with a dog show, there were eight entries: a German Shepherd Dog, two Labrador Retrievers, three Poodles, and two Springer Spaniels.

The requirements in the initial trials were as follows:

Walk at handler's side off leash

Retrieve a dumbbell on the flat and over an obstacle

Sit-stays and down–stays with handler out of sight

Come when called

Leap over a long jump on command.

These first competitors were watched and cheered on by more than 150 people. Robert Cart, a field–trial enthusiast, presided over this first event. The winning dog was a Labrador Retriever owned by William F. Hutchinson of Far Hills, New Jersey.

Prior to the first trial in 1933, owners had trained in groups, and had competitions and exhibitions, but the dogs involved were either German Shepherds or Doberman Pinschers. There were a number of professional trainers who would give private lessons or work on a "problem" dog. To mention a few, Carl Spitz trained dogs for movies, (for example, "Buck" in *The Call of the Wild*, and "Toto" in *The Wizard of Oz*); Hans Tossuttii, who wrote *Companion Dog Training* in 1946; and Josef Weber, who wrote *The Dog in Training* in 1939.

However, that first trial triggered an enthusiastic response among dog owners. Here was proof positive that one could train one's own dog. Enthusiasm over this novel concept took hold, prompting the North Westchester Kennel Club to offer an obedience trial at their all-breed show on June 9, 1934. This event included the following tests:

Heel on and off lead and figure eight

Sit-stays and down-stays with handler out of sight

Retrieve on flat, and over an obstacle

Long jump.

These individual events came to a total of 250 points for a perfect score.

Due to the persuasion of Mrs. Walker, Somerset Hills Kennel Club became the second club to hold a trial in conjunction with an all-breed show, in Far Hills, New Jersey, on September 22, 1934. In 1935 Mrs. Walker hosted a second private event on October 21, this time also incorporating tracking tests. Six obedience trials at all-breed shows were also held that year.

Obedience trials were extremely relaxed by today's standards with very little emphasis on handling, and nearly any method of getting a correct response from the dog being accepted. While we might consider this to be lax, it contributed greatly to the enthusiasm of potential exhibitors, and consequently the number of participants increased quickly. Even journalists took note, publishing accounts that added to the public's awareness of this new sport.

Around the same time, Mrs. Grace L. Boyd bought her Standard Poodles to America from England and demonstrated the skills which had them winning Britain. She wrote a brochure for beginning trainers that enjoyed wide distribution. In addition, Mrs. Walker produced a booklet "Obedience Test: Procedures for Judge, Handler and Show-Giving Club." She submitted this to the American Kennel Club, which in turn developed the "Regulations and Standards for Obedience Tests." Novice and Open classes were available only to amateur trainers. Professionals were allowed to also compete in the Utility classes, which at that time designated more than half of the points to tracking tests. A dog needed to earn two "legs" to qualify for a title, with a minimum number of dogs required in each class: six in Novice, four in Open and three in Utility.

The North Westchester Kennel Club held the first licensed trial in accordance with these regulations on July 13, 1936. The 12 entries were all at the Novice level, regardless of past competitions, as one had to have the two legs there before proceeding to Open. Eight out the 12 had qualifying scores. At the Orange Kennel Club the next day, eight out of 16 dogs qualified, and the first six Companion Dog titles were won by five Standard Poodles and a Miniature Schnauzer.

Six months later, AKC revised the regulations somewhat. Among other things, the Novice and Open classes were now divided into two sections, A and B, to separate amateur and professional trainers. In 1938 classes were broken down into individual exercises, clarifying points to be awarded for each part. The dogs were also now required to "clear" rather than "climb" jumps. In 1939 terminology was changed so that "obedience tests" became "obedience trials." Eighteen trials were held in 1936 with a total of 33 titles awarded to dogs in nine different breeds. Thirteen Standard Poodles won, twice as many as any other breed.

In 1937 the AKC *Gazette* began to publish detailed reports of obedience competition winners. That year 82 dogs earned CD degrees, 20 CDX degrees, and four UD degrees. Twenty-five breeds were now represented in obedience. Carillon Epreuve, a Standard Poodle owned by Mrs. Walker, was the first dog of any breed to earn all three degrees.

Novice class: heel on leash. Photography by Booth.

An early influence on obedience training and competition was the Obedience Test Club of New York (O.T.C.). They implemented and maintained an approved list of judges, especially important in those early days, as there was little or no standardization of judging criteria. This was remedied by establishing classes for judges and eventually, the majority of judges generally approached their assignments in a similar way. Never having joined AKC the O.T.C. dissolved in 1940. In 1946 AKC established an Obedience Advisory Committee, which worked to standardize judging. In fact, at this time, the section of the regulations titled "Suggestions for Obedience Trial Judges" was changed to "Standard for Obedience Trial Judging." That year

Tracking also became a separate class, with the requirement that a dog have a CD degree to be eligible to compete. Two hundred points were established as a perfect score for all three obedience levels, with a minimum qualifying score of 170 and more than 50% of the perfect score required in each exercise. Between 1947 and 1950, the regulations were defined and refined until they became essentially the standards with which we are familiar today, including the rule that points are to be deducted in multiples of one-half point. Tracking had also been redefined, growing from a one-paragraph description in 1938 to eight pages in 1947.

In 1969 the Directed Retrieve was added to the Utility class, replacing the See Back exercise. In 1975 AKC began to screen and scrutinize obedience judges more closely, and began to offer judges' educational seminars. In 1972 the "Guidelines for Obedience Judges" was first issued. On July 1, 1977 AKC began to offer an Obedience Training Championship or OTCh. to competitors. On July 24, 1977, Moreland's Golden Tonka UD became the first OTCh. on record. The advanced tracking test or TDX was approved by AKC in 1979 and implemented on March 1, 1980. The first TDX was won by a Dachshund, Gretel Von Bupp Murr UD, on March 15, 1980. In 1983, the 50th anniversary of obedience in the United States, the Board of Directors of the American Kennel Club adopted a resolution of gratitude and appreciation to Mrs. Helene Whitehouse Walker. Due to her initial persistence and diligence, the sport of obedience has grown enormously, with over 100,000 dogs competing each year, and several thousand titles earned annually.

TRAINING THE PET RETRIEVER

A study conducted by the Labrador Retriever Club a few years ago disclosed that the great majority of Labradors sold went into homes as pets and children's companions. Fortunately, because of the intelligence of the breed and its desire to please, many are self-trained, to a greater or lesser degree. Unfortunately, others train their masters. As a neighbor lady once said, "My dear little Weeinie is *so* obedient, he does everything I tell him to do...of course, I never tell him to do anything he doesn't want to do."

In our opinion a bad-mannered, untrained dog is a reflection of its owner. Every dog, whatever his role in life, be it house pet, hunting companion, or show dog should receive sufficient training to make it capable of self control, be amiable to discipline, and a welcome companion to its master without being a nuisance to other people.

There are certain things every house dog should be taught: submit to quiet handling, be clean in the house, learn to stay on his property without running-off, walk on a lead without pulling, come when he is called, sit or lay on command and know his place in the house.

Labrador puppies should handled at an early age; they should be taught by kindness and rewarded for their effort. All handling must be done quietly but firmly and the puppy should be talked to in a soothing but, when necessary, firm voice. It is most amazing how a dog that is accustomed to being handled with kindness and affection will submit to painful operations without the necessity of sedation. Many years ago one of our Labradors cut a pad on his foot while running in a water test at a field trial. The veterinarian put four stitches in the dog's foot while it lay perfectly quiet as I stroked his head.

HOUSEBREAKING THE LAB

Many people and especially "Mom" object to acquiring a new puppy because of the seemingly difficult job of housebreaking—not to mention the damage and expense of soiled floors and carpeting. Here is the easiest, most simple method of housebreaking, one that will take the "chore" out of the job and one that will make for a happy well-adjusted pup.

Housebreaking in theory is very simple. It is finding a means of *preventing* the puppy from doing his duties in the house and giving him *only* an opportunity to do it outside. A dog is a strong creature of habit and because he learns by association, he will soon know there is no other place to relieve himself but the great outdoors and good old *terra firma.*

Obedience begins at home. Teach your Labrador the ground rules from an early age lest you find your dog quickly becomes master of the house. Photograph by Vince Serbin.

The trick then is to find this magic means of prevention. Here we take advantage of a very natural instinct of the dog, his desire to keeping quarters clean, i.e., not to mess his bed. It only follows that if we devise a bed that he cannot get out of, then presto he is going to stay clean. Add to this a commonsense schedule of being taken from his bed to outside and we have the perfect answer to housebreaking.

First the bed that he cannot get out of—this is known as a crate —a folding cage large enough for him to comfortably lie down in. If you are appalled by the idea of confining him to a crate, let me dispel any idea of cruelty. You are actual catering to a very natural desire on the part of the dog. In the wild state, does a dog, when he beds down for the night, lie down in the middle of an open field where other animals can pounce on him? No, he finds a cave or trunk of a tree where he has a feeling of security, a sense of protection. With a crate, this is what you are providing. Then too, think of it as a means to an end. He is only going to use it for a few short weeks; as he comes to perform with greater consistency, he gains ever lengthening periods of freedom as he proves himself to be reliable.

And now to the important part: the commonsense schedule that is so vital to success in housebreaking. We'll start with the last thing at night, bedtime for the puppy. Take the puppy out and give him the opportunity to do his duties if possible and you are in a protected area let him go without the leash.

Very often to start with, the leash can be sufficient restriction to keep him from doing his duties. If necessary, use a suppository and be sure to praise him when he has completed his duties. Take him inside and put him in his crate.

The first thing in the morning (*and we mean the first thing*) pick him up and take him outside. He's been clean all night and holding it all night: he should do his duties in a hurry. Now bring him in and give him freedom, but in the kitchen only. A child's gate at the kitchen doorway is an excellent barrier to the other rooms in the house. Give him this freedom while breakfast is being prepared and while you are eating breakfast. After your breakfast, and when you have time to take him out, feed him his breakfast and take him out immediately. Remember the rule: take him outside after each and every meal.

Now bring him in and put him in his crate and go about your normal routine of the morning. He should stay in his crate until about 11:00 to 11:30 AM—then out of the crate and outside. Bring him in, and while you are preparing and eating lunch, let him have the freedom of the kitchen only, for an hour or two. Follow this with a quick trip outside then back in and into the crate until 4:00 or 4:30 PM.

It is now time to feed him dinner. To save yourself an extra trip outside, feed him in his crate and as soon as he has finished his last mouthful, take him outside. After he has completed his duties, bring him in and again allow him the freedom of the kitchen while you are preparing dinner and during the dinner hour. Give him another trip about 8:00 PM and again just before your bedtime.

Keep up this 24-hour schedule for at least two weeks, so that by prevention in the house and repetition of the habit of doing his duties outside, he has the firm association with the proper place to relieve himself. You can now start increasing his freedom out of the crate. Do this by first giving him freedom in the morning—but again only in the kitchen. If he remains clean, then the next day try freedom in the afternoon. It's only through these testing periods that you will know when he has arrived at the point of being reliable.

You should continue for a few weeks (depending on the individual puppy) to put him in the crate during the two most crucial periods: at night and when he is left alone in the house during the day (shopping periods, etc.). You should finally be able to not rely on the crate for housebreaking reasons. Don't be surprised now if your puppy considers his crate indispensable and still insists upon having it available at all times. This habit is handy for emergencies and solves the problem of what to do with the puppy on trips, etc.

Now that you have him reliable as far as the kitchen is concerned, start introducing him to the other rooms of the house, but under strict supervision. The best way to do this is with the aid of a leash. If you wish to have him in the living room while you are watching TV, put him on the leash and hook the handle end of the leash around your feet. In this way you'll know if he gets restless or mischievous. If he attempts any chewing, a jerk on the leash or a smart smack on the nose together with a sharp "no" will get your point home.

In addition to the proper routine, there are other factors involved for a successful housebreaking job—they are as follows:

1. **Worms.** Make certain that your puppy is free of worms. Have your veterinarian do a microscopic stool examination. A puppy with worms cannot control his eliminations.

2. **The proper diet.** Most puppies in good health can do very well on two and not more than three meals a day. Feed a bland nourishing diet that produces a well-formed stool. Stick to this diet religiously. Do not vary it for fear that you may upset his intestinal tract.

3. **Timing.** Do not give him any food after 6:00 PM. It takes a dog about six hours to digest his food and have an elimination as a result of that meal. Any food after 6:00 PM may give him an unexpected urge after he is put to bed.

4. **The use of water.** Do not leave water (or food) where he can help himself at any time. Offer him a drink when you are about to take him out or in the summer keep a pan of water outside. If you are to control output you must control intake too.

5. **Correction.** In spite of a rigid routine, your pup may have an occasional accident during his periods of freedom. Here is where correction is necessary. If you catch him in the act, give him a smart smack together with a loud "no" and put him outside at once. Remember a dog learns by association and in connection with any act of wrongdoing he must receive some form of discomfort in order to learn that he has done wrong. However, you must catch him in the act. It does absolutely no good to punish him for a mistake he has made an hour or even five minutes ago. This applies whether the mistake is messing on the floor or chewing your best pair of shoes.

6. **Puppy Signals.** During periods of freedom, watch for any circling around, sudden loss of interest in a toy, or going toward the door. These are signs that he needs to go out.

Any healthy pup eight weeks of age or older, even in cold weather, can go outside. Of course you don't leave him out long enough to get chilled. You take him out just long enough to complete his duties. Make good common sense the rule of the day.

All too often we receive a phone call from a person that has lost his dog which then ran out into the street and was hit by a car. We always recommend to anyone purchasing a dog to have a fenced-in yard or pen, but frequently someone will, inadvertently, leave the gate open and the dog will get loose and sometimes run into the street. All too often these dogs have not been taught to stay within the perimeters of their home and have not been taught basic obedience commands. These commands are those which your dog must learn, not only to be a useful retriever gundog but also to be a good citizen. These basic commands are sit, stay, come, heel and kennel. When teaching these commands, training sessions should be short, not over ten minutes (after all, you and I have an attentions span of only 20 minutes—ask your clergyman, if you don't believe us). And, importantly, make sure your training sessions are fun for both you and your puppy.

"Cotton" Pershall, probably the greatest Labrador Retriever trainer and handler of all times, starts training his puppies anywhere from seven to 12 weeks using a tennis ball. Cotton teases the puppy with the ball and then throws it a short distance away. Some puppies will return with the ball while others will pick it up and run with it and still others will lay and chew on it. When the puppy returns with the ball, either directly or through coaxing, he is praised and rewarded with a pat.

In a short time he will learn the commands "fetch" and "come," and be ready for a restraint either in the form of a rope lead or a training collar. We believe that both you and your new puppy, when he becomes old enough, will benefit by enrolling in a formal obedience training class.

Novice or Open class: heel free. Photography by Booth.

OBEDIENCE TRIALS

Obedience trials have undergone many changes over the years. They have grown to meet the changing demands of its competitors. Obedience trials consists of three levels of difficulty: Novice, Open and Utility. In order to advance through the levels in obedience, the dog and handler team must complete each level starting with Novice and ending with Utility.

171

The first level, **Novice** is divided into six separate exercises. To qualify the team must complete each section with at least half the points given for it and they must finish with at least 170 points out of the 200 points that they start with. Points are deducted for each error made by either the dog or handler. The Novice sections are:

1. Heel on leash with a figure 8: The team must follow the directions given it by the judge. They must work precisely.
2. Stand for examination: The handler removes the leash and stands the dog so the judge may run his or her hand down the dog's back. The dog should not move.
3. Heel free: This is done off leash and is the same as the heel on leash. There is no figure 8.

Above: Novice class: dog sitting in front for recall. Photography by Booth. *Below:* Novice or Open class: group long sit. Photography by Booth.

4. Recall: The handler leaves the dog sitting on one side of the ring and at the judge's command calls the dog to sit in front of him or her. The dog must also return to the heel position at the handler's signal.

5. Long sit: This is a group exercise usually with anywhere from six to 12 teams in the ring at the same time. The judge has the handlers sit their dogs on one side of the ring and they leave the dogs and go to the other side of the ring, turn and face them and wait for one minute before returning to the dogs at the judge's command.

6. Long down: This is also a group exercise. The handlers put their dogs in a down position and leave them for three minutes.

Above: Novice class: dog finishing. Photography by Booth.
Below: Novice or Open class: group long down. Photography by Booth.

Above: Utility class: signal exercise, sit. Photography by Booth. *Below:* Open class: drop on recall. Photography by Booth.

Once the team has qualified at three separate obedience trials under three different judges, the dog is given the title Companion Dog and the owner can place the letters CD at the end of the dog's AKC name.

The next level is **Open**, which is separated into seven exercises. The same rules apply for qualifying as in Novice.

The exercises are:

1. Heel free and figure 8: This is like the heel free in Novice except there is a figure 8 in it.
2. Recall with drop: The handler leaves the dog and calls it at the judge's signal. The dog is signaled to drop halfway into the handler. The dog must front and finish like in the Novice recall.
3. Retrieve on flat: The handler throws a dumbbell across the ring. The dog is sent to retrieve it and should front and finish as in the recall.
4. Retrieve over the high jump: The dog is sent to retrieve the dumbbell but it must jump a solid high jump, go to the dumbbell and return to the handler to front and finish.
5. Broad jump: The dog jumps over a long broad jump on the ground to front and finish at the handler.
6. Long sit: As in Novice this is a group exercise. The handlers are out of sight for five minutes.

After the dog qualifies in three trials with three different judges, the dog is given the title Companion Dog Excellent. The letters CDX can be placed after the dog's AKC name.

Open class: heel free, figure eight. Photography by Booth.

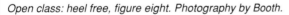

The last level is **Utility**, which has seven separate exercises in it. As in the other two levels, the same rules for qualifying apply. The exercises are:

1. Signal: Using only hand signals, the handler must have the dog heel, sit, stand, drop and recall with front and finish.

2. and 3. Scent discrimination: This is two separate exercises. The dog must choose an article which the handler has scented from a group of articles that are not scented by the handler. One of the articles must be made of leather and another, metal.

4. Directed retrieve: The dog is sent to get one white glove from a line of three white gloves. The judge decides which glove is to be retrieved.

5. Moving stand and examination: The handler and dog are given a heeling pattern by the judge and at the judge's signal the handler has the dog stop and stand as the handler moves across the ring to face the dog. The dog either is examined by the judge and then the dog must return to the heel position at the handler's signal.

6. Directed jumping: The dog is sent across the ring by the handler and must turn and sit at the handler's signal. The handler then sends the dog over one of two jumps in the ring at the judge's command. The dog must front and finish. The exercise is repeated and the dog jumps the second jump.

The title for this level is Utility Dog and the dog has the letters UD after its name.

Open class: broad jump. Photography by Booth.

Open class: retrieve on flat. Photography by Booth.

Above: Open class: retrieve over high jump going to the dumbbell. Photography by Booth. *Below:* Open class: retrieve over high jump returning with dumbbell. Photography by Booth.

An Obedience Trial Championship may be earned by a dog after it has achieved its UD. The Obedience Trial Championship or OTCh. is earned by acquiring 100 points. These points are given to dogs that take first or second place in either Open or Utility. The dogs must also have placed first in Open B and Utility at least once. They must have an additional first place in either class. The letters OTCh. are placed before the dog's AKC name.

The UDX title requires the dog to have a UD and then qualify in Open B and Utility B simultaneously, but not consecutively, in ten shows.

Non-Regular Classes: The AKC has recognized that obedience should be fun and has introduced classes which are interesting to both exhibitor and spectator. These include:

Graduate Novice: Open to dogs that have earned their CD degree and have not been shown in the Open Class.

Brace: Two dogs with one handler competing in the Novice routine.

Team: Five handlers and their dogs perform the Novice routine simultaneously.

Versatility: Handler assigned six exercises randomly—two Novice, two Open and two Utility.

Non-regular class: team heel on leash from novice. Photography by Booth.

The Labrador Retriever, without question or doubt, is the best overall land and water retriever. The breed has claimed far more field trial championships than all other breeds combined.

Retriever Field Trials

by Mary C. Knapp

Contemporary American field trialing evolved from the British method of employing "non-slip" retrievers (i.e., heeling at the handler's side) to recover fallen game when ordered to do so. They are not required to quarter and flush game, only retrieve it. Although the British dog is expected to retrieve both fur and feathers, his American counterpart is used exclusively on birds.

The American Kennel Club Standard Procedure for Retriever Field Trials booklet defines the purpose of a field trial: "to determine the relative merits of retrievers in the field. Retriever field trials should, therefore, simulate as nearly as possible the conditions met in an ordinary day's shoot." It further states that a dog "should sit quietly on line or in the blind, walk at heel or assume any station designated by his handler until sent to retrieve. When ordered, a dog should retrieve quickly and briskly without unduly disturbing too much ground, and should deliver tenderly to hand. He should then await further orders.

"Marking is of primary importance. A dog which marks the fall of a bird, uses the wind, follows a strong cripple, and will take direction from his handler is of great value."

Most trials are run on weekends and offer four different stakes. Each stake is designed to test dogs and/or handlers with various degrees of experience and is judged by a pair of amateurs who, between them, have judged a number of other stakes. Each stake presents three or four different test situations. Tests are usually divided equally between land and water. Judges use wind, terrain and distance to test dogs on marking ability, courage, nose, style and trainability. All dogs are tested on the first test or "series" of each stake. Those that pass are called back to the second for further judgment. After three or four tests (sometimes more) most dogs have been eliminated and, in many cases, less than ten complete all tests. Judges then designate four places in order of performance and award Judges Awards of Merit (JAM) to those that have done creditable work but did not place in the top four.

The most advanced stakes are the Open (Special or Limited) and

Amateur (Owner-handled). They are termed Major stakes as places awarded in them count toward Field and Amateur Field Championships. First place provides five points; second, three points; third, one point and fourth, one-half point. Judges of these stakes must have judged a total of eight other trials between them. If one has judged eight by himself, the other does not need any and a new judge can be initiated.

To obtain a Field Championship (FC) a dog must earn ten points in Open, Limited or Special Stakes, five of the ten must be the result of a win (excluding a breed specialty trial). To receive an Amateur Field Champion title (AFC) a dog must earn 15 points by placing in the Open, Limited, Special, Amateur and/or Owner-handled Amateur Stakes. Five of the 15 must be the result of a win in either the Open Stakes or the Amateur Stakes (excluding a breed specialty trial). Open points won by amateurs also count toward an AFC as well as an FC. Since it is difficult to place over professionally handled dogs, dual points are warranted.

The Open Stake is available to dogs over six months old handled by professionals or amateurs. Because of increasingly large entries, it can be limited if the previous year's entry was too large. A Limited Stake is only open to dogs who have taken a first or second in the Qualifying, or have taken a place or a JAM in the Open, Limited, Special, Amateur or Owner-handled Amateur Stakes. A Special Stake further limits eligibility to dogs who have placed in the same stakes as the above, but within the period comprised of the previous calendar year and current calendar year preceding the trial.

The Amateur Stake is open only to amateur handlers, although the dog may be professionally trained. At some trials it is limited to an Owner-handler Stake. This prevents amateurs from handling other dogs than their own. Since it is advantageous to run a number of dogs and "go to school" on each test, such limitation tends to keep the competition more equal.

Both Stakes have similar tests. Dogs are expected to arrive, work and leave the "line" (starting point) off leash. They must be steady to shot, work over decoys, and honor another dog's retrieve. Tests consist of marked retrieves—pheasants or mallards—thrown by gun stations located at various distances in front of the line. Birds are thrown or shot one at a time in numbers up to four. After all the birds fall, judges call the contestant's number and he is allowed to send the dog. In scoring marks, judges generally favor dogs which proceed directly to the "fall" area and recover the bird with a short, tight hunt thus disturbing little of the surrounding terrain. However wind, terrain, obstacles and distance can deflect a dog. Usually, the longer a dog hunts, the lower the score. If a dog forgets a mark, the handler will direct him to it through a series of whistles and hand signals. Generally, this is interpreted as failure to mark and severely penalized.

As competing dogs run, judges draw a small diagram of each performance in their books. (Each page gives the dogs' number for identification purposes.) They will also add notes such as good or poor style, poor line manners, handler, whines, etc., to refresh their memories. All the information is taken into consideration when they determine the final awards.

Marks may vary in distance from less than 20 to 300 yards or more. In some tests, a gun or two retires (hides) while the dog is recovering another bird. When the dog returns to line, he must be able to remember the retired bird fall(s) as there is no gunner in the field, visible from the line, to refresh his memory. Often marks are combined with blinds which add to the difficulty.

Besides marks, there are usually at least two "blind" retrieves: one on land and one on water. A blind retrieve is a dead bird which has been planted so that the dog does not know where it is but the handler does. The handler sends his dog in the general direction and, theoretically, since the dog has been trained to run a straight line, he should run until he arrives at the bird. Like the marks, however, the same distractions can influence the dog. When he veers from a fairly straight line, the handler stops him with a single whistle blast, then gives him a hand signal to indicate direction of the bird. Sometimes it takes a number of direction changes (whistles) to recover the blind. Since a straight line is desirable, the more corrections incurred, the lower the score.

NFC-NAFC Super Chief handled by August Belmont.

Dee's Dandy Dude.

Some All-Age test diagrams follow:

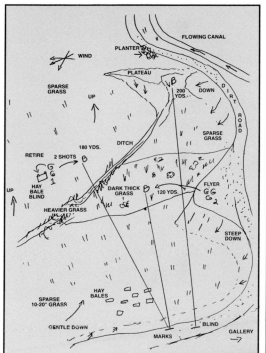

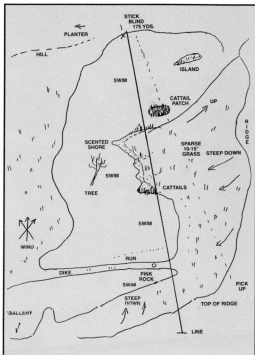

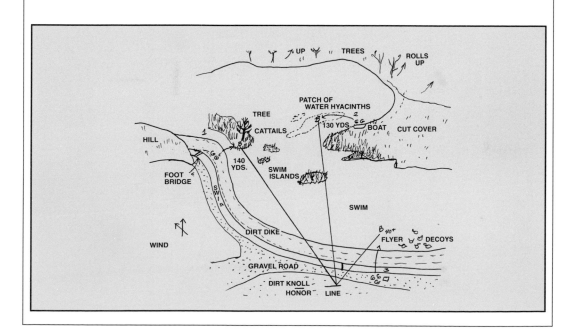

Growth of the All-Age Stakes are illustrated by *Retriever Field Trial News* statistics below:

OPEN ALL AGE AND AMATEUR ALL AGE COMPARISONS

	OPEN ALL AGE			AMATEUR ALL AGE		
	Trials	Starters	Avg.	Trials	Starters	Avg.
1992	204	11768	57.7	204	9679	47.4
1991	209	11846	56.7	209	9645	46.1
1990	207	11159	54.0	207	9141	45.0
1989	206	10936	53.0	206	8913	43.5
1988	196	10365	52.9	196	8513	43.4
1987	193	10580	54.8	193	8433	43.7
1986	187	9913	53.0	186	7960	42.8
1985	188	9770	51.9	188	7915	42.1
1984	185	9305	50.3	184	7242	39.4
1983	183	9056	49.5	182	7273	40.0
1982	177	8722	49.3	177	7218	40.8
1981	176	8762	49.8	175	7432	42.5
1980	175	8770	50.1	174	7412	42.6
1979	174	8991	51.7	173	7436	43.0
1978	169	9115	53.9	168	7191	42.8
1977	164	9149	55.8	163	7258	44.5
1976	161	8283	51.4	160	7178	44.9
1975	153	7670	50.1	152	6535	43.0
1974	151	7351	48.7	150	5821	38.8
1973	146	7754	53.1	145	5483	37.8
1972	139	6557	47.2	137	4818	35.2
1971	138	6010	43.6	135	4362	32.3
1970	134	5703	42.6	132	4134	31.3
1969	130	5430	41.8	128	3731	29.1
1968	127	4817	37.9	126	3798	30.1
1967	125	4332	34.7	120	3041	25.3
1966	123	4317	35.0	119	2958	24.8
1965	126	4281	33.4	118	3029	25.6
1964	119	4038	34.7	114	2889	25.3
1963	115	4006	34.8	109	2853	26.2
1962	111	3683	33.1	105	2685	25.5
1961	108	3562	32.9	99	2497	25.2
1960	106	3583	33.8	85	2277	24.0
1959	102	3301	32.4	95	2134	22.9
1958	100	3133	31.3	92	2079	22.6
1957	92	2939	32.0	83	1968	23.7
1956	84	2871	34.2	60	1502	25.0
1955	71	2369	33.5	39	967	24.0
1954	65	2114	32.5	37	976	26.3
1953	60	2324	38.8	35	891	25.5
1952	58	2071	35.7	39	855	22.0
1951	53	1950	36.0	32	727	22.0

The Qualifying Stake is the more demanding of the Minor Stakes. It is for dogs which can do multiple marks and some blinds, but not the difficulty of those required in the All-Age Stakes (Major). The *Standard Procedure* states that eligibility "shall be for dogs which have never won a first, second, third or fourth place or a Judges Award of Merit in an Open, Limited or Special All-Age Stake, or won first, second, third or fourth place in an Amateur All-Age Stake, or Owner-handler All-Age Stake, or won two first places in Qualifying Stakes at licensed or member club trials."

Usually marks and blinds are shorter and wider spread than All-Age tests, however, dogs must still honor another dog's retrieve, work over decoys and be steady to shot. Most likely the blinds will be planted outside the marks, rather than through them, or be run separately. Also, there can be an occasional retired mark. Dogs may be taken to and from line on leash, but must be run off leash.

In both Minor Stakes, a "controlled break" will not automatically disqualify a dog as it does in the Major Stakes. If a dog leaves the line to retrieve before judges release it and the handler can within a short distance call him back, the dog is penalized, but need not be eliminated from further competition.

The *Standard Procedure* states that "a Derby Stake at a Retriever Trial shall be for dogs which have not reached their second birthday on the first day of the trial at which they are being run."

Derby tests are usually single- and double-marked retrieves largely designed to test natural ability and some training concepts. The dog is expected to be steady to shot (controlled breaks allowed, but penalized) work over decoys, but does not have to honor another dog's retrieve. Although many are able to do blinds, they are not used in testing a Derby dog. Generally a retired mark is not used in this stake.

The Derby Stake does not carry championship points, but the *Retriever Field Trial News* does offer the Charles Morgan Memorial Trophy annually "to the dog that has accumulated the highest number of Derby points on either of the following basis: (1) during that calendar year or, (2) during its lifetime if it became two years of age during that calendar year, except that if a dog wins it under (1) above, it shall not be eligible to win it the next year under (2) if it is not yet two years old at the end of the calendar year in which it was the winner.

"All Derby Stakes, including Specialty Trials, will carry points provided they have ten starters. Points for the four places are 5-3-2-1." Charles Morgan was a professional trainer who was highly concerned about Derby dogs. After his death in the late '60s, this trophy was named for him. Previously, the old *Country Life* magazine had offered a similar trophy for many years.

187

Below are sample diagrams of Qualifying tests:

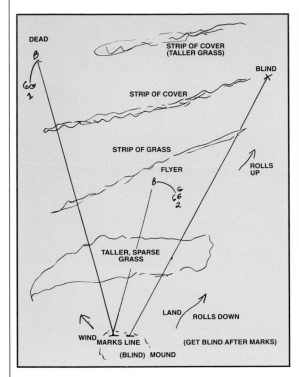

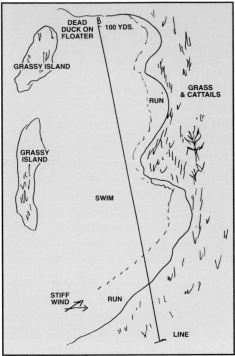

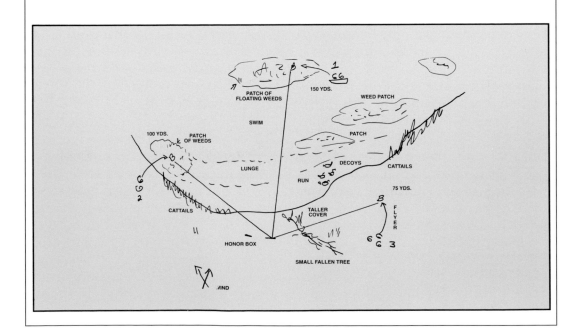

The growth of the Minor Trial Stakes is illustrated by *Retriever Field Trial News* statistics below:

DERBY AND QUALIFYING STAKE COMPARISONS

	DERBY			QUALIFYING		
	Trials	Starters	Avg.	Trials	Starters	Avg.
1992	220	4956	22.5	216	6467	30.0
1991	224	5856	26.1	218	5905	27.1
1990	224	5509	24.6	220	6304	28.7
1989	224	5417	24.2	218	6200	28.4
1988	217	5741	26.5	209	5735	27.4
1987	213	6045	28.4	203	5671	27.9
1986	209	6230	29.9	201	5662	28.2
1985	208	6319	30.4	201	6265	31.2
1984	204	6452	31.6	196	6061	30.9
1983	199	6782	34.1	189	5602	29.6
1982	193	6200	32.1	182	5084	27.9
1981	190	6664	35.1	178	5096	28.6
1980	189	6399	33.9	174	4936	28.4
1979	189	6591	34.9	175	5210	29.8
1978	188	7193	38.3	170	5515	32.4
1977	179	7067	39.5	166	5382	32.4
1976	170	6915	40.7	158	5213	33.0
1975	163	6677	41.0	145	4582	33.5
1974	152	6082	40.0	135	4423	32.8
1973	142	5748	40.5	130	4279	32.9
1972	136	5005	36.8	118	3876	32.8
1971	136	4879	35.9	114	3158	27.7
1970	131	4284	32.7	111	3170	28.6
1969	127	4343	35.0	107	2981	27.9
1968	122	3829	31.3	111	2831	25.5
1967	118	3015	25.6	114	2551	22.4
1966	119	3157	26.5	108	2267	20.9
1965	123	2647	21.5	108	2268	21.0
1964	115	2701	23.4	100	2111	21.1
1963	110	2369	21.5	96	1972	20.5
1962	108	2387	22.1	94	2037	21.6
1961	105	2365	22.5	92	2117	23.0
1960	91	2002	22.0	100	1825	18.2
1959	91	2080	22.9	95	2056	21.6
1958	85	1772	20.8	94	1850	19.7
1957	79	1661	20.0	86	1662	19.3
1956	70	1525	21.8	77	1516	19.7
1955	57	1404	24.6	61	1582	21.0
1954	52	1132	21.8	55	1098	19.8
1953	49	1157	23.6	46	848	18.5
1952	42	1110	26.4	43	747	17.0
1951	37	1069	28.9	39	725	18.0

If you would like more detailed information concerning rules, regulations and explanations of retriever trials, the *Standard Procedure* and *Recommendations of the Retriever Advisory Committee* booklets are available to individuals upon request, at no charge, from the American Kennel Club, 51 Madison Ave., New York, NY 10010.

There are also two National Championship competitions which are offered each year. The National Retriever Championship Stake is open to professionals and amateurs alike. It is sponsored by the National Retriever Club, Inc., an organization which consists of member clubs throughout the country. The Stake is held in mid-November and moves to an area within a different time zone each year. The first Stake was held in 1941. To be eligible to run this prestigious stake, dogs must qualify each year. To do so, a dog must win an Open, Limited or Special All-Age Stake, plus earn two other points. This must be accomplished in licensed trials sponsored by member clubs in good standing which begin with the first one after the last National to the last one prior to the next National Stake. In the last few years, records kept by the *Retriever Field Trial News* indicate that less than 100 of the 1500 or so dogs competing qualify for the coveted National Retriever Championship Stake.

The current National Champion and Canadian National Champion automatically qualify. If the National winner is handled by an amateur, the win also qualifies him for the next National Amateur Stake. Conversely, the current National Amateur winner is qualified to run the National, but the dog must be amateur-handled.

The National Retriever Club is the older of the two National-sponsoring clubs. In contrast, the National Amateur Retriever Club was established in the 1950s and presented its first Stake in 1957. It was organized by amateurs including W.W. Holes, Edward Spaulding, Lewis Greenleaf, John Olin, M.B. Wallace, Bing Grunwald and Guthrie Bicknell. They felt that a National title should be available to qualified competing dogs handled by amateurs only. To qualify for it, dogs must win an Open, Limited, Special, Amateur or Amateur-handler Stake and earn two other points in any of the same stakes; however, the dog must be handled by an amateur. Eligible trials begin with the first one after the last National Amateur Stake to the last one preceding the next National Amateur Stake. The current National Amateur Champion and Canadian National Amateur Champion automatically qualify. The Championship Stake is held in mid-June each year and also revolves through the different time zones. Since a dog can qualify by taking places in both All-Age Stakes, more qualify to compete in the National Amateur Stake than in the National Championship Stake. *Retriever Field Trial News* records indicate that 100 to 135 of the 1500 dogs competing qualify.

Both National Stakes are judged

Diagrams of several representative Derby tests are shown below:

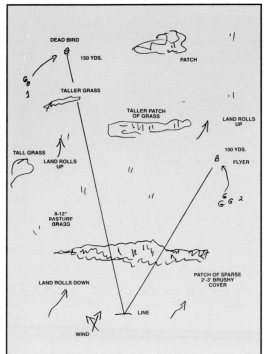

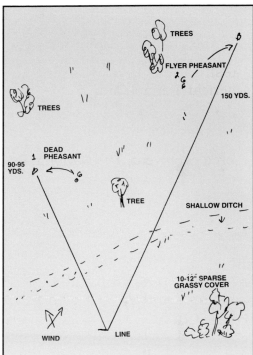

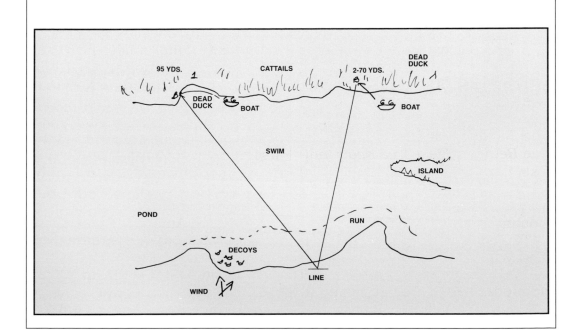

by three people, each having judged an excess of eight All-Age Stakes (usually many more). Often one of the three people has judged a previous National Stake. There are a minimum of ten different tests run during a six-day period. Tests are somewhat more difficult than weekend trials, and dogs are gradually eliminated until a winner emerges. Those that finish all series, but do not win are termed "Finalists." National winners and Finalists are highly regarded and may influence many generations of retrievers to come through their demand for breeding purposes.

Contemporary field trials have evolved from fairly short, simple hunting situations to complicated, highly competitive events today. Along the way, a number of dogs and people have contributed to the change and success of the sport. Early Labradors and their trainers were imported from Great Britain by prominent American patrons.

Marshall Field (Caumsett), W.A. Harriman (Arden), Franklin P. Lord (Blake), Dr. Sam Milbank (Earlsmoor) and Robert Goelet (Glenmere) were some of the active breeders, importers and trialers.

Groundwork for today's trials was laid in the 1930s and '40s when, according to the National Field Trial Club's 1941–1960 book, trials rose from one in 1931 to 21 in 1941. In 1935 *Field and Stream* magazine offered a trophy to be awarded each year to the dog which accumulated the greatest number of points in the Open All-Age Stakes. Points were five for first place, three for second, two for third and one for fourth. It was awarded from 1935 until its retirement in 1953. (After the National Championship began in 1941, it was awarded in addition to it.)

During the late '30s, the National Retriever Club was organized with the help of the American Kennel Club. Alfred Ely and Tom Merritt were instrumental in that venture. Tom served as an early officer and was also the owner of the great Labrador Dual Ch. Grangemead Precocious.

It was during this period, too, that J.F. Carlisle's (Wingan) British trainer/handler David Elliot introduced "handing" into the United States. Sheepdogs were directed by whistle and hand signals in his home country, and he determined it was useful in retrievers also. At the time, it was a revolutionary concept and eventually changed the way trials were run.

Prior to AKC sponsorship, early trials were held by invitation on private estates such as the one owned by Marshall Field. Most dogs were owned by influential and wealthy people who hired trainers; some also served as gamekeepers on their estates. Social barriers existed between owners and trainers to the extent that trainers ate and travelled separately from owners. These barriers remained until the late '50s or early '60s when professional people (amateurs with time available to train their own dogs) joined the ranks of enthusiasts.

During the '40s other names such as Ben Boait, Howes Burton, Mrs. J.M. Austin, Dr. and Mrs. Evans,

Dual Ch. Grangemead Precocious with his sons, FC Freehaven Muscles, FC Cherokee Medicine Man and Dual Ch. Cherokee Buck. Photography by E. Shafer.

Dr. George Gardner (Nelgard), Mr. and Mrs. D.E. Pomeroy (Blackpoint), Kathleen Starr Frederick (Timber Town), Mr. and Mrs. M. B. Wallace, Jr. (Casa Audlon) and Morgan Belmont dominated the scene. Many of these individuals donated their time and resources to the sport as well as competing.

Amateurs also trained and handled dogs, but not to the same extent as today. One name which appears repeatedly is that of Paul Bakewell, III (Deer Creek). In ten years, from 1939 to 1949 he won the National Stake seven times. Only once was one of his dogs handled by a professional, T.W. "Cotton" Pershall. The dogs included two-time NFC Rip, NFC Tar of Arden, NFC Marvadel Black Gum and the famous three-time NFC Dual Ch. Shed of Arden. The latter two dogs are still found in the ancestry of many contemporary field-trial dogs.

Some of the most successful professionals of the era were Charles Morgan, Frank Hogan, Orin Benson, Dave Elliott, M. "Snuffy" Beliveau, James Cowie, Ray Staudinger and William Wunderlich.

Although trials continued to grow in popularity, World War II limited any rapid growth for a few years during and after the conflict. A number of professional trainers were also recruited to train dogs for the K-9 Corps. Among them were

193

Charles Morgan, Billy Wunderlich, Dave Elliot, Roy Gonia and Cotton Pershall.

After the war, growth resumed at a rapid rate until the number of Open Stakes rose from 30 in 1946 to 100 in 1958. In 1951 the Amateur Stake achieved championship status, and many amateurs attended and ran the stake in hopes of earning an additional title on their dogs. Shortly after, the "Double Header" Club was formed. It offered special recognition to amateurs who had handled their dog to a win in both the Open and Amateur stakes during the same trial—a very difficult feat!

It was during the early '50s that John Olin (Nilo) began to run retrievers. In 1952 and 1953, his great NFC King Buck won the National Stake handled by Cotton Pershall. In 1965 Cotton again won the National with Olin's dog NFC Marten's Little Smokey. Always a strong competitor, John often handled his own dogs in the Amateur Stake. Although CEO of the Olin Corporation, he donated his time and talents to the sport. A staunch supporter of the National, it was his influence which prompted Winchester to donate ammunition to the event for many years. In 1963, after the death of John Fraser (editor of *Field Trial News*), John Olin promoted and arranged for acquisition of the *News* with the help of Bing Grunwald and others. In 1964 it was acquired by both the National Retriever Club, Inc., and the National Amateur Retriever Club and re-named *The Retriever Field Trial News*. It exists today as the only medium which informs field trialers of the results of American and Canadian field trials including the National and National Amateur Championship Stakes of both countries, trial dates, rule changes, judging suggestions, and other matters of interest and importance to the sport.

During the '50s and '60s, Mr. and Mrs. George Murnane were also formidable competitors. Their professional handler Joe Schomer won the Open National twice ('57 and '59) with NFC Spirit Lake Duke while NFC Whygin Cork's Coot repeated the feat ('66 and '69) handled by Joe Riser. In '71, he won it with their NFC Mi-Cris Sailor. Other successful professionals included D.L. Walters, Tony Berger, Roy Gonia, Ed Minoggie, J.J. Sweezey and Jim Weitzel.

Another great dog began to make his mark during this period. NFC Cork of Oakwood Lane, owned by Dr. Mork and handled by Tony Berger, is in the ancestry of many successful dogs running today. Fast and stylish, this 100-pound-plus Labrador Retriever is difficult not to notice!

In the mid '60s, August Belmont and NFC-NAFC Super Chief were the team to beat. They were also first to win a National "Double Header," by winning both the National Stakes back to back. (In '75 and '76, his daughter NFC-NAFC Wanapum Dart's Dandy would duplicate the feat.)

During the early '60s, a remote control "electric collar" appeared and was soon recognized as an effective training tool. It consisted of an electrical receiver attached to a collar and a handheld transmitter operated by the trainer. When the handler pressed a button on the transmitter, the dog received a mild electric shock.

"collar" dogs and, at the time, there was much interest from those not yet familiar with it. Rex Carr, a retired career military officer, was one of the pioneers who revolutionized retriever training by devising a system of using the collar combined

John Olin with King Buck.

Once the dog has been conditioned to respond in a positive manner to the electric stimulus, the handler could control his dog's behavior without touching him. The collar offered a safe, instant correction at distances farther than conventional methods provided.

Super Chief was one of the early

with a foundation of basic training. Older "conventional" methods employed a wide array of tools, most of which required physical strength and endurance for dog and handler alike. It also involved a good deal of leg work and skill with firearms. The collar method taught dogs basic concepts in a controlled yard-type situation, then transferred the knowledge gained into the field using electric stimulation to reinforce those concepts, rather than as a tool for discipline only.

Ramifications of the collar method were not fully understood at first, and incorrect applications produced dogs with little style or enthusiasm, although they were under control. Later, it was refined and enhanced by more sensitive equipment and training methods which revived stylish performances. Since many collar dogs became successful, the method was adopted by amateurs as well as pros. Women, especially, could train competitive dogs as the physical strength required of conventional methods was no longer required.

At approximately the same time, animal behavioralist Charles Pfaffenberger published his book *The New Knowledge of Dog Behavior.* He had done a study for the Seeing Eye organization to see if he could find a better way of predicting and increasing the number of pups who would become successful guide dogs. His study indicated that, contrary to the popular belief that dogs were not mentally mature until they were physically mature, dogs were able to accept some training as early as seven weeks of age. Also there were several distinct "stages" each pup went through that could influence future trainability. He found that early human socialization was also imperative to success. That knowledge, combined with collar conditioning, allowed dogs to be trained with better results, and at an earlier age.

Hip dysplasia, scourge of the working retriever, had been identified as a hereditary problem and influential people such as Dr. George Gardner, John Olin and others educated and encouraged breeders to have their dogs x-rayed and certified by the Orthopedic Foundation for Animals

Cork of Oakwood Lane, whelped April 27, 1951.

FC-AFC River Oaks Corky owned by Michael P. Flannery.

(OFA) in an effort to prevent its proliferation.

During the '70s knowledgeable amateurs remained active in all phases of the sport and it flourished. Several dogs which are dominant in pedigrees of today's field champions arose during this period. They are NAFC FC CNFC CAFC River Oaks Corky and NFC AFC San Joaquin Honcho. Corky was trained by his original amateur owner John Trzepacz, and polished by professional Billy Voigt after his sale to Mike Flannery. (His record of over 500 total All-Age points remains unsurpassed through 1994.) Rambunctious, stylish, and with uncanny marking ability, he was a real crowd pleaser.

Corky's most famous son NAFC FC River Oaks Rascal, owned and handled by Joe Pilar, soon followed in his dad's pawprints. His desire

NAFC-FC Trumarc's Zip Code owned by Ed and Judith Aycock.

producers of field and amateur field champions.

During this period, one of his sons, NAFC FC Trumarc's Zip Code (also trained and handled by Judy) began to challenge Honcho's record as a competitor and producer.

Several others are reflected in current pedigrees of successful competitors. They are NAFC FC Dee's Dandy Dude owned by Mike Paterno, NAFC FC Ray's Rascal, owned by Ray Goodrich, NAFC FC Piper's Pacer, owned by Roy McFall and NFC AFC Westwind's Supernova Chief, owned by D.J. and Nancy Esposito.

A number of breeding kennels have consistently produced competitive Labradors. Among them are: Candlewood, Mary Howley; Castlebay, Hank Mc Neil; Hawkeye, Bill and Mary Hillmay; Hiwood, Roy and Jo McFall; River Oaks, John and Cai Trezpacz; Royal Oaks, Laurel Allen; Shamrock Acres, Sally McCarthy Munson; Trieven, Jay and Val Walker; Trumarc, Ed and Judy Aycock; Westwind, Albert Uhalde; and Wanapum, Eddie Bauer.

for birds appeared to border on insanity. Galleries held their breath when he was on line as he seemed to be on the verge of breaking during most marking tests.

Honcho was trained by amateur Judith Weikel Aycock with methods taught by Rex Carr. Unfortunately, an illness forced Honcho into early retirement. It did not diminish his ability as a sire, however, and he became one of the all-time great

Right: NAFC-FC-CNFC-CAFC Piper's Pacer owned by Roy McFall. *Below:* NAFC-FC Kannonball Kate was the all-time high-point retriever bitch with a total of 255 points (as of April 1, 1979).

NAFC-FC Ray's Rascal owned by Ray Goodrich.

Other noteworthy events in the '70s included Dennis Bath's NAFC FC Lawhorn's Cadillac Mack, who won the National Amateur twice and the rise of highly competitive bitches in the sport.

From 1970 to 1980, seven bitches won National titles which was more than double that of all who had ever claimed a National title before. They were: NFC NAFC Wanapum Dart's Dandy (both titles), NFC AFC Creole

NFC-AFC Candlewood's Tanks A Lot.

Sister, NFC AFC Happy Playboy's Pearl, NFC AFC Euroclydon, NFC AFC Risky Business Ruby, NFC AFC Wanapum's Lucyana Girl, NFC AFC Yankee Independence and NAFC FC Kannonball Kate (the current high-point All-Age bitch with 410 $^1/_2$ points). It appeared the trend of "women's lib" had also invaded the retriever sport. Perhaps a change in training methods and/or the availability of medication to prevent heat cycles allowed bitches to be more competitive.

In the '80s collar-trained dogs posed a formidable challenge to the conventionally trained ones. They were difficult to beat. By the late '80s, it appeared most of the successful dogs had been developed by that method, and conventional trainers had diminished, replaced by young men and women using modified versions of the collar technique.

On the down side, although dogs could do amazing blinds and distant, complicated marks, there was criticism within the sport concerning a breeding trend which seemed to select dogs on the basis of their suitability to the method rather than on natural ability in general. Further, in the quest for more style, some dogs became too hyper to be easily trained. Concentrated linebreeding to a relatively few popular studs had reduced previously numerous gene pools to only a few.

Thus identified, these side effects of success are being addressed by the many influential, conscientious and dedicated breeders who carefully plan litters with an eye on the future of the sport.

In the '90s popularity and success of the sport were illustrated by the shattering of several records. In 1991, a record 109 dogs competed for the National Amateur Championship and a young Labrador female won the National Championship, an unprecedented twice in succession ('90 and '91). She is NFC AFC Candlewood's Tanks A Lot. NFC NAFC Candlewood's Super Tanker became one of the few to earn the coveted double National title.

Several yellow dogs earned over 100 All-Age points—a difficult feat for all dogs, but extremely rare for a yellow to date. They were: FC AFC Lakeridge's Charlemagne, FC AFC CNFC CNAFC The Marathon Man, FC AFC Candlewood's M.D. Houston and FC AFC Candlewood's Captain Kid. (It is interesting to note that three generations are represented. Charlemagne sired Houston who, in turn, sired Captain Kid.)

Over the years many great people and dogs (too many to have all been included in this short chapter) have contributed to the evolution of the sport as we know it. Some are easily recalled while others have faded into the past. However, their legacy remains and is appreciated and enjoyed by current participants. In the new century, we can only speculate and wonder what lies in the future for the people and dogs in the sport.

FC-AFC Lakeridge's Charlemagne handled by Corinne Thompson.

English field dogs differ slightly from American Labradors in conformation as well as working style. Photograph by Robert Smith.

The English Field-Trial Labrador and English Field Trials

by Jack Chojnacki and Christopher G. Wincek

English field trials differ from American trials in several respects and, for that matter, so do the dogs. There are a number of field trials held throughout Great Britain over the course of any year culminating in the Retriever Championship in December. However, entering these trials is the first difference that deserves comment. Trials are run as either a one-day trial, with an entry of 12 dogs, or a two-day event with an entry of 24 dogs. For many trials, as many as 100 dogs may seek to enter but by luck of the draw only 12 (or 24, as the case may be) are selected. In effect, one could train

Field trials in Great Britain are strongly geared toward the notion that these expeditions should closely imitate a typical day's shoot. Photograph by Robert Smith.

and work Labrador Retrievers for a number of years and theoretically never participate in a single trial. For this reason, people participating in trials generally enter multiple trials at any given time for any given week.

This limitation, while difficult for some, allows for a trial where dog work is carefully scrutinized and where there is no pressure to drop dogs.

A second major difference about the British trials is that they are more closely guided by the notion that a trial should simulate a typical day's shooting activity, which is a part of our American standard as well. Birds are wild birds and the stakes are either walk-up, a driven shoot or a duck shoot. A walk-up stake would be where a line of people walk through a field with four dogs at a time accompanied by six gunners, four judges and the beaters. A driven shoot would be where four dogs are set at a peg and the beaters coming in front of them are driving birds over the top, again for the six gunners to shoot the birds and then to be picked up following the flight.

The third stake, a duck shoot, would be where ducks are driven across a pond, lake or river

Photographs on this page of Labrador retrieving pheasant by Robert Smith.

tion in the trial is set up to evaluate the marking, training and hunting ability of the dogs.

A British field-trial dog is the prototypical non-slip retriever. Line manners and control at the line are of utmost importance. One sound from the dog and the dog is dropped from the trial. There is no whining, barking or other sound allowed to be made by the dog. The dogs are commanded to stay at heel whether it is heeling through a walk-up or sitting at a peg beside its handler during a driven shoot. Any creeping is grounds for immediate dismissal from the trial.

and the dogs, after being held steady and as the flight is completed, are sent out to retrieve.

The way the tests are set up is at the discretion of the gunner. For English field trials, which are generally held on estates and shooting estates, a complement of six gunners must be found who actually pay for the day's shoot for a fee from £12 to £18 per bird. Since they are paying sportsmen, the judges have to work within their desires of doing driven shoots or walk-up shoots, shooting birds only, and in most cases this would be partridge or pheasant, or combined birds and fur game, typically rabbits and hare. The competi-

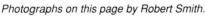

Photographs on this page by Robert Smith.

A TYPICAL DAY'S SHOOTING

The East Anglia and Labrador Retriever Club trial held on October 12 and 13, 1992 was attended by Jack Chojnacki. The opening stake was a walk-up. The gunners had elected not to shoot hare, so only partridge and pheasant would be the game shot and upon which dogs would be judged. This was a 24-dog two-day stake; it began at 9:00 AM when all of the handlers of the dogs were called together by the four judges, the chief steward and the steward of the beat, a gameskeeper. Three trophies were awarded: the Philray trophy for the winner of the stake, the Birdbrook trophy, also for the winner of the stake, and the Ditchingham Smith trophy presented for the runner-up in the trial. The prizes were £30 for first place, £20 for second place, £10 for third place, and £5 for fourth place. This practice of awarding cash prizes is another difference between trials in America and British trials.

The first stake was a walk-up. Four dogs were placed in line stretching out about 100 yards. The line consisted, going from left to right, of a gunner, a beater, a dog and handler, a beater, a gunner, a beater, a dog, a beater, a gunner, a gunner, a beater, a dog, a beater, a gunner, a beater, a dog and handler, a beater and a gunner. There were a total of six guns in line with the four dogs, each dog having a handler, and there were eight beaters, each flanking a dog.

The judges walked behind the dog and handler, so it is quite a sight to see as they start with 22 people in line. The other 20 dogs were about 20 yards to the left of the line and about 20 yards back following a steward who carried a large red flag on a pole. Spectators and all other dogs not under judgment cluster around this flag so as not to disturb the working dogs.

Beet fields had been harvested but were still covered in beet leaves approximately 1 to 18 inches high, very thick. The line proceeded through the cover until birds were flushed and shot by gunners. It was explained to the handlers that birds would be flushed and shot and then dogs would be selected to retrieve these birds. The dogs were expected to retrieve birds that flushed in front and flew away from the guns as well as birds that came back straight over the line and fell behind the gunners and dogs.

The judges explained that the dogs 1 and 2 to the left of an imaginary center line would be expected to retrieve birds to the left of that line, dogs 3 and 4 to the right of that imaginary line were expected to retrieve birds to the right. It was further explained that this would include birds flushed and shot out in front, over to either the left or right or dropped behind the line.

The group started out at a reasonably brisk pace, walking through the beet field. The first bird to be flushed was dropped about 40 yards in front of dog 3. This dog's number was called by the judge and the dog was sent out to retrieve this fallen bird which was a strong flying cock pheasant. The dog went generally to the area of the fall and hunted in that area. After a two- or three-minute hunt, the handler began sent generally to the left or to the right and allowed to hunt further. This particular dog would stop on a whistle and be given a very quick cast and then be allowed to hunt back in the area where the handler felt the bird had dropped.

The dogs must have complete control on line: the British field trial dog is a prototypical non-slip retriever. Photograph by Robert Smith.

whistling and handling the dog, much like an American trial, where the dog was asked to stop, was expected to sit and face the handler upon a long blast of the whistle. The handler then gave hand signals, also typical of American handling. The dogs however were not expected to handle in the precision-like manner that American field trial dogs are expected to handle. They were After another three or four minutes of handling, the dog failed to pick up the bird and was called in. Since the dog had worked the whole area of the fall, it was anticipated that this had been a runner. Runners are fair game in a trial and the dogs are expected to trail and pick up a runner. To this end, dog 4, who was on the side of the line where dog 3 had been sent, was

Yellow Labrador in pursuit of a felled bird in the water. Photograph by Robert Smith.

asked to retrieve the bird. Dog 4 went out and hunted about five minutes on his own and was then given four handles and handled very crisply. After a full ten minutes, that dog was brought back to the line and dog 2 was moved over to the position where dog 3 had been and was sent to the fall. After failing to pick up the bird, dog 1 was brought over and requested to pick up the bird.

Dogs 2 and 3 each took about five to six minutes and neither of them came up with the bird. By British standards, dog 3 was then dropped; he had been first to the fall, had been given the opportunity to go to the fall with a fresh scent and was expected to pick up a runner. Since dogs 4, 1 and 2 were not the first dog to fall, but in sequence followed dog 3, they were not eliminated from the stake. However, it was noted by the judge that had dog 1 or 2 found the bird, either trailed it or found it at the sight of the fall, dog 4 who was second to be sent would have missed it, that dog would have been "eye-wiped" by dog 2 or 1 picking up the bird, and dog 4 would also have been eliminated.

After all four dogs failed to pick up the bird, dog 3 was eliminated and dog 5 was brought into the spot vacated by dog 3. This was a continuing process as a dog either completed or failed, wherein another dog was brought from the gallery and put in the line so that four dogs were always in position to retrieve. These dogs were not working the field but were walking through the field under steady control by the handlers.

At the end of all four dogs failing,

the judges went to the spot of the fall, and with the beaters, looked over the area, and found no bird fallen and it was determined that it had been a runner, so only dog 3 was eliminated.

On the second series of the first day, after four dogs had failed to pick up the bird, the judges went to the area of the fall and found the bird. Consequently all four dogs running at the time were eliminated, being in effect "eye-wiped" by the judges. The trial proceeded in this manner until all 24 dogs either failed or retrieved fallen game. It is interesting to observe these dogs as true retrievers. It was demanded of them to retrieve the bird—and only the bird—for which they were sent. During some of the retrieves throughout the first day, while the dog was working the field, a bird would flush. The dog was expected not to follow the flushing bird, even if it were dropped by a gunner, but was expected to stay on the bird it had been sent to retrieve. It happens on occasion that while one dog is working, another bird is flushed and shot and then, after the working dog comes in, the next dog is sent to retrieve the bird that had been shot during the course of the first dog's hunt and retrieve. The dogs' control and discipline to stay in the area of the fall to which they are sent, as other hunting activity is occurring, is amazing.

Through the 24-dog course, on six occasions, dogs were sent to a fall, experienced a runner and successfully followed that runner for up to 100 yards and retrieved it. It is

Labrador retrieving on land. Photograph by Robert Smith.

very interesting to see these dogs being judged on what would be a day's shoot and that runners are part of the luck of the trial. The true hunting retriever is of utmost importance in a British field trial. For one's dog to gain a reputation of being a "gamefinder" is the highest of compliments.

Blind retrieves occur as they happen. A blind might have happened when four or five birds are shot, all going out at the same time before a dog was sent and the dogs might be looking to the left and a bird falls right, or in the case of birds that come over the line and were dropped behind the line where the dog had no way of watching the bird fall. Again, a major difference in han-

dling exists between American and British field trials. When a handler in an American field trial starts to handle a dog with whistles, that dog is expected to stop hunting and to be directed solely by the handler to the bird. In the British field trial, the dogs are sent to the area and then left to hunt some more with handles being used sparsely.

BRITISH TYPE AND TRAINING TECHNIQUES

In our combined experience, the British trial dog looks much more like our American trial dogs than what is more commonly represented to us in America as the prototypical British shooting dog, dogs commonly imported here for the conformation

British shooting dogs are surprisingly athletic in appearance and are probably more recognizable as Labradors than many lines of American field-trial dogs. Photograph by Robert Smith.

Retrievers in England are steady and natural in their work ethics, less programed than American retrievers. Photograph by Robert Smith.

ring, which have an abundance of substance, short legs with an emphasis upon close coupling to the effect that fronts are straighter. So many dogs are imported to America from Britain each year from "gundog kennels" with muzzles so short one wonders how they would pick up a cock pheasant or large drake effectively, and with heads so wide that the image of single-colored Rottweilers with tails sharply comes to mind.

The American public has been misinformed as to the appearance of the British shooting dog. The British shooting dogs are much more athletic in their type and their appearance. Remember, a British field trial is a true hunting scenario, not a remote imitation of hunting like an American trial. Wild birds are relied upon and much is left to luck and surprise, true components to what makes hunting so interesting.

Although the quality of being a sportsman and being in the outdoors and appreciating good dog work are somewhat ineffable, the beauty of a British field trial is embellished by the natural elements of hunting with the discipline, control and responsiveness of the British field-trial dog and by the partnership shared between the dog and its handler. The trialing has all of the earmarks of a great sport.

A few more words about British field-trial dogs. Although in form and structure, they may resemble American field-trial dogs, they are by and large, if we may be so brash

Temperament and biddability are paramount for retrievers. Photograph by Robert Smith.

to generalize, of a better type overall than our trial dogs. They are probably more recognizable immediately as Labradors than some of our more extreme representatives of trial dogs who have become rather whippety, snipey, with an impersonal, hard expression. We are not suggesting that British field trialers per se are more sensitive to type. We do note, however, that they do not expect the lining abilities, the physical challenges of our geography and distances, the water work and the almost robot-like performance that some of us prefer in the States. Perhaps our preferences in American trials affect our type of dogs.

Collar conditioning and training is relatively unknown in Britain. Additionally, were collar conditioning introduced, it may be crosscurrent with development of some of the natural abilities that British trialers prefer. One difference between American and British trial dogs' performance is marking. Although marking is of utmost importance in British trials, the lining ability so preferred in the States is not really met with the same interest in Britain. British trial dogs tend to quest in their progress towards a mark. Nose is a very strong feature in their working lines so there is an element of flushing towards a mark in their dog work.

Implicit in this discussion is to convey the value of a British field-trial dog's absolutely quiet, flawless line manners. It may be well worth our while in our outcrosses in American performance breeding to look to some of their working lines. This is not to suggest that we would be immediately breeding American field champions by doing so. It truly is a different kind of dog. One wonders whether English dogs would take the pressure of some of our training techniques. However, we can learn some lessons.

Temperament is such an unquestionable aspect of the English field–trial lines. One becomes aware readily of the relationship between temperament, training ability, responsiveness, heart and biddability in working with these lines. The lines provide very much

Black Labrador photographed by Robert Smith.

for a one-man type of dog, with intense desire to please and with equally intense loyalty. Heart, style, brains, marking ability, responsiveness, coupled with a deep-seated sense in the dog's heart of the partnership it shares with its handler, are what makes this line of Labradors compelling, desirable and respected shooting partners.

ACHIEVING A FIELD TRIAL CHAMPIONSHIP

To achieve a field trial championship in Great Britain, a dog must win a 24-dog two-day stake and a 12-dog one-day stake, or three 12-dog one-day stakes. In effect, then, a dog has to beat 36 different dogs to become a field trial champion in the United Kingdom. All dogs winning one 24-dog stake are entitled to compete in the British Retriever Championship. The British Retriever Championship is held in December and is often attended by the Queen. In 1992, the Championship was held at Sandringham, the Queen's shooting estate in East Anglia. If a dog were to win a British Retriever Championship but was not yet a field trial champion, he would by virtue of winning the championship acquire that title.

American retrievers, in general, possess more style and fortitude when hitting the water than British dogs. Photograph by Robert Smith.

In order to become a British field trial champion, a dog has to beat 36 different dogs. Photograph by Robert Smith.

Wayne Eliassek and his Chesapeake Bay Retriever, Chopper, demonstrate "concentration."

Hunting Tests

by A. Nelson Sills, Robert H. McKowen and John V. Carroll, Jr.

The advent of the American Kennel Club Retriever Hunting Test program in 1985 was an idea whose time had come. Few, if any other AKC programs, ever received such immediate acceptance and rapid growth.

In 1985 the Labrador Retriever was becoming the most popular dog in America. Many people bought Labs for hunting, showing and field trials; of course the majority were purchased as pets. By 1990, the Lab had the second highest number of registrations in the AKC stud book. In 1991, Labs reached the number-one position with 105,876 registrations. Labrador Rctrievers not only repeated as the most popular breed in 1992 but increased the lead substantially with a total of 120,879,

Labradors do a superb job on both waterfowl and upland game.

1993 Master National Qualifiers.

almost 15,000 registrations over the next highest breed, the Rottweiler. Continuing its reign as the number-one dog in America, the Labrador's 1993 registrations stack to an all-time high of 124,899, though only less than 5,000 registrations over the Rottweiler.

The reason for this immense popularity is the Labrador's pleasing and biddable personality and attractive appearance. But unless a means could be found to allow the breed to continue to prove its abilities in the field, there was fear that a lot of those very qualities that make the breed so popular would be lost.

True, Labrador field trials have existed since 1931 but because of the intense competition for place-ments and championship points in the number of trials that can be practically held, only those very select dogs with concentrated training could compete. Many Labradors are used for hunting both waterfowl and upland game where they do a superb job but this sport only accounted for a portion of the total number of dogs bred.

In many parts of the country, hunting seasons are short and, for most of the year, the dogs are not used in the field except for some training. Their owners sought some type of performance event other than trials. By this time the trial requirements far transcended the performance needed in an ordinary day's hunt. This group of hunters, as well as some former field trialers, and some people who only showed their dogs, were interested in a program that would more closely approximate conditions they would likely find while hunting.

That is why there was such great excitement when the AKC announced its new Retriever Hunting Test program in 1985 and some clubs began holding tests.

The two basic features of the hunting tests are that they approximate actual hunting situations and that they are not competitive. Dogs compete against a standard to qualify for one of three titles instead of competing against each other for placement.

The title structure also offered encouragement to newcomers as well as those who had experience in field trials. The entry stage is the Junior Hunter (JH), followed by an intermediate state called the Senior Hunter (SH) and finally the ultimate challenge, the Master Hunter (MH).

The JH level tests the dog on natural abilities. The dog can be lightly restrained with a leash at the line or point where it leaves for a retrieve. It must retrieve two single land marks and two single water marks. The dog must earn four qualifying scores in order to receive a JH title.

In the SH level, the dog must retrieve multiple marks from both land and water as well as retrieve two blind birds (birds which the

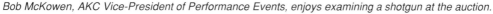

Bob McKowen, AKC Vice-President of Performance Events, enjoys examining a shotgun at the auction.

dog did not see fall and has to be directed to by its handler). It has to be steady on the line without a leash. A SH must have five qualifying scores; unless it has earned a JH, in which case it need only earn four qualifying scores. They must also be able to handle diversion shots and diversion birds, and the dogs must honor.

The MH is the ultimate test of a combination of natural ability, experience and training. Like the SH, the Master Hunter must also have multiple marks on land and water and blinds as well as diversion birds and shots, as well as honor. The Master dog's manners and performance, however, are judged much more stringently than either the JH or SH. Six qualifying scores are required for a title, unless the dog has earned an SH title which counts as one.

Although the first AKC Hunting Tests were held in 1985, the Hunting Test program actually began two years earlier, in 1983. In that year, a new organization called the North American Hunting Retriever Association (NAHRA) brought the concept of non-competitive testing to American Kennel Club staff members.

Representing the AKC at that meeting to consider the concept were A. Nelson Sills and David Merriam, both members of AKC's Board of Directors; A. Hamilton Rowan, Director of Field Trials; John V. Carroll, Manager of the Field Trial Department, and Robert A. Bartel, Field Representative. Ted Eldridge, another member of AKC's Board,

entered into the formative process at a later date. Representing NAHRA was Jack Jagoda of Virginia; Ned Spear, Vermont; Richard Wolters and Lewis Brothers.

A program was developed in consort with NAHRA in 1983, and a set of joint AKC/NAHRA regulations for sanctioned (non-licensed) events went into effect on January 1, 1984. About four sanctioned tests were held that year to iron out the wrinkles in the new program.

However, there emerged philosophical differences about the administration and direction of the program. In late 1984, NAHRA broke with AKC to go its own way.

AKC then issued its own set of regulations for Retriever Hunting Tests effective February 9, 1985, and shortly thereafter convened the first Retriever Hunting Test Advisory Committee. The recommendations made by that committee resulted in the orange book which became effective July 9, 1985 and remained in effect for seven years.

The second Advisory Committee meeting was convened in August 1991, under the direction of Performance Events Vice-president Robert H. McKowen, and the recommendations made by that committee resulted in the new regulations which took effect July 1, 1992.

Early in the program, participants began to voice a need for an activity (either a title or event) beyond the Master Hunter-title level. Support for the idea continued to grow and under urging from Nelson Sills, the

Animation. Nancy Sills and Yellowjacket's Sportsman MH.

AKC investigated the possibility of something to work for after obtaining a Master Hunter title.

In late 1989, AKC sent a survey to all clubs holding retriever tests. The majority of the respondents was in favor of an annual showcase event that would help keep Master Hunter titlists in the program and give owners an incentive to work for each year.

The AKC under direction of Bob McKowen and John Carroll, with advice from Nelson Sills, established the first Master National Test to be held the week of September 15, 1991, in Chesapeake City, Maryland.

At the same time, the AKC issued a call to a "Master National Associa-tion" organizational meeting which was held on September 15 prior to the start of the first Master National Retriever Test. The first Master National was sponsored by the AKC and hosted by the Del Bay Retriever Club, whose president was Nancy Sills. Larry Wharton served as chairman of the event and Nelson Sills was chief steward. This first event drew a surprising 94 entries, 26 of which qualified over the six-day event.

The organizational meeting to develop a Master National Association was chaired by Bob McKowen. Representatives from 59 clubs attended the meeting and a panel of officers and directors was elected to take over the reins of the second

Larry Wharton and Nelson Sills receive the prestigious Vision Award, presented by MNRC President Sonny Robertson.

Above: 1993 Master National in progress. *Below:* 1993 Master National judges Ed Haas and Milton Holcombe; Mike Diesio, AKC Director of Sporting Breeds; Chairman Northrup Larson, and judge Bob Klusman.

annual Master National. The Middle Tennessee Amateur Retriever Club was named host club and Bill Speck was elected president of the association. Linda Furr was elected secretary/treasurer. Jim Hall was appointed chairman. By the 1992 event, 110 clubs had become members and 65 were represented at the annual meeting held in advance of the test at the Percy A. Priest Wildlife Area in LaVergne, Tennessee.

At its initial meeting, the Master National Association voted to rotate the Master National among four regions across the United States. The third event was scheduled for Kansas City with the Kansas City Retriever Club serving as host. Sonny Robertson was elected president and Northrup Larson was named Hunting Test chairman.

The Master National serves as a culmination of the year's activities, a gathering of some of the best dogs that participated in the program the previous year and a test of the progress that has been made.

The Retriever Hunting Test program continues to grow yearly. It provides an activity for many hunters and other owners of retrievers who do not wish to participate in the highly competitive field trials. The Hunting Test program also provides workers to help retriever clubs and some of the more successful dogs are entered in both field trials and hunting tests.

At the first AKC-licensed Retriever Hunting Tests held in 1985 there were 13 events with a total of 681 starters. The distinction of holding the first events belongs to the Jayhawk Retriever Club and the East Texas Retriever Club which ran on the same dates in St. Joseph, Kansas and Lufkin, Texas, respectively. Since then, the AKC Retriever Hunting Test program has had spectacular growth as evidenced by the following statistics:

Year	Events	Starters
1986	44	3,227
1987	81	6,857
1988	119	9,250
1989	154	11,527
1990	188	13,427
1991	214	15,383
1992	202	16,188

Training a Retriever

by Fred Kampo

Probably the most important key to success in training a retriever is the matter of attitude—especially *your* attitude. Whatever the background of your puppy, you must realize from the start that training takes patience, composure and a lot of confidence on your part.

As for the puppy, he is right there, ready and willing to be trained. It is a whole new world he is being introduced into, and he can't wait to learn all he can about it.

How that learning is directed is up to you! Just keep in mind that to a puppy, life is one big game, and all the world is a playground. If you make learning a game, it will turn out to be fun not only for the pup but for you as well.

When is your dog old enough to begin his formal training? For some things, he is old enough the minute he is brought into your household. This is his early training. It will include some of the social graces such as housebreaking and the meaning of the words "No" and "Quiet." The dog should be at least seven weeks old when he starts these lessons. Then, when he has a good base in these ABC's, it will be time to enter the next stage of training where he will learn the specialties that will make him excel in hunting, field trials or hunting tests.

All of his lessons, and particularly his early lessons, must be accompanied by plenty of rewards (i.e., praise). It is not just a matter of what he is learning but also that he *likes* the whole idea of training.

Here are a few more tips to help set the stage for successful training:

Create a good learning atmosphere away from any distractions. It is important that you have your dog's complete attention.

Keep the commands simple. Use only one-word commands as much as possible, preferably a word of only one strong syllable, such as "Sit", "Come" or "Heel."

Always be firm and calculating. The dog will learn to recognize certain tones in your voice as well as words. He will also learn your attitude.

Unless you are deliberately trying to catch your pup's attention for a specific purpose, react and

227

talk slowly during training so he is not confused.

Never shout at your dog. You don't like it and it doesn't sound good in the neighborhood. Furthermore, it isn't necessary if you insist that your dog obey commands in a normal tone.

Begin training in 15-minute sessions. Have a specific plan for each session, concentrate on it without interruption during the full session, then immediately put the pup in his kennel or have some play time. If you are anxious to speed up his learning, it is all right to have several sessions in the day, but do not extend this to several hours of training in a single day. Keep an eye on your dog; do not allow him to become bored.

Repeat often! Do not assume your dog has retained everything he learned yesterday. Repeat it today! Repeat it again tomorrow and before every training session. The dog learns through the confidence he gains from repetition.

Always be sure your dog is well exercised before every lesson. He needs an opportunity to "air" and get his running out of the way before he must begin to concentrate.

Never settle for a sloppy response. Always insist on immediate obedience.

Always end each session with something the dog is good at so he can achieve success and receive praise. This is an important step in giving him confidence.

In the dog's early training, always have a collar on, even when he is only exercising. It doesn't hurt to have him drag a short rope from his collar. It is a reminder that he is not in complete control.

EARLY TRAINING

There is much your dog can learn even before he is old enough to begin his formal obedience training. It is also important that a strong human bond be developed between you and your dog. Dedicating yourself to his training in the beginning will help achieve both of these goals and bring you many rewards later in life. This is the period when he must not only learn basic obedience but also learn how to become a member of your household. It is when he develops his personality.

The Word Is "No!"

They're never too young to learn!

Your puppy's training can begin almost as soon as he is weaned, and one of the very first lessons should be recognizing the word "No!" He will not only learn its meaning but at the same time learn the many things in his big new world that are off limits...like a shoe to chew on, a corner of the garden to dig in, or a bed to get up on. There is no formal "No" lesson; it is a continuous process.

Every time the pup does something undesirable,
1. Restrain him.
2. Take the offensive object away from him (or move him away from it),
3. Say "No!" in a stern voice.

If your dog doesn't stop his transgression when he hears the

The proper way to put on a choke lead.

word "No," then sound the "rod"...the rod in this case being a rolled-up newspaper for a puppy, or the gripping end of a lead for an adult. (Too much cannot be said for the newspaper roll; it is harmless, yet makes so distinctive a noise that the sound of it slapping against your hand or leg has the desired effect.)

It probably won't take long for your pup to learn the meaning of the word "No," but it will take some time for him to learn all of the items on the "No" list. It calls for patience as well as firmness on your part.

The Collar and Lead

Place a small collar on the puppy as soon as he arrives. He should start getting used to it as soon as possible, and it gives you something to hold on to during training. Be sure the collar fits properly, not too tight so as to choke him, but not so loose that he might catch his paw in it, or pull out of it. You may have to purchase several collars as your pup is growing.

Next start teaching him to walk with a short nylon lead. Don't worry about heeling; he'll have plenty of time in the future to learn that. Right now just let him get used to the lead. He will soon learn that it means control, and that when it's on he can't get away and will have to do the things expected of him. Even though he may not like it at first, it won't take him long to learn that when the lead is on he will be getting plenty of attention. He will soon find it tolerable.

Housebreaking

Put this at the top of your list. It is important to bring the puppy into the house often, but while he is in, stay with him and keep him busy. Hold him and play with him, but don't let him sleep without putting him in his kennel or crate. When you see that he is tiring, put him out before he has a chance to mess. Then, put him into his crate, which conveniently may be moved from room to room.

Even when your pup does not seem particularly tired, put him out often: you will be surprised how he will tend to his business when he is outside, even when he has shown no particular signs while you were playing. Be sure to praise and pet him whenever he has performed correctly.

Teaching your dog that his kennel is his home goes right along with housebreaking. Using the kennel will not only keep him clean it will also help keep him out of trouble. But remember that he is very small and is eating several times a day, so do not make the kennel a prison. He must have attention, especially when he is going outside to do his job.

Manners

Every dog must learn his place. When he is young and learning his commands is the time to also be teaching him not to beg at the table, sleep on furniture, jump on guests, or commit any of the other indiscre-tions that will mark him a "bad dog." It all hinges on his learning the "No" command.

Being quiet is also a part of his manners. To stop a puppy from barking, simply hold his mouth firmly shut and tell him "No." Re-peat this using a little more pressure on his lips each time.

At night, keep the pup's kennel next to your bed, especially for the first few nights that he is with you. Be sure he has been out so that any nighttime barking will not be a sign that he needs to relieve himself. Then when he barks in the night reach out and shake or slap the kennel, saying "No" or "Quiet." It should take very little time before your puppy under-stands and gives you, and himself, a full night's sleep; he does not like the noise inside his home any more than you like his barking inside yours.

ELEMENTARY TRAINING

Remember to select a good, rela-tively quiet and distraction-free location where you will be able to concentrate on the business at hand without interrupting your lessons.

Remember also that these will be ten- or 15-minute lessons. No mat-ter how much fun you are having, stop when the time is up. If things are moving along well and you want to go further, fine, but only in short segments, and only with several hours rest between each lesson.

You can train a dog to respond to voice commands, hand signals or the whistle. In any event, the voice signal is basic and must be learned first. However, introduce the whistle fairly early, especially when it comes to sitting. A sharp blast on the whistle along with the word "Sit" will soon be associated together, which will help in the field later on. Use the voice for everyday commands around the house; use the whistle and hand signals in the field.

Use of a Whistle:

Voice command:"Sit"

Whistle command: one blast

Voice command: "Come"

Whistle command : four or five short blasts

To a retriever, several quick blasts means "come fast," and a single blast means "sit and wait for further instructions."

Equipment:
1. A lead (6 feet)
2. A choke collar
3. 30 or 40 feet of nylon rope
4. A whistle
5. White and red bumpers (substitutes for a shot bird, usually made of plastic or canvas)
6. A pistol with blanks
7. A kennel or crate

Lesson One: Sit

The command "Sit" is one of the most important for the working retriever. He is required to sit at your side while waiting in a blind; he will take his hunting or field-trial directions for a retrieve from a sitting position either at heel or while sitting at some distance from you.

"Sit" is a good word for a dog because the hissing sound of the S

SIT. Head up, push down on rump.

is clear even when speaking in a whisper, as in a duck blind or at a field trial when it is important to keep your dog steady without making a big fuss.

PROCEDURE:
1. Begin by walking the dog at your side, using a short lead.
2. Stop and command "Sit" in a firm tone. At the same time, hold his head up with the lead and with your other hand push down firmly on his rump. When he is settled in the sitting position, give the command "Sit" once more, repeat the command "Sit" several times, then release the pressure and praise him.

Each time you take him out, tell him to sit at once. After the first ten- or 15-minute session, he should know perfectly well what you mean, although he may not want to comply. Push him down as a reminder, and keep pushing him down until he does it freely without your help.

Making him sit should be the start of every lesson. At each session increase the time he spends in the sitting position until he is able to stay there for a minute or two without moving. When he seems comfortable with it, begin slowly moving away from him, all the time firmly commanding him to "Sit."

Continue this until you can move 20 or 25 feet away without the dog moving. If he tries to follow, put him back to the spot where he was sitting, scold him and tell him to "Sit." Don't ever let him get by with

Make him sit as you slowly move away.

moving away from the spot he is supposed to be in, or he will develop the habit of sneaking along the ground without ever getting up—annoying while hunting, and disastrous in field trials or hunt tests!

If you are going to use a whistle for your commands, do not start until your dog has learned to sit freely with the voice command. Then give the voice command "Sit," and as he is sitting, give one blast of the whistle. In a few days reverse the order, giving the whistle command first and then the voice command. Finally after a few more days, when he has mastered the whistle command, drop the voice command entirely. You will soon begin to alternate between the whistle and voice at your discretion.

Lesson Two: Come or Here

Either word, "Come" or "Here," is suitable. The choice is yours, but once you have decided, stick to either one or the other. Don't confuse your pup by expecting him to learn both.

"Come" is one of the most critical commands for you must depend upon your dog to return to you if he is heading for danger or his boundary lines. "Come" is also one of the easiest commands to teach, provided the trainer keeps his voice firm and friendly.

PROCEDURE:

1. Very soon after his first few lessons, the puppy should know the "Sit" command. When he is sitting well, begin his next command lessons by slowly moving away from him, about 20 feet in the beginning, then bending or kneeling on one knee, clapping your hands and calling your pup by his name, or the word "Come." When he responds, give him a lot of praise.

2. If your pup does not come to you, move quickly away from him, clapping your hands and calling his name. Let him chase after you...never chase him or it will soon become a game with him. Keep up this procedure, clapping your hands while running from him. When the pup has responded satisfactorily five or six times, try giving him the command and clapping without running. When he comes to you give him plenty of attention.

3. These simple steps may well be all that is necessary to teach the command "Come." However, if the pup starts to stray, give him the "Sit" command and attach a 30- or 40-foot rope to his collar while he is sitting. Slowly walk away from him until you reach the full length of the rope and command "Come" while giving the rope a sturdy tug. Keep giving short tugs, calling "Come" with each one. When he reaches you, be sure to be generous with your praise.

4. After two or three lessons, when he is responding well to the verbal command, begin to

introduce the whistle. Give the command, clap your hands, and at the same time give four or five blasts on the whistle.

Lesson Three: Heel

The command for a retriever to "Heel" is as basic as the command to "Sit" or "Come." Keeping his head at your knee is home base; it is where he starts and where he finishes, the focal point from which you put him through his hunting or field procedures. Because the command to heel requires slightly more discipline than the others, the dog should be more mature before his lessons begin, and he should be perfectly comfortable walking with the lead.

The first decision for the dog's master is to determine from which side the dog will work. If you hunt and are right handed, it is best to train your dog to walk on your left side so there is no danger of his interfering with the gun you carry on the right side. If you are left handed, it is vice versa. It is a personal decision based upon what is most comfortable for you. But once selected, stick with it. Don't run the risk of confusing the dog as to which side he should be on. If you plan to attempt conformation showing, you will need to choose your left side. Heeling is a command that requires constant maintenance if it is done correctly.

PROCEDURE:

1. As your dog is coming out of his kennel, begin his lesson with a brief refresher course before starting on the new command. Have him "Sit" a few times, then walk away and practice the "Come" command.

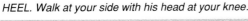
HEEL. Walk at your side with his head at your knee.

2. Keeping a short hold on the lead which is attached to his choke collar, start walking while giving the command "Heel." Repeat the command several times, always saying the word "Heel" very distinctly.

3. As the dog seems to become more comfortable walking at your side, loosen your grip on the lead to give him some lee-way. He will inevitably start to surge forward, away from you. When he gets out in front, give the "Heel" command again, pulling him back into position with a yank. He is wearing a choke collar, so yanking in quick tugs will apply the needed pressure to remind him where he is supposed to be. As soon as he is back in the right position, loosen the pressure on the collar to show him that he is now back into the comfortable walking position. Never give in to his desires. If he insists upon getting in front of you, keep pulling back.

4. Still another method is to walk with a little stick or switch in your free hand, swinging it back and forth in front of the dog's nose. As he gets out ahead, the switch will slap him across the nose. All the time this is happening, keep using the command "Heel." He will quickly get the message as to where you want him. If he starts to surge forward again, jerk him back into position telling him to "Heel."

5. If the dog lags behind or stops to investigate some smell that intrigues him, just give the lead a pull, repeating the command "Heel."

6. Once he has learned the basics, teach him to keep up with you by changing your pace and making

An airline or wire crate is a safe, comfortable place for your dog.

KENNEL. To call him to the car or crate.

right and left turns. All the while keep repeating the command "Heel."

7. Control your voice. When the dog is doing well, speak in a pleasant tone; when he is being stubborn, be harsh. You can even growl a little, but don't shout at him.

Once your dog is comfortable walking with you at the heel position, work with him without the lead. But the minute he sways, put him back on lead and put him through the paces again. Do not ever let him get sloppy at this command.

Lesson Four: Kennel

This is a useful command, not just to get your dog into his kennel, but also into the car, the boat, etc. There is no need for a special lesson for this command; just call his name and use the word "Kennel" every time he enters his kennel, dog crate, or the car. At first he may require a shove or a dog biscuit tossed in ahead of him, but he will soon catch on, and there will be no more need to shove.

Lesson Five: Swimming

Now that your young dog has had a sufficient background in the basics of becoming a good pet, it is time to introduce him to disciplines relating to his basic hunting instincts. These are things that come naturally to a well-bred Labrador. But to be an effective hunter or field-trial dog, they must be refined.

Get your retriever into the water at an early age, and get in there with him! Pick a nice warm day and shallow water where you can both play comfortably. Don't just throw a bumper out into the water and expect your pup to retrieve it. Play with him first, gradually moving him to deeper water. He will follow you and begin swimming before he knows it. Age is not as much a factor to swimming as the temperature of the water or the gradual slope of the bottom. Be sure it is a nice warm day.

RETRIEVING

Before your pup can make his first trip to the field, he should be thoroughly familiar with the commands to sit and come when he is called. He should also have gone through the simple task of retrieving a bumper in the yard and bringing it back to you.

When he is ready to go to the field, pick a location that is safe, away from traffic and has short cover. A cut hay field is excellent for this first trip to the field.

Equipment:

There are several training needs you will have:
1. Four to six white bumpers
2. A blank pistol
3. Blank cartridges
4. Choke collar
5. A short rope

One more needed ingredient is a training partner, someone to walk out into the field to throw bumpers to you.

When you have located your field, select the spot to run from. The first few times, try a cross-wind mark which will give your dog a better chance to wind the

Basic retrieving diagram.

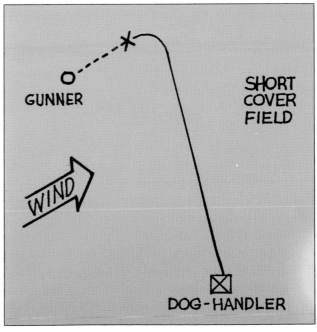

bumper if he does not see it. A "mark" is a thrown bumper or shot bird that the dog sees fall.

Before training always give your dog the freedom to go off on his own. This enables him to "air" and run off some energy, and to get ready to concentrate on training.

Lesson Six: The Single Retrieve with Bumpers

PROCEDURE:

Keep these first retrieves short so that you and your dog can concentrate. Keep all of the bumpers in a bag or plastic pail.
1. Have your partner ("gunner") walk out into the field 40 or 50 yards with the bumpers. Have him take one bumper out of the bag and be ready.
2. With your dog in a ready (sit) position at your side, and with a hold on the short rope lead, signal your partner with your free arm. The gunner can then yell "Hey! Hey!" and throw the bumper out 30 or 40 feet away from himself.
3. When the bumper has been thrown and the dog has seen it fall, release him immediately by dropping the lead and saying his name or "Back!" When he picks up the bumper, blow your "Come-in" whistle (three short blasts), clap your hands, call his name and encourage him to return to you with the bumper. Praise his efforts so that he knows he has done a good job.

In these first sessions, five or six retrieves is ample. As you proceed

you can retrieve longer and in a little more cover. Also work in down-wind marks as well as cross-wind marks.

Walking singles: Your training partner can change positions in the field with each retrieve by walking 30 or 40 paces and throwing into a different area.

In the beginning lesson it does not hurt for the cover to be short enough to allow the dog to see the bumper lying on the ground.

Lesson Seven: The Single Retrieve with Birds

When your dog is doing well on these single marks with bumpers, it may be time for real birds. Pigeons are a good bird for the young dog to retrieve. Introduce birds (pigeons) in a controlled location, such as a fenced-in area where he is comfortable with retrieving bumpers.

PROCEDURE:
1. First, have your partner toss a bumper for the dog to retrieve a few times, and then throw a dead pigeon. Your dog may drop it and smell it, but hopefully he will snap it up as he did the bumper and bring it to you.
2. As soon as he picks it up, encourage his speedy return by clapping your hands, walking backwards, and blowing the "Come-in" whistle, but don't let him chew or play with the bird. Always keep in mind that you want your retriever to proceed quickly to the bird, pick it up and return to his handler quickly and deliver it tenderly to hand.

3. When he is able to deliver birds to you in the controlled area, you can again go out into the field, using both dead pigeons and bumpers. The ability to mix the use of birds and bumpers is very important for future training when he will be required to retrieve a shot bird, dead bird and a bumper from three different stations. This is why it is critical that your dog retrieve on command, regardless of what he is asked to pick up.

Most trainers introduce a young retriever to dead birds in the yard at the young age of ten to 12 weeks just to get the dog's reaction to birds. However, introducing birds as a steady component in training at such an early age can sometimes result in lack of interest in bumpers.

Lesson Eight: Introducing Gunshots

The marking set-ups in the previous lesson are basic and should serve as a starting point for your youngster. When your dog is doing fine on these basic retrieves, it may be time to introduce him to the shot from a blank pistol (*not* a shotgun).

Usually gunshy dogs are the result of introducing a loud shotgun blast at close range at an early age. The classic example of this is someone with a new pup saying, "I think I'll take him out and and fire off the old 12-gauge a few times to see if he's gunshy." More times than not, he will come back with a pup that has a fear of the shotgun. That is why special care should be taken when you introduce your

youngster to his first loud shots. The introduction should be gradual: Cap the gun at first; use a .22 blank pistol at long distances; then a shotgun at long distances (75 to 100 yards), and always a retrieve (the reward) accompanying the gunshot.

PROCEDURE:
1. Place a gunner in the field with a number of bumpers (or birds) at about 50 or 60 paces.
2. Have the gunner throw a bumper with a "Hey! Hey!" and send your dog to retrieve.
3. When that retrieve is completed, line the dog up again, have the gunner throw another bumper and fire the pistol as your dog sets out. Because he will already be on his way to the retrieve, he will most likely pay little attention to the shot, since his mind is on the reward associated with retrieving a bumper or bird.
4. Repeat this procedure several times.

Once this procedure works and no problems develop, alter the routine slightly to the standard procedure of:
1. The gunner/thrower shoots the pistol.
2. He throws a bumper or bird.
3. You send your dog to retrieve.
4. He retrieves to hand.

Lesson Nine: Multiple Retrieves

Making more than one retrieve is a set-up done by placing more than one gunner/thrower in the field. Start with two gunners/

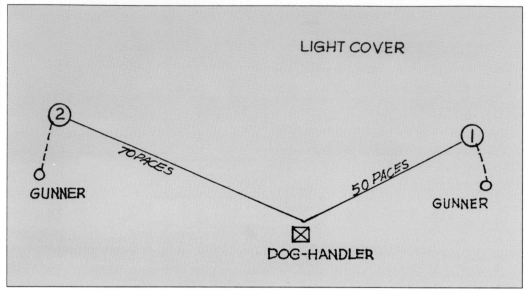

Multiple retrieves diagram.

throwers, placing one in the field to the left of a line about 70 paces away, and the other to the right of the line about 50 paces away. Do these marks as singles at first. The widespread double placement of the gunners allows you to intercept your dog if he tries to pick up the first bumper then run over to the second without delivering the first.

SINGLE PROCEDURE:

1. The right-hand gunner fires and throws a bumper.
2. Send your dog to retrieve it.
3. Now have the left-hand gunner fire his pistol and throw a bumper.
4. Send your dog to retrieve it.

After successfully completing both, do it as a double.

DOUBLE PROCEDURE:

1. Set your dog up to watch the right-hand bumper. Signal that gunner to fire and throw the bumper.
2. After it falls to the ground, slowly move your dog around to face the left-hand gunner. Signal for him to fire and throw a bumper.
3. After the second (left-hand) bumper falls, send your dog for it.
4. When he returns with the bumper, take it and carefully line him up for the right-hand bumper.
5. Send him for it.

You can reverse the order after completing the set-up. That is, throw the long bird first and the short bird second. If he should be confused, have one of the gunners get his attention and throw out another bumper. Keep working on this concept, and you will eventually teach your dog the principle of multiple retrieves.

6. Continue to keep the check cord on the dog and release him quickly to keep his enthusiasm

high. As time goes on you may wish to "hold" the dog a little longer before allowing him to retrieve.

Lesson No. 10: Whistle Stop Drill

Having taught your dog to sit on a single blast from your whistle will help you when you start the handling phase of his training. Work your dog on a long 20- to 30-foot rope lead during these drills.

PROCEDURE:

1. Snap the long rope lead to his choke collar, walk him at heel along a straight path or field, frequently stopping and saying "Sit" and giving a short whistle blast.
2. Make him stay in that position while you walk away from him, always facing him and maintaining eye contact.
3. If he tries to come toward you, raise your hand, blast on the whistle and say "Sit."
4. When he stays on the spot and you are 20 or 30 feet from him, give him the "Come-in" whistle as you tug on the rope. Bring him to the heel position.
5. Repeat this procedure with a "Sit" whistle, saying "Sit" and backing away from your dog, extending the distance each time you walk away.
6. Finally call him to your side with the "Come-in" whistle and the command "Here" or "Come." Do this drill from time to time for 15 or 20 minutes, but be careful not to overdo it or

Make your dog stay in the sit position. Walk away and keep eye contact. If he tries to move toward you, blow "Sit" whistle, raise your hand, and say "Sit."

lose patience with your youngster.

7. After many lessons with the whistle stop and sit drill, you will be able to walk away for 70 or 80 paces. Now call him with the "Come-in" whistle, stop him half way to you with a short, hard "Sit" whistle blast and with your flat hand extended as you say "Sit."

8. When he sits, make him stay there for a time (about 30 seconds).

9. Now call him to you.

You can repeat sections of the drill from time to time whenever you have ten or 15 minutes of training time available.

Lesson Eleven: Handling Hand Signals

At this stage of training you will begin to teach basic response to hand signals. The need for your dog to respond to basic hand signals not only is important in field trials but also is valuable in hunting where conditions of wind, distance, etc., may impair voice or whistle directions in retrieving fallen game that your dog has not seen down. There are basic steps to follow as he learns these handling skills.

BASEBALL:

This is a drill to teach taking directions from the handler: "Right," "Left'" and "Back" from a central point.

NOTE: When setting up blind retrieve drills use white bumpers. After your dog learns the drills, use orange bumpers for blinds and white bumpers for marks.

This drill is called "baseball" because the drill field resembles a baseball diamond with the handler directing from home plate. The first, second and third bases are where the bumpers are placed and the pitcher's mound is where the dog will be placed and cast from there.

Procedure:

1. Let's begin by placing six white bumpers at second base, allowing the dog to see them being set out.

Baseball diagram.

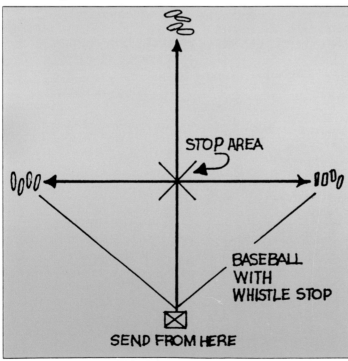

STOP AREA

BASEBALL
WITH
WHISTLE STOP

SEND FROM HERE

Line him up directly at the bumpers, arm extended, hand over his head: send him.

2. Now, with the dog at heel, walk him to home plate and line him up straight at the bumpers.
3. Here you will insert a key word that will convey to him that this is a different situation than a mark. Many handlers use "Dead" or "Dead bird" as this key word. Line up your dog, and quietly say "Dead bird."
4. When he has fixed on the bumpers, put your hand down in the direction of the pile of bumpers and give him the command "Back," which should also be in a normal voice. Do not yell or scream these commands—use your normal speaking voice.

THE "BACK" COMMAND:

The "Back" command releases the dog to retrieve the bumper.

After a few retrieves from the home-plate area, take him to the pitcher's mound and make him sit on the pitcher's mound facing you.

1. Blow the "Sit" whistle.
2. Walk or back up to home plate, stop, blow the whistle again (one sharp blast) to reinforce the "Sit" command.
3. Raise your right arm straight over your head and give the command "Back."
4. When the dog picks up the bumper, meet him at the pitcher's mound. After delivering the bumper, have him sit at the pitcher's mound again and repeat this "Back" command drill.
5. After he understands the drill, alternate between sending him from a heel position and the pitcher's mound.

THE "OVER" COMMANDS:

Now let's "Over" cast the same way by putting the bumpers at first base.

1. Send your dog from the heel position at home plate a few times.
2. Move him to the pitcher's mound facing you and use the word "Over," with your arm

bumpers at third base and repeat the drill with the Left overs.

When your dog understands this exercise, you can put him at the pitcher's mound and cast him to any of the three positions at will. It is advisable to work on one phase of this basic drill at a single training session. Don't try to rush through it.

Proper delivery of the bumper.

straight out horizontally to the side in the direction of the bumper.
3. Repeat the drill as you did the "Back" cast drill, only use the word "Over."

When you feel that he has absorbed this, go to the next drill, which is a Left over. Place the

1. Let your retriever watch you plant three or four bumpers at first, third and second bases.
2. Line him up to the second-base pile of bumpers, send him to it, and have him deliver one to you.
3. Next, line him toward the second-base pile.
4. Stop him at the pitcher's mound

Above: *Right hand "over."* ***Below:*** *Straight up arm back cast.*

Left hand over.

with a sharp whistle, make him face you, cast him to the right-hand (first-base) bumpers with a right-hand "Over" cast.

5. After retrieving a first-base bumper, line him again toward second base, stop him again at the pitcher's mound with a blast from your whistle, and cast him to the left-hand bumpers at third base.

6. Now, line him to the second-base bumpers without a stop whistle. You must mix up the lining and stopping so you don't create "popping" (stopping on his own in anticipation of the stop whistle).

7. Next, line him up again toward second base, send him to the pitcher's mound and stop him there.

8. Now cast him "Back" to the second-base pile.

Some trainers like to set up two baseball fields, one short and one longer.

Lesson Twelve: Lining Drills/Patterns

These drills teach your dog "lining"—to go where he is pointed. Pattern blinds are helpful in training your dog to utilize the skills he has learned in the whistle stop and baseball casting drills. Find a field with very little cover and set out a pattern of three blinds, one 75 to 100 yards to the right, one 100 to 200 yards down the center, and one to the left of that at 100 to 175 yards.

PROCEDURE:

This drill starts as a multiple lining drill, but can develop into many useful skill teaching drills.

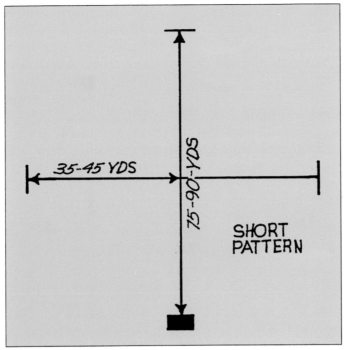

Short pattern baseball diagram.

Long pattern baseball diagram.

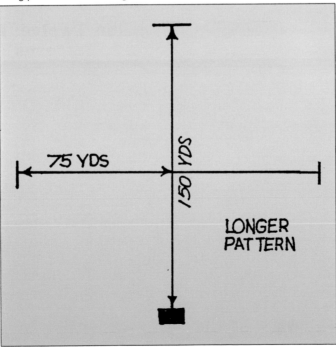

1. First, place the dog on the line while you and your training partner walk out and place a number of bumpers (four or five) at Position No. 1.
2. Now, put the dog back into your vehicle for a few minutes.
3. Take him out of his kennel and heel him to the line, getting him lined up properly to the pile of

The next time out use the same procedure, but place the bumpers at the far left blind, Area No. 2.

The third area to be identified is the center line, the longest one, No. 3. This drill should not confuse the dog; he should know that there are bumpers at these same places each time.

Send him to Area No. 3 first,

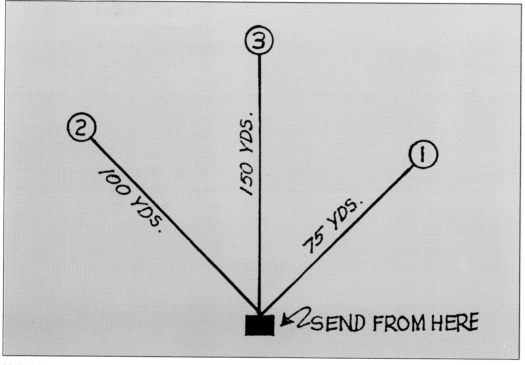

Lining diagram.

bumpers. He should remember where you put them and go directly to them.
4. Run this two or three times, then put him away and let him rest.
5. Bring him out again and repeat one more time. What you have done is given him a great deal of confidence in running a line to the blind area.

then to No. 1, then No. 2. Mix this up after he knows all three positions of the bumpers. He may wander off the line, but now you should be able to stop him and cast him to improve his line. Always put the bumpers in the same place.

There are other drills and exercises you can add to this blind drill.

One drill is placing a gunner in the field, throwing a mark away from the line to the blind. Pick up the mark and run the Pattern Line No. 1 in back of the gunner, then Pattern No. 2 and finally Pattern No. 3. This is where your set-up for a blind should be different than for a mark. Many trainers today send their dog for marks on their name and reserve a key word or words, such as "Dead bird" to set up the blind, and "Back" to actually send for blinds.

These drills are only a small part of training a retriever to handle. The best method to keep your interest up and learn as you proceed is to form a group or join other trainers so you can share ideas on various methods of achieving results. Consulting pro-

fessional retriever trainers to get answers to your questions is always worthwhile.

Drills should always be fun for your dog. Never overwork him to the point of boredom or exhaustion, and always quit your training on a good note. A little training at regular intervals is much better than overworking infrequently.

SIMPLE WAGON-WHEEL LINING DRILL:

This is a drill to help lining on blind retrieves.
1. Set out three white bumpers at Station Nos. 1, 2 and 3, placing them six to eight paces from the hub.
2. Set your dog at your side at the hub.

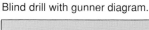
Blind drill with gunner diagram.

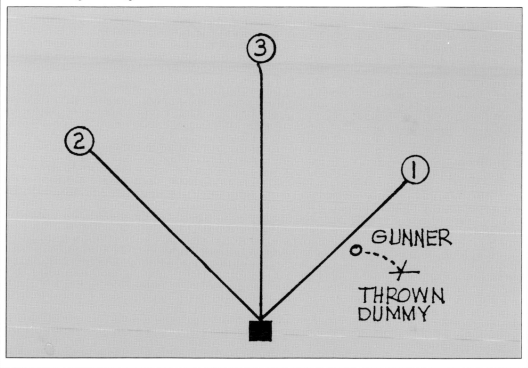

3. Send your dog from your side to the three white bumpers.
4. Replace each bumper as he retrieves it.
5. Repeat the drill, having him pick up the white bumpers several times.
6. Now place two red bumpers between the white ones and a little farther out, about 12 to 14 paces.
7. Send your dog from the hub to pick up the red bumpers.
8. Replace each bumper after it has been retrieved. There will always be five bumpers used in the drill.

Do this from time to time; it is a good lining drill, providing your dog with experience that gives you control at the line. You can move, and make him move with you to pick up whichever bumper you instruct him to pick up.

All of the drills and procedures you have put your dog through should also be done in the water as well as on land. This may be a little difficult at times, perhaps even requiring a boat, but your efforts will be well rewarded as your dog develops into a "complete" retriever.

The training procedures and comments provided in this discussion are basic in training a retriever to be a good, well-behaved companion in the home, yard or field. Your retriever is born with certain instinctive reactions. If you spend time with him and shape his behavior to suit your particular needs and lifestyle, you can mold these talents to a very high degree of perfection. It is up to the owner/trainer as to just how far he or she wants to develop these special talents.

Treat your retriever properly and he will do everything he can to please you.

Wagon-wheel lining drill diagram.

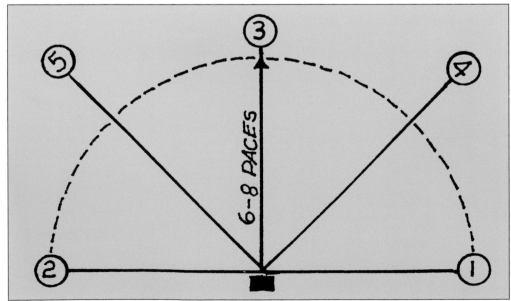

6–8 PACES

A handsome Labrador with his retrieve. Photograph by Isabelle Francais.

G.E. Ina is used as a brood bitch for Guiding Eyes For The Blind. Ina was sired by Ch. Franklin's Affirmed.

Labradors in the Community

by Jane Russenberger

INTRODUCTION

Dogs have helped mankind in their work and play for many years. In recent times, the versatile Labrador has become friend and helper to the physically disabled, law–enforcement agencies and commercial ventures. The special qualities of Labrador Retrievers have made them ideally suited for a wide range of tasks and likely they will find many more occupations in years to come.

GUIDE DOGS

Labradors Reign

Many people may be surprised to learn that throughout the world Labrador Retrievers are used more often for guide dogs than any other breed. When one thinks of a guide dog, the image of a German Shepherd often comes to mind. This is because German Shepherds were the first dogs to be used as guide dogs in America. Movies, books and the German Shepherd's special place in history keep this concept alive.

In time, guide-dog training schools throughout the world began experimenting with other breeds of dog. Collies, Bouviers, Boxers, Standard Poodles, Dobermans, Golden Retrievers, Flat-Coated Retrievers, Standard Poodles, Border Collies and others have joined the ranks of guide dogs in varying popularity but one breed, the Labrador Retriever, dominates guide-dog production today.

In many ways, Labradors are highly suited as trainees for guiding the blind. Their carefree coats, ideal size, intelligence and adaptable, willing dispositions make them naturals for the work. The gene pool of suitable dogs is also excellent and widely available.

History of Dog-Guide Use

In a primitive form, dogs have been associated with the blind as protectors and guides for at least 1,000 years, but it was not until World War I that someone started experiments in training dogs to act as guides for the blind. In a historical summary of guide dogs in Britain (*The Guide Dogs for the Blind Association*, 1992), it is told that the idea to train guide dogs came about by a doctor in Germany who was caring for soldiers wounded in the war. He was walking along the hospital grounds with a blind man and was called away. The doctor left his German Shepherd with the man and he was so impressed by the dog's behavior that he decided to try to actually train a dog to help guide the blind.

In 1923, the first guide-dog training center was started in Potsdam, Germany where several thousand dogs were trained within the next ten years. While living in Switzerland and breeding German Shepherds for law enforcement, Mrs. Dorothy Harrison Eustis, heard of this work and wrote an article for the October 1927 issue of the *Saturday Evening Post.*

When Morris Frank, a blind man in America, read the article he wrote to Mrs. Eustis, "I want one of those dogs. Thousands of blind people like me abhor being dependent on others. Help me and I will help them." (*The Guide Dogs for the Blind Association,* 1992). Mrs. Eustis arranged for Elliott Humphrey, who was in charge of her kennels, to study the work in Germany and then return to Switzerland to train a dog. Once this training was accomplished, Morris Frank was offered the guide dog Buddy, America's first guide-dog. The Seeing Eye, America's first guide dog school, was born of the efforts of Mrs. Eustis and Morris Frank.

Guiding Eyes for the Blind Boomer and Cashmeir with their litter of potential guide dogs are products of selective breeding combining dogs from Whygin, Groveton and Highland kennels. Photograph courtesy of Guiding Eyes for the Blind, Yorktown Heights, NY.

LABRADORS IN THE COMMUNITY

Worldwide, Labradors are the breed most commonly used for guide dogs. This dog was bred by the world's largest school, The Guide Dogs of the Blind Association, England, which is the courteous provider of this photograph.

Sources of Labradors

It is unclear exactly when Labrador Retrievers were first used as guide dogs. Although it is likely that somewhere in the world a few Labradors had been used as guide dogs by at least the late 1940s, it is known that in 1950 a litter of Labradors was bred by Guide Dogs for the Blind in San Rafael, California. By 1955 this same organization bred multiple litters, which is a likely sign that their first efforts with this breed were promising.

Correspondence from Cheryl Laughlin, the Records and Information Officer for The Guide Dogs for the Blind Association in Britain, indicates that five Labrador broods were in their colony at the end of 1961. In his book *Another Pair of Eyes*, which details the history of

255

The warm, intelligent expression of a guide dog speaks of his willingness to serve. This dog is a son of Ch. Coalcreeks Gimme a Break. Photograph courtesy of Guiding Eyes for the Blind, Yorktown Heights, NY.

this British school, Peter Ireson notes that before the breeding program was established, Labradors "had not been notably successful, possibly because many had come from gundog lines that had been bred and reared for a very different sort of life. But puppy-walked dogs from other sources soon began to show qualities that were more suited to guide-dog work."

Most of the guide-dog schools in the United States (approximately one dozen) and many internationally have their own breeding programs that provide a dependable supply of quality dogs. Donated puppies from quality bloodlines are accepted at many schools. An interested breeder wishing to make a donation should make contact with the school preferably at the time of or before breeding. The ideal guide dog is fairly calm, easy to handle, adaptable to change, has a low distraction level and is very self-confident. At many schools, hip, elbow and eye clearances are required of dogs used in their guide-dog and breeding programs. Virtually every line of Labrador has produced guide dogs; however, the greatest success rates have been achieved through generations of selective breeding for guide-dog traits.

A review of pedigrees from Guide Dogs for the Blind indicates early foundation stock originated from Sandylands lines with later additions of Briary, Braemar and other lines. Guiding Eyes for the Blind in

G.E. Indigo, bred by Guiding Eyes For The Blind, sired by Ch. Franklin's Affirmed.

Yorktown Heights, New York, which also has a long-standing Labrador colony, used the Whygin line for its original stock, adding Groveton lines and more recently Briary, Highland, Scrimshaw, Kresland, Franklin, Shataf, Beechcroft, Kerrybrook and others successfully. It is obvious from this list of fine kennels, Labrador breeders are not only very generous but also very important supporters of guide-dog schools.

The Making of a Guide Dog

A guide-dog's training begins at puppyhood with its puppy-raising family. Volunteer families raise potential dog guides from puppyhood through ages 12 to 18 months when they return to the school for formal training. A puppy raiser's job is to teach manners and basic obedience and to socialize their young charge to the noises, activity and ways of a complex world.

Formal training, lasting from four to ten months, begins by teaching specific voice and hand-directional commands that will one day be given by the blind owner to communicate to the dog which way to go. Dogs are taught to stop at curbs, go around obstacles, cross streets in a specific manner, ignore distractions and many other lessons. A guide dog must consider the height and width of its handler when maneuvering next to objects such as poles, people and overhead branches. In addition,

Volunteer puppy raisers provide a potential guide dog puppy with its first year of love, socialization and manners. This dog, Helen, is from Scrimshaw Labrador lines. Photograph courtesy of Guiding Eyes for the Blind, Yorktown Heights, NY.

Guide dogs help provide safe, independent travel. Finding doors and weaving through obstacles are part of a normal day's work for a well-educated guide dog. Photograph courtesy of Guiding Eyes for the Blind, Yorktown Heights, NY.

guide dogs are taught to slow down or go around broken, uneven surfaces or dangerous drop-offs. Traffic training is perhaps the most difficult for the dogs. They must learn to intelligently disobey a command such as refusing the forward command to enter the street when there is an oncoming car. Intelligent disobedience requires a self-confident and very stable dog.

Although training varies slightly from one school to another, in general the lessons are taught through repetition and praise. First the dog is shown what to do, much as one would teach obedience, then gradually the dog is expected to take over and develop a good working pattern without much help.

Blind individuals are matched with their guide dogs and undergo weeks of training to learn how to become a successful team. When working as a team, the blind person knows where they want to go and the dog helps them get there safely and quickly. Guide dogs enable a blind person to travel independently, travel to work or just to walk around the block. Moving about with freedom and independence with the aid of a loving, canine friend is what having a guide dog is all about.

By law, blind people using guide dogs within the United States are guaranteed access to all public places. Guide dogs can be identified by the special harness with a handle. If there is one disadvantage to using Labradors as guide dogs, it is the universal appeal of these dogs. The public can be an immense help to a guide-dog user by refraining from calling, petting or otherwise interfering with the dog while it is working.

HEARING DOGS

Also known as auditory assistance dogs and signal dogs, hearing dogs serve as the ears for their hearing-impaired owners. Al-though there are mechanical devices that can detect and alert a hearing-impaired person to various sounds, hearing dogs double as companion and helper thus bringing friendship as well as assistance.

Small mixed-breed dogs are preferred and most often utilized as hearing dogs because of client preference for a small dog. Labrador Retrievers are used occasionally as hearing dogs. Most schools training hearing dogs indicate that they obtain the majority of their dogs from pounds, shelters and rescue organizations. A high-energy, friendly and eager dog with good house manners is desired.

Red Acre Farm, Inc., writes in their *History of the Hearing Dog Program of the American Humane Association* (Red Acre Farm, 1981) that in 1976 the American Humane Association in Denver, Colorado began training hearing dogs as a pilot project. The pilot project resulted from a feasibility study conducted by specialists in the animal, hearing and speech fields and members of the deaf community. They were brought together by the Minnesota Society for the Prevention of Cruelty to Animals. The need for hearing dogs grew and, as

Hearing dogs signal a sound to a hearing-impaired person by getting his attention then leading the person to the source of the sound. Photo courtesy of Dogs for the Deaf, Central Point, OR.

a result, many regional programs for training hearing dogs have been established.

Hearing dogs are trained to respond to certain routine and emergency sounds such as an alarm clock, smoke detector, door knock, bell and a telephone/TTY. The actual sounds selected are usually tailored to the specific person who will use the dog. For most sounds, the dog will paw his owner to get his attention then lead the owner to the source of the sound. In the case of a smoke-detector alert, the dog gets the attention of his owner then drops immediately to the floor and lies still.

The training takes about four to six months and involves basic obedience using both voice and hand signals and "sound keying," which is teaching the dog to notice specific noises. Once the dog is trained, the dog owner receives about two weeks instruction to learn to work with the dog.

Throughout the United States, certified hearing dogs are guaranteed by law equal access into public facilities and on public transportation. A special identification card is carried by the owner and the dog usually has an identifying yellow or

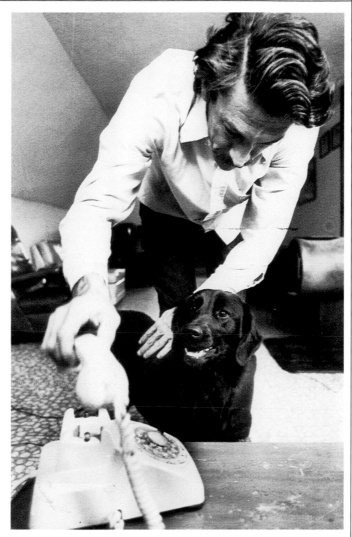

Hearing-impaired people can live more independent lives with the aid and companionship of a trained hearing dog. Photo courtesy of Dogs for the Deaf, Central Point, OR.

orange collar and leash. Some schools train "working companion dogs" that are trained to respond to sounds and are obedience trained but they work exclusively in the home and do not have legal access rights to go into public places where pets are not allowed. These dogs are typically placed with younger applicants and applicants who only need the dogs to work in their homes.

Service dogs wear a special backpack which is used not only for identification but also for storing items. Wallaby was placed with Margo by Canine Companions for Independence, the first service-dog organization. Photo courtesy of CCI.

SERVICE DOGS

Service dogs assist people with mobility limitations resulting from diseases such as multiple sclerosis and muscular dystrophy, congenital abnormalities and injuries caused by accidents. Whether wheelchair-bound or using walkers, crutches or canes, these people are in need of a canine friend to help them pick up dropped items, bring things that are out of reach and overcome obstacles such as curbs and doors. In addition to independence, service dogs provide constant unconditional love for their partners. As one of the staff at Support Teams for Independence, Inc. (*Support Teams for Independence*, 1993) stated, "they give them a reason to get up in the morning and, for many individuals, these dogs are the first living creatures that they are responsible for."

Labrador Retrievers and Golden Retrievers are commonly used as service dogs. Other large breeds such as Rottweilers, Bernese Mountain Dogs and German Shepherds have been used but, like guide-dog work, Labradors again demonstrate their versatility, trainability and willingness to serve by being a favored breed for this work.

Most service-dog organizations breed their own dogs, accept qualified donated dogs and puppies and obtain some dogs from dog pounds, shelters and rescue leagues. Like guide-dog schools, puppies are raised by volunteer puppy raisers until the dogs are around 18 months old.

A screening of service-dog organizations indicates most dogs are donated through the generosity of many quality breeders throughout the United States. Canine Companions for Independence (CCI) stated that show lines, especially dogs

from Braemar Kennels, have been very successful as service dogs. They noted that descendants of Ballyduff Marketeer were also of particular interest. Canine Working Companions in New York cited Snowden Hill Kennels as their main source of dogs.

The ideal candidate for service-dog training is a softer type dog that

Service dogs pick up and return dropped items, turn on light switches and get objects that cannot be reached from a wheelchair. Photo courtesy of New England Assistance Dogs, West Boylston, MA.

In this series of photographs, courtesy of Teammates Julian, NC, service dog Jo Jo helps master Dennis through a door. Jo Jo is out of Snakes Moses of Antioch breeding.

can easily be handled by the disabled. In addition, willingness to work and focus on their trainer, a strong retrieving instinct, adaptability to multiple handlers, confidence in public situations and a lack of any aggression are essential traits for a good service dog. Hip, elbow and eye clearances are required by most organizations.

The concept of a school devoted to train service dogs began in 1975 with Bonita (Bonnie) Bergin, the founder of Canine Companions for

Independence. Abdul, the first service dog, was a black male Labrador Retriever trained by Bonnie Bergin and placed with a quadriplegic woman in California. Now service-dog organizations exist throughout the United States, Canada, Australia, France and Japan. CCI reports that they receive many requests from all over the world to open chapters or help establish training schools in other countries, indicating that the demand for these special dogs is great.

Service dogs receive six to ten months of training where they learn

Sandy and Sam. Unconditional love provided by a social dog brings happiness and companionship. Photograph courtesy of Elaine Smith of Therapy Dogs International.

needs of the person. Some dogs, called specialty dogs, are trained for people with multiple disabilities such as a deaf person using a wheelchair.

Margo Gaithright-Dietrich has post-polio syndrome. Over a period of only a few years, she went from an active, physical lifestyle to needing an electric wheelchair to get around. When she first learned of Canine Companions for Independence (CCI), Margo saw an opportunity to regain the independence and self-respect she had lost. Her service dog Wallaby, trained by CCI, responds to more than 60 commands and assists Margo in countless ways. Still, the physical assistance Wallaby offers Margo is only part of the story. The two have formed a special bond of love and devotion that adds a unique dimension to the match between a canine companion and someone with a disability.

Service dogs have the legal privilege of access to public places and public transportation. They can be identified by either a backpack or a harness. As with guide dogs, the public should be careful not to interfere with the dog by petting or otherwise distracting it while working.

commands and an associated action such as retrieving, opening doors and operating switches. Each command is taught as a single unit then commands are added to one another to form an exercise. For example there are many individual commands in pulling a wheelchair. They are combined together to result in the pulling exercise. The actual training is customized to the

SOCIAL DOGS AND THERAPY DOGS

For anyone who has been confined to a hospital or nursing home, the lonely hours of isolation and boredom can be almost unbearable. There are programs throughout the United States where pet owners and breeders can become involved in community service to bring some joy and companionship to a lonely person. A few licks and a hug from man's best friend can mean so much. Labrador Retrievers, with so much love to share, are well suited for this special work.

What Social Dogs and Therapy Dogs Do

Pet therapy, more properly called animal-assisted therapy or pet-facilitated therapy, is divided into two forms. In its simplest form, a pet may live with or visit people with the goal of just brightening their day by meeting and greeting. Dogs that perform in this way are called Social Dogs. All that these dogs need to do is to be fairly obedient and most of all to enjoy interacting with strangers confidently.

Therapy Dogs have a more sophisticated role of working with a health-care professional assisting in a treatment process. The treatment goals focus on helping patients improve in their physical, social, emotional and/or cognitive functioning. Therapy Dogs need more advanced skills in obedience and need to be particularly confident, relaxed and personable.

Registered therapy dog Hershey (Highland's Hershey's Cocoa), owned by Elaine Smith, visits a patient. Photograph courtesy of Elaine Smith of Therapy Dogs International.

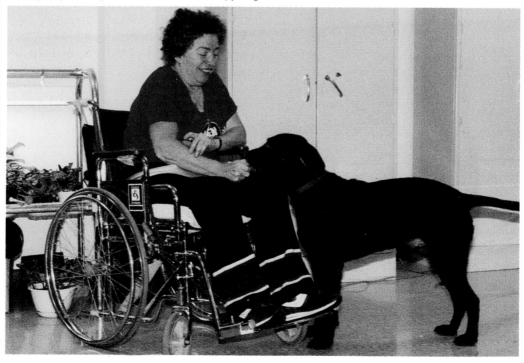

Becoming a Social Dog

There are almost a dozen organizations in the United States that promote the use of pet- or animal-facilitated therapy programs (*Cornell Health Newsletter*, 4/92). Most focus on preparing and certifying volunteers and their dogs as effective social dog and handler teams.

Pet-Partners is one program sponsored by the Delta Society, a non-profit organization. The Pet-Partner program has a screening and training process where pet owners and their dogs, cats, birds and other companion animals can become registered. Registered animal-people teams visit nursing homes, hospitals, schools, prisons, treatment centers and other facilities to share their animals and time with people in need. More information can be obtained by contacting the Delta Society at P.O. Box 1080, Renton, WA 98057, 206-235-1076.

Another pet therapy program is Therapy Dogs International (TDI). It was started in 1979 by Elaine Smith of New Jersey. Elaine believes TDI was the first organization of its type in the United States. Elaine recalls that the idea of starting TDI came to her when she was working as a nurse in England where pets were freely admitted to public places. After moving to the United States, she read an article in *Dog World* magazine about a person who wanted to bring their Samoyed into a nursing home to visit a patient. The dog was denied access to all but the lobby where the patients were overjoyed to have the company of a canine.

With four people in the King James, New Jersey area, Elaine started bringing the joy of man's best friend to people in nursing homes and other confinement situations where personal pets are not allowed. Now TDI has over 2,000 dedicated people and dogs who volunteer their time and love to make someone's day a little brighter.

The following story told by pet therapist Janet Vaughan tells firsthand a little of what benefit a therapy dog can do. "The residents were seated around the perimeter of the recreation room. My yellow Labrador Fonteyn and I would greet each resident then provide the resident with the opportunity to touch her if they wanted and engage in conversation. While moving from person to person, I observed that one of the women was staring straight ahead and appeared non-communicative with the ladies seated on either side of her. Her face was expressionless.

I greeted the woman but despite my efforts, she remained unresponsive. As I said good-bye to her and moved on, suddenly her hand shot out and tightly grabbed Fonteyn's leash. As her hand touched the leash, she began to reminisce about how her daughter had been a dog breeder. She spoke of the dogs they had had, giving a detailed description of the breed, names and a variety of tales about the dogs. She spoke with animation smiling and making eye contact with Fonteyn while stroking her head and all the while maintaining a very tight grip on the leash. It was as if the leash was a link to positive memories from her past. When she released her grip on the leash she lapsed back into the expressionless stare and silence."

tance of them and their multiple infirmities. It is so important for our residents to be able to express their feelings to Hershey. He does not judge their feelings or discard them, he allows them to feel and deal with those emotions. They really enjoy stroking and talking to Hershey as an all-accepting friend."

Hershey visiting a nursing home facility. Photograph courtesy of Elaine Smith of Therapy Dogs International.

As one nursing home wrote in a letter nominating Hershey, a chocolate Labrador owned by Elaine Smith, as the Delta Society Therapy Dog of the Year, "Their [our patient's] response to his gentleness, warmth and love is beyond words. He has the power to enable them to recall their own pets with his immediate accep-

LABRADORS AS DETECTION DOGS

Military and law-enforcement agencies have long known the benefit of dogs in sentry work. As the world changed, so did the need for different help from man's best friend. German Shepherds and breeds of similar type dominated early uses of dogs in the military and law enforcement. As time progressed, however, the special qualities of Labradors started to become appreciated.

Today Labradors are employed in many law enforcement fields as detection dogs aiding in detecting accelerants, explosives and illegal drugs. Through their keen sense of smell and willing nature, they have helped the world become a little safer.

History of Detection Dogs

The history of detection dogs dates back at least to World War I. World War II, however, was the time when the use of detection dogs became prominent in the United States. *Pure-Bred Dogs/American Kennel Gazette* (American Kennel Club, 1989) reported that a volunteer program called Dogs for Defense was established in 1942 to obtain suitable dogs for military work. Most were used as sentry dogs and messengers, but in 1944 the development of military mine-detection dogs, called M-dogs by American and British forces, was reported. "The dogs have proved particularly valuable in their ability to locate the non-metallic mines which defy the best of mechanical detectors." Even today with advanced technology, dogs outperform sophisticated scientific

Mattie, the world's first working accelerant-detection dog, is trained to detect and signal for 12 different accelerants. Mattie was donated by Guide Dog Foundation and trained by the Connecticut State Police. Photo courtesy of Connecticut State Police K-9 Training Unit.

Gabby, a drug-detection dog, can detect small traces of drugs hidden in cars, on people or in buildings. She was donated by the Guiding Eyes for the Blind and is from Shataf and Guiding Eyes bloodlines. Photo courtesy of Connecticut State Police K-9 Training Unit.

instruments developed to detect a wide range of compounds.

It is unclear how many, if any, Labradors served during World War II. Debby Kay, a noted detection dog trainer, had researched the topic and found reference in Dogs for Defense chronicles that Labradors were highly favored by the British Army for their nose, ability in the water, strength and endurance (*The Labrador Quarterly*, 1992).

Requirements for dogs donated to the Dogs for Defense program at the time the M-dog program began may have discriminated against the use of Labradors despite their availability in the United States and success in other countries. An excerpt from the *Pure-Bred Dogs/ American Kennel Club Gazette* (American Kennel Club, 1989) states "only longhaired dogs of a neutral color are now acceptable, 14 months to two years of age, strong and absolutely fearless .... Shorthaired dogs and black dogs the Army has found do not stand up under extremes of climate, while white dogs endanger their own lives and those of the men they serve by their conspicuous color."

In her article published in the summer 1992 edition of *Labrador Quarterly.* "The History and Use of Labradors as Detector Dogs,"

LABRADORS IN THE COMMUNITY

Debby Kay reports that Chief Cahill of the Washington DC Metro Police Department is credited with bringing the Labrador into popularity during the 1960s as a detection dog in the United States. Having come from Scotland Yard in England, Chief Cahill was familiar with the use of Labradors in detection work. To help combat the rising drug problems developing at that time, Chief Cahill

Above: Myrica and Keith are doing an article search in this training problem. *Below:* Leo is a detection dog in training. He is sitting to indicate to his handler that he has made a find for which he will receive a food treat and praise.

Labrador participating in a public demonstration to show the kind of work that detection dogs can do for police units. Photograph by Isabelle Francais.

enlisted the help of the ever-willing Labrador. Narco, the first Labrador drug-detection dog, did such a fine job that more Labradors were quick to follow.

Training Detection Dogs

Training methods vary widely but most involve two phases: discrimination and room-search behavior. Discrimination involves teaching the dog that it will get a reward, usually food, when it sniffs a container with a particular compound in it. After the dog makes the connection that he is to sniff and discriminate a particular odor from the scores of other odors, the dog is taught to alert its handler that he has made the discrimination and located the odor. The alert signal is usually a passive activity such as a sit when alerting to explosives. For other detection work, such as drugs, the alert may be a more active and aggressive communication such as pawing at the source of the odor. It takes daily workouts with many repetitions in varied situations to train and maintain a detection dog.

Training progresses to include multiple sniffing locations, which challenges the dog to find the odor. As soon as the dog has completed the discrimination training, the dog is encouraged to indulge its natural curiosity, to search, find, and sit when finding the training odor that was previously placed in the room without the dog being present. Room search becomes a hide and seek game and an enjoyable experience for an eager dog.

The level of complexity is gradually increased by lessening the amount of odor by having it age or providing smaller quantities, teaching the dog to discriminate multiple odors and having naturally occurring odors present to serve as distractions.

Praise, repetition, encouragement and use of the Labrador's basic instincts and drives make detection training and work a well-matched occupation. A note in the *Information & Training Manual, Explosive Detection Dogs, NY City Bomb Squad* (NY City Police Department, 1983) adds this important point, "It must be emphasized that these animals require considerable attention and affection during the training ses-

sion, while performing security searches and while off duty. The dogs work for their food reward and the praise they receive from their handlers."

The ideal candidate for detection work is a well-socialized, one-to two-year-old dog that is confident, friendly with other dogs, comfortable around crowds, and will stay focused on a task for extended periods of time for the food reward.

Drug Detection

In the United States, drug detection was the first official detection role for the Labrador. By 1970, the U.S Customs Service began its drug-detection program. Local law-enforcement agencies also began training dogs for drug detection.

K-9 Fred performing a demonstration with his handler at the Virginia State Corrections Department. The fastest, most effective, non-invasive package search is with a trained dog—the average dog can search 200 bags per hour. Photo courtesy of International Detector Dogs Ltd.

Although other breeds, such as the Golden Retriever and German Shepherd, have been and are still used, the Labrador is favored by many.

Gabby, a female black Labrador Retriever, works with Trooper Pete Naples of the Connecticut State Police. Gabby is trained to alert to odors of marijuana, cocaine and other illegal drugs. Her handler wrote the following to Guiding Eyes for the Blind, who donated Gabby for the detection program, "Gabby and I passed a six-week narcotic-detection program. She started out a little slow—but her finish was outstanding. She was first in her class of five dogs; scoring 100% on a very intense and difficult final on detection of a wide range of narcotics. Gabby and I have bonded very well and she trusts me 100% and I trust her. She works with me every day. Gabby has assisted U.S. Customs numerous times with ships coming in from foreign countries. Her largest find so far in our fight against narcotic trafficking was a seizure of $14,810 in a 1987 Nissan that had been carrying illegal drugs."

Contrary to some beliefs, the dogs do not get addicted to the drugs and in fact are carefully protected from inhaling harmful quantities. A careful search is first made by human investigators looking for large stashes of drugs that are not hidden in sealed containers or other hiding

Bo is searching a room for hidden explosives and weapons. A trained detection dog can search buildings, luggage, aircrafts and vehicles more quickly and accurately than a person can. Photo courtesy of Connecticut State Police K-9 Training Unit.

places. The dog is then allowed to conduct a search of the area designated by the handler. The dogs work on leash, and when a drug is located, the dog will sit to indicate its find. As with other detection work, the reward for finding the designated odor is a handful of food and lots of praise.

Bomb Detection

Explosive-detection canine programs are becoming more important to thwart international and urban terrorism. Training programs have existed worldwide for many years. A

Bo has made a find and is indicating this to his handler by sitting.

December 9, 1971 article published in the *New York Times* spoke of a research program conducted at the psychology department of the University of Mississippi and supervised by the United States Land Warfare Laboratories in Aberdeen, Maryland. In this program, bomb-detection dogs were trained or conditioned to respond to specific odors of explosives.

The dogs were then field tested in noisy congested areas. A Labrador named Sally was among the eight dogs in this program. The program was a success and helped fuel the training of bomb-detection dogs throughout the United States.

The New York City Bomb Squad is credited with having one of the earliest and finest bomb-detection programs in the United States. Many of the dogs used in this program were donated by Guide Dog Foundation of Smithtown, New York.

Although many breeds are used, Labradors are well suited for this work. The following true story speaks of the wonderful work these dogs do. "The success and value of this program was dramatically demonstrated on March 7, 1972 when Brandy, the explosive-detection dog, responded to a 707 Jetliner, which was airborne and had been recalled to JFK

International Airport in answer to a bomb threat. Within a minute the dog discovered a briefcase in the cockpit of the aircraft and gave a positive reaction indicating the presence of an explosive. The briefcase, which bore an airplane tag indicating it was crew baggage, was carefully removed from the cockpit and found to contain a highly sophisticated time bomb, with four-and-a-half pounds of plastic explosives. Within twelve hours, an identical bomb secreted in a first-aid kit exploded in an aircraft cockpit in Las Vegas, Nevada causing $1,500,000 in damage. This aircraft departed JFK International Airport but was not searched by the explosive-detection dogs, although several visual searches were conducted by the crewmen and mechanics of the jet airliner"(*Information & Training Manual*, Explosive Detection Dogs, NY City Bomb Squad, 8/83).

Explosive-detection dogs are commonplace in airports. Debby Kay's article on Labradors as detector dogs notes that dogs can search 200 suitcases per hour, which makes them the fastest, most effective, non-invasive package searchers. Most states have trained dogs to respond to bomb threats and also screen meeting locations for important dignitaries.

During a training exercise, K-9 Nikki investigates the inside of a building that had been the subject of arson.

Accelerant Detection

The idea of training dogs to detect and alert to accelerants commonly used by arsonists took hold in the late 1970s to the early '80s. A comprehensive study conducted by experts in the arson-dog training and forensic laboratory fields documented the reliability of accelerant-detection dogs and paved the way to make them a respected tool of the arson investigator.

The first canine accelerant-detection-training program evolved from collaboration among the Federal Bureau of Alcohol, Tobacco and Firearms and multiple Connecticut state agencies each contributing their expertise. It began as a feasibility study, which was first presented in 1983 to determine if dogs could detect accelerants and differentiate between accelerants and similar chemical gases normally present at a fire scene. Mechanical devices that are used in arson work have many false positive readings because of the similarity of accelerants to gases formed from combustion. If a dog could detect only the accelerant, better and fewer laboratory samples could be obtained that would hasten the investigation.

The first test dog was a yellow Labrador Retriever named Nellie. She was trained successfully to detect accelerants. With Nellie's success in field tests, in 1986, a black Labrador Mattie was trained as the first operational accelerant dog. Both dogs were donated by the Guide Dog Foundation in Smithtown, Long Island, NY.

This excerpt from a newspaper article that appeared in a canine accelerant-detection program report, published by the U.S. Department of Treasury, Bureau of Alcohol, Tobacco and Firearms and the Connecticut State Police in 1988, demonstrates how an accelerant-detection dog can be helpful. "Troopers Douglas Lancelot and James Butterworth entered the gutted store, listening as the Fire Marshall pointed out the probable place of the origin of the fire. Butterworth brought Mattie around to the back entrance as I positioned myself inside where I could take photographs of the dog working.

Mattie cast around the charred remains of what once had been a shoe store. She paid attention to several spots but moved on until she reached the sill of the inside back door leading from the back foyer to the showroom. She quickly sat and looked up at Butterworth. 'That's her indication of a hit,' Lancelot explained. 'You got something girl?' Butterworth questioned Mattie. 'Show me.'

The firemen used an axe to lift the tiles. They took a sample of the underflooring. But Mattie indicated it was negative when she checked the sample. Mattie sniffed the area again and indicated a spot just a few inches away from where the first sample had been taken. The fireman took another sample that met with Mattie's approval."

Cadaver-detection K-9 Jetta (Am-Can. Ch. Chilbrook Salitane CD, TDI, CGC) during a training exercise. Upon locating a cadaver scent, the dog will sit and bark at the source until the handler arrives. Photograph courtesy of Chilbrook kennel, Colonial Beach, VA.

Accelerant-detection dogs are now commonplace tools for the arson investigator. Small, energetic Labradors are deemed the best for the job. They must be confident and willing and love food, which is their reward for the work they do.

Other Detection Work

Labradors will continue to be challenged to apply their keen sense of smell in the aid of mankind. Some other uses include evidence searches, man trailing, cadaver searches, detection of toxic waste and gas pipeline leaks. They can even help biologists by detecting such things as the peak of the estrus cycle in cattle, the accurate timing for artificial inseminations and the whereabouts of gypsy moth egg cases and box turtles. There is no doubt that new jobs for the ever-willing and versatile Labrador will continue to be found.

SEARCH AND RESCUE DOGS

In the United States there are over 200 non-profit organizations comprised of well-trained volunteers and their dogs who stand ready to go out in any weather or terrain to help find lost and missing persons. Every week these hardy souls hike through the woods and fields honing their skills in the techniques of search and rescue.

Becoming a search and rescue team is not easy for dog or handler. It is an endeavor undertaken by a motivated few who are willing to invest two to three years of hard training just to be certified and possess a willingness to practice every week to remain proficient.

Labradors can be found among the other larger sized working and herding breeds used for this work. German Shepherds are the most used as rescue dogs; however, Rottweilers, Border Collies, Golden Retrievers, Australian Shepherds and other breeds have been used. The best rescue dogs are those with a higher energy level, higher prey drive and a confident, friendly personality. Dogs from working bloodlines usually have higher aptitudes for this work.

Training and Proficiency Testing of a Rescue-Dog Team

Each organization conducts its own training and proficiency-testing programs. Most have very similar standards and specific tests of the team's proficiency in locating missing persons. The basic training requires a handler/dog team to locate missing persons in a variety of settings often in large search areas ranging from 40 to 200 acres. Searches during the night in dense heavy brush cover and location of well-hidden articles of clothing and belongings are required.

Handlers not only must be very physically fit but also must receive training in search strategy, medical emergency care, wilderness survival and compass travel. Keith Heavrin, a member of the Maine Search and Rescue Dogs

organization, estimated that a person just starting in search and rescue faces an initial hefty financial investment for the necessary equipment, such as a radio, all-weather clothing and other essentials not to mention the continuing expenses of traveling to the working sites.

Dogs are trained to seek the scent of any human that is present in the air. This is in contrast to tracking, which is teaching the dog to follow a specific track on the ground. Air scenting had been found to be the most reliable search method since ground tracks become contaminated, deteriorate rather quickly and are more subject to weather conditions. Air scenters also tend to remain with the scent where a ground-oriented tracker could lose the track and also miss airborne scent thereby losing the scent completely.

The dogs are actually tuning into the human scent present on the 50,000,000 dead skin cells, called rafts, that are shed every minute by a person. Rafts are left behind wherever a person goes and the scent present on them and also the scent from exhaled breath disperses in the wind much like smoke would disperse.

A dog in basic wilderness search and rescue training is taught to seek the generic human scent rather than seeking a specific person. The lessons begin with simple exercises. The dog is praised for responding correctly and the exercise is repeated if the dog does wrong. No corrections are ever

Search dogs must be willing to travel in all types of transports. Here Alaskan search and rescue dog veteran Katie awaits her handler Bill Tai to leave for a search site. Photograph courtesy of Debby Kay, Colonial Beach, VA.

given. The emphasis on training is positive motivation, as the dogs perform solely because it is a game to them. Rewards include exuberant praise and whatever else the dogs might enjoy.

Eventually the rescue dog is taught to signal a find to its handler. The method for signaling varies considerably but is a specific communication that is only used for that purpose. Training becomes more complex in progressive stages and it can take about two years for the dog and person to become proficient. When actually searching, the dog works off lead ahead of the handler in a grid or figure-eight pattern and checks in with the handler periodically. If a find is made, the dog returns to the handler, communicates the find and moves back and forth between the victim and handler until the victim is reached by the handler.

Many handlers begin training their dogs as puppies ensuring that a positive, happy relationship develops where the dog's natural curiosity to find is nurtured and rewarded. Search and rescue dogs are highly trained in obedience where they and their handlers have a deep, effective communication system and are under finely tuned handler control.

Specialty Search Dogs

In recent years there has been a shift to a heavier reliance on volunteer search and rescue organizations to assist in all types of search and rescue. Andy Rebman, a canine specialty search and rescue trainer, began his career with the Connecticut State Police and now trains specialty search and rescue classes from his North Franklin, Connecticut home.

Andy noted with law-enforcement budget cuts there has been an increased demand for trained volunteer search teams to assist with searches for victims of drownings, suicides, disasters and even homicides. Although avalanche and other disaster victims may be alive, quite often the search is for a missing person who has died.

Dogs trained for a live-person search usually need additional training to alert to a cadaver. The scent of a cadaver is different and dogs not trained for cadaver work often react with avoidance, raised hackles or other responses not typical of the alert signal made when a live person has been found.

In 1974 the New York State Police first reported a departmental approach to training dogs for cadaver search and by 1977 Andy started training dogs in this specialty.

Andy Rebman is credited with pioneering much of the work of using chemicals rather than human flesh to train a specialty cadaver search dog. Cadaverene is a commercially prepared compound that simulates one of the breakdown products of decomposed human flesh. Cadaver dogs have found victims buried for prolonged periods even as long as 16 years as well as cadavers buried over four feet deep with a concrete slab over the body. It is unknown how long the various by-products of decomposition are detectable and experimentation in this area is ongoing.

The training is similar to other search work. The search may be in the rubble of a destroyed building, a large area of land, over water or virtually anywhere. Care must be taken when a find is made that the site is not disturbed in order to preserve any evidence used in a possible criminal case. Andy, after participating in over 1,000 missing-person searches and training scores of dogs and individuals, noted that Labradors are his second favorite breed for search and rescue work because of their excellent work ethic and ability to bond with the handler.

Getting Involved in Search and Rescue

The development of search and rescue dogs began rather slowly in

When searching the avalanche site for buried victims, a dog must work quickly yet accurately to locate persons. No time can be wasted digging in the wrong spot.

the 1960s. Although dogs had been used by individuals for many years prior to this time, it was not until 1961 when Bill and Jean Syrotuck of Washington State defined training techniques in writing and helped organize a group to train search and rescue dogs. The Syrotucks owned German Shepherds and got the idea to train their dogs to find lost people when they read a story of a family pet that helped find a missing child. Their first search took place in 1965 and by 1972 the first national search and rescue organization, the American Rescue Dog Association (ARDA), was founded. From this beginning until the mid-1980s, only a limited number of people were involved in search and rescue. By 1986 there were 25 organizations in the United States and in 1993 there were between 200 and 250 averaging from four to ten teams each.

For anyone interested in getting involved in search and rescue, a directory of search and rescue organizations can be obtained from the National Association for Search and Rescue (NASAR), P.O. Box 3709, Fairfax, VA 22038. NASAR is a non-profit national organization that encompasses all types of search and rescue, including but not limited to dogs.

BIBLIOGRAPHY

The History of Guide Dogs in Britain, The Guide Dogs for the Blind Association, Berks England, 1992, pages 1-8.

Lauglin, Cheryl, Records and Information Officer, The Guide Dogs for the Blind Association, letter, 2/10/93.

Johnston, Laurie, "For These Dogs, It's Bombs That Make Them Salivate," *The New York Times*, 12/9/1971, page 49.

"Animal-assisted therapy programs: evaluating the evidence," *Cornell University College of Veterinary Medicine Animal Health Newsletter*, Volume Number 3, April, 1992.

Search and Rescue Dogs Training Methods, American Rescue Dog Association, Howell Book House, NY NY, 1991.

Lee, Laura, Puppy Coordinator, Support Teams for Independence, Inc., P.O. Box 1329, Perris California 92572-1329, letter to Jane Russenberger, 1/7/93.

Charlie Creasy, Associate Director of Development, Canine Companions for Independence, Box 446, Santa Rosa, CA 95402-0446, letter, 11/80/93.

"Type of War Dog's Work Is Ever Changing," *Pure-Bred Dogs/American Kennel Gazette*, Madison Ave., NY, NY 1/16/89, pages 112-114.

Debby Kay, "Labradors as Detector Dogs," *The Labrador Quarterly*, Hoflin Publishing, Wheat Ridge, CO 80033-3299, page 124.

Information and Training Manual, Explosive Detection Dogs, New York City Bomb Squad, New York City Police Department, 1983.

Canine Accelerant Detection Program, U.S. Department of Treasury, Bureau of Alcohol, Tobacco and Firearms and Connecticut State Police, Meriden, CT, 1988.

Genetic Studies and the Labrador Retriever

by Autumn P. Davidson, DVM, Diplomate,
American College of Veterinary Internal Medicine

Dr. Davidson belongs to the American College of Veterinary Internal Medicine Veterinary Medical Teaching Hospital, School of Veterinary Medicine University of California, Davis.

The development of a unique type of dog, known as a "breed," is based on the manipulation of genetics, the science of heredity. Breeders take on the role of Mother Nature when mating select dogs with particular characteristics to produce offspring with similar traits. Individuals within a breed have reduced genetic variability,

The miracle of genetics: the birth of a yellow Labrador Retriever.

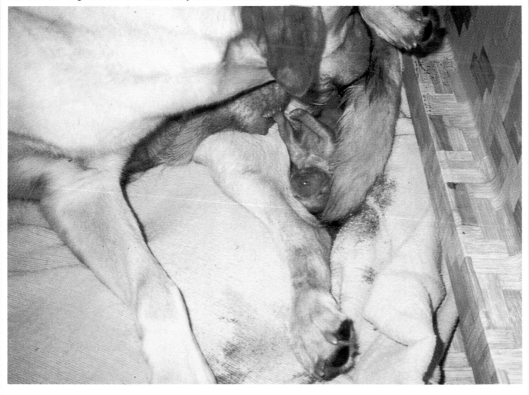

The Labrador breeder must be able to recognize desirable as well as undesirable traits in her line. This breeder examines her first chocolate puppy.

thus, all Labrador Retrievers tend to look and behave similarly. Unfortunately, limiting genetic variability also increases the likelihood that undesirable traits can surface, unless they are specifically selected against. The purebred dog fancier must have both a working knowledge of genetics and the ability to recognize desirable and undesirable traits in order to play the role of Mother Nature successfully.

The Labrador Retriever is a popular dog with characteristic behavioral and physical traits differentiating it as a breed. The Labrador is well known for its jolly, "eager to please" personality, kind and intelligent expression, short, dense-hair coat, and "otter" tail. These traits are easily recognized, and form the basis for the image of the dog brought to mind when one thinks about a Labrador Retriever. Breeders and fanciers of Labrador Retrievers recognize several additional qualities as being typical for the breed, such as "birdiness," drive, trainability, tail set, undercoat, angulation and topline. To the inexperienced lay person, Labrador Retrievers of the same color can all look and act alike, but to the breed fancier, they are quite different. Each individual dog has a unique set of traits. Recognition of these varied behavioral and physical traits allows the fancier to design breeding programs using only dogs with the most desirable characteristics.

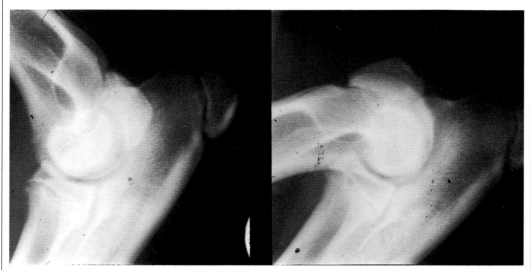

Above: *X-rays showing degenerative changes with elbow dysplasia.*
Below: *Poor forelimb conformation (straight shoulders) is evidenced in this yellow Labrador Retriever. This young dog additionally suffers discomfort from elbow dysplasia, as evidenced by his disinclination to bear weight on his forelimbs.*

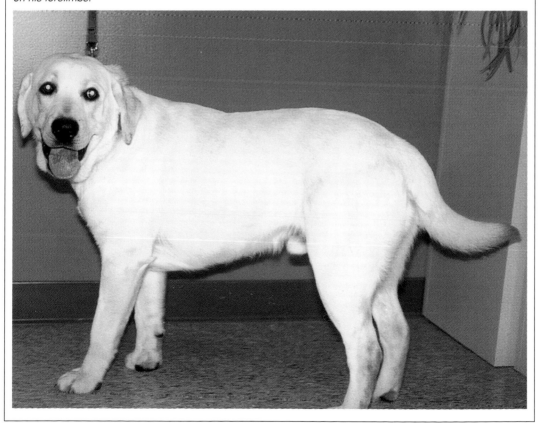

Similarly, breeding stock should be selected from individuals lacking undesirable characteristics, such as poor dispositions or instincts, orthopedic and ocular disorders, or faulty conformation.

Some traits are readily evident (conformation, hunting instincts) while others require specific examinations [hip dysplasia: radiography; progressive retinal degeneration (PRA): an ophthalmologic examina-

Carpal subluxation, seen in this four-month-old Labrador pup, is inherited as a sex-linked recessive trait, but can be exacerbated by obesity and inactivity.

By selecting superior individuals for breeding purposes, the Labrador fancier is increasing the likelihood that the puppies produced will display the same desirable characteristics and similarly lack undesirable traits. Environmental influences (training, diet, injuries, etc.) can influence how the various traits appear in individuals, but their origin is still inherited.

tion]. The heritability of a trait is a measure of the degree to which a trait is under genetic control, as opposed to environmental influences. Heritability scores range from 0.0 to 1.0. Traits with heritability scores greater than 0.5 are under a large degree of genetic influence, their incidence can be greatly modified by selective breeding.

The uniqueness of the Labrador Retriever is maintained because "like produces like." Offspring resemble their parents, both in personality and physical characteristics, because these traits of individuals are inherited, transmitted from generation to generation, following the laws of genetics.

Gregor Mendel discovered the basic laws of inheritance in 1866, by conducting experiments with peas grown in the garden of an Austrian monastery. The fundamental laws governing inheritance discovered by Mendel apply to dogs as well as to peas.

The inheritance of coat color in the Labrador Retriever serves as a convenient model for describing the Mendelian principles. The actual unit of transmission responsible for Mendelian inheritance is the minute gene. Physically, genes consist of deoxyribonucleic acid (DNA), a biochemical substance whose molecular and physical structure was discovered by Nobel Prize laureates J.D. Watson, F. Crick and M.H.F. Wilkens in 1962. Genes reside in chromosomes, tiny structures found within the nucleus of cells. Approximately 100,000 genes are present in the canine chromosomes. The entire compliment of genes in the dog is collectively called the genome. Chromosomes, obtained from cells

The brood bitch class illustrates continuity among generations of Labradors. Ch. Clarion's I've Arrived, owned and bred by Drs. Patty Debrick and Autumn Davidson, is shown with her get, half-siblings Huchu's Parker (by Ch. Belnaboth Tom of Edgewood) and Huchu's Naught By Nature (by Ch. Slateridge Sir Locksley).

during their replication, are visible under the microscope by the use of special stains. Each gene resides at a specific physical site in a chromosome, known as its locus. Genetic mapping is the process by which the actual locus of a particular gene is identified, accomplished by test breedings or specific biochemical tests involving DNA. Genes and chromosomes occur in pairs. Each unit of a pair of genes occurring at one locus is called an allele, and is designated by a letter of the alphabet. Alleles may be alike, homozygous (HH), or dissimilar, heterozygous (Hh). One member of each pair originated from each of that individual's parents. For example, the yellow Labrador is homozygous at the yellow locus (ee), while a black Labrador carrying chocolate is heterozygous at the black-chocolate locus (Bb). The yellow Labrador had to receive one yellow allele (e) from each parent, while the black Labrador carrying chocolate received a black allele (B) from one parent and a chocolate allele (b) from the other. A mutation is a random, usually deleterious, change in a gene, which generally occurs during DNA replication preceding cell division. Mutated genes will subsequently be inherited by the following generations, if they were not lethal (producing a change that caused death before reproduction could occur). Selective breeding utilizing mutations having no deleterious consequences has led to many of the traits associated with the various pure breeds (such as the variety of ear shapes).

Most canine cells contain 78 chromosomes, which occur in 39 pairs. Germ cells (eggs and sperm) normally contain 39

The blue iris color in this yellow Labrador Retriever's right eye is most likely the result of a spontaneous mutation.

The yellow, chocolate and black Labrador Retriever. Coat color genetics in the Labrador provides a good example of the laws of Mendelian genetics.

unpaired chromosomes. The biological process that creates germ cells in the parents (meiosis) arbitrarily selects one of the two alleles present for each gene, thus reducing the total chromosome number by one-half. Fertilization then combines these germ cells' chromosomes, resulting in the usual 78 chromosomes in pairs, with one half of each pair originating from one of the parents. Genes do not mix or blend, they are sorted by this precise biological mechanism, which enables prediction of the likely outcome of matings of individuals with known genetic makeup. For example, the black Labrador (BB) bred to the chocolate Labrador (bb) will predictably produce black puppies carrying chocolate in their genes (Bb).

The detectable physical characteristics or traits of an individual dog are defined as its phenotype (brown eye color, dysplastic elbow). The actual underlying genetic makeup of the dog, which will be passed on to subsequent generations, is defined as its genotype. Unfortunately, knowing the phenotype does not always predict exactly what the underlying genotype is. Not all genes in an individual's genotype are reflected by its phenotype. Whether or not the black Labrador carries the chocolate gene is not apparent by looking at the dog. The most straightforward genetics involve traits that are determined by one set of genes, found on one pair of chromosomes.

Autosomes are all of the

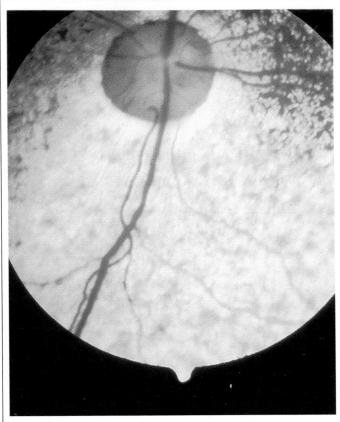

Attenuation of retinal vessels and a thinning of the tapetum, as seen in progressive retinal degeneration (PRA).

seen more frequently in males. Females have a second X chromosome which can carry a normal gene that counteracts that deleterious trait. Males inherit sex-linked traits from their dam. Hemophilia B (Christmas disease), a bleeding tendency seen in the Labrador secondary to a depletion of the coagulation protein IX, is a sex-linked trait carried on the X chromosome.

Sex-limited traits are seen in only one gender, although the genes responsible for the traits can be present in both. Cryptorchidism is an example of a sex-limited trait. Females can carry and transmit the gene without any phenotypic expression. Autosomal dominant forms of alleles override the expression of recessive forms when an individual is a heterozygote (a dog with Bb on the black-chocolate locus will be phenotypically black, as black is dominant to chocolate). Dominant traits passed from one generation to the next are clearly detectable in the offspring, making dominant traits more readily manipulated in a breeding program. Because the dominant trait is usually expressed in any individual possessing the gene, breeders can select for or eliminate the trait in one generation, by subjecting their dogs to whatever

chromosomes except the pair determining the gender of an individual, the X and Y sex chromosomes. Autosomal inheritance is therefore not linked to the gender of the dog. PRA is an example of an autosomally inherited trait.

Sex-linked characteristics are determined by genes found on the X chromosome. Females have a pair, XX, while males have only one, coupled with a Y chromosome, XY. Y chromosomes do not carry any genes. Because males receive only one version of the X chromosome (from their mother), deleterious traits caused by genes on the X chromosome tend to be

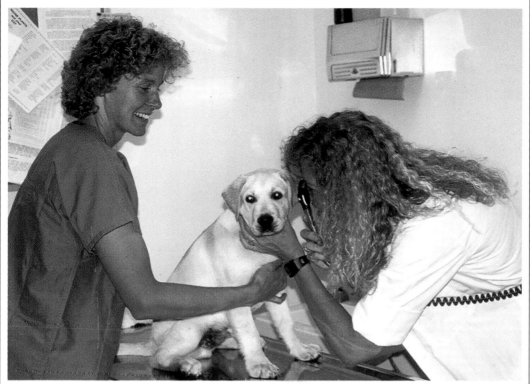

Above: Ophthalmologic examinations of the retina and lens for inherited eye disorders requires special equipment and expertise. ***Below:*** This yellow Labrador Retriever is undergoing x-ray evaluation of his elbows, an examination necessary to assess the phenotypic presence of elbow dysplasia.

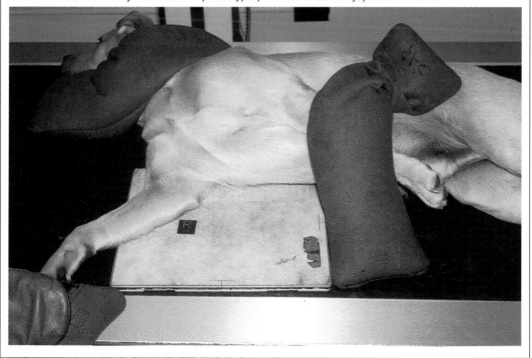

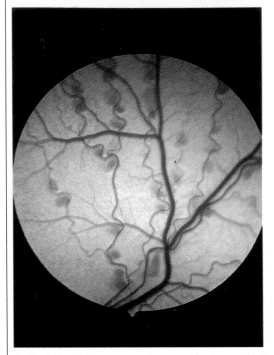 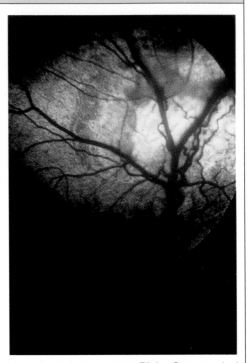

Left: Retinal folds, as seen in the milder forms of retinal dysplasia in the heterozygote. *Right:* Severe retinal changes, with retinal separation, as seen in more severe forms of retinal dysplasia in the homozygote.

scrutiny is necessary to detect the trait (radiograph, ophthalmologic examination), and using or eliminating affected individuals from the breeding pool.

Recessive forms are expressed only when they are present in a homozygous state, lacking the dominant form (a dog with bb on the black-chocolate locus will be chocolate). A recessive gene can be passed along in the heterozygous state, hiding without expression, for several generations until two such carriers are mated, producing a homozygous individual expressing the recessive gene. (Breeding two dogs carrying the chocolate gene, Bb x Bb, can produce some chocolate offspring, bb.)

Some traits do not fall into either category of simple recessive or dominant modes of inheritance, but have more complicated genetics. Incomplete dominance results in partial expression of a trait when the alleles are heterozygous. In some instances, more than one body system is affected by a single gene. Retinal dysplasia with associated skeletal abnormalities can occur in the Labrador Retriever, and is caused by a single autosomal gene with recessive effects on the skeleton and incompletely dominant effects on the eye. Heterozygous Labradors have phenotypically normal skeletons and mild ocular abnormalities. Homozygous individuals have limb deformities and eye abnormalities that range from mild to severe.

Incomplete penetrance occurs when a dominant trait is expressed only in a percentage of the individuals possessing the dominant allele (seen in von Willebrand's disease, a genetic bleeding disorder). Modifier genes can alter the degree to which a trait is expressed. Several modifier genes affect the expression of coat color in the yellow Labrador Retriever, resulting in shades of yellow that range from solid white to foxy red.

The expression of one pair of alleles can be suppressed by the presence of a particular other pair, by a process known as epistasis. For example, a Labrador Retriever that is homozygous for yellow in the recessive form, (ee), will be phenotypically yellow in color, regardless of what is present on the black-chocolate locus. The homozygous recessive yellow locus (ee) is epistatic to the black-chocolate locus. If the yellow locus has dominant homozygous alleles (EE), or is heterozygous (Ee), the color determined by the black-chocolate locus will be expressed, and the dog will be phenotypically black or chocolate. Although the homozygous yellow locus is epistatic to the black-chocolate locus, the eyelid and nose coloration of the yellow Labrador are dependent upon alleles at the black-chocolate locus.

The pattern of coat color is determined by another pair of genes, distinct from the color genes, located on the "A" locus. The solid

Chondrodystrophic skeletal abnormalities seen accompanying ocular changes in homozygous form of retinal dysplasia.

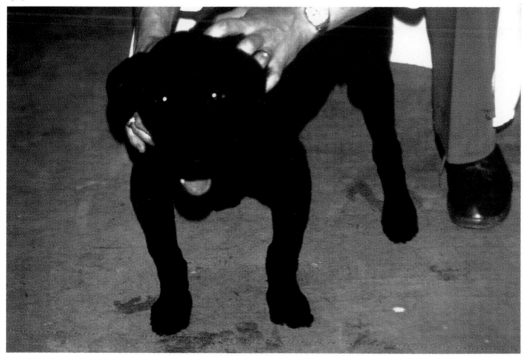

Above: Variation in shades of yellow in two four-week-old Labrador Retriever littermates. **Below:** Variations in shades of yellow in four related adult Labrador Retrievers. Such variation is the result of modifier genes.

coat color pattern allele (S) is autosomally dominant to the tan-point coat color pattern allele (s). A Labrador with the coat pattern genotype that is homozygous dominant, (SS), or heterozygous, (Ss), will be solid in color.

The homozygous recessive genotype (ss) produces a tan-point color pattern. The tan-point color pattern is not expressed in the yellow are polygenic traits, as are problems with dentition and malocclusion.

Polygenic traits are much more difficult to manipulate by selective breeding. An individual's genotype for a polygenic trait is best evaluated by the phenotype of its siblings. A dog with one dysplastic littermate in a litter of ten is less likely to have or produce dysplasia than another

Dark brown or black eyelid and nose coloration, as seen in the yellow Labrador Retriever homozygous for black, BB, or heterozygous, Bb, at the black-chocolate locus.

Labrador, but can be carried in their genotype.

Traits having more complicated genotypes are polygenic, where more than one gene determines the phenotype. Hip and elbow dysplasias with four dysplastic littermates in a litter of ten. The phenotype of parents and grandparents provides a limited amount of additional information about the likely genotype of an individual.

Above: Liver-colored eyelid and nose pigment seen in the yellow Labrador Retriever homozygous for chocolate color, bb, at the black-chocolate locus. *Below:* A phenotypically solid chocolate Labrador Retriever puppy.

Unfortunately, for polygenic traits, the existence of several generations of phenotypically normal individuals does not guarantee phenotypically normal offspring. Geneticists can calculate with acceptable accuracy the number of siblings in which phenotype must be evaluated in order to assign the relative risk that an individual dog will have or produce a particular trait.

DNA fingerprinting is a technology that compares specific sequences of chromosomal DNA between individuals, allowing definite analysis of parent-offspring relationships. Through DNA fingerprinting, the actual sire of a puppy can be identified if a bitch was bred to more than one stud. The American Kennel Club (AKC) has specific guidelines for the registration of purebred litters under such circumstances. Currently, the technology is available to breeders and veterinarians through International Canine Genetics, a company based in Malvern, Pennsylvania. DNA fingerprinting enables us to see that the genetic differences between different breeds, although profound phenotypically, are subtle genotypically. Dr. Joe

Templeton, a geneticist at Texas A&M College of Veterinary Medicine, reported that DNA fingerprinting could not be used to distinguish between breeds, although it could distinguish individual dogs from one another.

Traits controlled by autosomal dominant genes and genes carried only on the X chromosome (in males) are the easiest to eradicate from a breeding program, because they are apparent in all individuals carrying the gene. Recessive traits are more difficult to eradicate because they may be masked in individuals carrying the gene in a heterozygous state, enabling those dogs to be used in breeding programs unless careful pedigree analysis or genetic screening is performed. A high number of individuals carrying a deleterious recessive gene can occur in a breed if a popular sire, who is a carrier of that gene, is used as a mate with multiple bitches. Such a sire is known as a "matador" among geneticists. Subsequent line-breeding efforts, utilizing individuals with common ancestry including this popular sire, results in a high number of homozygous offspring with resultant

Above: A tan-point black Labrador Retriever phenotype, homozygous recessive for the tan-point gene. *Below:* A tan-point chocolate Labrador Retriever phenotype, homozygous recessive for the tan-point gene.

expression of the trait, seen as an epidemic of a genetic disease. Efforts to maximize variation in breeding programs, utilizing different sires, helps to avoid this situation.

Armed with a working knowledge of genetics, the Labrador fancier depends on veterinarians and animal research scientists for guidance concerning the recognition, definition and control of genetic diseases. Breed fanciers and practicing veterinarians are often the first to notice that a particular abnormality seems to

Above: The number of teeth is a polygenic trait. Here an extra upper premolar is present.
Below: Missing teeth threaten to become a common problem in the Labrador. Here several upper premolars are missing.

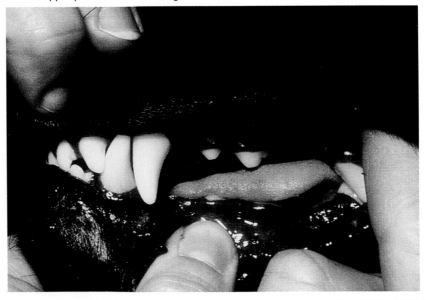

occur more frequently in a certain breed than it should.

Criteria by which a disease is suspected to be genetic include: (a) one or more breed(s) have a greater frequency of a disease than other breeds (the disease occurs with a greater frequency in related individuals); (b) there is an increase in that disease frequency with inbreeding; (c) a disease has a characteristic clinical appearance (phenotype), age of onset and clinical course, and involves the same anatomic site in different individuals. Once a disease or disorder has been identified as a potential genetic problem in a breed, specialists in various fields of veterinary medicine, working with geneticists, can then study the disease, its incidence, associated pathology and mode of inheritance.

Recently, a substantial increase in the level of interest in purebred dog genetic disease control has occurred, supported by concerned breeders and veterinarians and a better educated public. The field of medical genetics has advanced to the point where the technology capable of analyzing many genetic diseases is in place. Adequate time, resources and finances are necessary for such work to progress. Additionally, computer science has advanced dramatically, enabling data banking for detailed subsequent analysis on a large scale,

Veterinarians must maintain a high index of suspicion for genetic disorders when examining purebred dogs.

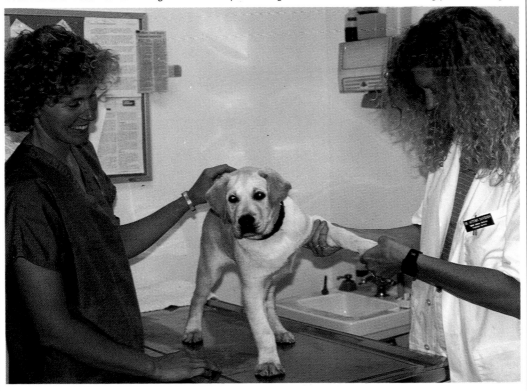

and facilitating pedigree and statistical analyses. Retrospective pedigree analysis utilizing carefully kept records can delineate a disorder's mode of inheritance in many circumstances, avoiding the use of live dogs for prospective test breedings. (With good records, the test breedings have already been done.) The discovery of the genetic basis of an inherited disease and subsequent reduction in its incidence depend on appropriate diagnostic screening tests, test breedings and data banking. Large centralized data-recording schemes, which keep the names and pedigrees of affected, carrier and normal individuals, and test large numbers of individuals on a regular basis, offer a route to lowering the incidence of a disorder. Several organizations exist which record genetic-disease information in the purebred dog. It is encouraging that ongoing scientific research in genetic diseases of the purebred dog is evolving on a daily basis.

Two such programs in the field of genetic-disease data banking hold great promise for breed fanciers and veterinarians interested in purebred-dog inherited disorders. The first, the Canine Genetic Disease Information System, developed by Dr. Donald Patterson at the University of Pennsylvania's School of Veterinary Medicine, is a computerized system that collects and stores information of known and suspected genetic disorders in all breeds, in conjunction with the American Kennel Club. Information will be available to veterinarians and breed fanciers concerning the incidence and current knowledge of such diseases. The second, the Institute for Genetic Disease Control (GDC), based in Davis, California was founded in the summer of 1990. GDC provides an alternative to test breeding for breed fanciers wishing to evaluate their stock for inherited disorders. The GDC is an open, centralized registry of proven genetic disorders which banks the names and pedigrees of phenotypically normal and affected individuals. Additionally, research dam banks were created to study the incidence and patterns of transmission of disorders suspected, but not yet proven, to be genetic. All-breed registries exist at GDC for hip and elbow dysplasias, and osteochondroses of the shoulder and hock. A registry exists for inherited sebaceous adenitis, a skin disorder in Poodles. Work is in progress to develop genetic registries for progressive retinal degeneration, dwarfism, portosystemic liver shunts, medial patellar luxation, osteonecrosis of the femoral head (Legg-Perthes disease) and craniomandibular osteopathy. Research dam banks exist for epilepsy and for osteochondroses of the stifle in the Labrador Retriever. The GDC will also record information derived from other registries, such as the Orthopedic Foundation for Animals (OFA). For a nominal fee, breeders, veterinarians and scientists can obtain

The phenotypes of these litter mates predict more about the genotype of the individual Labrador than that of its parents and grandparents.

progeny and sibling phenotypic reports for a dog they might be interested in using for breeding, gaining valuable information about that dog's potential for genetic problems (its genotype). The inclusion of affected individuals is encouraged.

The Veterinary Medical Data Base (VMDB) compiles animal disease data from nearly all North American veterinary medical colleges. At least 281 different canine diseases have been documented as being genetic in nature. The mode of inheritance is known for approximately 50%, most commonly found to be autosomal recessive. Localization of the gene(s) responsible for inherited disorders within the dog chromosome can be accomplished by the use of DNA "markers," which indicate a gene's presence on the chromosome. Once the location of the deleterious gene(s) is known, DNA "probes" can be developed to permit widespread genetic testing of individuals, using blood cells, to identify those "affected" (before they become apparent clinically) and those who are "carriers." Such genetic mapping and screening are possible even before the actual DNA sequence of the disorder's gene(s) is known.

Currently several projects concerning general mapping of the canine genome exist. Scientists under the guidance of Dr. Jasper Rine at the University of California, Berkeley, and Dr. George Brewer at the University of Michigan are pursuing identification of the canine genome. The Scott-Ritchey Research Center, at the College of Veterinary Medicine at Auburn University, is a new program studying the genetics of companion animal disease, focusing on gene mapping and gene therapy. Dr. George Padgett, a pathologist with special interest in genetics at the School of Veterinary Medicine, Michigan State University, has studied inherited diseases of the canine for several years, providing valuable information to breed fanciers concerning tracking of inherited disorders. The James A. Baker Institute for Animal Health at the New York State College of Veterinary Medicine has a long history of valued contributions to the field of canine infectious disease, and more recently has developed important programs studying genetic diseases. Ophthalmologic disorders are being pursued under the leadership of Dr. Gus Aguirre, well known among Labrador fanciers for his work with PRA. Dr. George Lust has studied canine hip dysplasia at the institute since 1968, and currently is studying the impact of environmental effects (such as diet and medications) on the development of hip dysplasia, as well as searching for a genetic marker for dysplasia in white blood cells.

Several organizations and individuals are working to collect data on genetic disorders in the Labrador Retriever. These groups provide a centralized, standardized method by which dogs can be evaluated for inherited disorders.

The Canine Eye Registration Foundation (CERF), located at the Purdue University's School of Veterinary Medicine, and a subsidiary of the VMDB, was established in 1974 by a group of concerned purebred dog owners and breeders. CERF's stated goals are to eliminate heritable eye diseases in purebred dogs through registration, research and education. CERF cooperates with the American College of Veterinary Ophthalmologists (ACVO), maintaining a registry of purebred dogs they have examined and found free of heritable eye disease, as well as a closed (confidential) research data base of all ACVO examinations, which tracks breed abnormalities. PRA Data, Inc., is a non-profit organization dedicated to compiling voluntary pedigree data on Labrador Retrievers which have been clinically confirmed as having progressive retinal degeneration. The pedigrees of affected dogs are published and made available to interested individuals for a nominal fee.

The Orthopedic Foundation for Animals (OFA) was established in 1966 with the following objectives: to collate and disseminate information concerning orthopedic diseases of animals; to advise, encourage and establish programs to lower the prevalence of orthopedic diseases; to encourage and finance research in orthopedic diseases of animals; and to receive funds and make grants to carry out these objectives. The OFA has operated under the guidance of

Dr. E.A. Corley, and currently maintains registries for both hip and elbow dysplasia. A consensus report, arrived upon by three veterinary radiologists (out of a field of approximately 20) is given for each dog. The hip joint is evaluated and graded as "normal" (excellent, good, fair), "borderline," or "dysplastic" (mild, moderate, severe). The elbow joint is evaluated as normal or dysplastic, with grades of severity progressing from I to III. An evaluation of "normal" in either the hip or the elbow can be made permanently at an age of 24 months. The OFA is currently the world's largest hip registry and as such has been able to generate remarkable data. A tremendous increase in the level of lay-person awareness concerning hip dyspla-

sia, and subsequently a motion among breed fanciers to incorporate hip evaluations in the breeder's code of ethics, occurred in large part because of the OFA. A specific technique (ventro-dorsal view, pelvis symmetric, hind legs extended and parallel) for positioning the dog for hip evaluation was adopted and promoted by the OFA based on findings of the American Veterinary Medical Association (AVMA), published in 1961.

Wide-scale use of this technique by veterinarians has standardized hip evaluations and generated important comparative data concerning hip dysplasia. The OFA is a closed registry, making information public only on normal individuals.

This yellow Labrador Retriever is positioned properly for pelvic limb (hip) x-rays by the standard AVMA-recommended technique.

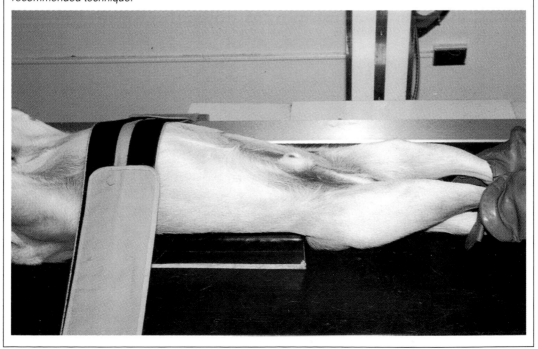

During the past 15 years, it has become apparent that severe problems exist with heritable orthopedic disorders in the elbow, shoulder and hock of the Labrador, as well as in the hip. In response to breeders' concerns and requests for assistance with dysplasias of the hip and elbow, and osteochondroses of the shoulder and hock, the Wind-Morgan Program was initiated in 1990. The Wind-Morgan Program is associated with the School of Veterinary Medicine's Department of Radiology, at the University of California, and is administered by the GDC. Dr. Alida Wind, the veterinary orthopedic surgeon credited with the discovery of elbow dysplasia (in Bernese Mountain Dogs), and Dr. Joe Morgan, a veterinary radiologist specializing in hip dysplasia, together evaluate x-rays of Labradors' hips, elbows, shoulders and hocks. Permanent evaluations are offered for individuals 12 months of age or older, and a "Wind-Morgan number" is awarded if a dog is found to be phenotypically free of disease in all four sites. The criteria of normalcy in the Wind-Morgan Program are tough, and only "normal" or "dysplastic" evaluations are given. The evaluation of littermates, progeny and geriatric individuals is encouraged. The Wind Morgan Program is an open registry, providing progeny and sibling analyses to concerned individuals via the GDC. Guide Dogs for the Blind, in San Rafael, California utilizes the program extensively in evaluating their breeding stock.

Across the country, several individual programs studying specific genetic disorders occurring in the Labrador Retriever can be found. New and important studies evolve each year.

At the School of Veterinary Medicine, University of California, Davis, Drs. Terrell Holliday and Autumn Davidson, with neurotechnologist Collette Williams, have embarked on a prospective study to identify electroencephalogram (EEG) characteristics of epilepsy in Labrador Retrievers. Epileptic and apparently normal individuals, as well as their relatives, are under study. Data concerning specific details of their seizures, response to anti-epileptic medication and pedigrees are recorded. GDC is recording the resultant statistics in its research database. A working criteria for inheritable epilepsy in the Labrador has been established, including the following: the seizures must have started between the ages of three months and seven years; multiple seizures must have occurred, separated by at least one week; the seizures must be symmetric and typical for epilepsy; the dog must be free of serious heart, lung, liver or kidney disease, and not be hypoglycemic. At the College of Veterinary Medicine, Texas A & M University, Dr. Dawn Merton-Boothe is studying alternative means of controlling seizures in epileptic dogs who do not respond to the sole use of phenobarbital, the "gold standard" drug for suppressing seizures.

At the Inherited Eye Disease Studies Unit within the Section of Medical Genetics, School of Veterinary Medicine, University of Pennsylvania, recent advances as to the categorization of PRA in several purebred dogs have been made. Through test breedings, Drs. Gustavo Aguirre, Gregory Acland, Larry Stramm, James Lindsey, and Bennett Hershfield have shown the specific genetic defect causing PRA is the same in Labrador Retrievers, English and American Cocker Spaniels and Poodles. This information will greatly facilitate further work towards creating diagnostic genetic markers for individuals with the defective gene, because results obtained already from years of work on the Poodle can be applied to the Labrador with confidence. Currently, Drs. Aguirre and Acland are continuing their studies to identify the genes responsible for PRA at the Center for Canine Genetics and Reproduction, College of Veterinary Medicine, Cornell University, with hopes to develop a dependable blood-based test to differentiate the normal, carrier or affected status in the Labrador.

Drs. George Lust, Nancy Burton-Wurstor, Kathy Beck and Gail Rubin, with Alma Williams, at the College of Veterinary Medicine, Cornell University, recently published findings concerning the reduction of symptoms of hip dysplasia, studied in four litters of Labrador Retrievers, following the administration of glycosaminoglycan polysulfates. Dr. R.D. Kealy, in collaboration with scientists from the Schools of Veterinary Medicine at the University of Pennsylvania and Cornell University, the School of Public Health, University of North Carolina, and the Laboratory for Comparative Pathology in Sweden, has a recently published work which found a reduction in the incidence and severity of hip dysplasia with either limited food consumption or varied dietary electrolyte (sodium, potassium and chloride) composition in growing Labrador Retrievers. Dr. Gail Smith, at the University of Pennsylvania School of Veterinary Medicine, has published extensively concerning the impact that the methods of x-ray positioning and the use of sedation or anesthesia have on the accuracy of the diagnosis of hip dysplasia. Specifically, Dr. Gail has correlated hip laxity (joint looseness) with the development of hip dysplasia, and found that the standard technique of evaluating the canine hip (the standard leg-extended view) failed to detect significant laxity in many cases. Dogs diagnosed by OFA as being "fair" (normal) were uniformly found to have excessive hip laxity when examined by Dr. Smith's distraction x-rays. Distraction x-rays require anesthesia and position the hip in a fashion that simulates their weight-bearing orientation, with a fulcrum between the thighs. Meaningful findings can be made in dogs as young as four months of age. Interestingly, all dogs found to be dysplastic by the OFA were also found to have excessive hip laxity by the distraction x-ray technique. Studies analyzing the relationship between Labrador Retrievers certified as free of hip dysplasia by the more stringent Wind-Morgan Program, and subsequently x-rayed by the distraction technique, are underway.

The study of Drs. Ulreh Mostosky, George Padgett and Curtis Probsts on the inheritance of elbow dysplasia at Michigan State's College of Veterinary Medicine has recently been completed. The study was based on three generations of test breedings using Labradors Retrievers affected with elbow osteochondroses and/or fragmented coronoid processes. Their results supported the disorder's proposed polygenic mode of inheritance. The study failed to detect osteochondroses in the elbow without an accompanying fragmented coronoid process, suggesting that the former might be caused by the latter, in the elbow.

The Labrador Retriever recently became the number one AKC registered dog in the country, nudging aside the American Cocker Spaniel, who held the post for many years. Most breed fanciers wonder what took people so long to discover what they have known all along, the Labrador is simply the greatest dog in the world. Unfortunately, the role of being the most popular dog in the United States is

Puppies delivered from yellow bitch. Bred by Windanna Kennels.

Labradors owned by contributing author Dr. Autumn P. Davidson.

a treacherous one. Many veterinarians found the previous "number one breed in America" to be one of their least favorite patients. Cocker Spaniels have, in the last decade, become notorious for poor dispositions, with a tendency toward fear-induced aggression, submissive urination, defecation and worse! A marked increase in physical flaws, such as skin allergies, ear problems, eye disorders and malocclusions occurred as well. "Nice" healthy Cockers were considered valuable and uncommon. Popular purebred dogs invite unscrupulous breeders to produce puppies for an eager market. The puppy-buying public must become informed about genetic disorders so they can support reliable breeders. The reputable breeder must not only keep abreast of new developments in veterinary medicine and purebred dog genetics but meet an obligation to educate the public as well. Breeders should support (both financially and with patients) investigators interested in their breed's disorders, instead of viewing them with suspicion or disinterest. The science of genetics created our Labrador, it will provide us with the knowledge to minimize its flaws, and keep it the great breed we all love.

Can. Ch. Beautawn's Inside Information CDN, Am. CD, WC is out of Bill Gugin's first homebred bitch Beautawn's Brandy on the Rock CDX, WC.

The Labrador Retriever in Canada

by M. Judith Hunt

LABRADOR RETRIEVER CLUB OF CANADA

In the spring of 1979, letters were sent to breeders and clubs across Canada regarding the formation of a national breed club. During the summer of 1980, Sandy Briggs and Mike Lanctot started the ball rolling to form the Canadian national club. A constitution committee was formed consisting of Sandy Briggs, Charles Hunt, Hugette Beattie and Frank Jones. An ethics and aims committee consisted of Charles and Judy Hunt, Bud and Merle Milsom and Ed and Jill Schafer.

Application was made to the Canadian Kennel Club for recognition, at which time there were 40 charter members who had passed the proposed Code of Ethics, Aims, Constitution and By-laws. Official club recognition was not received from the CKC until January 1982. The first executives of the Labrador Retriever Club of Canada were: Chairperson, Sandy Briggs; Vice-chairperson, Mike Lanctot; and Secretary-treasurer, Monica Briggs. The Regional Directors included: Carole Bernier (Atlantic Provinces); Michael Beattie (Quebec); Reg Beard (Eastern Ontario); Robert Gibson (East-central Ontario); Frank Jones (West-central Ontario); Dale Haines (Southwest Ontario); Marie Prosperi (Northern Ontario); Kay Nemeth (Manitoba); Tom Hynes (Saskatchewan); Charles Hunt (Alberta); and Ruth Raper (British Columbia).

At the annual general meeting in August 1985, the regions were changed to West (British Columbia and Alberta), Central (Saskatchewan, Manitoba and N.W. Ontario to, but not including Sault St. Maria) and East (Sault St. Marie and East).

The executives are elected for a three-year term on a regional rotational basis with all executive members from one geographic location.

The first national specialty and Working Certificate Tests were held in Winnipeg, Manitoba in July 1982 and hosted by the Labrador Retriever Club of Manitoba. The national specialties also rotate through the three regions on a yearly basis with the annual general meeting being held in conjunction with the specialty.

Not until July 1992 in Quebec was an obedience trial held in conjunction with the national specialty.

ESTABLISHED BREEDERS IN CANADA

The following kennels have bred significant dogs in the areas of conformation, field trials and/or obedience. Each breeder has had an influence on the Labrador Retriever breed in Canada as well as the United States and has been breeding Labradors for at least a decade.

Can. Ch. Amaranth's Talisman CD, WC, known as Taylor, was breeder-owner-handled by Joan Calder to number-two Lab in Canada in 1986 and number one in 1987. He is a Raleigh grandson.

Amaranth Labradors was established in 1978 in Shelburne, Ontario, by Joan Calder. The

Can. Ch. Northriding Raleigh CD, WC was the foundation stud for Amaranth Labradors. He was bred by A. J. Wintjes.

A smiling Taylor photographed by Alex Smith. Owner, Joan Calder.

purpose of this breeding establishment is to produce show Labradors that would rather retrieve. Ch. Northriding Raleigh CD, WC was the foundation stud dog who lived to the age of 13 years. His dam was a South African field-trial champion who goes back to the Zelstone and Sandylands lines. His sire was a Wimberway dog with a Castlemore and Liddly background. In 1986 a Raleigh grandson, Ch. Amaranth's Talisman CD, WC, was breeder-owner handled to number-two show Labrador in Canada with a Group third win at the very large Credit Valley Show in Toronto. He became the number-one show Labrador in Canada in 1987 and number-five Sporting dog. The same year a Raleigh daughter, OTCh. Amaranth's Silver Moon, Am. UD, became Canada's top obedience Lab and number-four Sporting dog,

Can. Ch. Springfield's Native Fancy CD, WC was Bill Gugins's first bitch and is the dam of Ch. Beautawn's Inside Information CDN, Am. CD, WC.

and then number two in 1988. Amaranth Labradors have bred over 50 show champions and four obedience trial champions.

Beautawn Labradors William (Bill) Gugins's first fascination with Labradors began in 1966 while living in the Calgary, Alberta area when his friend and hunting partner purchased a dog for hunting. Bill's first acquisition of a registered Labrador Retriever was in 1970, and it was purchased as a hunting companion and family member. Eleven years later, after the passing of this first Labrador, both the opportunity to purchase a daughter of Am. Ch. Lockerbie Brian Boru and the moving to the Okootoks, Alberta area happened, and the true inception of Beautawn Labradors had arrived. In 1981 Beautawn's first bitch, Ch. Springfield's Native Fancy CD,WC, was bred to Am. Ch. Braemar's Oakmead Dillon CD, WC, producing Beautawn's first homebred brood bitch Beautawn's Brandy on the Rock CDX, WC. Among Brandy's many impressive achievements was the winning of three regional specialties and the Canadian National Specialty for Dam and Progeny, each time competing with different progeny would rank among her best. Two of

Brandy's progeny have done her very proud, Ch. Beautawn's Inside Information CD, Am. CD, WC was the number-three Labrador in Canada in 1990, and his litter sister Ch. Beautawn's Instant Replay CDX, WC has won BISS and BOS at regional specialties. Another one of Brandy's progeny Ch. Beautawn's High Country Taffy was a multi-group placement winner, BPIS winner and number-two female Labrador in Canada before she was ten months old. Brandy's progeny have been the backbone of many new and existing Labrador kennels in the U.S. and Canada, and her name keeps appearing on quality pedigrees throughout the Labrador world. The influence of Brandy on Labradors of Beautawn is still very evident in all puppies produced there today. Brandy has consistently produced type, temperament, trainability and versatility, all goals that Beautawn Labradors continues to strive for today.

Cedarbrae Kennels James Girvan purchased his first Labrador in 1981 from a local breeder. Although the dog gained his show

Beautawn's Brandy on the Rock CDX, WC became the foundation bitch of Beautawn Labradors.

Above: Can. Ch. Beautawn's Instant Replay CDX, WC is the litter sister to Ch. Beautawn's Inside Information CDN, Am. CD, WC and has won best in specialty show awards at regional shows. Below: Can. Ch. Beautawn's Inside Information CDN, Am. CD, WC on the day he gained his championship in July 1988.

championship, he was not an outstanding specimen. The dog did provide the Girvans, however, with the opportunity to become involved in Labs and to the eventual purchase of foundation bitch, Trixie, from Ellie Ellis. Trixie, formally Ch. Gleneagles Joie de Vivre CDX, WCI, was the 1987 LOC Neville trophy winner for outstanding versatility at the national level, having achieved all of her titles before the age of two. She was field trialed at the junior level in the same year and, although she never placed, she made it to the final series in several trials. She went on to win best of opposite sex at the 1990 Labrador Retriever Club of Canada national specialty at the age of five. Trixie was bred to Ch. Windanna's Midas Gold CD, WC (which was a linebreeding on Am. Ch. Raintree Braemar Baliff CD, WC) and two bitches, Kelsey and Skeeter, were kept for the program. Registered Ch. Cedarbrae's Tranche de Vie CD, WC, Kelsey matched her dam's distinction by winning the 1990 LOC Neville trophy, including a high in trial. She was also trained as a weight puller and for three years competed on an international level through the International Weight Pullers Association. Her best pull was in 1992 of 1350 pounds (on wheels) at a pulling weight of 75 pounds—that's 18 times her weight! Skeeter or Ch. Cedarbrae's Touch of

Gleneagle Joie de Vivre CDX, WCI, a Neville trophy winner, taking BOS at the Canadian national in 1990. Owner, James Girvan of Cedarbrae Kennels.

Trix CD, WC was Canada's top female Labrador show dog in 1992 and ranked number six for all Labradors that year. She won over 25 BOBs and was BOS at the LRC of BC specialty in 1992. Cedarbrae was established with the objective of producing a sound, versatile, good-looking dog that will fit into any home, be it for show, obedience or field. Cedarbrae only produced five litters in its first decade of existence, carefully watching the offspring and breeding only those dogs that exemplify the qualities that make the Labrador Retriever unique among dogs.

Above: Kelsey or Can. Ch. Cedarbrae's Tranche de Vie CD, WC, the 1990 Neville trophy winner, in pulling harness. *Below:* Kelsey in action at the 1992 Luxton Fair Weight Pull. Kelsey weighed in at 69 pounds and pulled 1340 pounds.

The all-time top champion-producing sire in Canada, Am-Can. Ch. Ebonylane's Aslan, bred by Mike and Pat Lanctot and owned by Dr. Ken Bentley.

Ebonylane Labradors is found in Fall River, Nova Scotia and is owned by Pat and Mike Lanctot. Established in 1974, the Ebonylane foundation consisted of best in show winner and producer Am-Can. Ch. Shamrock Acres Ebonylane Ace CDX, WC. The most cherished award won by Ace was the Neville trophy, awarded in 1980 by the Labrador Owners Club for the top all-around Lab in show, field and obedience. Best in show winner Am-Can. Ch. Hollyhock Sam (an Ace son on lease to Ebonylane) was top Labrador in Canada in 1980. Ace daughter, Ch. Ebonylane's Shadow, when bred to Australian import Ch. Astroloma Joshua (linebred on Ch. Sandylands Tan), produced Am-Can. Ch. Ebonylane's Aslan, who became Canada's top producing sire of all time with over 100 champions to his credit in 50 breedings. Aslan was instrumental in Ebonylane's becoming the top producing Canadian kennel of all time. This combination of Josh and Shadow also produced Am-Can. Ch. Ebonylane's Midnite Bandit, a multiple best of breed winner at specialties in the U.S., Am-Can. Ch. Ebonylane's Caviar, a winner of the puppy sweeps at the American national specialty in

The foundation of Ebonylane, best-in-show winning and top-producing Am-Can. Ch. Shamrock Acres Ebonylane Ace CDX, WC doing what he loved best. Owners, Mike and Pat Lanctot and bred by Sally McCarthy and Jackie Childs.

1981, and Am-Can. Ch. Ebonylane's Northern Trooper CD, a back-to-back group winner in the U.S. Of special pride to the Lanctot is the fact that they produced the top Labrador in Canada in 1984—Am-Can. Ch. Ebonylane's Buccaneer Gold CD—and the top Labrador in the U.S. that same year—Am-Can. Ch. Ebonylane's Yellow Poplar. Both of these top dogs were out of the same bitch, Am-Can. Ch. Ebonylane's Cotton Candy. Bucky was sired by Aslan and Pops was sired by Bandit. In 1983 the Lanctots purchased Ch. Waterdog's Raider of Ebonylane CD. Bred to Aslan daughters, Raider produced many specialty, breed and obedience winners as well as over a dozen certified Seeing Eye dogs for the blind. The Lanctots operated a small kennel of eight to ten adults producing 65 litters in 20 years and attribute much of their success to the cooperation and support received from their puppy owners. Since their move from Hemmingford, Quebec to Fall River in 1989, Pat and Mike have semi-retired from breeding to allow more time for travel and judging.

Above: Can. Ch. Waterdog's Raider of Ebonylane CD owned by Mike and Pat Lanctot. *Below:* Can. Ch. Ebonylane's Trademark at two years of age is the culmination of 18 years and five generations of Ebonylane breeding. Owners, Mike and Pat Lanctot.

321

Can. Ch. Lindenhall's Bold Eagle CD is an important sire at Lindenhall Kennels. Owners, Wayne and Peggy Donovan.

Lindenhall Kennels was established by Peggy and Wayne Donovan in 1977 with the purchase of several Labs from strong field lines. In 1982, after trying unsuccessfully to show field dogs, the Donovans purchased a yellow male puppy from Ebonylane Kennels and, as they say, the rest is history. The puppy grew up to be Am-Can. Ch. Ebonylane's Buccaneer Gold CD, the number one Lab in Canada in 1984 and '85 and is the top-winning show Lab in Canadian history with a record 13 bests in show. Bucky passed on his winning ways to his sons: Can. Ch. Rathamill Angus At Lindenhall CD, who won the Canadian national specialty in '89, Am-Can. Ch. Beaumans Goldchip At Lindenhall, who was the number one Lab in Canada in '88, '89, and in '90 was the top Sporting dog, and Am. Ch. Lindenhall's Grandquest Rebel who was one of the top Labs in the U.S. for '92. All the Labradors at the Donovans', with the exception of two chocolates, are related to Bucky. Now that Bucky is retired, Can. Ch. Lindenhall's Bold Eagle CD is the top stud along with Bucky son Ben and grandsons Chuckie and Jimmy. Lindenhall Kennels has produced over 40 champions, including many Labs with obedience and working titles. Several have

Above: Am-Can. Ch. Ebonylane's Buccaneer Gold CD won a record 13 bests in show, making him the top-winning Labrador in Canada. *Below:* Bellsen's Bun at Rahontsi at age ten, owned by Dale Speck.

been placed as guide dogs and some work in hospitals and homes as therapy dogs. With each new generation, Lindenhall continues to breed sound, multi-purpose Labrador Retrievers bred to the Canadian standard.

Selamat–Rahontsi Labradors started in 1969 primarily as a working kennel by its owners, Jim and Dale Speck of Harley, Ontario. The working lines were based on Can. FTCh. Pelican Lake Toby and to this day his line is still in some of their dogs. Over the years the kennel became known for quality chocolates, beginning with the importation of Can. Ch. Castlemore Bramble and his litter sister Ch. Castlemore Pride WC from Ireland. At approximately the same time, the kennel imported a six-year-old male from the U.S. Wanapum-Dart's Puget-Power was shown for the first time at the age of seven years and finished his title quite handily. Brown was on the top derby list in the U.S. as a youngster and his working ability is still coming through in his descendants. The kennel still has a Castlemore Bramble son at limited stud, two of his grandsons and a great-grandson of both Castlemore Bramble and Wanapum Dart's Puget

Can. Ch. Castlemore Bramble at age two, owned by Dale Speck.

Can. Ch. Shwarzenberg Chico Son WC owned by Dieter and Ursula Dohmen.

Power. Rahontsi's Luger WCX is a grandson of Puget Power and a great-grandson of both Castlemore Bramble and Castlemore Pride. The kennel's bitch lines primarily go back to Ch. Castlemore Pride and Ch. Castlemore Bramble. The Rahontsi-Selamat Labrador kennel has owned and bred specialty show winners, Master Hunting retrievers, as well as many champions and working-titled dogs. The kennel is constantly striving to breed dogs free of hereditary defects while main-taining breed integrity. All breeding stock is carefully screened for hips, eyes and other known defects.

Shwarzenberg Labradors are located at Castlegar, British Columbia. They are owned by Ursula and Dieter Dohmen. The kennel name has been registered since 1975 with the Canadian Kennel Club. Shwarzenberg breeds one litter each year or every second year. Dual Ch. and AFTCh. Duke Von Shwarzenberg CD was the first hero of this kennel which has always

FTCh.-AFTCh. Shwarzenbergs Lucky Dee CDX owned by Dieter and Ursula Dohmen.

Above: The family with the WhistInwings dogs: Can. Triple Ch. WhistInwings Kitty Magee WCX, FTCh. Sundee's Pacemaker, and Ballad of the WhistInwings CDX, WCX owned by Kerry and Lori Curran. **Below:** Can. Triple Ch. Kenosee Jim Dandy WCX at eight weeks of age in the arms of Lori Curran.

strived for dual-purpose Labradors. Am-Can. Ch. Proud Chico Von Shwarzenberg was imported from Sweden in 1976. He was a dark chocolate and sired many good chocolate offspring. A recent litter sired by him produced Ch. Shwarzenbergs Chico Son. FTCh.–AFTCh. Shwarzenbergs Lucky Dee CDX was trained and campaigned in trial by Ursula. She is now retired and a daughter has taken her place. Shwarzenberg tries to keep the number of Labradors at the kennel down to five at a time so as to be

able to give each dog the attention he desires. Dieter and Ursula both teach obedience and field-trial classes.

Whistlnwings Labradors, owned by Kerry and Lori Curran of Langdon, Alberta, is the proud home of Canada's only Triple Champion Labradors—dogs that have achieved a show championship, an obedience trial championship and a field trial championship. The first one, Triple Champion Kenosee Jim Dandy WCX (Dandy), was given to Lori as a seven-week-old puppy by her breeder, Jim Harkness. She was field trial dog by pedigree, although both her parents (FTCh.-Am.FTCh. Pelican Lake Andy and Kenosee Jo) were good-looking Labradors. Her grandsire was all-time high point open dog in Canada '75, '81 CNFC-FTCh.-AFTCh.-FC-AFC Pelican Lake Petey Two. Whistlnwings's second Triple Champion is a homebred daughter of Dandy by Am-Can. Ch. Monarch's Black Arrogance CD, WC, Triple Champion Whistlnwings Kitty Magee WCX (Kitty). The Currans have done all of Dandy and Kitty's training and handling at shows and trials themselves, and both girls earned all their championships before their fifth birthdays, with limited showing and trialing. The Currans are basically field trialers who love the breed and are dedicated to

Can. Triple Ch. Kenosee Jim Dandy WCX in March 1986 before she earned her field trial championship.

Can. Triple Ch. Whistlnwings Kitty Magee WCX at almost five years of age.

Above: Can. Triple Ch. Whisltnwings Kitty Magee WCX finishing her show championship with a four-point win handled by Lori Curran. *Below:* Burbury Stuff'd Shirt owner-bred by LauraLee Burdick.

Above: Ironwood of Whistlnwings (FC-AFC-FTCh.-AFTCh. Ironwood Tarnation x Triple Ch. Kenosee Jim Dandy WCX), owned by the Currans. Below: Kerry Curran and FTCh. Sundee's Pacemaker with Lori Curran and Can. Triple Ch. Kenosee Jim Dandy WCX.

keeping it a dual-purpose breed where the great majority look and work like Labradors should. While the Currans have been involved in the breed for many years, they have bred very sparingly, not breeding their first litter until 1985. Kerry has been field trialing for 30 years and is a popular field-trial judge who had the honor of judging the 1982 Canadian National Retriever Championship. Lori has been field trialing for nearly 25 years and has delved into obedience and conformation as well as professional training. The Currans' great challenge is to produce the show and field-trial Lab in one package. Towards this end, they have crossed field and show lines. Each litter is planned with the aim of achieving a step closer to the ultimate goal of producing a line of Labs which has the qualities to make dual or triple champions. The Currans have produced nine litters of which seven

Am-Can. Ch.-OTCh. Wimberway's Wateaki Am. CDX born in 1962 was the top Labrador in Canada in 1965 and number two in 1966.

progeny are qualified all-age field trial dogs, two of which are field trial champions, two obedience trial champions and two show champions, one Senior Hunter, and many dogs with points or legs towards new titles. A definite highlight of Whistlnwings Labradors was at the 1991 Canadian National Specialty when Ch. Whistlnwings Autumn Thunder WC went BOS and litter sister Triple Ch. Whistlnwings Kitty Magee WCX earned her first open field trial win. The Currans feel strongly that breeders should train and work their dogs because it is very easy to lose those "unseen qualities," such as intelligence, heart and desire to retrieve, qualities that are just as important as expression and the otter tail!

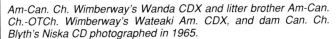

Am-Can. Ch. Wimberway's Wanda CDX and litter brother Am-Can. Ch.-OTCh. Wimberway's Wateaki Am. CDX, and dam Can. Ch. Blyth's Niska CD photographed in 1965.

Wimberway Kennels is the breeding establishment of Sandy Briggs, a CKC member since 1960 who began breeding Labradors in 1962. Wimberway has produced over 175 Canadian show champions, over 150 CD title holders, plus 50 with CDX or UD, and over 75 with working titles. Many of the Wimberway dogs have been pointed toward field trial championships. Among the significant Labradors that have been associated with Wimberway are Wimberway's Norseman CD, winner of the Purina Gold Whistle, Dual Ch. Looncall's Tony's Mr. Jay, Dual Ch. Black Lobo, Dual and AFTCh. Win-Toba's Maximum, FTCh. Glenlogie's Peter. Sandy Briggs has bred, handled and owned many specialty winners including multi-BIS Am-Can-Ber. Ch. Wimberway's Friendly Freddy, Canadian BIS winner Am-Can-Ber. Ch. Wimberway's Elosca Excole CDX, WC, Am-Can. Ch. Wimberway's Odin CD, Am-Can. Ch. Williston Blacksmith, and Am-Can. Ch. Banner's Cole Younger, Am-Can. Ch. Wimberway's Wanda CDX. Wimberway has bred many all-'rounders including Am-Can. Ch.-OTCh. Wimberway's Wateaki Am. CDX, who had points towards field trial championship and was Canada's top Labrador in 1965, Ch. Wimberway's Colros Radar CDX, WCX who shined as a puppy group winner, and

Am-Can-Ber. Ch. Wimberway's Max of Bernfield with Bob Forsth, en route to his American championship. Breeder, Carole Bernier.

Above: Can. Ch. Wimberway's Petchief Apiper CD, WC with handler Carole Bernier in 1982. **Below:** Am-Can-Ber. Ch. Wimberway's Friendly Freddy WC was a multiple best in show winner and specialty winner. Owner, Sandy Briggs.

Can-Ber. Ch. Huntingdon Chester O Wimberway Am-Can. CDX, Ber. CD, Can. WCX, Am. WC. Sandy was the first breeder to travel to Bermuda and therefore had the first Canadian-owned Bermudian champion. Many of the Wimberway dogs have been placed in community service roles. These dogs can be found with the Swiss Seeing Eye school, Swiss police department, American police officers, Canada Customs, Canine Vision Canada, and various security companies throughout North America.

Windanna Kennels of Charles E. and M. Judith Hunt is located in Calgary, Alberta. The Hunts bought their first Labrador in 1975, a fox-red bitch puppy named Gemini's Anna (Ch. Halsinger's Laddie x Ch. Wimberway The Treasured Tam). Windanna has produced over 50 homebred champions, 32 CD-titled dogs, 10 CDX-titled dogs, and two obedience trial champions. Additionally there are some 20 dogs titled in field and working. In 1988 Ch. Windanna's Burgundy Bertie CDX, WCI won the Neville trophy, owner-breeder-handled. The Windanna bitch line goes back to BPIS Ch. Windanna's Snow Queen CD (Ch. Ghillie's Jeep x Gemini's Anna CD), who produced seven champions in two litters, was second top producing Labrador bitch in 1985. Her daughter BPIS Ch. Windanna's Betsy Paramore (Am. Ch. Raintree Braemar Baliff CDX x Ch. Windanna's Snow Queen CD) produced four champions, including a third-generation BPIS. A daughter, Windanna's Pallas Athena CD (Ch. Finchingfield Ivan of Oaklea x Ch. Windanna's Betsy Paramore), produced eight champions and

Can. Ch. Windanna's Bergundy Bertie CDX, WCI, won the Neville trophy in 1988. Owners, Charles and Judith Hunt.

Can. Ch. Windanna's National Dream (Am-Can. Ch. Rainell's Dynasty x Can. Ch. Windanna's Molly Melody). Owners, Charles and Judith Hunt.

Judith Hunt handles Can. Ch. Windanna's Molly Melody (Am-Can. Ch. Braemar Oakmead Magnum Force x Windanna's Pallas Athena CD) to Best Puppy in Breed at the Canadian national specialty in 1988.

BPISS Ch. Windanna's Molly Melody (Am-Can. Ch. Braemar Oakmead Magnum Force x Windanna's Pallas Athena CD), a group-placing, Award of Merit bitch who produced eight champions from two litters. Windanna believes in breeding its bitches to the best possible stud dogs who are compatible with their lines and only using breeding stock which has been certified clear for hip, eye and blood problems. Windanna received the Canadian Kennel Club's Top Labrador Retriever Breeder Award in 1991. The Hunts are founding members and past executives of the Labrador Retriever Club of Canada as well as members of the Labrador Owners Club, the Westwind Sporting Dog Club, the Alberta Kennel Club, the Labrador Retriever Club, Inc., the Labrador Retriever Club (U.K.) and the Labrador Retriever Club of Scotland. The Hunts have recently begun to enjoy careers as judges, and Judy had the honor of judging the LRC of British Columbia's first regional specialty.

Above: Can. Ch. Windanna's Snow Queen CD is one of the foundation bitches at Windanna, owned by the Hunts. *Below:* Can. Ch. Windanna's Betsy Paramore in the ribbons at the 1986 American national specialty, handled by Judith Hunt.

Windanna Great Orion in the great outdoors. Orion is by Am-Can. Ch. Finchingfield Ivan of Oaklea x Can. Ch. Windanna's Betsy Paramore. Orion is six months old and a working partridge and water retriever.

Above: *A five-week-old brood from Windanna—in every color of the Labrador rainbow! These puppies by Am-Can. Ch. Barbury Stuff'd Shirt Am-Can. CD, TT, WC x Windanna's Wiliston Polly Toodle.*
Below: *At three years old, Windanna Klondike Buck (Am-Can. Ch. Rainell's Dynasty x Can. Ch. Windanna's Molly Melody) working one snowy Canadian day.*

Above: Windanna's Northern Light at eight weeks old, sired by Can. Ch. Windanna's Opus Won out of Windanna's Tiger Lily. **Below:** Ch. Windanna's Opus Won (Am-Can. Ch. Braemar Oakmead Magnum Force x Windanna's Pallas Athena CD). Breeders, Charles and Judith Hunt.

Above: *Can. WR-OTCh. Windanna's Wild Hollyhock WC (Ch. Salin's Cajun's Casanova WC x Windanna's Pallas Athena CD).* **Below:** *The three-year-old Windanna's Wayward Winchester.*

Above: Can. Ch. Wimberway's Leymuf Lively CD, WC into the pool retriever-style. Owner, Sandy Briggs. **Below:** Judy Hunt gaiting Can. Ch. Windanna's Betsy Paramore on the weekend she gained her championship: three five-point majors and a best puppy in show to boot!

Above: Can. WR-OTCh. Windanna's Wild Hollyhock WC doing what comes naturally. **Below Left:** Can. Ch. Windanna's Pippin O Bucklebury CD, WC with some of her trophies, including the prestigious Neville award. **Below Right:** Windanna's Wayward Winchester at three months with Jesse Best and her first duck retrieved out of water.

Two handsome black Labrador Retrievers photographed by Robert Smith..

Genetic Diseases of the Labrador Retriever

by Frances O. Smith, DVM, PhD
Diplomate, American College of Theriogenology

MUSCULAR DISEASES

Labrador Retriever Myopathy (Type II myopathy)

Type II myopathy is a simple autosomal recessively inherited disease of Labrador Retrievers. Affected animals show stiff gait and bunny-hopping. Muscle atrophy (especially in the rear) is common. Signs are not progressive but are worsened by cold and exercise.

Sire and dam of affected animals are obligate carriers. Siblings of affected animals have a 67% chance of being carriers of the disease. Affected animals may be suitable as pets but are unsuitable for performance events. To eliminate the disease, affected and known carriers should not be bred.

Diagnosis of the disease is muscle biopsy (Type II fibers are usually deficient) and electromyography. Muscle enzyme levels may also be affected.

NERVOUS SYSTEM

Epilepsy

Epilepsy is a recurrent seizure disorder associated with non-progressive brain disease. Idiopathic epilepsy (cause unknown, probably heritable) is a seizure disorder occurring most commonly in purebred dogs from six months of age to three years of age (rarely to five years) without underlying metabolic, toxic or systemic causes. The fundamental event in a seizure is a disturbance in the excitability of the central nervous system that results in a focus of excessive neuronal discharge.

Epilepsy is a recognized hereditary problem in the Labrador Retriever. Affected animals should not be bred. Breedings producing seizures should not be repeated. Siblings of affected animals are at higher risk of producing seizures than are siblings of normal animals. Ovariohysterectomy of intact females may help in seizure control.

Narcolepsy and Cataplexy

Narcolepsy and cataplexy are rare nervous-system diseases of the Labrador Retriever. Narcolepsy is excessive daytime sleep sometimes triggered by activity. Cataplexy is acute hypolonia associated with narcolepsy. The result of the syndrome is an altered sleep-wake cycle. The syndrome is inherited as a simple autosomal recessive.

EYE DISEASES

Progressive Retinal Atrophy

Labrador Retrievers have an excessive risk of developing this disease. Preston estimates the number of carriers as 1% of the population. In 1952 the disease was first reported in the United States in a dog imported from England. That dog was blind at five years of age. Prior to his death the dog was widely used at stud.

Early signs of PRA include nightblindness and dilated pupils. Ophthamologic signs are tapetal hyperreflectivity, vascular attenuation and optic disbatrophy. An electrorinogram may be abnormal prior to signs visible to the ophthamologic or clinical (visual) changes.

The disease is very similar to PRA in the Miniature Poodle and occurs at the same gene locus and is thus a progressive rod cone degeneration. PRA is inherited as a simple autosomal recessive. Affected dogs should be removed from the breeding population. Parents of an affected dog are obligate carriers and should not be bred. Offspring of affected dogs are at least obligate carriers and should not be bred. Unaffected siblings of affected dogs have a 67% chance of being carriers. Dogs affected with PRA will totally lose vision. Some adapt well to blindness and may remain suitable as pets.

In 1991, 0.84% of examined and CERF reported Labradors were diagnosed as either having generalized retinal atrophy or suspicious retinal atrophy.

Because this is a late onset disease in the Labrador, it would be very desirable to have a test that detects the disease in the young animal. Current progress in DNA fingerprinting is very encouraging and in the future may serve as a method for identification of affected and carrier dogs.

Reference: Schelle, G.B.; Progressive retinal atrophy in a dog. JAVMA 121:177-178, 1952

Cataracts

Posterior polar cataracts in the Labrador Retriever usually appear as bilateral posterior subcapsular triangular or posterior polar subcapsular inverted V-shaped cataracts first seen at six to 18 months of age. The cataracts progress slowly seldom causing much adverse effect on vision. Affected dogs are usually functional as pets and hunting dogs. Affected dogs should not be bred. The mode of inheritance is a simple dominant with incomplete penetrance.

Retinal Dysplasia

Complete retinal dysplasia is congenitally abnormal development of the retina. Affected animals are blind at an early age. The disease is inherited as a simple autosomal recessive.

Retinal and Vitreal Dysplasia with Skeletal Abnormalities

Carrig, Nelson and MacMillan have identified a genetic condition in the Labrador with association between eye and skeletal defects. There are three eye conditions: normal eyes, multifocal retinal dysplasia and total retinal dysplasia; and two skeletal conditions: abnormal and normal.

Visual difficulties occur at eight weeks and both eye and skeletal defects are more apparent as puppies grow. The skeletal defects include shortened forelimbs with elbows in and a bowing of the carpus. Hind limbs are very straight, and tibial growth may be regarded. These animals have abnormal elbows and hips. Severely affected dogs have larger than normal eyes.

In multifocal retinal dysplasia, the abnormal portion or portions of the retina are usually located above the optic disc. Nelson and MacMillan have found this type of multifocal retinal dysplasia in about 20% of field-trial Labs. Vision may or may not be affected. In some dogs small folds disappear with age.

The skeletal and eye defects appear to be inherited together. The skeletal lesion segments as a recessive trait and the eye lesion acts as an incomplete dominant. Because dogs with severe eye abnormalities and multiple skeletal defects can be produced by breeding mildly affected individuals, even mildly affected dogs should not be bred. Dogs with skeletal defects and severe eye involvement should be culled.

Author's Note: Other eye problems occur less commonly in the Labrador Retriever and can be detected when present at ophthamologic examination.

Ref: Rubin, L.F., *Inherited Eye Diseases in Purebred Dogs*, pp 182-192 Baltimore, Williams and Williams 1989.

SKELETAL SYSTEM

Canine Hip Dysplasia

The most commonly reported genetic disease of the Labrador Retriever is canine hip dysplasia. CHD is a developmental hereditary disease involving the rear limbs of a dog resulting from the failure of the head of the femur to fit tightly into the acetabulum (a ball and socket-like arrangement). Lameness, degenerative joint disease, arthritis and abnormal movement often result from the defect. The lameness may be intermittent or constant and tends to worsen with age. Young dogs with dysplasia commonly suffer acute lameness between six and 12 months. Clinical signs may resolve only to resurface in middle to older years.

The only definitive diagnosis of hip dysplasia is radiographic evaluation of the pelvis. Ideally, radiographs will be combined with palpation. The radiograph must have good pelvic definition with the pelvis not tilted, femurs must be extended and parallel.

Canine hip dysplasia is the genetic result of the action of an undetermined number of genes (a polygenetic trait). The incidence of hip dysplasia can be decreased by breeding normal to normal.

Even better results can be obtained by breeding normal to normal with normal grandparents and normal siblings. Because the radiograph is a phenotypic model of a genotypical trait, normal animals (based on radiographs and palpation) can produce abnormal animals. The reverse is also true.

As of December 1992, 52,828 Labradors have been certified as normal. During the period from January 1974 through December 1992, the Labrador has shown a significant increase in the percentage of excellent hips and a significant decrease in the percentage of dysplastic individuals. Recognize that there is selection bias because many animals are never radiographed and many radiographs from dysplastic dogs are never submitted for evaluation. Based on the cream of the crop, progress is very encouraging. Of the 52,828 animals evaluated, 12.6% of those evaluated received excellent hip ratings and 14.2% received a rating of dysplastic.

Hip dysplasia can be influenced to some extent by such factors as diet, exercise and possibly even by litter size. Other polygenetic traits are also affected by such environmental factors. This knowledge should not be used as an excuse to breed an obese animal who demonstrates radiographic evidence of canine hip dysplasia.

Elbow Dysplasia

Elbow dysplasia is a developmental disease manifested as degenerative joint disease of the elbow. Elbow dysplasia has been recognized as a cause of forelimb lameness in the Labrador. The most common cause of elbow dysplasia is ununited radial coronoid process of the ulna although ununited anconeal process can also be identified. Based on current research, elbow dysplasia is inherited as a polygenetic trait. Affected animals should not be bred.

Diagnosis is by radiographs of the elbow, lateral and AP views. Many dogs with elbow dysplasia exhibit foreleg lameness at seven to 12 months of age. Some dogs are totally asymptomatic. As of 1992, 727 Labradors were found to have elbow dysplasia.

Osteochondritis Dissecans or OCD

OCD is a cartilage disease of dogs due to a disturbance of indochondial ossification. The end result is that cartilage gets thicker than normal and under situations of pressure or tension develop small fissures. The fissures may reach the surface of the cartilage resulting in the condition called osteochondritis dissecans.

OCD can occur in the shoulder, elbow, hock and stifle joint. The shoulder joint is most commonly affected in rapidly growing dogs. Males are more often affected than females.

Rapid growth, nutrition (especially excessive) and trauma all contribute to the syndrome. There is no consensus as to the heritability of the disorder.

Bilateral Carpal Subluxation

This disease causes extreme bending of the carpus. Rarely seen, it is inherited as an x-linked recessive.

Craniomandibular Osteopathy

Craniomandibular osteopathy is a bone disorder involving formation of excessive dense bone on the mandible or lower jaw. Recessive inheritance has been proven in the terrier breeds studied. Mode of inheritance in the Labrador is likely the same; incidence of occurrence is very low.

BLOOD DISORDERS

von Willebrands Disease

VWD is an inherited bleeding disorder that can result in unexpected hemorrhage following stress, trauma or surgery. The disease is inherited as a dominant with incomplete penetrance. Measurements of certain factors in blood can be used to assess whether a dog is normal or abnormal with respect to canine VWD. VWD occurs in the Labrador Retriever. Normal score is 70–180% borderline is 50–69% and abnormal is 0–49%.

Hemophilia A

Hemophilia A (Factor VIII) deficiency is a sex-linked recessive trait causing bleeding. The disease is carried by females; males are affected. The hallmark of the disease is unusual bleeding in male puppies. The disease can be detected in both affected and carrier animals by blood testing. Affected and carrier animals should not be bred.

GENETIC DISEASE CONTROL ORGANIZATIONS

Orthopedic Foundation for Animals (OFA)

The Orthopedic Foundation for Animals was established in the 1960s under the influence of John Olin. Located in Columbus, Missouri, the organization functions as a nonprofit organization dedicated to control of genetic orthopedic disease in animals. The OFA certifies dogs 24 months of age or older as normal with respect to hip dysplasia or elbow dysplasia based on consensus evaluation of normality by three board certified radiologists. Normal hips are evaluated as excellent, good and fair compared to others of the same breed and age and are assigned an OFA number.

Elbows are evaluated as normal and assigned a number or graded I, II, III and not assigned a number.

The OFA has a screening service for dogs under two years of age and can be valuable to the breeder. Based on data on preliminary evaluation of 425 Labradors, a high percentage of Labradors with normal evaluations received an OFA number (hips) at age two years. Of 425 preliminaries 90.35% (384) OFA certified at age two. Fourteen animals with abnormal preliminaries later OFA'd (3.3%). Twenty-seven animals with normal preliminaries failed to OFA at a later date.

Orthopedic Foundation for Animals, Inc.
2500 Nifong Blvd.
Columbia, MO 65201
314-442-0418

INSTITUTE FOR GENETIC DISEASE CONTROL (GDC)

The Wind-Morgan Program initiated in 1990 hopes to provide a mechanism for orthopedic improvement of the Labrador Retriever. This organization certifies Labradors free of elbow dysplasia, shoulder OCD and hock OCD. In animals 12 months of age or older, a Wind-Morgan number is assigned if the radiographs demonstrate that the dog is normal.

Wind-Morgan
c/o Dr. Autumn Davidson
Small Animal Clinic
University of California
Dairs, CA 95616

CANINE EYE REGISTRY SERVICE OF CERF

The files of CERF are located within the Veterinary Medical Data Base at Purdue University. The organization tabulates data on inherited eye diseases in purebred dogs and assigns CERF numbers to normal dogs. A CERF number is issued yearly as many ocular diseases occur in mid to later life. Thus a dog should be re-CERF-ed throughout its breeding life. A CERF number is assigned based on a complete ophthalmic examination by a board certified veterinary ophthamologist.

CERF
South Campes Court Bldg. A
Purdue University
West Lafayette, IN 47907

VETERINARY HEMATOLOGY LABORATORY

This lab runs assays for hereditary and non-hereditary bleeding disorders.

Veterinary Hematology Laboratory
New York State Department of Health
Wadsworth Center for Laboratories
Albany, NY 12201
518-869-4507

Veterinary Care of the Labrador Retriever

by Ann L. Huntington, DVM

YOU AND YOUR VETERINARIAN

Your veterinarian can be a source of help and information vital to the health and longevity of your Labrador. The following information, which may help guide you through the complexity of veterinary care, is no substitute for a sound relationship with a veterinarian. Space doesn't allow an encyclopedia of medical conditions, so only those commonly seen in Labradors are discussed.

SELECTING YOUR VET

Most veterinarians are well-trained, caring professionals. How do you pick the veterinary practice for your dog? Ask friends, neighbors and breeders for recommendations. You might ask a veterinarian in a nearby community whom he or she would recommend in your town. Once you have narrowed it down, visit the practice and chat with the staff. Determine if the hours, ambience and fees are compatible with your needs. If so, make an appointment to have your pet examined.

During examination you should ask the veterinarian about hospital policies, interest in purebred (show or performance) dogs, what type of medical work is done at that facility and what is referred to other practices, medical centers or teaching hospitals and the availability of emergency coverage. Did you think your dog was given a thorough examination and was it handled with kindness and patience? If the answers and the "feel" of the practice are not right for you, consider checking out another practice.

It is important to establish a rapport with a veterinarian *before* you need emergency services. Do this by maintaining regular contact for routine services and examinations.

ROUTINE MAINTENANCE AT HOME

Many problems can be avoided or detected early by consistent care at home. Feeding adequate (not excessive!) amounts of good-quality food is vital. Fresh water should be readily available. The importance of regular exercise cannot be over-emphasized.

Even though the Labrador Retriever's coat is one of the easier coats to maintain, it should be brushed or combed at least twice a week. This is not just to remove dead hairs and stimulate the skin but, more importantly, the time to go over your dog routinely and systematically, looking for possible health problems. Run through the following "Home Health Checklist" each time you groom your Labrador. While the list may seem long, with practice you will be able to do a complete home health exam in under two minutes. And you may detect problems in their first stages that, if neglected, could cost your dog unnecessary discomfort or perhaps its life!

A sometimes overlooked but vital aspect of home care for your Labrador is training and socialization. The number one cause of euthanasia (putting to sleep) of dogs in the United States is not cancer, not arthritis, not old age, not any a disease at all. It is behavior problems. Labradors love to be with people and are eager to please. But they must know the rules, and they must be socialized. Spend as much time with your dog as possible. Take advantage of puppy kindergarten classes, obedience classes and training groups. Your veterinarian can help you find these resources. Any time that you invest in training and socializing your puppy during his first year of life will be rewarded you with a lifetime of dividends.

VETERINARY MAINTENANCE

If your home health exam reveals a problem by all means have your veterinarian investigate it further. But what if your Labrador is healthy? It is still important to have your dog be given a thorough physical examination every year. For most, this is best done at the time of annual vaccination and parasite checks. This examination could reveal the early onset of disorders that would be missed by your home examinations, such as heart murmurs or changes in the size or shape of abdominal organs.

All dogs should be vaccinated yearly for canine distemper, infectious canine hepatitis, parainfluenza and parvovirus. These are usually given as a single injection in a combined vaccine. This combination vaccine may also provide important protection against leptospirosis and/or coronavirus.

Rabies vaccines are vital, and should be kept up to date according to the type of vaccine given and local law. You will be issued a tag and certificate of rabies vaccination. Keep these in a safe place as you will need them for licensing in many areas, and as proof of vaccination when traveling.

Other vaccinations are available that provide protection against Lyme disease and infectious tracheobronchitis (kennel cough). Ask your veterinarian about risk factors for these diseases in your area, and areas you travel through, to determine if your Labrador needs that protection.

In addition to a thorough physical examination and boosters on needed vaccinations, your dog's yearly routine should include a blood test for heartworms and testing a sample of feces for parasites.

As your Labrador Retriever gets older, many veterinarians advise more extensive testing of urine and blood to screen for diseases that commonly accompany the aging process.

HOME HEALTH CHECKLIST

This list involves two types of check-ups: a home physical examination and careful observation of your pet's behavior and actions.

A home physical examination does not have to be done in a formal way by placing your Labrador on a table. On the contrary, the best thing is not to make a big deal of it. Instead, when giving your dog his grooming and petting, nonchalantly do some explorations. He won't even realize what you're really up to.

Examination:

1. The Eyes. They can be checked unobtrusively as you're giving your dog some affection. Make sure the eyes are clear and bright and have no discharge. The "whites of the eyes" should not be reddened or discolored.
2. The Mouth. Check for abnormal coloration of the gums. Sores, reddened gums or gums where the pink area are very pale could indicate a problem. Are the teeth free from tartar and growing

normally? Is the breath foul-smelling?
3. The Ears. Make certain they're clean, have no abnormal swellings, and are odor-free.
4. The Nose. An easy one to check. Make sure there is no discharge and no raw areas.
5. The Feet. Are the nails properly trimmed? Check for redness between the toes and for normal pads. A light squeeze of each foot could reveal tenderness and a problem.
6. The Coat. Use a flea comb to check for fleas, ticks, lice or mites. The coat should be glossy. The skin should be free of flakes or sores as well as odors.
7. The Genitals. There should be no protrusion or drainage from the anal or genital areas.
8. The Body. Run your hand over the entire body to see if there are any lumps or tender spots.

Observations:

9. The Appetite. Eating more or less than usual can indicate a problem. Water consumption should also be noted. Increased water consumption is an early symptom of several diseases.
10. The Feces. Check your dog's stool to make certain that it's the normal color and consistency, and that there is no blood, mucus or tapeworm segments. Watch for changes in frequency and for difficulty in passing feces.
11. The Urine. Try to see the color of the urine to make certain there is no blood present and it is not abnormally dark. Does he strain

to pass urine, empty his bladder more frequently or have accidents in the house?
12. The Gait. Is your dog walking and running normally, neither holding back nor limping?
13. The Demeanor. Watch for changes in alertness and attitude. Sleeping more, acting restless, tiring easily or getting uncharacteristically grouchy could indicate a problem.

COMMON INFECTIOUS DISEASES

These are the diseases that are controlled by the most common vaccines. By buying your puppy from a conscientious breeder, maintaining a clean premises, avoiding high-risk situations and keeping vaccinations current, you can limit the risk of these conditions.

Canine Distemper

This viral scourge most cruelly attacks the young or infirm. Symptoms begin with pneumonia, fever, and discharge from the eyes and nose. They often end with tremors, seizures and death. While some dogs survive with aggressive medical treatment, most do not. Vaccines are highly effective.

Canine Parvovirus and Coronavirus

These two distinct viruses cause severe bloody diarrhea in infected dogs. Parvo is the more deadly, while dogs with corona often will recover on their own unless other factors (parasites, for example) are present. Puppies six weeks and older are at highest risk, and intensive care is often needed to pull them through. The parvovirus is very hardy and can often survive in the environment for several months or longer. For this reason it is unwise to take puppies anywhere until they have received their first series of immunizations.

Leptospirosis

This bacterial disease is picked up by contact with urine from infected dogs. The severity ranges from mild to extremely debilitating or even fatal. Symptoms include fever, nasal discharge, vomiting, muscle soreness, and a yellow discoloration most easily seen in the eyes, gums and skin. Humans are also susceptible to leptospirosis, so careful handling of infected dogs is vital.

Infectious Canine Hepatitis

A viral disease that especially attacks puppies, infectious canine hepatitis is not related to the hepatitis that can infect human beings. Symptoms include fever, drowsiness and loss of appetite, but in many cases of unprotected puppies, there is death without recognizable warning signs. Risk of this disease striking a litter of young puppies is one compelling reason to make certain brood bitches have current vaccinations prior to breeding.

Kennel Cough

Also called infectious canine tracheobronchitis, this is a single disease caused by a complex of organisms, both viral and bacterial. In this regard it is similar to the common cold of humans. The infection irritates the windpipe so severely that the dog develops a loud, persistent deep cough. The cough is so bad that many owners, when they first hear their dog coughing with kennel cough, feel sure that something must be caught in his throat. Like a cold, most cases of kennel cough must "run their course," lasting seven to ten days. Symptomatic treatment with cough syrups or cough suppressants, coupled with antibiotics in severe cases, will ease recovery. This disease is airborne, so the risk is higher wherever dogs congregate. If your dog will be boarded, groomed professionally, attending puppy or obedience classes or dog shows, a vaccine specific for this disease is recommended.

Lyme Disease

This tick-borne bacterial disease is spreading rapidly over the world. It affects a wide variety of animals, including humans. The most common symptoms in the dog are fever, malaise, and severe lameness. In most cases, prompt treatment with antibiotics will cure Lyme disease. Prevention is best attained by avoiding ticks. In areas that are at risk for Lyme disease, a vaccine is beneficial. Ask your veterinarian for his recommendation in your locale.

Rabies

The saliva of rabid animals is the only source of this always fatal disease. Unfortunately wild animals, especially foxes, skunks, raccoons and bats, are often infected. A single bite is all it takes. All dogs should be vaccinated against rabies, both to protect them and to protect the humans with whom they live.

DIGESTIVE SYSTEM

The digestive system begins with the mouth and progresses through the esophagus, stomach, intestines and colon, ending at the anus. Since it is responsible for processing food, it makes sense that disorders of this system are reflected in food-related symptoms: difficulty eating, vomiting, diarrhea, or weight loss.

Dental Disorders

Good digestion begins with the ability to chew food well. While an underbite or an overbite may be an undesirable trait in Labrador Retrievers, be assured that these conditions will not affect your dog's ability to eat. Poor dental health, however, can cause serious problems. Plaque and tartar build-up leads to gingivitis and periodontal disease, painful conditions that cause difficulty eating, bad breath, tooth loss, and increased risk of age-related disorders such as heart and kidney failure. If your dog has these symptoms, your veterinarian may recommend having your dog's teeth scaled, polished and sealed. To prevent tartar build-up and gingivitis, feed dry food, provide acceptable chew toys, and consider brushing his teeth. Excellent brushes and toothpastes developed specifically for dogs are available from most veterinarians.

Vomiting and Diarrhea

It is likely that any dog owner will have to deal with vomiting or diarrhea at some time during the pet's life. Minor causes include eating too fast, minor viruses, motion sickness, anxiety or eating non-food items such as twigs, tree bark, rocks or bits of cloth. Most cases are not serious and can be treated symptomatically. Withhold food for 12 to 24 hours and administer an antidiarrheal at a dose of one tablespoonful per 20 pounds of weight. For the next 48 hours, offer only a very bland diet. Boiled rice with a little chicken or beef cooked in works well, as does a prescription-diet formula. If this does not control the vomiting or diarrhea, or if your dog is acting sluggish or is in pain, consult your veterinarian.

Intestinal Parasites

Many parasites reside in the intestinal tract of dogs. Roundworms are the most common worm in young puppies, and are often transmitted prenatally from mother to offspring. These worms are 3 to 6 inches long, reside in the first portions of the small intestine, and are often found mixed with vomited material in puppies. Symptoms are vomiting, unthriftiness and a pot-belly.

Hookworms are another small intestinal parasite. Less than an inch long, these little vampires attach to the lining of the intestine and live off blood. Severe infestation can lead to diarrhea, weakness from anemia, and even death.

Whipworms live in the lower portion of the small intestine and in the cecum and colon. They rarely affect young puppies, but can be a significant cause of weight loss and chronic diarrhea in older dogs.

Tapeworms are small intestinal parasites with an unusual life cycle. They are transmitted only through an intermediate host, most commonly the flea or small rodents. In order for your dog to develop tapeworms, he must swallow the intermediate host, releasing the tapeworm. As it develops in the intestine, the tapeworm begins to shed small segments that pass down through the colon and rectum and emerge, still slowly wiggling, from the anus. Within a few minutes the segments dry out, looking like small grains of rice stuck to hairs around the anus, or settling on your dog's bedding. The most common symptom of tapeworm infection is licking at the anal region or "scooting" the fanny along the ground.

Coccidia and Giardia are two protozoal parasites that commonly cause diarrhea in puppies and dogs. All the parasites described above should be treated by, or in consultation with, your veterinarian. Have parasite checks run on your dog's feces at least once a year, and whenever you see vomiting or diarrhea. Some wormers are effective against more that one type of worm, others are more specific. Prevention is very important. Some of the medicines developed to prevent heartworms will also effectively prevent some types of intestinal parasites. Pick up your dog's stools, and avoid areas that may be highly contaminated by stools of other dogs.

Bloat

Not all digestive-system diseases are characterized by vomiting and diarrhea. One of the most deadly actually involves the sudden inability to vomit! Gastric dilatation and volvulus (GDV), commonly called bloat, is a disorder in which the stomach rapidly swells and flips over within the abdomen. This usually occurs during the first one to two hours after eating or drinking a large amount. The effect of the stomach twist is blockage of the exit routes from the stomach. The food, fluid and gas rapidly expand, causing damage to the stomach wall, choking off the major blood supply to the spleen, shock and ultimately death. Untreated, bloat is usually fatal within four to six hours. Only immediate veterinary intervention can save a dog with GDV. If you find your Labrador retching but producing nothing, restless, anxious and uncomfortable, and with an abdomen that is visibly enlarging before your eyes, call your veterinarian immediately. Minutes count in trying to rescue your dog from this terrible disorder. To help prevent GDV, feed more than one meal per day, have fresh water available at all times so your dog doesn't suddenly overindulge, and limit

exercise for two hours after each meal.

Stomach or Intestinal Foreign Bodies

All puppies and dogs explore their world with their mouths. And Labradors seem to especially relish chewing on things! Unfortunately, many times these items don't stop at the mouth, but wind up being swallowed. Rocks, clothing, hardware, leashes, toys, bones, parts of furniture or rugs—the list of things Labradors will swallow is endless. If you know your dog has swallowed something unusual, call your veterinarian and alert him or her to the possible problem. Many things will either be vomited or passed in the feces without any injury to the dog. Small items can be helped through the bowel by temporarily increasing the amount of fiber in the diet. Whole wheat bread, bran cereal or fiber-type laxatives can be mixed in the food. Larger items may require surgical removal. The dog who swallows something larger than a walnut, loses its appetite or has persistent vomiting must be evaluated by a veterinarian. Prevention is the key. Puppy-proof your home and discourage chewing anything but a few selected toys.

Obesity and Pancreatitis

What is the number-one nutritional disorder of Labrador Retrievers? Hands down, the winner is obesity. The majority of Labradors have been or are overweight. Our

357

breed loves to eat! But that does not mean that obesity is correct or healthful. Overweight puppies are far more likely to have developmental bone and joint disorders. Overweight adults develop more arthritis, cruciate ligament rupture, diabetes and heart disease than normal-weight dogs. They tire more easily and are more prone to heatstroke. Pancreatitis, a painful, sometimes fatal cause of acute illness and vomiting, occurs largely in overweight dogs. How do you know if your dog is obese? Try to feel his ribs about halfway down his sides. While they shouldn't be visibly sticking out, you should be able to easily count them with your fingers through a thin layer of padding. If the ribs have disappeared beneath a blanket of fat, it's diet time!

There are conditions, such as hypothyroidism, that can contribute to obesity. If you believe that your dog's weight problem could be due to more than simple overeating, ask your veterinarian to investigate further.

It is impossible to say exactly how much to feed a Labrador, because metabolic rates, exercise levels, types of foods and environmental factors all contribute to caloric needs. If your dog is healthy but overweight, weigh him, then cut his intake by one-third and re-weigh him in two months. If he is still overweight, cut his intake by another one-third. I know healthy active Labradors who will gain weight if they are fed more than one and one-third cups of good-quality food per day.

RESPIRATORY SYSTEM

Compared to those purebred dogs in which very short noses are preferred (Bulldogs, Pugs, etc.), our Labradors are in great shape in the respiratory department! There are few respiratory disorders that are seen frequently in Labs. Bronchitis and/or pneumonia may strike dogs of any age, often due to kennel cough or distemper. A vaccination will limit the risk of this. A cough or breathing difficulty that persists more than one or two days, or accompanied by sluggishness or inappetence, should be investigated by your veterinarian.

Laryngeal Paralysis

Some older Labradors develop a very loud, raspy throat noise that is audible whenever the dog is panting. The noise disappears when the mouth is held shut. This is usually due to laryngeal paralysis, an aging change in which the cartilages that guard the opening to the windpipe lose their mobility. Over several weeks or months, this progresses to a point where breathing is difficult, and doing any exercise is impossible. While surgery is possible, prognosis is poor. Because other conditions can resemble laryngeal paralysis, a veterinarian should carefully examine the dog's throat while it is under anesthesia to confirm the diagnosis.

Heatstroke

One major function of the canine respiratory system is to help prevent overheating. Dogs don't have sweat glands covering their bodies as we do to allow evaporation of perspiration to keep cool. Panting cools the body through the evaporation of moisture off the tongue and inside of the mouth. In very hot temperatures, or when the humidity is high, panting will be an inadequate response, and heatstroke will likely follow. The dog's body temperature can quickly climb to 104°, 106° or even higher. Death can follow. It is vital to quickly bathe the dog in cold water or alcohol to bring the temperature back down to the normal 101–102° range. Placing ice packs on the throat can reduce swelling of the airway, and speed recovery. Any sign of weakness, disorientation or sluggishness should be evaluated quickly by a veterinarian. Clearly, prevention is preferred. Never leave dogs confined in unshaded areas or without fresh water. Closed cars, even with the windows cracked open, can become death traps on hot summer days. Never leave your dog in a closed vehicle.

Bee Stings

Most Labradors can easily tolerate an occasional bee sting or insect bite. Some, however, will have a dramatic allergic reaction. This can cause swelling around the face, nose, lips and ears. That reaction is called angioneurotic edema. Mild cases can be treated with ice packs on the swollen areas and oral antihistamines. An adult Labrador can be given an over-the-counter antihistamine containing Benzhydramine in a dosage comparable to an adult human's; always check with your druggist or veterinarian first. The swelling often takes six to ten hours to subside. In more severe cases, the swelling may extend into the throat as well, threatening respiratory collapse. Treatment with cortisone or epinephrine injections may be needed.

CIRCULATORY SYSTEM

The circulatory system includes the heart and blood vessels, and the blood that flows through them. Problems of this system are serious ones, often requiring aggressive veterinary care. The symptoms range from simply tiring more easily than usual, to weakness, cough, collapse, or death.

Heartworms

One of the most common heart diseases in dogs is also the most preventable: heartworm disease. These parasitic worms are several inches long and live in the chambers of the right side of the heart and its neighboring large vessels. They are transmitted from one dog to another by the bite of a mosquito. Undetected and untreated, heartworms will usually kill the canine victim slowly. The first noticeable signs are cough and weight loss, but by the time these symptoms are obvious, the disease is quite advanced. Early detection with a blood test by your veterinarian will increase the chances for successful cure of heartworm disease. But with recent advances, prevention couldn't be simpler. Medicine to prevent heartworms is available as tablets, chewables or liquids that can be given daily or monthly. Many also include ingredients to prevent several types of intestinal worms. Prevention in the form of a yearly injection may be on the horizon. There are very few areas in North America in which the climate totally prevents mosquitoes. Everywhere else, all dogs should be taking heartworm preventative.

Heart Disease

Labradors are blessed with fairly trouble-free hearts. The congenital and inherited heart conditions common in other breeds are rare in the Labrador. But occasionally puppies will be born with birth defects affecting the heart, or older dogs will acquire heart conditions that require veterinary treatment. Diagnosing these conditions requires careful listening with a stethoscope, along with x-ray, electrocardiogram (ECG) and ultrasound studies. To detect these conditions early, all puppies should be examined by a veterinarian prior to being placed in new homes. Adult dogs should have complete physical examinations yearly, or more often if weakness, coughing or fainting is noted. The prognosis and treatment vary.

Anemia

The role of red blood cells is to carry oxygen from the lungs to all the tissues of the body. Anemia is a condition in which there are too few red blood cells. Because the cells are not getting enough oxygen, the dog becomes very weak and usually shows labored breathing. Anemia can be due to blood loss. Hemorrhage can result from a cut, internal bleeding or those miniature blood suckers—fleas and hookworms are common examples. Otherwise, anemia can be due to red-blood-cell destruction, a condition usually associated with immune-system disease. Finally, anemia can be due to faulty production of red blood cells by the bone marrow, associated with some cancers and poisons. An easy-to-detect warning sign of anemia is unusual paleness of the gums. If you note this while going through your regular "Home Health Checklist." Or, if you see the typical symptoms, call and discuss it with your veterinarian. Tests will be done to determine the severity and cause, and treatment instituted.

Leukemias

It is a misconception that leukemia is a single specific disease. Leukemia literally means an abnormally high number of white blood cells in the blood. In reality, there are many types of leukemias, depending on which type of white cell is present, and the characteristics of the abnormal cells. Typical symptoms are fever, sluggishness and weakness, often with enlarged lymph nodes ("swollen glands"). While some types of leukemia are relatively mild, most forms are life-threatening. As yet, the cause of leukemia (like the cause of cancer) is still poorly understood. The diagnosis is based on blood tests, biopsies and bone-marrow studies, and treatment generally involves chemotherapy.

THE SKIN

Did you know that more dog owners seek veterinary care for skin problems than for any other type of ailment? Skin conditions are both very common, and very obvious! Even relatively minor skin conditions can cause a dog to look and smell bad. Worse, even minor problems can make the dog suffer with itching or pain or both. Here are just a few of the most common skin disorders seen in Labradors.

Fleas, Ticks and Mites

Far and away the most common skin disorders of dogs are due to these tiny parasites. They can cause itching, rashes, scabs, patches of hair loss and a bad smell. The theory behind treatment is simple—get rid of those bugs! In truth, it is not always an easy task.

Fleas are a nearly ubiquitous parasite. They seem to have found a niche in almost every environment. The adults live, feed, mate, and lay eggs on the dog. They produce large amounts of tiny black speck-like feces ("flea dirt") that help confirm an infestation. Recent studies show that adult fleas very rarely leave the animal which they have selected as host. Rather they move from place to place over the dog, sucking tiny blood meals several times a day. Their eggs are shiny white specks about the size of the period at the end of this sentence. Each egg rolls and drops off the dog, landing on the ground, carpet, upholstery or floor. A larva hatches out, munches on fallen flea dirt and dust, then spins a cocoon, entering the pupal stage. Fleas emerge from the cocoons, and leap onto the next warm body that comes near. This entire cycle can take from several days to several months, depending on temperature and humidity.

Dogs infested with fleas will scratch and bite at themselves frequently, usually concentrating on the armpits, abdomen, and area just above and around the base of the tail. In severe cases, or in dogs that are allergic to flea bites, there can be large sores and areas of hair loss.

Treatment involves removing the fleas from both the pet and the environment. Treating your dog alone will not solve the problem! There are literally hundreds of flea-control products and methods available, each with advantages and disadvantages. Currently, control of fleas in the home is best achieved by a combination of foggers, sprays and diligent vacuuming, or by professional application of a non-toxic mineral powder marketed commercially. Flea control on your dog can involve sprays, collars, foams, powders, dips, topical liquids, tablets, repellent mists, etc.! Your veterinarian is best able to address the needs of your own pet, and is a good source of advice on which products to use.

Ticks rarely cause the extreme rash and itch wrought by fleas. They wreak their havoc in other ways, most seriously by transmitting Lyme disease and Rocky Mountain Spotted Fever. Hopping on board when your dog walks through grass or brush, ticks find a choice site (around the ears is a favorite), take a big bite, and don't let go. They stay attached, gradually sucking enough blood to fully engorge, then eventually drop off. To remove a tick attached to your dog, grasp it firmly close to the skin with a pair of tweezers, and pull slowly straight up without any rocking or twisting motion. Then swab the site with some alcohol or antiseptic. Large numbers can be dealt with by using sprays or dips. Repellent sprays and collars and topical liquids will provide some protection against tick bites, but prevention is best achieved by avoiding tick-infested areas whenever possible.

Mites are microscopic parasites that live within the skin itself, or just on its surface. There are three common types:

Demodex mites are not itchy, cause patches of baldness and are most common in immature dogs. They are not contagious to other animals or to people. Diagnosis is made by scraping the surface of the skin and looking at the scraped-off material under the microscope. The majority of cases are localized, that is limited to a bald patch or two on the head or legs, which can be treated with a topical cream. Generalized demodex, in which the affected regions begin to cover larger and larger areas, is much more serious and difficult to treat. Frequent drenching with a powerful pesticidal dip is necessary. Dermatologists have confirmed that generalized demodectic mange is due to an immune deficiency, and strongly advise against breeding these dogs, even after successful treatment.

Sarcoptic mange, or canine scabies, is an intensely itchy mite disorder. Dogs literally scratch themselves raw, concentrating most on their face, ears, neck and elbows. This type of mange is highly contagious, both to other dogs and to humans. Diagnosis is based on finding the mite on skin scrapings. Unfortunately, this mite is more elusive than the demodex mite, and may require many scrapings. For that reason, many dermatologists now recommend that if you suspect sarcoptic mange, go ahead and treat for it. A good response to treatment is considered a conclusive diagnosis. Treatment involves either a series of parasiticide dips or oral administration of a fairly high dose of ivermectin (the active ingredient in some monthly heartworm preventatives). In most cases it is advisable to treat all animals in the household.

The third type of mange is Cheyletiella, a commonly missed diagnosis. A common mite among puppies, Cheyletiella is signaled primarily by an intense itch and very flaky skin. The pups appear to be covered with dandruff. But examination of the flakes under a microscope will reveal that many of them are actual mites. This type of mange can also spread to other animals in the family and to people. Fortunately, these mites, because they are not buried in the skin, are very sensitive to treatment. Frequent bathing in a simple flea shampoo will usually eliminate the mites.

Tumors and Cysts

Throughout their lives, dogs are subject to developing many lumps and bumps on or just under the skin. The vast majority of these are harmless and require no treatment. Among these are a variety of warts, sebaceous cysts, fluid-filled cysts, callouses, lipomas and harmless skin growths. Once accurately diagnosed, unless they grow rapidly, become raw on the surface, or cause the dog to lick or scratch at them, just leave them alone. They can always be removed later if a problem develops. There are other surface growths that are not so benign, however. Mast-cell tumors, some types of melanomas and mammary growths fall into this category. Because it is difficult for the inexperienced eye to tell just from casual inspection which lump is insignificant and which is serious, it is best to have any suspicious changes evaluated by your veterinarian.

Allergies

Next to parasites, allergies are the most common cause of itching in Labradors. That's a simple statement, but tracking down the source of an allergy is far from easy. Allergies can be caused by pollens, fungi, dander, fleas, components of foods, contact substances such as wool or cleaning products...the list is nearly endless. Prime sites for allergic itch and rash include the inner thighs, abdomen, feet, face, fanny and lower back. Ear infections can be triggered by allergies in some cases. The itch and rash can be treated or soothed by special shampoos or rinses, antihistamines or even corticosteroids, given as an injection or in tablet form. Often secondary bacterial infections may set in, making antibiotics vital to assuring relief.

Whenever possible the underlying allergenic substance should be determined. This may involve intradermal skin testing, blood tests for special allergy antibodies, strict elimination diets or patch tests. If your pet is prone to allergies, consult with your veterinarian or a veterinary dermatologist to try to develop a means of long-term control.

There is some evidence that a tendency toward allergies could be inherited, so animals with severe allergies should be used for breeding only with great caution.

Non-itchy Skin Diseases

Certain diseases cause an unhealthy, unthrifty, even smelly coat without causing any itching. Endocrine diseases (hypothyroidism, Cushings disease, diabetes mellitus) also may be counted among these. Seborrhea is a condition in which the normal development of cells on the skin's surface is altered, producing extra crusting and flaking, often with a greasy or waxy texture and a strong odor. While treatment with some nutritional supplements and medicated shampoos will help alleviate seborrhea, the relief is usually only temporary. Therefore it is wise to have your veterinarian search diligently for any possible underlying cause.

Diseases of the Anal Area

If your Labrador sits and then scoots his bottom along the ground, check out the following common causes:

1. Tapeworms. These parasites release rice-sized segments that wriggle from the anus onto the surrounding tissue, then dry up and either drop off or stick to a few hairs. Watch for the tell-tale segments, and bring one or two to your veterinarian for identification and medication.

2. Anal sac problems. Dogs have sac-like glands just under the skin on either side of the anus, about the size of lima beans. These sacs become intensely itchy when they fill up with secretions (impaction) or if they become infected or abscessed. In addition to scooting, expect persistent licking or biting when the sacs are infected or abscessed. Simple impaction can usually be treated by manually expressing the contents from the sacs. Most people prefer to have the veterinarian do this, but if you're not at all squeamish, ask for a demonstration. Infections and abscesses require more aggressive treatment, either by infusing antibiotics into the glands or by surgically draining the abscess.

3. Fleas. Yes, this little vampire crops up again as a common cause of anal itch. One of the areas that fleas seem to prefer on dogs is the section just around the base of the tail. Any dog that scoots should be carefully checked for fleas.

In addition to those conditions causing an itchy anal area, this region should be checked regularly for growths and swellings. A number of tumors develop in the skin around the anus. Most are benign, but some are malignant. The incidence of malignancy in perianal tumors is much higher in intact males than in females or neutered males. Perineal hernias, another condition "favoring" intact males, will appear as soft bulges on one or both sides of the anus. The presence of any visible abnormality in this region is cause to have your veterinarian investigate further.

Cuts and Burns

As careful as we try to be with our pets, at some point an accident can happen. Cuts most often occur when dogs are running in a field or wading in a pond or river, and step on a hidden piece of glass or metal. Fights with other animals are another common cause. Small cuts (less than an inch long, not too deep and with little gaping or blood) will generally heal well with thorough daily soap and water cleaning. Larger ones often require stitches. If bleeding is profuse, apply a temporary bandage or direct pressure to the cut area, and transport your dog to a veterinarian or veterinary emergency hospital. It is always wise to phone ahead to alert the staff that you are on your way. Deep cuts, or cuts that we automatically consider contaminated such as bite wounds, will usually require antibiotics to prevent infection. After your Labrador has been discharged, complete with stitches and bandage, the real fun begins. It is *your* responsibility to try to keep bandages intact while the wound heals. If your dog worries the bandage or stitches, ask about anti-chew sprays that can coat the bandage, or about the advisability of borrowing an Elizabethan collar. This is an incredibly awkward plastic device that looks like a lamp shade and sticks out from the dog's neck, thus forming a mechanical barrier between his mouth and his stitches. As clumsy as it is, your dog will get used to it, it's only temporary, and it is much better than needing to resuture!

Burns are less common, most often caused by spilling hot liquids on the dog. Minor burns will be helped by running lots of cold water over the burned area. Don't apply butter or any greasy ointments. Severe burns or burns that cover a larger area should be seen by a veterinarian right away.

THE EAR

Ear Infections

Infections of the ear canal are extremely common in Labrador Retrievers. Dogs have a long ear canal with a distinct bend before ending at the ear drum. Couple that with an ear flap that droops over the opening to the canal, and you can understand why these infections are so common. Air does not circulate well into the depth of the canal, and moisture is often trapped there. Dogs that love to swim complicate the picture by adding excess water, often water that is dirty. The mois-

ture in the warm ear canal sets up a perfect environment for infections to take hold.

The signs of an ear infection are painfully clear. The victim will vigorously shake its head, sometimes almost constantly. The ear will itch, making the dog scratch at the affected side of the head, sometimes causing sores. Quick visual inspection will show a reddened, thickened ear opening, usually with tan, brown or black smelly discharge building up in the canal.

There are three common types of infections: bacterial, yeast (or fungal) and parasitical (ear mites). Allergies may complicate any of these. Examination of the ear with an otoscope, often coupled with looking at some of the debris from the canal under a microscope, is necessary to determine which treatment is best. Thorough cleansing is the first step in treatment, followed by the application of appropriate ointment or drops. Some severe cases require antibiotics or anti-inflammatory medicines systemically as well. In the worst cases of chronic ear infections, surgery may be the only way to provide lasting relief from the misery.

Prevention is important. Watch for early signs by examining your dog's ears regularly. If there has been an infection in the past, the chances for recurrence are great. Applying a few drops of a mildly acidic ear-cleaning solution once or twice a week can greatly reduce chances for another flare up. Ask your veterinarian for a good commercial product, or mix up some simple "swimmer's mix"—equal parts water and white vinegar.

Ear Hematomas

When injured, the ear flap (pinna) of a dog can suddenly swell like a balloon. This is due to a tear in one of the veins in the ear which allows blood to fill the pinna. The condition is painful and unsightly. If left untreated, the swelling first enlarges, then over several weeks causes the ear to shrivel into a wrinkled scar. Surgery is best performed within the first few days. The fluid is carefully drained, and measures taken to prevent recurrence.

Deafness

Fortunately, Labradors are not dogs with a high incidence of early age deafness. However, many "senior citizens" gradually lose their hearing. By age 15, most dogs hear very little. This is a time to show extra consideration to your old friend. Try to approach from the front rather than from the rear. Before patting your sleeping dog, stomp the floor next to him a couple of times to alert him to your presence. Take extra precautions outside, always having him leashed or confined. Many deaf dogs are tragically killed when they hear neither their master's warning shout nor the sound of the oncoming car.

THE EYE

Inherited Eye Disease

There are several inherited eye conditions of the Labrador Retriever, most common among them being disorders of the lens (cataracts), the retina (PRA and retinal dysplasia) and the eyelids (entropion and ectropion). Following are the most frequently seen non-inherited eye problems.

Eyelid Disorders

Many dogs develop cysts or benign tumors along the margins of the eyelids as they get older. When they remain small, they usually require no treatment. However, if the growth reaches a size that it rubs against the cornea, it should be removed. Watch for any increased redness or discharge in the eye with the growth. These are signs that the tumor is starting to cause trouble for the dog, and should be checked out by your veterinarian.

Conjunctivitis

The conjunctiva is the tissue lining the inside of the lids and surrounding the eyeball. It can become red and inflamed from infections, allergies, or irritants, such as dust or sprays. Symptoms are a green or yellow discharge, redness to the inner lids and sclera, sometimes along with mild discomfort. Minor cases can be treated by gently cleansing the eye with a saline solution or weak boric-acid solution three times a day. If the condition persists longer than 48 hours, or if the eye is painful enough to cause any squinting or pawing, a veterinarian must be consulted. While an occasional case of mild conjunctivitis is common, one simple way to reduce the risk of irritant conjunctivitis is to never permit your dog to ride in a car or truck with its head out the window.

Corneal Injuries

A scratch, laceration or ulcer on the cornea is a true medical emergency. Lengthy delay in obtaining veterinary care can lead to loss of vision, or even loss of the eye. Look for excessive tearing, blinking and squinting in the affected eye. The dog may paw at the eye in pain. Treatment may involve eye ointments or solutions, surgery or therapeutic contact lenses. Expect to make several visits to your veterinarian to monitor healing and adjust medications.

Corneal Disorders

The clear surface of the eye is sometimes marked by either white patches or black pigmentation. Scar tissue, response to chronic irritation, and conditions called corneal dystrophy and pannus can appear as changes in the eye surface that do not seem to cause the dog any distress. If the rest of the eye is not red or painful, these conditions are not emergencies. But examination by your veterinarian or veterinary ophthalmologist will help determine the cause, prognosis for the future, and treatment needed, if any.

THE LOCOMOTOR SYSTEM

Lameness

Just as with people, dogs limp for a myriad of reasons. Most lameness is minor and short-lived: a stubbed toe, twisted joint, blistered foot, or pulled muscle are typical examples. If you see your dog favoring one leg, and don't know why, start to investigate!

Spread the toes and look on both upper and lower surfaces for swelling or redness. Squeeze each toe to see if it hurts. Then work your way up the limb, gently squeezing and feeling for heat and swelling. Flex each joint. In this way you should be able to localize the problem. Cuts, punctures, or severe redness or swelling should be evaluated by your veterinarian within a few hours. More subtle problems can wait a day or two. Restrict exercise to quick trips outside and give your adult Lab one buffered aspirin two to three times a day. (Consult your veterinarian for advice on an aspirin dose for your puppy.) If the lameness persists, have your veterinarian check your dog over. If the lameness is relieved, gradually increase exercise levels back to normal over several days.

Diseases of Bones and Joints

There are many bone and joint disorders that are common in Labradors. Some, such as hip dysplasia and elbow dysplasia, are discussed under inherited disorders. The conditions described below are either not considered inherited, or inheritance has not been proven.

PANOSTEITIS. This mysterious condition causes severe pain and lameness in dogs between the ages of five and 15 months. The lameness is intermittent, and usually shifts from one leg to another. A tell-tale sign is extreme tenderness when one of the long bones in the sore leg is gently squeezed in the middle. To accurately determine this, be careful not to bend the leg or handle other joints while you are giving the squeeze. A yelp from gentle pressure to the mid-shaft of the bone is highly suggestive of panosteitis. Treatment is rest, pain relievers such as aspirin, and knowing that time is on your side. Panosteitis generally disappears on its own with time. Severe or confusing cases must be confirmed with radiographs (x-rays) of the limbs.

OSTEODYSTROPHY. Another disease of young growing dogs, osteodystrophy (also called hypertrophic osteodystrophy or HOD) affects the limbs just above the joints. The most common and severe site is above the carpal joint, equivalent to our wrist. The affected area is hot, swollen and very tender to the touch. Many times the dog runs a high fever and won't eat or move around. Radiographs are important in establishing this diagnosis, and potent anti-inflammatory treatment may be needed. The prognosis is usually good, but some cases are so severe they respond poorly or not at all. While the cause of HOD is unknown, most experts feel that over-supplementation of puppies with excess calcium may be a factor.

OSTEOCHONDRITIS DESSICANS (OCD). This is a disease of cartilage within the joint, in which the cushioning cartilage is eroded or broken away, leaving exposed, tender bone. The shoulder is the most common joint involved, but the stifle, elbow and hock may also be affected. Most cases of OCD are diagnosed in dogs between six and 20 months of age. The lameness is usually slow developing and persists for weeks or longer. Radiographs are crucial to making the diagnosis of OCD in Labradors. Except in mild cases, surgery is the treatment of choice for OCD.

RUPTURED CRUCIATE LIGAMENT. This is the most common cause of sudden rear-leg lameness in middle-aged to older Labradors. The cruciate ligament is one of the major supporting structures in the dog's stifle joint (equivalent to our knee). When torn, the joint no longer supports weight in the usual fashion, causing the dog to hold up the leg. Surprisingly, the injury does not appear to be very painful. Other than limping, these dogs act perfectly normal, and rarely wince, even when you poke and prod the lame leg. The diagnosis is made with careful joint manipulation, often under anesthesia or tranquilization. Radiographs also help pinpoint the problem. Treatment is surgical, both to correct the instability and to deal with any damaged cartilage. Dogs that don't have the ruptured ligament repaired will usually begin to walk normally again within a few months as scar tissue builds up, providing stability. Unfortunately, arthritis develops later, and over the years the problem with the neglected joint will continue. The major predisposing factor in cruciate ligament rupture is obesity. While any-age dog can be affected, middle-aged to older victims are more common. The injury that causes the ligament to tear can seem minor. Many dogs do it under severe stress running through a field, but other times it can happen by simply jumping down off the couch.

OSTEOSARCOMA. The major type of bone cancer, osteosarcoma affects larger breeds of dogs far more commonly than those under 50 pounds. There is pain and firm swelling at the cancer site, usually near the end of one of the long bones of the legs. Radiographs and biopsy specimens are needed for diagnosis. Treatment involves amputation and chemotherapy, but prognosis remains poor for long-term survival. Even relatively young dogs can develop osteosarcoma. The cause is as yet unknown.

NERVOUS SYSTEM

The nervous system is made up of the brain, spinal cord, and all the peripheral nerves that make muscles move and allow the senses to work. This complex, integrated circuitry is vital to all life's functions. Fortunately, the nervous system is one of the most reliable of the body's systems. Most nervous system diseases are quite rare in Labradors.

Diseases of the Brain

The brain is the control center for the dog. With the exception of epilepsy, it rarely causes trouble. Only as our pets become quite elderly do we start to see signs of failing. One such condition is called "senile vestibular syndrome." With little

warning, your pet may suddenly list to one side, circle in one direction, and tilt its head at a severe angle. Close observation of the pupils will reveal eyes that jerk regularly back and forth. Your veterinarian can confirm the diagnosis. Fortunately, this condition will usually resolve within a few days even without treatment. Other brain problems include blood clots and brain tumors, again conditions generally affecting older dogs. Fortunately, congenital brain malformations are uncommon in Labradors.

Diseases of the Spinal Cord

Most spinal cord disorders in Labrador Retrievers are caused by injury. Spinal fractures usually result from severe trauma such as automobile accidents. Slipped discs occur many times from less dramatic circumstances. A dog may jump for a ball and land wrong, causing enough damage in some cases to completely paralyze the victim. These conditions require immediate medical and/or surgical attention if there is to be any hope of restoring use of the rear legs.

Another spinal condition seen occasionally in Labradors is meningitis. This severe, rapidly developing disease of the tissue surrounding the spinal cord and brain usually affects puppies less than 18 months. If your young dog suddenly is reluctant to move, cries when its neck is moved, and runs a high fever, consider meningitis and seek help immediately. Treatment instituted rapidly will usually cure most cases.

Seizures

Unfortunately, seizure disorders are the exception to the rule that says Labradors have few nervous-system problems. Seizures (convulsions or fits) can be so mild that the dog barely trembles, or so severe that it lies thrashing on its side for several minutes, often passing urine and feces, and vomiting. While seizures can be caused by literally dozens of distinct disease entities, the most common cause in Labradors is epilepsy. Epilepsy is showing up in many Labradors from many lines. Before diagnosing epilepsy, your veterinarian will want to run a complete battery of tests to rule out the other causes of seizures. These other causes include a variety of infections, tumors, metabolic diseases, parasites, and poisonings.

URINARY SYSTEM

Without a functioning urinary system, your pet would die within a few short days. The kidneys are the "heart" of this system, filtering and extracting waste products from the bloodstream. The resulting solution, urine, passes from the kidneys to the urinary bladder through two tubes called ureters. The bladder serves as a storage reservoir, then empties the urine from the body through a single tube called the urethra.

Diseases Causing Increased Thirst

As dogs get older, they often need to drink more water each day in order to help their aging kidneys remove waste chemicals from the blood. This condition, called "compensated renal failure," allows most dogs to live several more months or years than they would if the body was unable to compensate for the changes in the kidneys. Therefore, the main message is this: If your dog is suddenly drinking much more water than usual, let it drink! Restricting water can be serious or even life-threatening. In addition, when you note such an increase in thirst, it is vital that you and your veterinarian discover the root cause. Chronic kidney failure is only one of many causes of increased thirst. Diabetes, Cushing's disease, uterine infections, abscesses, poisonings, liver, blood and kidney disorders and some cancers all can have increased thirst as the first symptom.

Diseases Causing Blood in Urine

Blood in urine is a common sign associated with several different diseases, all of which must be treated. Each winter, when there is the first snow covering the ground, we get calls from people that see blood in the snow. Often the condition is chronic, but never noticed by the owner because the urine disappeared into the grass or dirt. Don't let this happen to your dog! At least once a week, crane your neck enough to watch the color of the urine. If you have any question, catch a small amount in a sauce pan (for males) or pie plate (females) and submit it to your veterinarian for analysis. Among the disorders causing bloody urine are bladder infections, tumors or stones; kidney infections, tumors or stones; prostate problems; vaginal conditions; and certain poisonings. Each is treated differently, so your veterinarian will need to run tests to pinpoint the cause.

Diseases Causing Incontinence

Urinary incontinence is the unconscious leaking of urine. Dogs that knowingly have accidents in the house are not incontinent. The most common form of incontinence involves older, usually spayed, females, who dribble a little urine in their sleep. Although less common, males also can be incontinent, sometimes dripping a little as they walk. Most cases of incontinence can be controlled medically with little difficulty. An exception is the incontinence seen in puppies, sometimes associated with malformations of the urinary tract. In the case of malformations, surgery may be needed. Your veterinarian will want to test the urine, and perhaps do radiographs or other tests before deciding which treatment is best.

REPRODUCTIVE SYSTEM: MALE

The male reproductive tract is a sperm-production and processing system. These tiny cells are formed in the testicles, undergo some maturing in the twisting ducts that leave the testes, are stored and mixed with fluid in the prostate, and exit the body through the urethra as it passes through the length of the penis. Males usually become fertile at about seven months of age, and can continue to be potent sires into their early teens.

Disorders of the Testicles

The most common testicular conditions of concern are monorchidism and cryptorchidism. These are the terms used when one or both testes fail to descend into the scrotum from the abdomen. It is rare for one or both testes to be actually missing. If they are not in the scrotum, in most cases they are in the groin area or within the abdominal cavity. Most testes have descended into the scrotum by six weeks of age. It is rare for Labradors to have a retained testicle descend after five months.

The tendency toward monorchidism is considered inherited, so affected dogs should not be bred. In addition, the rate of cancer in retained testicles is many times higher than in those that are properly descended. For this reason, we strongly urge neutering dogs with one or both testes still undescended at six months.

Disorders of the Prostate Gland

This walnut-sized gland surrounds the urethra in the pelvic region. It can become infected (a cause of infertility), swell with age, or develop cancer. Signs of prostate disease include bloody urine, or drops of bloody fluid dripping from the end of the penis; standing to urinate for a long time, only passing a thin stream; and difficult or painful bowel movements. Neutered animals have no prostate problems as the gland becomes inactive without the influence of the hormone testosterone. Evaluation of prostate disease may include examination of urine or semen, cultures, rectal examination, and radiographs or ultrasound. Treatment often involves long courses of antibiotics, neutering, and surgery directly on the prostate. Neutering is a good method of preventing prostate disease and is highly recommended in dogs not to be used for breeding.

Disorders of the Penis and Sheath

It is common for male dogs to have a small amount of greenish yellow discharge at the opening of the sheath. It develops within the sheath itself and has little or no affect on the general reproductive health. Copious amounts of discharge, or discharge that is blood-tinged, should be investigated by your veterinarian.

Castration

Unless your male is to be used for breeding, it is advisable to have him neutered. This can be done at any age over about two months, although traditionally the surgery is usually performed at around six months of age. There are many benefits to this. Prostate infections or cancers, tumors of the testicles or area surrounding the anus, and certain types of hernias are all extremely rare in neutered animals. Particularly if your dog is aggressive, or territorial, or tries to run off, consider neutering as one part of your behavior-correction program. Finally, the humane issue of too many unwanted puppies must be acknowledged. The best and kindest step to take with your pet Labrador is to have him neutered.

REPRODUCTIVE SYSTEM: FEMALE

This is where life truly begins. The two ovaries produce eggs, which are released and pass into the oviducts, where fertilization by the male's sperm occurs. The fertilized eggs start to divide and grow. They pass into the uterus and become attached to the soft uterine lining where, over the course of about nine weeks, they grow and develop into Labrador puppies.

Breeding

Most Labradors are easy breeders. They breed naturally, whelp (deliver puppies) with little assistance, and have strong mothering instincts. That doesn't mean that they don't need supervision! In any given individual, something could go wrong requiring help from you or your veterinarian. Artificial insemination, Caesarean section to deliver the litter, or bottle-feeding puppies may be necessary, so you must be on your toes.

Females generally have their first estrus season (or heat cycle) between nine and 15 months, and then continue to have seasons every six to eight months. The first signs of heat are swelling of the vulva (the tissues that surround the opening to the vagina), soon followed by spotting of a bloody discharge. Most seasons last approximately three weeks, with the fertile period falling between days ten and 16 on the average. It is important to stress that these numbers are all averages. Your female may have cycles that are much shorter or longer than is typical and still be quite normal.

During breeding, the male mounts the female from the rear and thrusts until his penis has completely penetrated the vagina. At this point a tie usually occurs. The penis has become so engorged and swollen that it is trapped within the vagina. Generally the male slides off, swings a rear leg over, and stands panting, stuck rump-to-rump with the female. During this time, do nothing except steady the animals so they don't try to thrash or lie down. The tie will end naturally on its own in 15 to 45 minutes on the average. In most cases it is best to breed two or three times during the fertile period, skipping a day or two between breedings.

In cases where the male and female are separated by a great distance, semen can be collected from the male using a fresh chilled process, and shipped to the female's veterinarian for insemination. The heat cycle must be closely followed using vaginal smears and blood tests to determine the best days for insemination. It helps if these breedings are planned well in advance so that dog owners and veterinarians in both locations are prepared.

Semen can be collected and frozen from valuable males for use in the future, for export to other countries, or for use when the male is temporarily unavailable. Not all veterinarians are comfortable with fresh chilled or frozen semen techniques. If necessary, ask your veterinarian for referral to a practice that utilizes these advanced reproduction technologies.

Disorders of the Ovaries and Uterus

The major life-threatening condition of the reproductive tract is pyometra, a severely infected, pus-filled uterus. This usually occurs six to nine weeks after a heat cycle. Symptoms include increased thirst, fever, a weakened condition, and in many cases a foul-smelling discharge from the vagina. This is one of the reasons that females not used in a conscientious breeding program should be spayed! The best treatment for pyometra is to spay her. There are, however, alternative treatments now available to treat pyometra in valuable breeding animals.

Ovarian cysts sometimes occur. Most are harmless and remain unnoticed. Some, however, secrete hormones that cause a female to stay in heat for several weeks longer than usual. If it doesn't subside on its own, this condition must be treated by your veterinarian.

Disorders of the Vagina

Many female puppies have a slight yellowish vaginal discharge. This is called juvenile vaginitis, and is quite normal. The discharge will subside when the female is spayed, or when she has passed her first heat.

Disorders of the Mammary Glands

Two serious conditions involving the mammary glands (breasts) of the dog: mastitis or mammary cancer. Both can be avoided by spaying your dog prior to her first heat.

Mastitis occurs during the period that a female is nursing her puppies. One or several glands become infected, often abscessing. Aggressive treatment with hot soaks and antibiotics is vital.

Mammary cancer is very common in unspayed female dogs over the age of ten. As many as 30% of these grand old girls will develop some type of breast tumor. It is important to check for these on your weekly examinations, and have your veterinarian remove any that is considered suspicious before the cancer has spread to other parts of the body.

False Pregnancy

Approximately eight weeks after a heat cycle, some females may develop enlarged mammary glands, even to the point of dripping a little milk. Often her behavior changes as well. She may seek closed quarters, dig and scratch like she is nesting, even grab one of her toys and carry it with her everywhere. This is called a false pregnancy, and the behaviors you see are triggered by the hormonal changes that typically occur at this time. False pregnancy is not considered a harbinger of infertility, and usually will cease without treatment within about two weeks.

Ovariohysterectomy

Ovariohysterectomy is the proper term for the operation commonly called spaying. "Ovario" meaning ovary, "hister" meaning uterus, and "ectomy" meaning removal. Both ovaries and the entire uterus are removed surgically. The advantages to this surgery are many. You avoid the mess of regular estrus cycles and the risk of unwanted pregnancies. Such life-threatening diseases as pyometra and mammary cancer are avoided as well. And you won't be contributing to the pet-overpopulation tragedy that leaves millions of dogs in shelters or killed each year for lack of a loving home.

ENDOCRINE SYSTEM

The endocrine system is comprised of a number of glands scattered throughout the body that secrete a variety of hormones vital to normal body function. Among these are the pituitary gland, thyroid gland, pancreas, parathyroid, and adrenal glands. Malfunction of these glands leads to the slowly developing conditions generally grouped as endocrine disorders. While there are many such disorders, there are four most commonly encountered in Labradors.

Thyroid Disorders

Hypothyroidism is a common condition in which the thyroid gland fails to produce an adequate amount of thyroid hormone. The condition is frequently seen in Labrador Retrievers. Symptoms to watch for are weight gain despite a moderate diet, reduced energy, chronic skin problems, infertility and a tendency to seek out warm places for napping. Diagnosing the condition requires blood analysis for thyroid hormone levels. When they are too low, treatment is thyroid hormone tablets, usually given once or twice a day. Some types of hypothyroidism may be inherited, so caution should be taken in deciding whether or not to use these animals in any breeding program.

Diabetes Mellitus

Sugar diabetes, properly termed diabetes mellitus, is not infrequent in Labradors. Overweight animals seem to be most commonly affected. These dogs drink water insatiably and produce a very large urine output. Their appetites are increased, and they have poor coats and poor body condition. Diabetic dogs have a higher incidence of cataracts than other dogs. In advanced cases, loss of appetite, vomiting and shock can occur. Fortunately, diagnosis of diabetes is straightforward: samples of blood and urine will reveal the high glucose levels. Treatment of diabetes in dogs requires strict dietary regulation, a consistent exercise regimen and injections of insulin. These injections are given once or twice a day at home by the dog's owner. And while this may sound impossible, even the most squeamish and needle-shy owner can rise to the challenge of administering insulin in an efficient manner. Follow-up monitoring of blood and urine sugar levels is critical to long-term success at controlling diabetes in dogs.

Cushing's Disease

While rarer in Labradors than other endocrine diseases, Cushing's disease, more properly termed hyperadrenocorticism, nonetheless can cause serious problems. The basic problem is an overproduction of cortisone-type hormones by the pituitary glands. The symptoms mirror diabetes in many ways: excessive thirst and appetite, poor hair coat and weakened condition. Diagnosis is based on a series of blood samples taken over the course of a day or two. Depending on the type of Cushing's disease, treatment may be in tablet form, or may involve surgery on the adrenal glands.

Addison's Disease

While Cushing's disease is an overproduction by the adrenal glands, Addison's is the opposite: underproduction of adrenal hormones. The symptoms of recurrent stomach upset are non-specific, resembling chronic gastroenteritis or even parasites. In advanced cases the vomiting can be so severe that shock can ensue. Blood tests will reveal characteristic imbalances in blood electrolytes, and specific deficits in cortisol levels. Treatment is to replace these missing hormones with supplements in tablet form.

The American Kennel Club

by A. Nelson Sills and Robert H. McKowen

The American Kennel Club was over 30 years old in 1917 when Scottish-bred Brocklehirst Floss, owned by Charles G. Meyer of New York City, became the first Labrador Retriever to appear in the AKC Stud Book. This was a momentous moment, as AKC recognition not only brought the prestige of being a registered breed but also meant the Labrador could compete and earn titles in a myriad of licensed and sanctioned events with consistent regulations across the country.

Founded in 1884, the AKC was quite small and the nature and extent of its operation had not been defined when it elected its fourth president, August Belmont, Jr., in 1888. Mr. Belmont served as president for 26 years, and by the end of his tenure in 1916, the AKC supervised the sport of purebred dogs throughout the nation and resembled the organization it is today. Years later, in 1977, Mr. Belmont's grandson, August Belmont, an esteemed name in Labrador Retriever history — his honors included being the first to win the National Amateur twice with the same dog (1967 and 1968) and first to win the National Retriever Championship and the National Amateur Retriever Championship in the same year (1968) — was elected Chairman of the Board of the American Kennel Club.

A "club of clubs" with no individual members, the American Kennel Club's charter mandates that it "do everything to advance the study, breeding, exhibiting, running and maintenance of the purity of thoroughbred dogs." In compliance with these high ideals, the AKC registers well over 1.2 million dogs a year in its stud book and licenses many activities Labradors participate in, such as dog shows, field trials, hunting tests, obedience trials, and tracking tests. It also licenses activities for specialized breeds, such as lure coursing, herding, and coonhound events, and maintains the official records of all these tests and competitions and awards the title certificates.

AKC EVENTS AND TITLES

The American Kennel Club is the principal registry for purebred dogs in the United States as well as the leading regulatory agency for dog shows and performance events. Every year more than 9,000 events are held under AKC license or sanction, and in most of our country, there is some type of competition or test nearly every weekend. The following is a summary of the events in which Labrador Retrievers are eligible to participate.

Dog Shows

Dog shows judge a dog's conformation (appearance). This is determined by how well the dog's structure, movement and temperament comply with the standard for the breed. The standard is a kind of "blueprint" in words of what constitutes the ideal dog in each breed. The title awarded to dogs earning 15 points in the prescribed manner at dog shows is Champion (Ch.).

Obedience Trials

Obedience trials judge a dog and handler's ability to perform a prescribed set of exercises as a team. There are three levels in obedience: novice, open, and utility, and each has a higher level of difficulty.

There are two ways to succeed in obedience competition. Performing the exercises well enough to pass earns the exhibitor a "leg," and three "legs" under three different judges earns the title of Companion Dog (CD), Companion Dog Excellent (CDX) or Utility Dog (UD). The highest titles for an obe-dience dog is Utility Dog Excellent (UDX). In addition, awards are presented to the top four scorers.

Tracking

AKC awards two tracking titles, Tracking Dog (TD) and Tracking Dog Excellent (TDX).

Hunting Tests

Held under simulated, natural hunting conditions, hunting tests give dogs the opportunity to demonstrate their instinct, ability and trainability in the field. Owners do not have to be hunters to succeed at these tests. At these non-competitive events, the dogs are judged against an acceptable standard of performance and can earn titles at three levels: Junior Hunter (JH), Senior Hunter (SH), and Master Hunter (MH).

Field Trials

Field Champion (FC) and Amateur Field Champion (AFC) are titles that can be won at field trials. Also held under simulated, natural hunting conditions, field trials are competitive and dogs have to beat other dogs in order to earn points toward these championships.

LEGISLATION

A leader in the fight against anti-dog legislation, the AKC has joined the American Veterinary Medical Association and responsible state and local organizations to urge the adoption of reasonable, enforceable and non-discriminatory laws governing the ownership of dogs...the kind that regulate by deed, not breed. A 24-hour toll-free hotline, 1-800-AKCTELL may be used by concerned individuals who want to report dog legislation developments in their locale.

AKC's Canine Good Citizen program was developed as a positive outreach program with the objective of making good citizens out of our nation's dogs in order to gain greater public acceptance for our canine friends and to help thwart anti-dog legislation. It rewards mannerly dogs and responsible owners and is the only AKC program that includes mixed-bred dogs. Several state legislatures have passed resolutions endorsing the Canine Good Citizen program.

AKC PUBLICATIONS

The AKC provides many publications to educate dog fanciers and the public in the sport of dogs:

Launched in 1888 and first published in January of 1889, *Pure-Bred Dogs/American Kennel Gazette* is a monthly, full-color magazine dedicated to helping owners of all registered breeds enjoy and learn about their dogs. The *Events Calendar*, a supplement to the *Gazette*, lists upcoming shows, trials and tests.

Show Awards, another monthly publication, lists new titleholders as well as results of the events.

The *AKC Hunting Test Herald* is a bimonthly publication for those interested in the hunting test programs for retrievers, pointers and spaniels. It features training articles and interpretations of the regulations in addition to announcing new titleholders and coming events.

The American Kennel Club also publishes *Puppies*, a magazine to help the new dog owner understand the joys and responsibilities of dog ownership.

An AKC classic, *The Complete Dog Book*, is frequently updated. It gives the history and standard of every registered breed as well as vital information on dog care.

AKC's newest book, the softcover *AKC Dog Care and Training*, helps prospective new dog owners choose the right breed for their lifestyle and provides the basic education necessary to keep a dog healthy and mannerly.

Publications are also available for those involved in lure coursing, pointing-breed field trials and herding.

In addition, numerous books and pamphlets are published by the American Kennel Club on subjects as varied as disaster planning, Canine Good Citizenship, and responsible breeding.

An extensive collection of educational videos to help dog enthusiasts learn more about registered breeds, dog shows, field trials, hunting tests, obedience and many other subjects is also available.

The AKC's specialized library (at 51 Madison Avenue, New York, NY) contains over 16,000 volumes and is open to the public for research Monday through Friday from 9:00 a.m. to 4:00 p.m.

OTHER AKC ACTIVITIES

A leader in all aspects of dog sports and education, the American Kennel Club:

- Makes the rules and regulations for the registration of purebred dogs, dog shows and all the performance events and maintains a field staff to observe and assist at dog shows and performance events. It sanctions and licenses dog clubs throughout the nation to hold events under its rules.
- Maintains the high caliber of dog-show and performance judges through judges' education and seminar programs.
- Contributes to and supports research for the improvement of canine health.
- Creates programs teaching responsible dog ownership to our nation's grade-school children because good habits begin with the young.

AKC REGISTRATION

A certificate of registration with the American Kennel Club identifies a dog as the offspring of a known sire and dam, born on a known date. If your dog's "papers" are an application for registration, fill out the form and submit it to the AKC with the correct fee. Soon you will receive your dog's individual registration, making your dog eligible to participate in the exciting activities that make up the world of the American Kennel Club.

Forty Years of Field Trials: Recollections

by Robert N. Wolfe

The AKC *Gazette* , *Retriever Field Trial News* and various newsletters, etc., report and record the accomplishments of our dogs in the field trial and show ring. The information that is published is generally limited to "Who Won What Where." The story as recorded represents a small part in the lives of those dogs and their human associates. In the countless hours that we trainers, handlers, and owners spend with our dogs and each other, many things happen or are said or done that would be interesting, and perhaps amusing to those with similar interests.

Presented here are some of these tales. We have collected them in our minds over many years in the sport. We hope you enjoy them.

THE KING'S ENGLISH

A. Wells Wilbor has been active in retriever trials for nearly 50 years. He has judged over 100 major stakes and three Nationals. He was judging a blind retrieve. The handler took a long time to get his dog lined up, heeling and reheeling several times. Wells stepped forward, and in his crisp Boston accent, said,

"Young man, you have stretched our patience to the very breaking point. Now will you please send your dog or pick him up?"

JUDGING IN THE RAIN

There is hardly any experience as frustrating as judging a field trial in the rain. On one occasion Bill (Shanty) Hogan was paired with "Doe" Hoffman. It was windy and rainy. Shanty was having a bad time with his wet book; pages were sticking together and coming loose. His pencil would not work on the wet paper, and finally, in total frustration, he threw the book into the back of the pick-up and said, "There, Doe, now you get in the truck and draw the 'pictures' and I'll call the numbers."

WE ALL MAKE MISTAKES

When a dog makes a mistake we make a big thing over it, yet handlers make mistakes and think nothing of it. A handler was running two derby dogs, and he brought the first dog to the lane and signaled for the birds. When the last bird was down he sent the dog. The judge stepped forward, tapped him on the shoulder, and said, "I'm sorry but I didn't call your number—please pick up your dog."

The handler brought his second dog to the line, called for the birds, and sent the dog when the last bird was down. Again the judge stepped forward, tapped him on the shoulder and said, "I'm sorry but I didn't call your number this time either, please pick up your dog."

ANOTHER HANDLER'S ERROR

It was the derby stake and when the birds were down, the dog leaned eagerly toward the bird. In the excitement the handler shouted "Heel!" The dog burst forth about ten feet, skidded to a stop, and wiggled back to the handler's side. The judge said, "Please pick up your dog."

TENDERLY TO HAND (OR COUNSEL FOR DEFENSE)

It's been said that a handler's job is to do whatever he can to make the dog look good in the eyes of the judge. In short, he is the advocate of the dog. He should accentuate the positive and minimize the negative. Dick Hecker of Tucson, Arizona trained and handled the 1960 National Champion, Dolabrans Smoketail, along with other fine Labradors. By profession Dick was a criminal lawyer. On the line he usually had a comment intended to minimize the faults and accentuate the strengths.

In 1958 the Ohio Valley Club held its trial in Lebanon, Ohio.

Dick was handling Frances Fishtail in the amateur stake. The test was a cold, single land blind, marked by a stake. In Dick's case the blind had not been planted. Fish took a perfect line and responded beautifully to Dick's directions but of course there was no bird. The judge asked Dick to recall the dog and the blind planter to check for the bird. Of course there was none. He was asked to plant another bird. The judge said that Dick would have to repeat the test, however he had already been scored based on the first run. The dog had been given top score for this series. When the dog returned on the second run, her jaws were firmly locked on the bird. Nothing that Dick could do or say caused any relaxation of her jaws. Dick finally had to remove the bird in pieces. All the while Dick was talking to the judges, complimenting them on their good knowledge of dog behavior by recognizing that any good bird dog that worked so hard seeking a bird that wasn't there would be overly possessive of the bird when she found it. The dog was called back for the next series and was awarded second place when the stake was finished.

GAMESMAN

It was at the Minnesota Field Trial at North Oaks, Minnesota, and Allen Williams and Bob Wolfe were judging the open stake. The test was a water blind. There was a very boggy island about 75 yards off shore in a large lake. The previous test had a mark thrown on the island. The dogs had great difficulty maneuvering on the island.

A number of decoys were set off the island, leaving an open water channel about 12 feet wide between the island and the decoys. The line to the blind was through the channel, between the island and the decoys and well "out to sea."

Billy Wunderlich was running four dogs, including Duxbak Scooter. All of these were qualified by the National except "Scooter," who needed a win. Of Billy's four dogs, Scooter would run last. The judges gave no instructions. Billy, professing to know what these judges wanted, convinced virtually all of the handlers that the judges wanted to see the dog cast off the boggy island. When Billy ran his first three dogs, he sent them to the island, let them get well up on the island and into the bird scent from the previous test. Then he gave them a couple of whistles and casts, to which the dog did not respond cleanly. Then he called them in. Then in a loud voice he exclaimed, "My dogs will either do this right or I'll pick them all up." He picked up three of his dogs. Most of the other handlers followed suit. Most of the dogs were picked up. Scooter was the last to run. When he reached the island Billy didn't let him get onto the bog and bird scent. Billy quickly stopped him and cast him back toward the blind. Scooter won the trial. The only handlers that escaped the trap were Cotton Pershall, Tony Betget, and Gene Cohn (amateur).

DON'T ARGUE WITH A BULL MOOSE

The water terrain at the Duluth Retriever Club is a man-made pond with the usual points, channels, bays, and a small creek that runs through it. The water is shallow and lush green foliage grows in the pond. One year a family of moose adopted the area, presumably attracted by the food in the pond. The bull moose had antlers with a spread of at least six feet. The dog training continued, moose or no moose. However, the training exercises were designed to avoid conflict with the moose. A fairly compatible relationship resulted. At the licensed field trial a marking test was set up in which one of the marks fell about 60 yards from the feeding moose. The moose showed little concern for the field-trial activity except to raise his head now and then when the guns were fired. After an hour or so, he sauntered off into the forest.

Some time later, Bob Bolles, a well-known field trialer from Virginia, Minnesota, arranged for a training session at the pond. When they arrived the moose was feeding in the pond. Bob said he was tired of having the moose preempt our full use of the pond, and he would chase him out. So he followed the dike around the pond and approached the moose, shouting and waving his arms. The moose charged him, Bob turned and ran with the moose in pursuit close behind. When Bob turned off the dike to get to the clubhouse, he tripped crossing a shallow ditch and fell flat on the ground. When he turned over he could feel the hot moist breath of the moose. Bob reached for his training pistol and emptied the gun in the moose's face. When he fired the last shot, the moose backed off and trotted away.

CHARLIE MORGAN

I saw and met Charlie Morgan for the first time at the Manitowac Field Trial in 1958. My son and I suffered a long drive and ferryboat ride from Detroit, Michigan to run my dog in the amateur. I had heard of Charlie and read of him so it was a thrill to meet him. The last series in the amateur was a very difficult (for those days) water blind. Mine was the only dog to complete it in accord with the judge's instructions. Charlie came to the line, took my hand, and said some very nice words about my dog. I quickly flew up to "Cloud 9" (and stayed there for some time). In the years following I judged him many times and had many conversations with him. My respect for him kept growing. He was always the competitor but always the gentleman.

The last time I saw Charlie was at Minnesota in the fall of 1967. I had a hot young dog and was invited to run test dog for the open; it was a long land blind in a hay field with a small patch of uncut hay at the end. My dog took a good line, but ran around the patch of clover. The next day Charlie and I met on a narrow road and he signaled me to stop. He said, "you have a fine young dog, I like him very much and I know you are a very good trainer and handler. I watched your dog run that blind yesterday, he ran around that patch of clover. He should have gone through it. I also noted that he's carrying his ears too high. If you bring those ears down a bit, he will go through the clover; and the judges will like it better."

A few months later Charlie suddenly dropped over dead at an informal trial in Wisconsin. He was on the line running his dog. One of the judges of the stake was Dr. Dick Keskey. Dick and Charlie were good friends. Charlie had trained and handled Dick's dogs. Dr. Keskey pronounced the death and had him placed on the seat of his truck overlooking the trial, while others took care of arrangements.

The Charles Morgan Memorial Trophy is awarded each year to the owner of the High Point Derby Dog.

WINTER TRAINING

A Minnesota field trialer decided to send his Lab to Arizona with a pro trainer for the winter season. Upon learning of this plan, his wife challenged him with, "How come the damn dog gets to go south for the winter and I have to stay here in the ice and snow?" He replied, "Honey, if I thought you would come back trained I'd send you along too."

WE MELLOW WITH AGE

Lawrence "Marti" Martens, of Sauk Rapids, Minnesota, has spent most of his life breeding, training and trialing fine Labrador Retrievers, with the kennel name prefix "Martens." He bred and developed a number of field champions, including the 1965 National Champion, Martens Little Smoky. One day a young man asked him why he didn't have any good dogs like he used to have. Marti responded with, "I believe that the dogs are just as good but since I retired, the training routine has changed. I used to train diligently every day. Now I find it hard to find the time to train. I sleep later in the morning, I have a leisurely breakfast, and by the time I finish reading the paper, it's time to go to town for coffee with my friends. I get and read the mail, have lunch, maybe rest for a while and do some chores. By then it's too late to take the dogs out. Maybe we can do that tomorrow or the next day."

When asked about punishing his dogs, he said, "When I have a dog that needs a lickin' I always do it in front of all my dogs so they can all benefit by it. However, in these later years, I don't lick them, instead I just swear at them."

FIRST THINGS FIRST

When arriving home after work each day a well-known Minnesota field trialer had a set routine. First he would let the dog out of the kennel and through a few plugs. Then he would march through the house to see what the mailman had brought. Then he would recognize family members.

One day his wife stopped him and said, "the trouble with this place is, that unless one wags one's tail, or comes in the mail, one doesn't get any attention around here."

ALL FOR THE PRICE OF ONE

There was a good sportsman, dog man and breeder of good Labrador Retrievers who lived in Long Lake, Minnesota. His name was Don Furen. Don was looking for a well-bred brood bitch, and he found one in a kennel near Fargo, North Dakota owned by Max Talbert. A deal was made and Don took the bitch home. Shortly thereafter, he determined that the bitch was with pup. He was quite concerned over this situation, and called the seller. The seller said, "Oh! didn't I tell you about that? I meant to but must have forgot. Fact is I have a young male here, a nice young dog—a little crazy perhaps, but a fine dog that somehow got over the fence and bred your bitch. I'm sure she's going to have a fine litter of pups and I'm not going to charge you a damned dime extra for the pups or the stud service."

Well the bitch was Little Peggy Black Gum, and she did have a fine litter. Several of them were good trial dogs. The best of them was FC-AFC Yankee Clipper of Reo Ray. Roger Reopelle haggled the price down to $60.00 for the pup. Roger developed him into one of the nation's top performers. He passed his genes on to many fine Labradors. Among the best was FC-AFC My Rebel, owned by A. Wells Wilbor and trained by Roger.

BARGAIN DOG

George and Edith Murnane lived on Long Island, New York. Joe Schomer and later Joe Riser were the trainers and handlers. Theirs was certainly one of the winningest strings on the field-trial circuit, winning five Nationals. George was a New York investment banker.

All of his dogs were field-trial competitors; all were males. All were purchased and well beyond the derby level when he acquired them. Only dogs owned by George were kenneled on the property. Even bitches to be bred were not allowed at his kennel. Stud service was available only when his dogs were on the road trialing. George did not handle the dogs in trials, but Edith did handle some in amateur stakes. The two Joes traveled the circuit with two big Chrysler station wagons, loaded with crates and dogs. A friend and business associate told George about a Labrador that he had with outstanding natural ability and field-trial potential. At a later meeting the friend again discussed the dog, and said the dog had so much potential that in the interest of advancing the breed it should get professional training. He proposed that George take it to his kennel for this training. George explained his policies and said that he could not take the friend's dog into his kennel or get involved in the training of the pup. George was not interested in the pup. Every time they met, George would have to listen to the attributes of this "great" field-trial prospect. At George's suggestion the friend tried to sell the dog. When asked what price he should expect, George's somewhat snide response was "if it's as good a dog as you say, it is probably worth $1000." Later the associate told George that he had not found a buyer and proposed that George buy the dog. To maintain the friendship, George decided to buy the dog and find a home for it. When the associate asked the price George was willing to pay, George said, "I'm afraid I've already established that —$1000."

The deal was made. George had the dog picked up, Joe Riser took a liking to the pup and started to fool with him; and in due course started to train him. The dog was FC-AFC Whygin Corks Coot. He went on to win the coveted National Championship in 1966 and again in 1969. George said, "I've bought a lot of dogs, and I've paid a lot of money, but I never bought so much dog for so little money."

SPLASH

At a trial of the Maine Retriever Club, the test was a blind retrieve with dry diversion shot out of a boat. The dog was on line. The judge signaled. The gunner fired, then promptly fell backward into the water.

SMILE YOU'RE ON CANDID CAMERA

When I arrived at the St. Cloud, Minnesota trial to run the amateur, I met my good friend Billy Wunderlich, and he told me about the open that had one more series to go. It seems he had two dogs in "good shape." They were Playboy and Nemo. According to Billy's observations, Playboy was leading the pack and Nemo was in second place.

Playboy was already qualified for that year's National and Nemo needed a win to qualify. If Nemo could put down a good job on this last series, and Playboy commit an error, Nemo could probably win. The test was a triple mark on land. The last bird down was a big cackling cock pheasant from guns about 50 yards out. Junior Betget and I were the gunners. The judges requested that we carry the bird well out. Nemo was a very spirited, unpredictable dog. He put down a perfect performance on this last test. Now the only dog that could beat him was Playboy, who came to the line and obediently sat down with the look of control and confidence. The judge signaled, and the birds were put down. As our bird hit the ground we heard Billy shout, "Heel!" Playboy broke. Billy let out a tirade accusing us gunners of causing the break by intentionally carrying the bird farther than the other dogs. It almost sounded like this speech had been rehearsed. Nemo won the trial because Playboy broke. How come?

Playboy never breaks. Did he make a mistake and go with being sent or did he hear, see, or feel something that he interpreted as a release? Was it made advertently or inadvertently? In the years following, several times I have asked Billy what really happened. The only answer I've ever received was a pleasant smile.

THE BEST LAID PLANS

There is nothing so important in conducting a field trial as good mechanics, especially at National Championship Stakes. The field-trial chairman spends a lot of his time over two or three years planning every detail and providing for contingencies.

The 1968 Amateur National was held in Auburn, Maine. Mac Filson was field-trial chairman, and no one had ever worked harder to provide the best mechanics. For the field-trial headquarters, he had selected a new Holiday Inn. It had suffered three complete changes in management and staff prior to the date of the trial. With each change the service got worse. The field-trial committee met the judges to plan the tests. Someone had driven the vehicle they were to use into the pool. They rented a Hertz station wagon. As they were studying the grounds the wagon stalled. They had to find a phone to call for a cab to take them back to the motel. At lunch the waitress dumped a large tray of drinks on the group. The day before the trial was to start it was learned that two dogs owned by Clif Tennant of Seattle, Washington were not entered because the entries had not been received. The committee and the club officers worked all night trying to find an answer to the problem. What to do for this man who came all the way from Seattle to run his dogs? They devised a procedure that everyone thought would work. Every contestant was asked to sign an agreement to let Clif run his dogs without objection. All contestants signed the agreement. The matter was referred to AKC, and AKC disapproved the proposal. The

Tennant dogs could not run the trial. On the first day of the trial everything stopped. The land that had been selected for the first test with the landowner's permission was not available because the owner had changed his mind and now wanted a cash payment in advance. With the help of several people the money was raised and the trial began. The man that was to bring the food truck passed out and was taken to a hospital. A family member tried to deliver the food but got lost and couldn't find the trial. On the second day the caravan was routed to approach the test site from the proper side, but the police sergeant who led the caravan chose a shortcut that led to the wrong side of the site. They had to go to the next town to work it out. The service at the motel got worse, but things went well the remainder of the trial; except that the winning dog (Super Chief) was off servicing a bitch when called to be recognized.

BAD WEATHER SOLVES PROBLEM

The Maine Retriever Club put on their first licensed trial in the 1950s. The field-trial committee thought they had an answer for every contingency. They ordered more than 100 pheasants from a game farm with whom they had no previous experience. When they went to get the pheasants, the breeder had only 25 ringnecks, the remainder were a conglomerate of various exotic birds. AKC would not recognize them as game birds, and the club had a lot of pressure to use ringneck pheasants for the land marks. The weather came to the rescue. A Nor'easter (heavy rain and wind) came up suddenly. The pheasants got were wet and wouldn't fly so the use of ducks was justified.

ROYAL VISITORS

The Swamp Dog Licensed Field Trial was to be conducted at the Bishop Estate. Mac Filson and George Stebbins were scheduled to judge. The King and Queen of Nepal were visiting our country, and the State Department was looking for some activity that would occupy the royal entourage on that weekend. Someone at the State Department was aware of the field trial, and a call was received by the club president requesting permission for the royal guests to attend the field trial. They were given the green light. A large contingent of FBI and State Department officials moved in to complete the arrangements. They proceeded to erect a tent and reviewing stand, along with much electronic equipment for communication and security, all of which were to be on the front lawn of the Bishop Estate. A crisis developed when they learned that the trial would be conducted at several sites throughout the estate. Their efforts to get the judges to agree to conduct the trial from the one site failed. Meanwhile one of the FBI people asked if there would be any guns used or any cars. Alice Lewis, in her characteristic strong voice said "Hell yes! There will be guns in most of the vehicles, as well as the guns in the field shooting the live birds." That was the last straw; certainly non-negotiable. They left and were not seen again until the Sunday night news on TV. There were the royal visitors, viewing a bench show in New York with reviewing stand, electronic security, and communications gear. The problem had been solved, much to the relief of the Washington Starlets as well as the Swamp Dog Field Trial Committee.

THE LATE ARRIVALS

The practice of running in order of the draw has always been religiously enforced at National Stakes. At the 1981 Amateur National, the dog handled by Roger Reopelle was not to be found as his turn to run approached. March (Bob Wolfe) reported it to the judges John Morgan, Jack Hogue, and Bill Sabbag. They instructed the marshal to "put a clock on Reopelle, skip him, and proceed with the trial. When Reopelle arrives determine his reason for being late, and report to the judges for instruction." On arrival Reopelle reported that his car battery was dead and he had to call for service. This was reported to the judges, who instructed the marshal to work him into the running sequence as soon as possible. Soon there was another late handler (Chuck Bang). He reported that he "sort of" had car trouble too. When that response was reported to the judges, they instructed the marshal to "work him in, but tell Chuck he better 'sort of' get his car fixed by tomorrow morning."

FINALLY IT'S HIS TURN

Val (Fisher) Walker had FC-AFC Misty's Sun Gold Lad, one of the truly great Goldens. He had campaigned under all kinds of conditions for many years. On one occasion in his later years, he was being handled in a trial by Jay Walker (Val's husband) on a triple water mark. As the last duck fell, Lad strained to go. However, instead of the usual "back" he was ordered to "sit-stay." Jay ran to the shore, dove in, swam to the duck and delivered the bird to Lad, tenderly to mouth.

MORE THAN READY

At the 1973 National Amateur, Ken Cory was running his very eager Lab. The holding blind was about 50 yards behind the line and when called from the blind, the dog bolted to the line; then sat down taking cognizance of the guns in the field. Ken didn't want to draw any more attention than necessary so he chose to walk quietly rather than run to the line. On arrival at the line, a judge said, "We knew you were coming sooner or later."

SMART DOG

Back in 1971, we were moving to our new house in Easton, Maryland, and in the process were having the creek that goes by the house dredged. One day Louise was walking along the edge of the creek, accompanied by a lady friend and my aging Retriever Bomarc of South Bay. The poor old dog for some reason went out in the water and soon was in trouble, mired in the bottom struggling, but unable to get back ashore. He was beyond reach, so after trying various strategies, Louise and her friend fashioned a sort of rope out of their petticoats, and were able to throw the end of it to the dog. Old Bo was smart enough to take advantage of it and grabbed his end of the rope and held on to it while being pulled to dry land.

CLOSE CALL

The "Women's" Trial was held in East Hampton, Long Island. Augie Belmont had recently acquired a four-hole dog trailer. At the end of the day he loaded his dogs and drove to the motel. When he arrived he noticed that one of the doors was open and there was no dog. Soupy (Super Chief, winner of three National Championships) was way gone. It was dark, and traffic was heavy. Augie remembered a lighted intersection, so he returned there and called. Out of the dark and through the traffic came the dog destined to win a National and two National Amateurs.

THOSE LOVABLE OUTLAWS

E.C. (Al) Christensen of Minnesota was a very active participant in the training and trialing of Labradors. He also was frequently called on to judge. He was very much oriented to the style and attitude of the dogs. He frequently stated that the winning dog should be the one that the judge would most want to take home.

Al was judging the amateur stake of the North Dakota R.C. of Fargo. After the last series was run, the surviving handlers sat in the clubhouse making book on who the winner would be. John Cross of Minnesota had a hard-going litter mate of FC-AFC My Rebel. His chances were generally discounted because he was less than responsive on the blinds, rough on birds, and had poor manners. After a long wait the judges came into the clubhouse and Al said, "You people would never guess who won this field trial." John said, "Well, who did win it?" Al said, "You did." John said, "You must be kidding —how come?" Al said, "Because he's a goddamn outlaw, and I love those outlaws."

WET PANTS

To most competitors in a field trial, handling a dog is a very stressful experience. On one occasion a group was discussing this and comparing their individual reactions. One great lady from California confessed that she invariably wets her pants when running her dog on a test. She handled great dogs over many years.

TOO LATE

When two persons judge a field trial, they ultimately must agree on every issue relating to the test design and dog performance. This calls for sincere and thoughtful consideration of the co-judges' opinions and perhaps a compromise of the two opinions. At the 1974 National Championship Stake, the field-trial chairman presented a plaque to the judges. It read "It's Too Late to Agree with Me—I've Already Changed My Mind".

GOOD NIGHT

After a long and tiring first day of the field trial, the visiting judge excused himself from the usual festivities and retired early. At about 10:00 p.m. he was awakened by a knock on the motel door. He arose and answered the knock, an attractive young lady who politely explained that she owned a dog in the open stake. She was not able to attend this first day of the trial, but D.L. Waiters handled the dog. On arrival this night she learned that the dog had been eliminated from further competition and she wanted to know why. The judge, obviously resentful of the interruption, very deliberatively got the book and found her dog's sheet. After a studied inspection he replied very casually, "The first test was a marking test. Your dog didn't mark. The second test was a handling test, your dog didn't handle; unless there are further questions, I bid you goodnight."

UNFAIR ADVANTAGE

The 1965 National Amateur Retriever Championship Stake was held in Park Rapids, Minnesota. Dr. Parker, Jimmy Jackson, and Sid Eliason were the judges. A certain attractive young lady from the East was a contestant. She was on the line running her dog, attired in a very spotty outfit including a pair of very tight stretch pants. Sid complimented the contestant on the outfit. She replied, "Wait until you see what I'm going to wear tomorrow if I'm called back for the next series." She was.

Another attractive lady also from the East, with somewhat more experience with dogs and with more conservative attire, was asked why she no longer wore those outfits that stir men's interest. She replied, "After I got good dogs I didn't need them."

GOOD ADVICE

Unfortunately, field-trial judges are subject to a lot of criticism — most of which is unfair. Cotton Pershall represented the Nilo Kennels of East St. Louis, Illinois. He spent nearly a lifetime training and working Labradors. Shortly after he retired and regained amateur status, he was invited to judge a field trial. Before he accepted, he discussed the matter with Mr. John Olin, his boss and close associate for many years. Mr. Olin said, "Cotton, perhaps more than any other person, you have the respect, admiration and love of the people in the sport. You have spent nearly your whole life earning this reputation. Why would you want to screw it all up in one weekend?"

BUT I DO

An active field-trial trainer on the West coast always had big, strong and tough dogs. In fact he admitted that he needed tough dogs because he was a hard trainer. One occasion he was administering punishment when a member of the training group said, "Why are you doing that? He doesn't know why he's getting punished." The trainer replied, "That really doesn't matter because I do!"

POPULAR JUDGES

Two field-trial enthusiasts were jokingly boosting their popularity as field-trial judges. Lawrence Martens, of St. Cloud, Minnesota, was standing by. One said, "You said you'd like to run under me, didn't you Marti?" Marti replied, "No, you misunderstood. I said I'd like to run over you."

MAYBE THE JUDGE CAN HELP

It was in November of 1969 when Mac Filson and I were judging the Lab Club Specialty Trial on Long Island. The early story of a Nor'easter was blowing across the South. We were concerned of the approaching storm. The test was a land blind. Roger Vasselais was handling one of his fine Labs. The dog chose to hunt the bird without Roger's help, so we asked Roger to pick him up. Roger blew many whistles without response. Perhaps showing more anxiety than needed, I sharply asked him to please get the dog under control. He gently hung his whistle lanyard around my neck and said politely, "I've done my best, perhaps you would like to try it for a while."

BIRCH LOGS FOR THE FIREPLACE

It was at the National Amateur Championship Stake at Park Rapids, Minnesota in 1965. The S.G. Borden Tenents of Houston, Texas were lodged at Timberlake, where the grounds were covered with white birch trees. The Tenents were returning from a party and it was well after midnight. Borden was determined to get his station wagon parked close to his cabin. In doing so he crashed into the birch trees in front and back, several times. His wife said, "Borden, when I said I wanted to take home some birch logs for the fireplace I didn't mean for you to chop them this way."

BREAK ON A BLIND RETRIEVE

Jack Fraser was the originator, developer, editor and publisher of *Field Trial News*. He judged over 100 trials. He was a judge at a trial in Manitowoc, Wisconsin. The test was a water blind. The handler was to follow a path to the shore of the marsh, with his dog at heel and a loaded gun in hand. When he reached the water he was to raise the gun and fire it, then handle his dog to retrieve a duck that had been planted in the marsh. One of the contestants was one of the most active field trialers in the country. He had judged a great many major stakes, trained and handled several good open dogs, etc. He was also a long-time friend of Jack Fraser. His dog was dropped after the water blind.

The next morning Jack was having breakfast when this handler came into the restaurant and was invited to join Jack at the table. After friendly greetings, the handler asked if they could discuss his dog's performance. He said he thought he had very good work and was surprised when he was dropped after the water blind. He asked Jack if he would tell him why he dropped the dog. Jack replied, "When the gun went off, your dog charged into the water intent on making the retrieve without having been sent. You stopped him, ordered him to 'heel' and sent him. We called it a controlled break. In an all-age stake, that calls for automatic elimination."

The handler countered, "Your instructions were that the handler was free to send the dog at will after the shot was fired. How could you conclude that I had not sent the dog?" Jack replied, "When the dog charged out you quickly responded by loudly exclaiming 'No! Get in here! Heel!' Now you would have no cause to do that if you had intentionally sent him, would you?"

GOT TO FIND 'EM BEFORE YOU CAN EAT 'EM

Some years back there was a common expression used to emphasize the importance of marking and finding the bird. It was used to put other infractions in perspective. For example, if one asked how serious dropping and muzzling a bird would be, the answer would be, "You got to find 'em before you can drop 'em."

Lawrence "Lornie" Martens of St. Cloud, Minnesota is a highly respected and loved "character." He was handling a dog at the Wisconsin trial in early April. The weather was rain, sleet, and snow. The birds were immature and only partially feathered hen pheasants. When the dog was sent to retrieve the shot bird, he marked it well and found it. However, for some time he made no effort to pick up the bird and come in. The judge was concerned and asked, "What's that dog doing out there?" Lornie replied very casually, "I believe he's eating the bird." The judge, now really upset, exclaimed, "Get that dog in here—that's terrible— that's the worst thing a retriever can do!" Still calm and casual, Lornie said, "Oh, I don't know— you got to find 'em before you can eat 'em."

IT'S HELL TO GET OLD

My brother and I were duck hunting. I had my two Labs, 11-year-old Duke (AN/AFC) and derby dog George, in my blind. My brother had his own boat blind 100 yards away. I shot a duck and sent Duke to retrieve. George broke and was quickly ahead in the swimming race to the bird. George retrieved the bird. Duke tried to take the bird from George but failed, then Duke swam over to my brother's boat, took one of his ducks, and delivered it to me.

ONE HAND DELIVERY

Bill Chilcott from Bellingham, Washington and I were to judge the Southern Arizona Trial at Bullhead City. Bill owned the great bitch, Gradys Shadee Ladee. This was to be Bill's first experience judging a championship stake. He had attended a trial the previous week and watched Ray Staudinger take delivery from Jaguar. Ray had a routine for getting the bird.

He would use both hands: one on the bird and the other picking feathers from the dog's mouth (or from the bird direct). At the opportune moment he would take the bird. Bill was concerned about it, so much so that he could not accept it. Guy Burnett, the Field Trial Chairman, suggested that on one test we require the handler to hold a gun while taking delivery, thus having only one hand to take delivery. Bill allowed that we would accept that. We set a triple mark in which the handler fired one shot (popper) at the last bird down as it was thrown in the water. His dog was sitting at his side, and the handler held the gun throughout the test. Ray Staudinger got all three birds cleanly. However, we noted that some of the dogs, including some hard-going ones, were obviously very nervous about the gun. Several dogs, when going for the marks, would stop several times and look back to the handler to be reassured that all was well.

YOU RUN AND I'LL SCORE

Dick Hecker, owner, trainer and handler of Dolabrans Smoke Tail, who won the National Championship in 1960, was judging a trial. He and his co-judge had set up a blind retrieve with a poison bird. A contestant, coming to line, asked Dick how he was going to score the test. Dick replied, "Why don't you just concentrate on running your dog the very best you can, and I'll concentrate on scoring and do the best I can!"

WHAT DID THAT DOG DO?

I was scheduled to judge the Memphis Field Trial. I arrived at the Memphis terminal very late on a Wednesday night. I took a cab to the motel where I was to stay. I knew that the trial was to be held at the Shelby County Penal Farm. I was interested in the distance between the motel and farm because we would be driving there every day. I asked the driver if he knew where the Penal Farm was. "Oh yes sir," he said, "in fact we will be going right through the farm on the way to the motel on this circle route." I asked him to let me know when we reached the farm so I could measure the time to the motel. After a pause he asked, "What you got to do with that Penal Farm?" I explained that there was going to be a dog trial out there and I was going to be the judge. After a long pause he said, "What did that dog do that you got him on trial?"

SERVES HIM RIGHT

At a Spring Trial in Minnesota the water was still very cold. The test in the amateur stake was a cold water blind to start the day. The line to the floating blind was down a wooded hill, across a pond, then across an isthmus of land, then halfway across a second pond. Many of the dogs were reluctant to get in the water and some refused the second pond. Before running his dog one of the handlers hurriedly left the grounds. He went to another area that offered a similar land-water, land-water terrain, and did some training exercises to reinforce his water entry. When he returned to perform the test, and took his dog to line, the dog would not look at the water. He would swing his head to the side. Finally the handler ordered him to go. He ran off into the woods and had to be picked up.

HERE WE ARE

We were returning from a hunting trip on a charter DC-3. I had my amateur field champion with us. He would sit in a seat and watch the goings-on through the window. The pilot saw him and asked if he would sit in the pilot's seat. His plan was to have the dog take the pilot's seat after the plane landed, and remain there while the co-pilot taxied to the parking position. The DC-3 has a window that opens for the pilot's use. The pilot wanted to see the look on the ground attendant's face when he saw the dog "piloting" the plane. Everything worked!! The dog sat attentively. At the last moment the dog stuck his black head out the window and surveyed the area. The expression on the ground attendant's face should have been in pictures.

THANKS TO PROCRASTINATION

After my many years of working with Labs and field-trials, my wife confided with me that many times she had considered offering an ultimatum, "It's going to be either the dogs or me; either they go or I go," and now she's afraid she waited too long.

A MATTER OF CHOICE

We were having a meeting of the Minnesota Field Trial Association Board of Directors. After disposing of the club's business problems, the group got into the more enjoyable activities of dog talk, gossip, drinking, etc. One of the items of the discussion related to a man who had been very active in the sport. He had owned several field champions and had been involved in national affairs, but was now quitting the sport. There was speculation as to why he was getting out. The consensus was that his wife was the cause. Apparently she disliked going to field- trials and objected to having to stay home when he went without her. His solution was to quit going.

One of the group was off by himself and wasn't involved in the conversation. We all thought he was asleep. Surely he had consumed a few. Someone said we ought to wake him up. "Hey, Bill, what do you think about this situation of Joe and his wife?" Bill raised his head and very clearly replied, "I am a very lucky person. I have both a good wife and a good dog (FC-AFC). If I had to lose one of them, I think it would be harder to replace the dog than the wife."

FIRST THINGS FIRST

Guy Burnett and I were scheduled to judge the Duluth, Minnesota Trial. We had prearranged that Guy would fly to Minneapolis and I would pick him up and drive to Duluth. Things started to go bad early that day. I had to go to work, and as I was dressing I noticed a small leak in the plumbing in the bathroom. I got a wrench and attempted to tighten the fitting. In my haste I split the fitting and had water all over the bathroom. I rushed to close the valve that supplies the whole house. I hurried off to work, leaving instructions to call the plumber. Later in the day a problem came up that would necessitate my staying at work a couple of hours later than planned. I got word to Guy to take a cab to my home and meet me there. When I arrived home I learned that the plumber couldn't come that day, but Guy was there. I found Guy under the bathroom fixture working on the plumbing. I said, "Come on, we have to get to Duluth. The plumber will probably be out tomorrow." Guy responded, "Calm down, we are not going to leave this house until the plumbing is fixed and the water is on. Now get out of my way so I can get it fixed." Guy was truly a great guy!

COOL AS A CUCUMBER

In 1969, Miss Valerie Fisher (later Mrs. Jay Walker) came all the way from Oregon to Burlington, Wisconsin to compete in the Amateur National Championship. Her dog was Misty's Sungold Lad. Val was without doubt the youngest handler in the trial, and probably the youngest handler ever to compete in a National, before or since. My guess is that the was 16 years of age.

As the trial progressed, people became more and more impressed with the dog and the handler. Val was as cool as a cucumber, no emotion, very professional. Lad was putting down outstanding work. The ninth series was running, and Val and Lad were still in. The tension was building, but Val showed no emotion. The marshals were lining up the contestants as their numbers approached. Where was Val Fisher? No one had seen her. Finally they found her. She was asleep in the back seat of the car. She completed the ninth and tenth tests and became a finalist in the National Amateur Championship.

FUN TRIAL

In 1965 the National Amateur was to be run in Park Rapids, Minnesota. The Duluth Field Trial was to be held on the previous weekend. Guy Burnett and I were scheduled to judge in previous years, when the Amateur National was held in Park Rapids. Many of the competing dogs ran the Duluth Trial as part of the pre-trial training program. The Duluth Club expected about 40 of these dogs in the open stake. They ordered extra birds and even scheduled the trial to start a day earlier. When the entries closed, they had only 16 dogs entered in the open stake. The National crowd went directly to the Park Rapids area for pre-trial training. Almost all of the dogs entered at Duluth were field champions handled by pro-handlers Billy Wunderlich, Tony Betget, Roger Reopelle and Jake Baird. We decided to have some fun. We ran seven series, and, except for mandatory eliminations, we carried all dogs to the end.

A RETRIEVER MAKES A CONVERT

My brother invited my father and I to join him and his friend Fred to hunt ducks. This friend had a cabin on a lake in Northern Minnesota. It was the last weekend of the season. My brother explained that my AFC Lab would have to stay outside as the owners objected to having dogs in the cabin. I fed my dog outside and he stayed the night in the wagon. By morning the temperature dropped to well below freezing. The lake was covered with ice. We loaded the boat and in the dark we crossed the lake, breaking ice all the way. We chose a point with a strong offshore wind. We assembled a makeshift blind and put out the decoys while birds were splashing into the water. A late flight of blue-billed ducks was in. Every few minutes a flock would strafe our set. We shot 24 ducks (limit). My dog, Duke, retrieved every one out of the icy water. Some floated well out to sea with the off-shore wind. Our host finally awakened to the fact that we had a dog. He had never hunted with a working retriever. He was amazed with the dog's performance. He never stopped talking about the dog. When we arrived back at the cabin he insisted that the dog be brought in. He proceeded to fix a bed for the dog in front of the fireplace and put an extra steak on the grill. Until the day Fred died, he was still talking about the dog.

CROSSCOUNTRY TOUR

Bob Pepper of Bellevue, Washington had his Lab, Pepper's Jiggs, qualified for the National Amateur Stake of 1960. It was held in Batavia, New York. Bob had a foreign sports roadster which he drove from Bellevue, Washington to Batavia, New York with Jiggs sitting beside him. Three years later at the 1963 National Amateur Stake, held in Sheridan, Wyoming, Bob and Jiggs won the National title, with an unusual display of courage —he did it on three legs.

LOVE IS A MANY-SPLENDORED THING

It was at the fall National in St. Louis in 1970. The members of the marshal's committee were socializing in the chairman's room after a long day in the field. As the night wore on, and the bottles became "dead soldiers," some were talking, some sleeping, few were listening. One member was going on and on about how much he loved his wife. He repeated it several times. Then after a long pause he said, "You know, as much as I love my wife, I believe I love my dogs more." He did have two field champion Labradors.

Shooting Over a Labrador

by J. W. McAssey

Many years ago some of our present Labrador's ancestors were working in Newfoundland in the fishing industry and occasionally helping their owners on hunting trips. Word spread to the English regarding the versatility and temperament of these fine dogs. Many were purchased to use for hunting and shooting activities by the English.

Eventually, hunters in the eastern part of the United States began importing retrievers from England. In 1931, field and conformation events were started and some 60 years later continue to grow and prosper.

In the United States today, the Labrador Retriever is number one in registrations by the American Kennel Club and a popular choice for those hunting upland game and waterfowl. In an ever increasing number, several hundred retriever clubs have been formed to sponsor training and trials which test and evaluate retrievers in various field activities. Labradors are used in many other phases of our society although his principal activity remains in the field.

Labradors have won all but one of the last 75 National and National Amateur Retriever Championship Stakes. It is therefore logical to assume this breed could also excel in the field, and they do. Disregard remarks and rumors that field trial champions or field-trial dogs do not make good hunting dogs. Many field trial champions and a large majority of those retrievers participating in field trials and hunting tests are used as hunting companions.

River Oaks Corky, elected to the Retriever Hall of Fame on the first ballot, high-point retriever to date and winner of United States and Canadian National Championships, was an outstanding hunting dog. Not only did Mike hunt Corky the normal trial season but, time and conditions permitting, they competed in several Canadian National Championship Stakes as well.

Many field trial champions are used by their owners for hunting—some during the trial season and others after the National is completed. Much depends upon the age and experience of the dog. It would certainly be poor policy

397

and counterproductive to hunt every dog while competing in field trials. It would be equally frustrating to attempt to win a field-trial event carrying championship points with an excellent hunting dog without ample training. Another farce is the "self-trained" retriever that never had a lesson and learned to do it all on his own. I wouldn't rely on being fortunate enough to find one of those rare critters. Yet I have seen dozens of them, but seldom one that was as gifted as his master boasted.

Taking a dog hunting, or releasing him in a field with little or no training, is a poor policy. For the dog's safety, he should do several things well: heel, sit, stay and come when called. He should do them consistently, not when it just pleases him.

Many parts of the country, particularly in the West, have large and varied areas of hazardous terrain. Occasionally the best hunting is in those areas where the conditions are less than ideal. Dogs, like their owners, have to learn how best to take care of themselves. It is no place for beginners—man or beast.

The following is from an article recently released by the Associated Press; Idaho was the state heading "Dog survives 100-foot fall at Shoshone Falls": "Whittaker's two-year-old black Labrador Jolly survived a fall of almost 100 feet when she jumped over a rock wall. The falls had grown from a trickle to a torrent by the first abundant water supply in years. Jolly apparently heard the water but a low rock wall prevented her from seeing how far away it was. The dog bolted over the wall. A trip to the veterinarian on Friday revealed no major injuries." Fortunately Jolly wasn't hunting in the Hells Canyon area—6000 feet to the bottom. If DL reads this I'm confident he would say (or think), "Hey man, that's the kind of dog I've been looking for all my life." So much for the self-trained hunting dog — if you really like him—train him or have him trained.

A good start towards having a good hunting companion is to purchase a pup from proven bloodlines and a couple of "how-to" books at the same time. If you don't have the experience as a trainer, or the inclination or time to learn, there are many good professional trainers available to do the job. Another option, and generally a reliable course of action, is to find a young (one to two year old) field trial "drop out" who has good basic training. They generally make outstanding hunters with a minimum of maintenance. Keep in mind they forget (conveniently) faster than they learn, soon pick up the habit of "doing it my way" and most can forget one year of training in one month of hunting on his own.

For many, an important part of some types of hunting depends directly on the quality and ability of the hunting dog. Over the years it was my good fortune to have friends who had good dogs. Though Clive, long-time friend and hunting companion, never succeeded to train a field trial champion, he did train two outstanding hunters. Clive's Babe was his second top hunting dog, but number one to him in many ways and for various reasons. She was one of the better looking bitches regardless of breed, an entertainer and a pleasure to have around. Babe was a talented hunting partridge, grouse, quail and ducks. Also a noted retriever of rocks thrown into ponds, creeks, irrigation ditches, swimming pools, etc., plus a few parlor tricks just to keep everyone awake.

Once or twice a season Babe would go off the deep end for no apparent reason and it would take five to ten minutes to pick her up. We always thought she put on that act so she wouldn't be taken for granted—a true bitch. Also a joy to be around and just about everything a Labrador is expected to be. Clive's Murph was number one—a unanimous vote by everyone who had the pleasure of hunting with him. Murph hunted where you asked him to, stopped on command and could trail a crippled pheasant like a Walker Hound after a rabbit. It wasn't unusual for him to hunt an entire season without losing a cripple. A remarkable performance for 30 to 40 pheasant hunts per year.

Murph was fortunate enough to hunt with some of the experienced hunters and best wing shots in any league. Almost without exception, all in that group would manage to hunt at least 100 days each year—and did so for many years.

I have known a few outstanding hunting teams (men and retrievers) that would lose only a few birds during a lengthy season lasting from September through February. Varied terrain from Canada to the Mexican border, and a mix of game, including doves, grouse, partridge, quail and waterfowl, provided unusual and difficult challenges to the dogs.

A conservative estimate would be a recovery rate in excess of 90% of downed game. A notable number when compared to several state and federal surveys that indicated less than 50% of game was recovered when dogs were not used. A recovery rate of 90% would probably be higher than the average group shooting over retrievers would achieve. When multiple hunters shoot over one dog, many factors determine how efficiently that dog and/or team will perform.

Experienced hunters who have shot together over a number of years generally establish a routine of gunning procedures, responsibility as to which sectors each individual shoots plus assisting the dog(s). This atmosphere not only is beneficial to the hunters but is crucial to get good performance from the dog—particularly one that may be young and has had limited exposure to actual hunting conditions.

When more than one hunter shoots over a dog, many factors determine the ability of that dog to perform efficiently. Even the best retriever can only be expected to mark the birds he sees fall. With several shooters firing simultaneously in different directions it is near-impossible for one dog to mark all the falls. Each shooter should be responsible to a great degree to mark the birds he shot to enable him to assist the retrievers. If an inexperienced hunter with marginal shooting skills is involved in a covey rise, frequently birds downed are not well marked and there is also a good chance for runners to cause additional problems.

Failure to mark a fall is not limited to beginners or those with limited field experience. A surprising number of hunters *never* learn to mark their birds accurately after having hunted hundreds of days over a period of years.

Two cronies of mine, Clive and Louie, frequently hunted together for some 30 years. Clive always had one or two hunting dogs on hand that couldn't make it on the field-trial circuit. Louie was an excellent shot, and many times over the course of a season would make multiple kills when shooting conditions were ideal. Louie seldom had even a reasonable mark on any downed bird unless it was the one that fell to his final round. After finding that bird he would only have a vague recollection of any other fall. This problem would always cause a "time out" while Clive and the dog(s) were pressed into service.

After some 20 years of pleading, coaching and threatening, Clive finally convinced Louie to try the old method of placing his hat on the ground in the vicinity of the fall. All went well for a few days until we spotted a covey of Hungarian partridge in a large field of wheat stubble. The shooters went out and left the dogs in the crates.

Several birds were shot and Louie watched the flight of the departing which flew in a long wide circle before landing some distance away. After marking them down, Louie found himself completely turned around and was uncertain as to his original position, and was now looking across a flat stubble field that appeared the same for a half mile in every direction.

Clive picked up his two birds while Louie was wandering around muttering to himself about his ability (or lack thereof) to mark birds. Clive baited him with the suggestion to put his hat down to mark the area, go look for the other bird, and he would get the car and the dogs. Clive drove the car down and parked it directly over Louie's hat without Louie noticing what he was was doing. Clive took a dog and proceeded towards Louie. In short order his dog found the first of Louie's birds and Clive inquired as to the location of the other fall.

Louie advised that he had put his hat down as directed, but it wasn't in sight. While the needling was in progress that now he couldn't even find his hat, and possibly parts of his anatomy at times, the dog came up with the missing bird—only 20 feet or so from the car and Louie's hat.

When first hunting Canada and parts of the United States many years ago, it was unusual to encounter another party hunting with retrievers. This is no longer true, particularly when hunting waterfowl. The drastic reduction in game, seasons and available areas to hunt makes it more important today to own a retriever. Good dogs not only will produce more shooting opportunities to the hunters but will put more birds in the bag. It is now, and always has been, important to find every bird that falls to the gun. This is the primary purpose of the retriever.

All things considered, today's Labrador Retriever is probably the most outstanding retriever of waterfowl and upland game birds. It is one of the most versatile and possibly best of all breeds to use when hunting a combination of waterfowl and upland game birds.

Gene Hill's one-liner in his *Field and Stream* article "Wishful Thinking" summarized what I've spent hours trying to portray, "Why don't they finally admit that other gundogs just aren't as good as Labradors?"

Judge's Anthology

by Dr. Bernard W. Ziessow

I believe all judges are asked, at one time or another, how they ever became involved in judging dogs. Whenever this happens to me, I'm reminded of this story:

A young man meets a "lady of the evening." Some time during their encounter, he asks, "How did a lovely girl like you ever become involved in this way of life?" She responds, "Just lucky, I guess."

Over the past 50 years I have met many judges. Each came from a somewhat different background but all shared a similar love for dogs and most believed they were making a contribution. Very few became judges for selfish reasons. Maybe, we're "just lucky."

When I first became a judge, my colleagues were such authorities as Alva Rosenberg, Percy Roberts, Louis Muir, Darek Rayne, Sadie Edmonson, Bea and Major Godsel, Vince Perry, Max Riddle and many others; most are no longer with us. Having breakfast or dinner with them was a real learning experience. And watching them judge was a lesson in itself.

I remember one time I was judging in the East. A well-known handler had shown a really outstanding Pointer to great success. At the particular show, the good Pointer was not present so the handler showed another dog with similar markings and won best of breed. When the dog was shown in the Group, the judge, Alva Rosenberg, whispered in the handler's ear, "Where did you ever find this one?" To the handler's dismay, the dog was left out of the Group ribbons. No one ever slipped a "ringer" on Alva; he never forgot a dog once he had seen him.

One of my favorite people was all-breed judge Joseph Fagel. Joe and I were members of Oakland County Kennel Club. We lived quite close to one another and often traveled to shows together. One time we were both judging at Phoenix. We had breakfast and traveled to the show site. When we arrived, the show secretary Helen Seder noticed that Joe's shoes were different—one shoe was black and white, the other brown and white. When she pointed this out to Joe, he responded "Yes, I know, I have another pair at home just like them."

I also have fond memories of training field dogs (English Springer Spaniels) with Maxwell Riddle. When it became too dark to work, we would return to Max's home and "skinny dip" in his pond, to be followed by a few drinks and a good steak. Then we would sit up half the night talking about dogs.

Becoming a judge in the early days was no easier but somewhat less involved than it is today. You filled out a multi-page application, provided references, and wrote a 100-word description of the breed or breeds applied for. If you were able to obtain approval from Albert Dick, for many years Executive Secretary of the American Kennel Club, you were permitted to apprentice under three different judges; each of whom sent a critique to the AKC. You then could be approved as a provisional judge and remained as such for three successive shows. But, in those days, there were fewer judges, fewer shows and fewer dogs. A really big show was 1000 dogs, and judges could judge 200 dogs a day. Accordingly, the only judges that charged a fee were those approved for more than one Group. And if you were not approved to judge a group, you couldn't even charge expenses. The learning process could be quite expensive.

The first breed for which I was approved was Labrador Retrievers, and my first assignment was the Heart of America Show at Kansas City. The club paid for my dinner and room but I had to cover my own air transportation from Detroit (and I was accompanied by my wife Madge). We flew from Detroit to Chicago and then changed planes to Kansas City. Our plane got to Kansas City (1000 feet straight up) but we did not land; the airport was engulfed in a blinding snowstorm. We flew back to Chicago and preceded to Kansas City via rail; arriving at 11:00 p.m., too late for the judges' dinner.

My first judging experience was unforgettable. Most of the dogs were shown by professional handlers: Hollis Wilson, Dick Cooper, Ed Bracey, Tom Crowe, Larry Downey and others of equally high reputation. I remember putting Hollis up with a really good-looking black Labrador that, I later learned, finished his Dual Championship that day. His name was Nilo Possibility, a great field dog that went on to win the National Championship Stake in 1958. In those days, it was not uncommon to see top field dogs winning in the show ring. And, many of the Sporting Group judges were actively engaged in field work: Joe Quirk, Vergil Johnson, Ray Beale, Fred Hunt, Max Riddle and Jack Spears—to name a few.

At that time, professional handlers were truly "professionals." Showing dogs was their only job and, like judges, they required AKC approval to handle dogs. Few, if any, of the really good ones "picked up" dogs at shows. Most insisted upon examining a dog before they agreed to handle it. And they trained and conditioned their dogs before they would take them into the show ring. Yes, they were truly "professionals." Many went on to become judges and, because of their experience and backgrounds, were knowledgeable and respected.

Fortunately, my judging experience began after air travel was the common mode of travel to most shows; in the real early days, judges traveled by car or rail. While I (and most judges) have "war" stories about the early days of air travel, my most memorable experience happened only a few years ago.

Several of us were judging a cluster of shows in Wisconsin and were scheduled to fly a commuter plane back to Chicago, en-route to our final destination. We boarded our plane, the doors were closed and the port engine was started. When they attempted to start the starboard engine, nothing happened. It was dead. After several unsuccessful attempts to get it going, the pilot and co-pilot deplaned and walked around to inspect the engine. Soon, a mechanic arrived and the cowl was opened to permit better examination. In due time it was closed and the pilot and co-pilot re-boarded the plane. After several coughs, the engine started and a puff of black smoke emitted from the exhaust. It was "revved-up" and we started down the runway for take off. After we were airborne, the stewardess came over the loud speaker and gave a most reassuring announcement: "You have nothing to worry about, the plane never gets above 2500 feet." And, there was no beverage service aboard.

Another time, Isadore Shoenberg and I were scheduled to judge in Texarkana. The Dallas Airport was virtually closed because of ice storms and our flight was canceled. We decided the only way to get to our destination was via bus so we took a taxi to the bus depot. Have you ever been in a Dallas bus depot? If you haven't, don't. After about a two-hour wait, we boarded our bus, a "local" that stopped in every borough and hamlet between Dallas and Texarkana.When, at 12:30 a.m., we finally arrived at our destination, the bus driver took pity on us and, rather than taking us to the bus depot, dropped us off in front of our hotel. And, he refused a ten-dollar tip.

But to me the time wasn't wasted; no one could spend seven hours with "Izzy" Shoenberg without learning something.

Memorable travel experiences are not always limited to air travel. Many years ago I was assigned to judge the Battle Creek Kennel Club Show, an easy two-hour drive from my office in Dearborn. The show was held in March and to say March weather in Michigan is unpredictable is a gross understatement. It started to rain in the early afternoon on the day before the show so I left my office about 3:00 p.m. because of possible adverse driving conditions. By the time I reached Ann Arbor (about 30 miles from my office), the rain turned to sleet and the highway soon became a sheet of ice. Cars and trucks were in the ditches and semi-trailers were jack-knifed; on the highway driving degenerated from skill to a game of chance—the longer you drove the greater your chance of ending up in the ditch.

At 8:30 p.m. that evening I finally arrived at my motel. I parked my car, checked in and started to my room. As I passed an open door, I heard someone call "Berney." I looked in to see Louie Muir. He said, "You look like you need a drink" and proceeded to pour a water tumbler half-full of Anton Korbel's private stock brandy. (Mr. Korbel , a long-time all-breed judge and famous vintner, used to send Louie a case of his brandy every Christmas.) That was one drink I shall never forget.

If one believes as a judge he will always be treated as an honored guest, he will, somewhere along the line, be subject to a rude awakening. However, "if you can't stand the heat, stay out of the kitchen." Dog shows are run by people, most are very kind and considerate; unfortunately, others treat judges as "hired hands" and are convinced that a judge's one aim in life is to cheat on his or her expense accounts. But, it has been my experience that these people are in the minority, and most show-giving clubs extend themselves to make the judging experience a pleasant one. And as someone once said "this is a frcc country," no one is forcing you to accept an assignment.

Long before I ever judged dog shows, I judged hunters and jump-ers at horse shows. I also ran dogs in field trials and judged both English Springer Spaniel and retriever trials. Frequently my wife Madge and I would travel to Wadsworth, Illinois for long weekends. She would fox hunt with the Mill Creek Hounds and I would train Labradors with Cliff Wallace. Cliff was one of the top field-trial handlers in the country and was engaged at that time by Mr. James Simpson (Stonybroke). As an aside, Cliff won the National Retriever Stake with NFC-Dual Ch. Shed of Arden when Shed's owner and regular handler Paul Bakewell was in service during World War II.

Whenever Jim Simpson got word of our visits to Mill Creek, he would ask that I stop by to see him. I would be met by the butler and ushered into drawing room. Soon after Jim arrived he would summon the butler saying, "Mr. Ziessow would enjoy a drink and I will join him." I never did determine if Jim wanted to see me or just didn't like to drink alone.

As long as I can recall, there were AKC representatives. Except today there are many more of them. The first one I remember was Billy Lang, an old-time handler. He was followed by Joseph Storey. Since there was only one or two reps to cover the entire country, one rarely saw them at shows. But, when they did, everyone was on his good behavior. I can still see Joe Storey in the superintendent's office, sitting at his typewriter.

And I remember having breakfast with Joe and his wife Mary at

Darby Chambers place in Stowe, Vermont while on the New England circuit.

This brings to mind my long-time friend "Charlie" Meyer. He was a handler in those days and a good one. One time, Ken Golden, who handled Sam of Blaircourt for Mrs. Grace Lambert, asked Charlie to take a class dog that had gone winners for the best-of-breed judging; Ken was handling "Sam." Maybe Ken should have known better because Charlie had a reputation as a great "kidder." All during the judging procedures Charlie called the other dog "Sam." Yes, Ken won but after much consternation and no little worry.

Forty years ago, there were only a handful of dog publications, compared to over one hundred today. The proliferation is due in part to the increased number of dogs and dog shows. It is also attributable to the number of dogs being "campaigned" and the apparent need to create a dog's reputation so that he can do top winning. While there are many very excellent dog publications, others are merely picture books with page after page of photographs of dogs winning this or that, here or there, under so and so; interspersed with articles written by someone you never heard of about topics you couldn't care less.

There is an often used expression that old judges never die, they just fade away. I really don't know if it is true, but the older a judge gets, the fewer assignments he will take. He becomes more selective regarding shows, remembering unpleasant experiences; it become less and less rewarding to gamble with plane schedules and the weatherman; and with each successive show, he sees fewer and fewer of his old friends.

They tell a story of a dog-show judge that died and went to Heaven, while waiting for his accommodations at the Pearly Gates, he met a Methodist minister that passed away on the same day. Saint Peter first called the minister and had him escorted to his living quarters, a lovely townhouse, beautifully furnished and with a brand new Ford Taurus in the driveway. After a few days, the minister, wondering how his new friend, the dog-show judge, was doing, decided to drive out to see him. He received directions and when he arrived at the judge's residence he was amazed. A beautiful villa, complete with swimming pool and formal gardens and, parked in the driveway was a Lincoln Town Car. After he had completed his visit, the minister called Saint Peter. He explained that he had devoted his life to being a faithful servant of the Lord and, while he was not complaining, he couldn't understand why the dog-show judge was so much better off than he in the "life hereafter." Saint Peter was most understanding, he explained "Reverend, this place is full of Methodist ministers, but very few dog-show judges ever make it!"

Official Standard for the Labrador Retriever

General Appearance–The Labrador Retriever is a strongly built, medium-sized, short-coupled dog possessing a sound, athletic, well-balanced conformation that enables it to function as a retrieving gun dog; the substance and soundness to hunt waterfowl or upland game for long hours under difficult conditions; the character and quality to win in the show ring; and the temperament to be a family companion. Physical features and mental characteristics should denote a dog bred to perform as an efficient retriever of game with a stable temperament suitable for a variety of pursuits beyond the hunting environment.

The most distinguishing characteristics of the Labrador Retriever are its short, dense, weather-resistant coat; an "otter" tail; a clean-cut head with broad back skull and moderate stop; powerful jaws; and its "kind," friendly eyes, expressing character, intelligence and good temperament.

Above all, a Labrador Retriever must be well balanced, enabling it to move in the show ring or work in the field with little or no effort. The typical Labrador possesses style and quality without over-refinement, and substance without lumber or cloddiness. The Labrador is bred primarily as a working gun dog; structure and soundness are of great importance.

Size, Proportion and Substance—*Size*—The height at the withers for a dog is $22^1/_2$ to $24^1/_2$ inches; for a bitch is $21^1/_2$ to $23^1/_2$ inches. Any variance greater than $^1/_2$ inch above or below these heights is a disqualification. Approximate weight of dogs and bitches in working condition: dogs 65 to 80 pounds; bitches 55 to 70 pounds.

The minimum height ranges set forth in the paragraph above shall not apply to dogs or bitches under twelve months of age.

Proportion—Short-coupled: length from the point of the shoulder to the point of the rump is equal to or slightly longer than the distance from the withers to the ground. Distance from the elbow to the ground should be equal to one half of the height at the withers. The brisket should extend to the elbows, but not perceptibly deeper. The body must be of sufficient length to permit a straight, free and efficient stride; but the dog should never appear low and long or tall

407

and leggy in outline. *Substance*—Substance and bone proportionate to the overall dog. Light, "weedy" individuals are definitely incorrect; equally objectionable are cloddy lumbering specimens. Labrador Retrievers shall be shown in working condition, well-muscled and without excess fat.

Head—*Skull*—The skull should be wide: well developed but without exaggeration. The skull and foreface should be on parallel planes and of approximately equal length. There should be a moderate stop—the brow slightly pronounced so that the skull is not absolutely in a straight line with the nose. The brow ridges aid in defining the stop. The head should be clean-cut and free from fleshy cheeks: the bony structure of the skull chiseled beneath the eye with no prominence in the cheek. The skull may show some median line; the occipital bone is not conspicuous in mature dogs. Lips should not be squared off or pendulous, but fall away in a curve toward the throat. A wedge-shape head, or a head long and narrow in muzzle and back skull, is incorrect as are massive, cheeky heads. The jaws are powerful and free from snippiness–the muzzle neither long and narrow nor short and stubby. *Nose*—The nose should be wide and the nostrils well-developed. The nose should be black on black or yellow dogs, and brown on chocolates. Nose color fading to a lighter shade is not a fault. A thoroughly pink nose or one lacking in any pigment is a disqualification. *Teeth*—The teeth should be strong and regular with a scissors bite; the lower teeth just behind, but touching the inner side of the upper incisors. A level bite is acceptable, but not desirable. Undershot, overshot or misaligned teeth are serious faults. Full dentition is preferred. Missing molars or pre-molars are serious faults. *Ears*—The ears should hang moderately close to the head, set rather far back, and somewhat low on the skull; slightly above eye level. Ears should not be large and heavy, but in proportion with the skull and reach to the inside of the eye when pulled forward. *Eyes*—Kind, friendly eyes imparting good temperament, intelligence and alertness are a hallmark of the breed. They should be of medium size, set well apart, and neither protruding nor deep set. Eye color should be brown in black and yellow Labradors, and brown or hazel in chocolates. Black or yellow eyes give a harsh expression and are undesirable. Small eyes, set close together, or round prominent eyes are not typical of the breed. Eye rims are black in black and yellow Labradors; and brown in chocolates. Eye rims without pigmentation is a disqualification.

Neck, Topline and Body—*Neck*—The neck should be of proper length to allow the dog to retrieve game easily. It should be muscular and free from throatiness. The neck should rise strongly from the shoulders with a moderate arch. A short, thick neck or a "ewe" neck is incorrect. *Topline*—The back is strong and the topline is level from the withers to the croup when standing or moving.

However, the loin should show evidence of flexibility for athletic endeavor. *Body*—The Labrador should be short-coupled, with good spring of ribs tapering to a moderately wide chest. The Labrador should not be narrow chested; giving the appearance of hollowness between the front legs, nor should it have a wide spreading, bulldog-like front. Correct chest conformation will result in tapering between the front legs that allows unrestricted forelimb movement. Chest breadth that is either too wide or too narrow for efficient movement and stamina is incorrect. Slab-sided individuals are not typical of the breed; equally objectionable are rotund or barrel chested specimens. The underline is almost straight, with little or no tuck-up in mature animals. Loins should be short, wide and strong; extending to well developed powerful hindquarters. When viewed from the side, the Labrador Retriever shows a well-developed, but not exaggerated, forechest. *Tail*— The tail is a distinguishing feature of the breed. It should be very thick at the base, gradually tapering toward the tip, of medium length, and extending no longer than to the hock. The tail should be free from feathering and clothed thickly all around with the Labrador's short, dense coat, thus having that peculiar rounded appearance that has been described as the "otter" tail. The tail should follow the topline in repose or when in motion. It may be carried gaily, but should not curl over the back.

Extremely short tails or long thin tails are serious faults. The tail completes the balance of the Labrador by giving it a flowing line from the top of the head to the tip of the tail. Docking or otherwise altering the length or natural carriage of the tail is a disqualification.

Forequarters—Forequarters should be muscular, well coordinated and balanced with the hindquarters. *Shoulders*—The shoulders are well laid-back, long and sloping, forming an angle with the upper arm of approximately 90 degrees that permits the dog to move his forelegs in an easy manner with strong forward reach. Ideally, the length of the shoulder blade should equal the length of the upper arm. Straight shoulder blades, short upper arms or heavily muscled or loaded shoulders, all restricting free movement, are incorrect. *Front Legs*—When viewed from the front, the legs should be straight with good strong bone. Too much bone is as undesirable as too little bone, and short-legged, heavy-boned individuals are not typical of the breed. Viewed from the side, the elbows should be directly under the withers, and the front legs should be perpendicular to the ground and well under the body. The elbows should be close to the ribs without looseness. Tied-in elbows or being "out at the elbows" interfere with free movement and are serious faults. Pasterns should be strong and short and should slope slightly from the perpendicular line of the leg. Feet are strong and compact, with well-arched toes and well-developed pads. Dew claws may be removed. Splayed feet, hare feet, knuckling over, or feet turning in or out are serious faults.

Hindquarters—The Labrador's hindquarters are broad, muscular and well-developed from the hip to the hock with well-turned stifles and strong short hocks. Viewed from the rear, the hind legs are straight and parallel. Viewed from the side, the angulation of the rear legs is in balance with the front. The hind legs are strongly boned, muscled with moderate angulation at the stifle, and powerful, clearly defined thighs. The stifle is strong and there is no slippage of the patella while in motion or when standing. The hock joints are strong, well let down and do not slip or hyper-extend while in motion or when standing. Angulation of both stifle and hock joint is such as to achieve the optimal balance of drive and traction. When standing the rear toes are only slightly behind the point of the rump. Over-angulation produces a sloping topline not typical of the breed. Feet are strong and compact, with well-arched toes and well-developed pads. Cow-hocks, spread hocks, sickle hocks and over-angulation are serious structural defects and are to be faulted.

Coat—The coat is a distinctive feature of the Labrador Retriever. It should be short, straight and very dense, giving a fairly hard feeling to the hand. The Labrador should have a soft, weather-resistant undercoat that provides protection from water, cold and all types of ground cover. A slight wave down the back is permissible. Woolly coats, soft silky coats, and sparse slick coats are not typical of the breed, and should be severely penalized.

Color—The Labrador Retriever coat colors are black, yellow and chocolate. Any other color or a combination of colors is a disqualification. A small white spot on the chest is permissible, but not desirable. White hairs from aging or scarring are not to be misinterpreted as brindling. *Black*—Blacks are all black. A black with brindle markings or a black with tan markings is a disqualification. *Yellow*—Yellows may range in color from fox-red to light cream, with variations in shading on the ears, back and underparts of the dog. *Chocolate*—Chocolates can vary in shade from light to dark chocolate. Chocolate with brindle or tan markings is a disqualification.

Movement—Movement of the Labrador Retriever should be free and effortless. When watching a dog move toward oneself, there should be no sign of elbows out. Rather, the elbows should be held neatly to the body with the legs not too close together. Moving straight forward without pacing or weaving, the legs should form straight lines, with all parts moving in the same plane. Upon viewing the dog from the rear, one should have the impression that the hind legs move as nearly as possible in a parallel line with the front legs. The hocks should do their full share of the work, flexing well, giving the appearance of power and strength. When viewed from the side, the shoulders should move freely and effortlessly, and the foreleg should reach forward close to the ground with extension. A short, choppy movement or high knee action indicates a straight shoulder; paddling indicates long, weak pasterns; and a short, stilted rear gait indicates a straight rear assembly: all are serious faults. Movement faults interfering with performance, including weaving; side-winding; crossing over; high knee action; paddling; and short, choppy movement, should be severely penalized.

Temperament—True Labrador Retriever temperament is as much a hallmark of the breed as the "otter" tail. The ideal disposition is one of a kindly, outgoing, tractable nature: eager to please and non-aggressive towards man or animal. The Labrador has much that appeals to people: his gentle ways, intelligence and adaptability make him an ideal dog. Aggressiveness toward humans or other animals, or any evidence of shyness in an adult, should be severely penalized.

DISQUALIFICATIONS
1. Any deviation from the height prescribed in the Standard.
2. A thoroughly pink nose or one lacking in any pigment.
3. Eye rims without pigment.
4. Docking or otherwise altering the length or natural carriage of the tail.
5. Any other color or a combination of colors other than black, yellow or chocolate as described in the Standard.

Approval Date: February 12, 1994

Effective Date: March 31, 1994

© *The American Kennel Club, Inc., 1994*

LRC Constitution and By-Laws

CONSTITUTION
ARTICLE I
Name and Objects

SECTION 1. The name of the Club shall be Labrador Retriever Club, Incorporated.

SECTION 2. The goal of the Club shall be to encourage and promote quality in the breeding and performance of pure-bred Labrador Retrievers and to do all possible to bring their natural attributes as working retrievers to perfection.

SECTION 3. In furtherance of its goal the Club will:

(a) encourage the organization of independent local Labrador Retriever clubs to promote performance and conformation events;

(b) encourage members and breeders to accept the Standard of the breed as approved by the American Kennel Club as the standard of excellence by which Labrador Retrievers shall be judged;

(c) seek to protect and advance the interest of the breed and to encourage sportsmanlike competition at field trials, hunting retriever tests, obedience trials and conformation events;

(d) conduct, sponsor and encourage, on behalf of the Labrador Retriever breed, events including: field trials, hunting retriever tests, obedience trials, and conformation events under the rules of the American Kennel Club.

SECTION 4. The Club shall not be conducted or operated for profit and no part of any profits or remainder or residue from dues or donations to the Club shall inure to the benefit of any member or individual.

BY-LAWS
ARTICLE I
Membership

SECTION 1. ELIGIBILITY. There shall be one type of voting membership, open to persons of legal age who are in good standing with The American Kennel Club, and who, by virtue of their involvement with and demonstrated commitment to the Labrador Retriever, have shown their dedication to the purposes and goals of this Club.

SECTION 2. DUES. Membership dues shall be fixed from time-to-time by vote of the Board of Directors and shall be due and payable on or before January 1 of each year. Only members whose dues are current may vote. The Treasurer shall send to each member a notice of dues for the ensuing year. Failure to receive such notice shall not excuse non-payment of dues.

SECTION 3. ELECTION TO MEMBER-SHIP. Each applicant for membership shall apply on a form as approved by the Board of Directors. That form shall provide that the applicant agrees to abide by these Constitution and By-Laws and the rules and regulations of the American Kennel Club. In addition, the application shall state the name, address and occupation of the applicant and shall provide opportunity for the applicant to set forth detailed information intended to satisfy the eligibility requirements set forth in Section 1 of this Article. The application shall be accompanied by sponsoring letters from at least two members in good standing who have personal knowledge of the qualifications of the applicant for membership. Forms for membership application shall be provided promptly by the Secretary upon receipt of a written request. Completed applications, including the sponsoring letters and a non-refundable application fee, shall be returned to the Secretary for submission to the Board. The amount of the application fee shall be fixed by the Board of Directors in an amount reasonably calculated to defray the expenses of processing the application. Applicants may by elected to membership by written vote of the Directors acting in person or by mail. Affirmative votes of at least two-thirds of the Directors voting shall be required for election. At reasonable intervals, and at least every 120 days, the Secretary shall submit copies of the completed applications and sponsoring letters to the Directors for their consideration and vote. If an applicant fails election by the Board, the Board need not reconsider an application by the same applicant sooner than three years.

SECTION 4. TERMINATION OF MEM-BERSHIP. Memberships may be terminated:

(a) by resignation. Any member in good standing may resign from the Club upon written notice to the Secretary; but no member may resign when in debt to the Club. Dues are considered a debt to the Club and the obligation to pay dues accrues on the first day of each fiscal year.

(b) by lapsing. A membership will be considered as lapsed and auto-matically terminated if such member's dues remain unpaid 90 days after the first day of the fiscal year; however, the Board may grant an additional 90 days of grace to such delinquent members in meritorious cases. No person whose dues are unpaid as of the date of any Club meeting shall be entitled to vote at such meeting.

(c) by expulsion. A membership may be terminated by expulsion as provided in Article V of these By-Laws.

SECTION 5. HONORARY MEMBERS. In addition to voting members, hon-orary members may be elected from among those who have rendered valuable aid to the Club or to the furtherance of the Club's purposes and goals. Such honorary members may be elected by vote of 75% of the Directors or by vote of 75% of the members present and voting at an annual meeting. Honorary members shall be exempt from dues and shall be entitled to all the privileges of the Club, except that they may not vote or hold office.

ARTICLE II
Meetings

SECTION 1. ANNUAL MEETING OF MEMBERS. The annual meeting of the Club shall be held in October or November of each year at such location and on such date as may be determined by vote of the Board of Directors. Written notice of the time and place of the annual meeting shall be mailed by the Secretary to each member of the Club at least 30 days prior to the date fixed for such meeting. If, for any reason, the Board of Directors determines that the annual meeting cannot, or should not reasonably be held as aforesaid, the Board by vote may determine to hold a special meeting in lieu of the annual meeting provided that such special meeting shall be held on a date prior to the end of the calendar year. Hereafter any reference to annual meeting in these By-Laws shall include any special meeting held in lieu thereof. A quorum for the annual meeting or for any special meeting held in lieu thereof shall be 100 members or 10% of the membership, whichever is less.

SECTION 2. SPECIAL MEETINGS OF MEMBERS. A special meeting of the Club may be called by the President; or by a majority vote of the members of the Board; and shall be called by the Secretary upon receipt of a petition signed by 100 members of the Club who are in good standing. Such meeting shall be held at such place, date and hour as may be designated by the President with the approval of a majority of the Board of Directors. Written notice of such meeting shall be mailed by the Secretary at least 14 days and not more than 60 days prior to the meeting. The notice of the meeting shall state the purposes of the meeting. The quorum for such a meeting shall be 100 members or 10% of the membership, whichever is less.

SECTION 3. VOTING AT MEETINGS OF MEMBERS. At the annual meeting or at a special meeting of the Club, voting shall be limited to those members in good standing who are present at the meeting—except that the annual election of Directors and the vote on amendments to the Constitution, the By-Laws and the Standard for the breed shall be decided by written ballot cast by mail. Voting by proxy shall not be permitted. The Board of Directors may authorize submission of other specific questions for decision of the members by written ballot cast mail. The affirmative vote of a majority of those present and voting at an annual meeting or a special meeting will be required to adopt any matter brought up for consideration and vote at the meeting unless another provision of these By-Laws calls for a different level of favorable vote. All votes at meetings of the Club shall be by a show of hands unless the meeting shall adopt a secret ballot.

SECTION 4. BOARD MEETINGS. The Board of Directors shall meet immediately following the meeting of the Club at which the election of Board members for the ensuing year has occurred to elect the officers and the Delegate for the coming year, to appoint the Nominating Committee for the coming year, and to discuss the transition of Club governance. Other meetings of the Board of Directors shall be held at such times and places as may be designated by the President or by majority vote of the Board of Directors. Notice of each such meeting shall be mailed by the Secretary to each Director at least 14 days prior to the date of the meeting. The Board may hold meetings on shorter notice or without notice upon waiver of such notice by at least two-thirds of the Directors. A Board meeting may be held by teleconferencing or similar technology; and a Director unable to attend a meeting in person may participate in such meetings by telephone or may register a vote by mail. A quorum for a Board meeting shall be one-third of the Directors whether present in person or participating by telephone or by mail.

ARTICLE III

Officers and Directors

SECTION 1. OFFICERS. The officers of the Club shall consist of a President, one or more Vice-presidents, a Secretary and a Treasurer each of whom shall be elected by the Board of Directors from among the members of the Board. The office of Secretary and Treasurer may be held by the same person. They shall be elected for one-year terms as hereinafter provided and shall serve until their successors are elected and qualified.

(a) The President shall preside at all meetings of the Club and of the Board, and shall have the duties and powers normally appurtenant to the office of President in addition to those particularly specified in these By-Laws.

(b) The Vice-president or Vice-presidents shall have such powers and duties as may be assigned by the Board of Directors or by the President with the consent of the Board.

(c) The Secretary shall keep a record of all meetings of the Club and of the Board and of all votes taken by mail, and of all matters of which a record shall be ordered by the Club. The Secretary shall have charge of the correspondence, notify members of meetings, process applications for membership, notify new members of their election to membership, notify officers and Directors of their election to office, keep a roll of the members of the Club with their addresses, and carry out such other duties as are prescribed in these By-Laws.

(d) The Treasurer shall collect and receive all moneys due or belonging to the Club; shall deposit the same in a bank approved by the Board in the name of the Club; shall maintain books and records at all times open to inspection of the Board; and shall report to the Board, as requested, regarding the condition of the Club's finances. At the annual meeting the Treasurer shall render an account of all moneys received and expended during the previous fiscal year. The Treasurer shall be bonded in such amount as the Board shall determine.

SECTION 2. BOARD OF DIRECTORS. The Board of Directors shall be comprised of 21 persons all of whom shall have been members in good standing for at least three years prior to their election. The Directors shall serve for staggered terms of three years each so that one-third of the Board of Directors will stand for election at each annual meeting after the meeting in which the transition to a staggered Board is adopted. To accomplish the transition to a staggered Board, a slate of members shall be nominated for election as Directors at the annual meeting in the year 1993 and such slate shall be classified into three groups each containing seven persons who will serve, if elected, for terms of 1, 2 and 3 years respectively. At least one person resident in each time zone shall be nominated for the office of Director in each of the three groups, so that each of the time zones shall be represented in each grouping of Directors. No more than 8 persons resident in one time zone shall serve on the Board of Directors during any year. No more than 3 persons resident in one time zone shall serve in the same group of Directors during any year. Each time zone shall be represented by at least 4 residents of that time zone at all times. Any

such Directors shall serve for the term to which they were elected and thereafter until their successors are duly elected and qualified.

SECTION 3. VACANCIES. Any vacancies occurring on the Board or among the officers during the year may be filled, until the next annual election, by a majority vote of all the then members of the Board. Any vacancies filled pursuant to this section shall comply with the geographic distribution requirements set forth in Section 2 above.

SECTION 4. POWERS OF THE BOARD. The control and general management of the Club shall be vested in the Board of Directors who shall have full power to conduct the business of the Club, to deal with the Club property, to determine Club policies and to otherwise manage the affairs of the Club with the objective of furthering the purposes and goals set forth in the Club's Constitution. At the meeting of the Board held immediately following the annual meeting of the members, the Board will elect the President, the Vice-president(s), the Secretary, the Treasurer, the Delegate to the American Kennel Club, and will appoint the Nominating Committee for the ensuing year. In addition to the matters specifically reserved to the members for determination at Club meetings by these By-Laws, the Board of Directors may refer to the members for discussion and/or vote or ratification other matters which the Board in its discretion determines should properly be put before the members.

SECTION 5. DESIGNATION OF ADDITIONAL ADMINISTRATIVE OFFICERS AND COMMITTEES. The Board may each year create offices and positions of administrative responsibility within the Club and may designate persons to fill those positions for the purpose of assisting the Club's Directors and officers in carrying out their responsibilities. In addition, the Board may appoint Standing Committees to advance the work of the Club in such matters as performance events, dog shows and other activities of interest and concern to the Club. The duties and responsibilities of such appointed officers, administrative personnel and committees shall be determined by the Board of Directors and the conduct of persons appointed to such positions shall always be subject to the final authority of the Board. Special committees may also be appointed by the Board to assist on particular projects. Any appointment made pursuant to this section may be terminated by a majority vote of the Board upon prior written notice to the appointee and the Board may appoint a successor to any persons whose service has been so terminated.

SECTION 6. DELEGATE TO THE AKC. The Delegate of the Club to the American Kennel Club shall be elected by vote of the Board of Directors annually for a term of one year and thereafter until a successor has been elected. Such Delegate shall take direction from the Board of Directors and shall represent the interests of the Club at meetings of Delegates of the American Kennel Club.

ARTICLE IV
Club Year. Nominations and Elections.

SECTION 1. CLUB YEAR. The Club's fiscal year shall be the calendar year. Officers and Directors elected in connection with the annual meeting prior to the end of a calendar year shall take office on January 1 of the year following their election. Each retiring officer shall turn over to his/her successor in office all properties and records relating to that office as soon as possible so that the newly elected officer may be fully prepared to perform his/her duties effective January 1.

SECTION 2. NOMINATIONS. Only persons who have been members of the Club for at least three (3) years shall be eligible for nomination and election to the office of Director. No otherwise eligible person may be a candidate for the office of Director who has not been nominated by the Nominating committee or by petition as herein provided.

SECTION 3. NOMINATING COMMITTEE. A Nominating Committee shall be appointed each year by the Board of Directors at the meeting immediately following the annual meeting of members. The committee shall consist of not less than five or more than seven persons who have demonstrated their commitments to the purposes and goals of the Club and who have substantial experience with the activities of the Club. Such committee should be appointed with due regard to geographic representation; however, no particular geographic distribution is required. For the years beginning after 1993, two members of the committee shall be members of the Board of Directors whose terms of office do not expire in the current year. One of said Directors shall serve as chairman. The Nominating Committee may conduct its business by telephone and by mail, as well as in person.

(a) The Nominating Committee shall nominate from among the eligible members of the Club, one candidate for each position on the Board of Directors for which the term will expire at the end of the then current year and shall procure the acceptance of each nominee so chosen. The committee shall make nominations that ensure compliance with the requirements for geographical representation on the Board as set forth in the provision, of Article III, Section 2. The committee shall submit no later than June 15 its slate of candidates to the Secretary who shall mail the list, including the full name of each candidate and the name of the state of residence, to each member of the Club on or before July 1, so that additional nominations may be made by the members if they so desire.

(b) Additional nominations of eligible Club members for positions on the Board of Directors may be made by written petition addressed to the Secretary and received on or before September 1, signed by 100 members or 10% of the membership, whichever is greater and accompanied by the written acceptance of each such additional nominee signifying willingness to be a candidate. Nominations by petition shall comply with the requirements for geographical representation on the Board as set forth in the provisions of Article III, Section 2.

(c) Nominations cannot be made from the floor at the annual meeting or in any manner other than as provided above.

(d) If no valid nominations by written petition are received by the Secretary on or before September 1, the Nominating Committee's slate shall be declared elected at the time of the annual meeting, and no balloting will be required.

(e) If one or more valid additional nominations are received by the Secretary on or before September 1, the Secretary shall, at least 30 days before the annual meeting, mail to each member in good standing a ballot listing all of the nominees for each position in alphabetical order, with the names of the states in which they reside together with a blank envelope and a return envelope addressed to the Secretary and marked "Ballot" and bearing the name of the member to whom it was sent. So that the ballots may remain secret, each voter, after marking his ballot, shall seal it in the blank envelope which in turn shall be placed in the second envelope addressed to the Secretary. The Secretary shall check the returns against the list of members whose dues are paid for the current year prior to opening the outer envelope and removing the blank envelopes, and shall certify the eligibility of the voters. After the vote has been tabulated, the Secretary shall announce the results of the voting at the annual meeting.

SECTION 4. TABULATING THE VOTE. To be valid, ballots must be received by the Secretary or an independent professional firm (designated by the Board) at least three business days prior to the meeting. Ballots shall be counted prior to the meeting by three inspectors of election who are Club members in good standing appointed by the Board. Such inspectors shall be neither members of the current Board nor candidates on the ballots to be counted. In any year the Board may by vote designate an independent professional firm to send, receive and count the ballots in time for a report of the results at the annual meeting. The person whose residence complies with the requirements for geographical representation set forth in Article III, Section 2, and who receives the largest number of votes for each position on the Board of Directors shall be declared elected. If any nominee, at the time of the meeting, is unable to serve, for any reason, such nominee shall not be elected and the vacancy so created shall be filled by the new Board of Directors in the manner provided by Article III, Section 3.

ARTICLE V
Discipline

SECTION 1. AMERICAN KENNEL CLUB SUSPENSION. Any member who is suspended from the privileges of the American Kennel Club automatically shall be suspended from the privileges of this Club for a like period.

SECTION 2. CHARGES. Any member may proffer charges against another member for alleged misconduct prejudicial to the best interests of the Club or the breed. Written charges with specifications must be filed in duplicate with the Secretary together with a deposit of $10 which shall be forfeited if such charges are not sustained by the Board or a committee appointed to hear the matter in accordance with Article III, Section 5. The Secretary shall promptly send a copy of the charges to each member of the Board or present them at a Board Meeting, and the Board shall first consider whether the actions alleged in the charges, if proven, might constitute conduct prejudicial to the best interests of the Club or the breed. If the Board considers that the charges do not allege conduct which would be prejudicial to the best interests of the Club or of the breed, it may refuse to entertain jurisdiction. If the Board entertains jurisdiction of the charges, it shall fix a date of a hearing by the Board, or a committee of not less than three members of the Board, not less than three weeks nor more than eight weeks thereafter. The Secretary shall promptly send one copy of the charges to the accused member by certified mail together with a notice of the hearing and an assurance that the defendant may personally appear and may bring witnesses.

SECTION 3. BOARD HEARING. The Board or committee shall have complete authority to decide whether counsel may attend the hearing, but both complainant and defendant shall be treated uniformly in that regard. Should the charges be sustained after hearing all the evidence and testimony presented by complainant and defendant, the Board or committee may by a majority vote of those present suspend the defendant from all privileges of the Club for not more than six months from the date of the hearing, or until the next annual meeting if that would occur after six months. And, if it deems that punishment insufficient, it may also recommend to the membership that the penalty be expulsion. In such case, the suspension shall not restrict the defendant's right to appear before fellow members at the ensuing annual meeting which considers the recommendation of the Board or committee. Immediately after the Board or committee has reached a decision, its findings shall be put in written form and filed with the Secretary. The Secretary, in turn, shall notify each of the parties of the decision and penalty, if any.

SECTION 4. EXPULSION. Expulsion of a member from the Club may be accomplished only at the annual meeting of the Club following a hearing and upon the recommendation of the Board or committee as provided in Section 3 of this Article. The defendant shall have the privilege of appearing and addressing the meeting provided that no evidence shall be taken at this meeting. The President shall read the charges and the findings and recommendations, and shall invite the defendant, if present, to speak. The meeting shall then vote by secret written ballot on the proposed expulsion. A two-thirds vote of those present and voting at the annual meeting shall be necessary for expulsion. If expulsion is not so voted, the suspension shall stand.

ARTICLE VI
Standards for Use of the Title

SECTION 1. No member of the Club shall use the title "CH" in front of the name of a registered Labrador Retriever dog until said dog, having won a conformation championship, shall also receive a Working Certificate or the equivalent as defined in this Article.

SECTION 2. The minimum working certificate requirements shall be designed to establish that the dog is not gun-shy. Accordingly, the dog will be expected to retrieve a shot game bird at a distance of 50 yards or greater on land; further, the dog will be expected to retrieve two ducks from swimming water either as a double mark or in immediate succession to establish the dog's willingness to reenter water. Shackled birds shall not be used for a Working Certificate test. Only shot birds shall be used on land, and only shot birds or freshly killed birds shall be utilized on the water. Steadiness is not required so a dog may be held on line, however the dog may not be released for the retrieve until the bird has fallen. Any reasonable command and gesture may be used to direct the dog to retrieve and return. Nothing may be thrown and no coercion may be used to encourage completion of a retrieve once the dog has been initially released to retrieve.

SECTION 3. Any dog that has satisfactorily completed both a land and water series in a field trial licensed by the American Kennel Club; or has received a placement or judge's award of merit in a field trial sanctioned by the American Kennel Club; or has successfully completed an AKC Junior Hunter title shall be deemed to have satisfied the Working Certificate requirements. In addition, a Working Certificate requirement may be satisfied by establishing to the satisfaction of any current member of the Club's Board of Directors that the dog in question has performed in accordance with the minimum requirements set forth above.

ARTICLE VII
Amendments

SECTION 1. Amendments to the Constitution and By-Laws and to the Standard for the breed may be proposed by the Board of Directors or by written petition addressed to the Secretary signed by 20% of the membership in good standing. Amendments proposed by such petition shall be promptly considered by the Board of Directors and must be submitted to the members with recommendations of the Board for a vote at the next meeting of members following the date when the petition was received by the Secretary.

SECTION 2. The Constitution and By-Laws and the Standard for the breed may be amended at any time without a meeting of members provided a copy of the proposed amendment has been mailed by the Secretary to each member in good standing on the date of mailing accompanied by a ballot on which such member may indicate a choice for-or-against the action to be taken. Notice with such ballot shall specify a date not less than 30 days after the date of mailing by which date the ballots must be returned to the Secretary to be counted. The favorable vote of two-thirds of the members voting within the time limit shall be required to effect any such amendment.

SECTION 3. No amendment to the Constitution and By-Laws or to the Standard for the breed that is adopted by the Club shall become effective until it has been approved by the Board of Directors of the American Kennel Club.

ARTICLE VIII
Dissolution

SECTION 1. The Club may be dissolved at any time by the written consent of not less than 75% of the members. In the event of the dissolution of the Club, other than for purposes of reorganization, whether voluntary or involuntary or by operation of law, none of the property of the Club nor any proceeds thereof nor any assets of the Club shall be distributed to any members of the Club, but, after payment of the debts of the Club, its property and assets shall be given to a charitable organization for the benefit of dogs selected by the Board of Directors.

The Labrador Retriever Club Working Certificate Program

Effective January 1, 1992, LRC, Inc. will allow any AKC registered Labrador Retriever which meets the performance requirements to receive the Certificate. It is no longer necessary to be a member of LRC, Inc. or to have a bench or obedience champion in order to obtain the Working Certificate.

When LRC, Inc. was founded in 1931, the members intended the Working Certificate program to parallel The Kennel Club of England's requirements that a Sporting Dog pass a working test before earning its conformation title. The American Kennel Club does not require working aptitude evaluation for Sporting Dogs who earn their conformation titles.

The Board of Directors of the LRC, Inc. felt it was necessary to encourage "grass roots" involvement in the Working Certificate program by making it more widely available to the Labrador-loving public. The Working Certificate program provides a way for Labrador owners to experience and develop an appreciation for the natural working abilities of their dogs without the sometimes lengthy and expensive commitment the competitive performance events require.

PERFORMANCE REQUIREMENTS FOR AN LRC, INC. WORKING CERTIFICATE

To be eligible for a Working Certificate, a Labrador Retriever must demonstrate the following:
1. The dog is not gun shy.
2. The dog will retrieve a shot bird at approximately 50 yards on land.
3. The dog will retrieve two shot ducks from water, either as a double or in immediate succession (back to back), to prove willingness to reenter the water.
4. Steadiness is not required, so a dog may be held on the line.
5. These requirements may be satisfied by completing land and water back to back series in a field trial under AKC rules; by completing a WC test held by a regional club; by acquiring an AKC Junior Hunter (or higher) title; or by completing successfully one AKC hunt test provided that the dog shall have met the requirements set forth above. The owner of the dog is responsible for

making arrangements with the judges and the hosting club *before* the test, and for providing a form for their signature upon completion of the test to verify the "pass."

IMPORTANT GUIDELINES FOR THE EVALUATION OF A DOG'S PERFORMANCE IN A WORKING TEST

1. Although delivery to hand is not required, the word "retrieve" in the performance criteria means that the birds should be returned to the handler. Accordingly, it is suggested that an area of delivery within easy reach of the handler be established by the judges before the test.

2. The WC is *not* a marking test and it is not to indicate the extent of training the dog has received, so the following should be considered:

   a. Land test: bird should fall in light cover.

   b. Water tests should be set up to show courage to reenter the water. Angled entries, excessive distances in the water, and "lines" set way back from the water are to be discouraged.

   c. One bird should be retrieved from swimming water if at all possible.

   d. Tests are generally run on pheasant and ducks, but pigeons and ducks are acceptable. AKC recommendations and local rules on the use of live birds should be followed.

   e. The dog need not be steady; the

collar may be held until a number is called. Line manners are not to be judged. As long as the bird is delivered to the area of the handler, the exercise is marked as a completion.

WHO CAN JUDGE A WORKING CERTIFICATE TEST?

Any Director of the LRC, Inc. or any judge of an AKC licensed field trial (need not be a point judge; may have judged only a minor stake), or any judge of an AKC licensed Hunting Retriever Test may officiate at a Working Certificate Test.

WHO MAY HOLD A WC TEST?

Any regional Labrador Retriever Club or other organized group may sponsor a WC test as long as the judge or judges meet the LRC, Inc. requirements for such a test. Tests for individuals may be set up if the judge, gunners and required facilities are agreeable and no other group testing is available. Dogs competing in hunt tests or field trials may also qualify for a WC if prior arrangements have been made with the judges and the hosting club for approval and certification.

WHICH DOGS ARE ELIGIBLE TO RECEIVE A WORKING CERTIFICATE?

Any AKC-registered Labrador Retriever which successfully completes the Working test must ask his or her owner to provide the LRC,

Inc. with the requested verification materials and fee in order to receive an official Labrador Retriever Club, Inc. Working Certificate.

HOW TO OBTAIN A WC

The following material is required in order to process a request for a Working Certificate:

1. Copy of dog's registration certificate. If you wish the WC to reflect current titles, then copies of the title certificates must also be enclosed.
2. Copy of the AKC Junior Hunter title certificate *or* a copy of the judges sheet showing completion of the test and signed by the judge indicating his qualifications.
3. Owner's name and current address.
4. Check to LRC, Inc. for $25.00.
   Mail the requested material to:
   Dr. Pat Crockett, WC Chair
   P. O. Box 80081
   Austin, Texas 78727

Please allow four weeks for processing. Working Certificates are done on an individual basis in order to ensure quality and this takes time. The certificates are well suited for framing. Funds generated by this program help support the increasing variety of LRC, Inc. activities.

If you need any further information regarding the program please contact the Conformation Affairs Committee Time Zone Chairperson in your area or your regional Labrador Retriever Club's area representative.

STEPS IN PLANNING A WC:

1. Appoint a committee for the event.
2. Obtain copies of the WC brochure. The *AKC Hunt Test Procedure Manual* is of great value as well.
3. Select and confirm the judges. *Be sure the judges have copies of the WC brochure in advance of the test!*
4. Make arrangements for the necessary land, birds, gunners and work crews.
5. Prepare a catalogue or official list of dogs running the test that includes space for the judges' statement and qualifications.
6. Be ready to provide owners whose dogs pass with the information they need to acquire an official LRC, Inc. Working Certificate.

WORKING CERTIFICATE REQUIREMENTS:

1. A land single retrieve of approximately 50 yards in light cover.
2. Back to back singles or a double in the water. One bird should be retrieved in swimming water if possible.
3. The dog is not required to be steady or deliver to hand; however, the judge(s) may designate an area for delivery.
4. The dog should not be gun shy.

Information on applying for a Working Certificate may be obtained from: Dr. Pat Crockett, P.O. Box 80081, Austin, Texas 78727.

Dual Champion Labradors

Michael of Glenmere
Gorse of Arden
Shed of Arden
Braes of Arden
Little Pierre of Deercreek
Youdel of Moreexpense
Bracken Sweep
Matchmaker for Deercreek
Grangemead Precocious
Hello Joe of Rocheltree
Cherokee Buck
Bengal of Arden
Treveilyr Swift
Dela-Winn's Tar of Craignook
Nilo Possibility
Beau Brummel of Wyndale
Boley's Tar Baby
Penney Oaks Corky
Kingswere Black Ebony

Alpine Cherokee Rocket
Markwell's Ramblin' Rebel
Krooked Kreek Knight
Burnham Buff
Problem Boy Duke of Wake
Danny's Cole Black Slate
Calypso Clipper
Ridgewood Playboy
Torque of Daingerfield
Sherwood's Maid Marion
Happy Playboy
Petite Rouge
Shamrock Acres Super Drive
Royal Oaks Jill of Burgundy
Warpath Macho
Hiwood Shadow
Shamrock Acres Simmerdown
Rinneys Cumula Nimbus
Little Miss Timber

National Best of Breed Winners

Conducted by The Labrador Retriever Club, Inc.

1933 - Boli of Blake, F. B. Lord
1934 - Drinkstone Pons of Wingan, Jay F. Carlisle
1935 - Bancstone Lorna of Wingan, Jay F. Carlisle
1936 - Raffles of Earlsmoor, Dr. & Mrs. Samuel Milbank
1937 - Ch. Banchory Trump of Wingan, Jay F. Carlisle
1938 - Ch. Earlsmoor Moor of Arden, Dr. & Mrs. Samuel Milbank
1939 - Ch. Earlsmoor Moor of Arden, Dr. & Mrs. Samuel Milbank
1940 - Ch. Earlsmoor Moor of Arden, Dr. & Mrs. Samuel Milbank
1941 - Ch. Earlsmoor Moor of Arden, Dr. & Mrs. Samuel Milbank
1942 - Ledgelands' Black Swan, Ledgelands Kennels
1943 - Ch. Earlsmoor Moor of Arden, Dr. & Mrs. Samuel Milbank
1944 - Ch. Michael of Wynward, Mrs. Edmund W. Poor
1945 - Wynward Whiskers, Mrs. E. W. Poor
1946 - Hugger Mugger, Joan W. Redmond
1947 - Dual Ch. Little Pierre of Deercreek, Mr. & Mrs. P. Bakewell III
1948 - Ch. Stowaway At Deercreek, Mr. Gerald Livingston
1949 - Ch. Chidley Spook, Mrs. Curtis Read
1950 - Toots of Dunecht, Mrs. James Austin
1951 - Hobbimoor's Merganser, T. Horner
1952 - Ch. Chidley Spook, Mrs. Curtis Read
1953 - Port Fortune Smoke Screen, J. G. Hinkle
1954 - Chidley Genii, R. Goold & Mrs. C. S. Read
1955 - Gunner of Land Fall, Land Fall Kennels
1956 - Whygin Skier of Southdown, Mrs. N. Tuttle
1957 - Golden Chance of Franklin, Mrs. G. B. Lambert
1958 - Ch. Golden Chance of Franklin, Mrs. G. B. Lambert
1959 - Ch. Ore Hill's Sunday Punch, Allen Buck
1960 - Ch. Dark Star of Franklin, B. W. Ziessow
1961 - Ch. Whygin Campaign Promise, Mr. & Mrs. James McCarthy
1962 - Ch. Whygin Gold Bullion, Helen W. Ginnel
1963 - Ch. Sam of Blaircourt, Grace L. Lambert
1964 - Ch. Sam of Blaircourt, Grace L. Lambert
1965 - Ch. Sam of Blaircourt, Grace L. Lambert
1966 - Lewisfield Chimney Sweep, Harry K. & Polly Proctor
1967 - Ch. Lockerbie Kismet, Lockerbie Kennels & J. F. Lewis III
1968 - Ch. Lewisfield Gunslinger, Mr. William A. Metz
1969 - Ch. Lockerbie Goldentone Jensen, Mr. William A. Metz
1970 - Ch. Spenrock Sans Souci, John G. Valentine
1971 - Ch. Hillsboro Wizard of Oz, Mrs. R. V. Clark, Jr.
1972 - Ch. Hillsboro Wizard of Oz, Mrs. R. V. Clark, Jr.
1973 - Ch. Barnaby O'Brian, Robert B. Matthews & Larry Worth
1974 - Ch. Kimvalley Picklewitch, Mrs. R. V. Clark, Jr.
1975 - Ch. Springfield's Musette, Mrs. R. V. Clark, Jr.
1976 - Ch. Shamrock Acres Benjamin, Dr. Richard Whitehill
1977 - Ch. Ravenwood Brigadier, Joe & Kay Fasekas
1978 - Ch. Kimvalley Picklewitch, Mrs. R. V. Clark, Jr.
1979 - Ch. Braemar Duggan, Wayne & JoAnne Ludvigson-Cain
1980 - Ch. Starline Special Occasion WC, Greg & Diane Wehrheim
1981 - Swedish & Am. Ch. Puhs Superman, Mary Ellen Pfeifle
1982 - Ch. Leyward Softly Softly At Lawnwood, Gary & Margaret Maxwell
1983 - Ch. Wingmasters Chism Trail, Jerry Limbourne
1984 - Ch. Briary Bell Buoy Of Windsong, Betty Dunlap
1985 - Can. Ch. Oaklea Gala, Dr. Olev & Hannelore Harm
1986 - Ch. Ramblin's Amaretto, Anne K. Jones
1987 - Ch. Cambellcroft's Angus CD, Donald & Virginia Campbell
1988 - Ch. Tabatha's Windfall Abbey, Annie & Ron Cogo
1989 - Ch. Davoeg's Irish Gold, Bob & Sylvia Shandley
1990 - Ch. Chelon's Firestorm, Cherl & Ron Ostenson
1991 - Ch. Chocorua's Seabreeze, Marion Lyons
1992 - Ch. Breezy's Whirlaway, J. A., Jackie McFarlan & Gordon Sousa
1993 - Tabatha's Dazzle, Carol Heidl

National Open Stakes Winners

Conducted by National Retriever Club, Inc.

Year	Winner	Owner–Handler	Breed–Sex
1941	Ch. King Midas of Woodend	E. W. Hodge–Frank Hogan	Golden Male
1942	Dual Ch. Shed of Arden	Paul Bakewell III	Labrador Male
1943	NFC-Dual Ch. Shed of Arden	Paul Bakewell III–Cliff Wallace	Labrador Male
1944	FC Shelter Cove Beauty	Dr. L. M. Evans–Charles Morgan	Golden Female
1945	Black Magic of Audlon	Mahlon B. Wallace, Jr.–Charles Morgan	Labrador Female
1946	NFC-Dual Ch. Shed of Arden	Paul Bakewell III	Labrador Male
1947	Dual Ch. Bracken Sweep	Daniel Pomeroy–T. W. Pershall	Labrador Male
1948	FC Brignall's Gringo	Cliff Brignall–Roy Gonia	Labrador Male
1949	FC Marvadel Black Gum	Paul Bakewell III	Labrador Male
1950	FC Beautywood Tamarack	Dr. L. M. Evan–Charles Morgan	Golden Male
1951	FC Ready Always of Marian Hill	Mahlon B. Wallace–William Wunderlich	Golden Male
1952	FC King Buck	John M. Olin–T. W. Pershall	Labrador Male
1953	NFC King Buck	John M. Olin–T. W. Pershall	Labrador Male
1954	FC Major VI	Mrs. Fraser M. Horn–Ray Staudinger	Labrador Male
1955	FC Cork of Oakwood Lane	Dr. Harold A. Mork–Tony Berger	Labrador Male
1956	FC Massie's Sassy Boots	William T. Cline–Roy Gonia	Labrador Male
1957	FC Spirit Lake Duke	Mrs. George Murnane–Joe Schomer	Labrador Male
1958	FC Nilo Possibility	K. K. Williams–William Wunderlich	Labrador Male
1959	NFC Spirit Lake Duke	Mrs. George Murnane–Joe Schomer	Labrador Male
1960	FC-AFC Dolobran's Smoke Trail	Richard H. Hecker	Labrador Male
1961	FC Del-Tone Colvin	L. J. Snoeyenbos–Tony Berger	Labrador Male
1962	FC-AFC Bigstone Hope	Mr. & Mrs. Bing Grunwald–D. L. Walters	Labrador Female
1963	NFC-AFC Del-Tone Colvin	Louis Snoeyenbos–Tony Berger	Labrador Male
1964	FC Ripco's V. C. Morgan	J. D. Ott–Paul E. Shoemaker	Labrador Female
1965	FC Martens Little Smoky	John M. Olin–T. W. Pershall	Labrador Male
1966	FC Whygin Cork's Coot	Mrs. George Murnane–Joe Riser	Labrador Male
1967	FC-AFC Butte Blue Moon	Mr. & Mrs. Bing Grunwald–D. L. Walters	Labrador Male
1968	NAFC-FC Super Chief	August Belmont	Labrador Male
1969	NFC Whygin Cork's Coot	Mrs. George Murnane–Joe Riser	Labrador Male
1970	FC-AFC Creole Sister	Donald Weiss	Labrador Female
1971	FC Mi-Cris Sailor	Mrs. George Murnane–Joe Riser	Labrador Male
1972	FC-AFC Royal's Moose Moe	William D. Connor	Labrador Male
1973	FC-AFC Baird's Centerville Sam	Mrs. Mahlon B. Wallace–Tom Sorenson	Labrador Male
1974	FC-AFC Happy Playboy's Pearl	David & Gretchen Crow–John Honore	Labrador Female
1975	FC-AFC Wanapum Dart's Dandy	Charles L. Hill	Labrador Female
1976	FC-AFC San Joaquin Honcho	Mrs. Judith S. Aycock	Labrador Male
1977	FC-AFC Euroclydon	Don Strait	Labrador Female
1978	FC-AFC Shadow of Otter Creek	Bob Kennon, Jr.	Labrador Male
1979	FC-AFC McGuffy	T. J. and Debby Lindbloom	Labrador Male
1980	FC-AFC Risky Business Ruby	Jeffrey L. Copeland, DDS	Labrador Female
1981	FC-AFC Orion's Sky	John W. Martin	Labrador Male
1982	FC Westwind Supernova Chief	D. J. and Nancy Esposito–Bachman Doar	Labrador Male
1983	FC-AFC Trieven Butch of Big Jake	Joseph and Gloria Boatright	Labrador Male
1984	FC-AFC Wanapum's Lucyana Girl	John Parrot	Labrador Female
1985	FC-AFC Dynamite Duke IV	Marshall and Linden Dunaway–Hugh Arthur	Labrador Male
1986	FC-AFC Jubilashus T. C. Malarky	John Larkin–Felix Mock	Labrador Male
1987	FC-AFC-CFC-CAFC Yankee Independence	Gunther Rahnefeld–William Eckett	Labrador Female
1988	FC-AFC-CFC PP's Lucky's Super Toby	Fred Kampo and Charles Hays	Labrador Male
1989	FC-AFC Otus of Redfern	Aurelia Rice–Danny Farmer	Labrador Male
1990	FC-AFC Candlewoods Tanks A Lot	Mary Howley and Randy Kuehl–Mike Lardy	Labrador Female
1991	NFC-AFC Candlewoods Tanks A Lot	Mary Howley and Randy Kuehl–Mike Lardy	Labrador Female
1992	NAFC-AFC Candlewoods Super Tanker	Joyce Williams–Mike Lardy	Labrador Male
1993	NFC-AFC Candlewoods Tanks A Lot	Mary Howley and Randy Kuehl–Mike Lardy	Labrador Female

427

National Amateur Stakes Winners

Conducted by National Amateur Retriever Club, Inc.

Year	Winner	Owner-Handler	Breed-Sex
1957	1954 NFC-AFC Major VI	Mrs. Fraser M. Horn–J. Fraser Horn	Labrador Male
1958	FC-AFC Boley's Tar Baby	Bing Grunwald	Labrador Male
1959	FC-AFC Braken's High Flyer	George L. Dudek	Labrador Male
1960	FC-AFC Queenie of Redding	Rolland Watt	Labrador Female
1961	FC-AFC Ace's Sheba of Ardyn	Dr. B. L. Finlayson	Labrador Female
1962	FC-AFC Carr-Lab Hilltop	Glen B. Bump	Labrador Male
1963	FC-AFC Pepper's Jiggs	Bob Pepper	Labrador Male
1964	AFC Dutchmoor's Black Mood	A. Nelson Sills	Labrador Male
1965	FC-AFC Rebel Chief of Heber	Gus Rathert	Labrador Male
1966	FC-AFC-CFC Captain of Lomac	Rudy R. Deering	Labrador Male
1967	FC-AFC Super Chief	August Belmont	Labrador Male
1968	1967 NAFC-FC Super Chief	August Belmont	Labrador Male
1969	FC-AFC Guy's Bitterroot Lucky	Guy P. Burnett	Labrador Male
1970	FC-AFC Andy's Partner Pete	Mrs. Clifford B. Brokaw, Jr.	Labrador Male
1971	FC-AFC Dee's Dandy Dude	Michael Paterno	Labrador Male
1972	FC-AFC-CNFC River Oaks Corky	Michael R. Flannery	Labrador Male
1973	1971 NAFC-FC-AFC Dee's Dandy Dude	Michael Paterno	Labrador Male
1974	FC-AFC Ray's Rascal	Raymond & Dorothea Goodrich	Labrador Male
1975	1972 NAFC-FC-CNFC River Oaks Corky	Michael R. Flannery	Labrador Male
1976	1975 NFC-AFC-CNFC Wanapum Dart's Dandy	Charles Hill	Labrador Female
1977	FC-AFC River Oaks Rascal	Joseph M. Pilar	Labrador Male
1978	FC-AFC Kannonball Kate	Peter Lane	Labrador Female
1979	FC-AFC Lawhorn's Cadillac Mack	Dennis Bath & Gerald Lawhorn	Labrador Male
1980	1979 NAFC-FC Lawhorn's Cadillac Mack	Dennis Bath & Gerald Lawhorn	Labrador Male
1981	FC-AFC Dude's Double or Nothin'	Delma Hazzard	Labrador Male
1982	FC-AFC-CFC-CAFC Piper's Pacer	Roy & Jo McFall	Labrador Male
1983	FC-AFC Beorn's Blazing Hydropsyche	Dr. William & Cynthia Howard	Labrador Male
1984	FC-AFC Trumarc's Zip Code	Judith Aycock	Labrador Male
1985	FC-AFC Topbrass Cotton	Jeff and Bev Finley & Jackie Mertens	Golden Male
1986	FC-AFC Winsom Cargo	Cal Cadmus, DVM	Labrador Male
1987	FC-AFC-CFC-CAFC Westwind Jemima Super Cake	Eva Proby	Labrador Female
1988	FC-AFC Honky Tonk Hero	Jerry Wickliffe	Labrador Male
1989	FC-AFC The Little Duke of Fargo	Dean Troyer	Labrador Male
1990	FC-AFC Candlewood's Super Tanker	Joyce Williams	Labrador Male
1991	FC-AFC Cody's R. Dee	Larry Bergmann	Labrador Male
1992	FC-AFC Gusto's Last Control	J.M. & L.K. DuBose	Labrador Male
1993	FC-AFC MD's Cotton Pick'N Cropper	Newt Cropper & Karen Rabeau	Labrador Male
1994	FC-AFC Lady Andrel's Nighthawk Lady	Gordon L. & Christine Kurz	Labrador Female

Glossary

Reprinted with permission of the American Kennel Club

Abdomen: The belly or undersurface between the chest and hindquarters.

Acetabulum: The concave lateral portion of the sacrum that articulates with the head (proximal portion) of the femur. Anatomically important in evaluating hip dysplasia.

Achondroplasia: A form of genetic dwarfism specifically characterized by arrested development of the long bones. A defect in most breeds and a requisite in others (e.g. Dachshunds, Basset Hounds).

Action: A term used to describe component functions of locomotion (e.g. "action of the hock"), or as a synonym for gait in some standards.

AKC: American Kennel Club.

Albino: A relatively rare, genetically recessive condition (cc) characterized by the inability to synthesize melanin, consequently resulting in white hair and pink eyes.

Almond eyes: An elongated eye-shape describing the tissue surrounding the eye itself.

Amble: A relaxed, easy gait in which the legs on either side move almost, but not quite, as a pair. Often seen as the transition movement between the walk and other gaits.

Angulation: The angles formed by the appendicular skeleton, including the forequarters [shoulder (scapula), arm (humerus), forearm (radius, ulna), wrist (carpus), pastern (metacarpus), toes (phalanges)] and hindquarters [hip (pelvis), thigh (femur), second thigh (tibia, fibula), hock (tarsus), rear pastern (metatarsus), toes (phalangcs)].

Ankle: *See* Hock.

Ankylosis: Abnormal immobility and fusion of a joint. Noted as a cause of faulty tails in the German Shepherd Dog standard.

Anterior: The portion carried foremost during normal locomotion.

Apple head: A domed top skull rounded in all directions.

Apron: Longer hair below the neck on the chest. Frill.

Arm: The anatomical region between the shoulder and the elbow, including the humerus and associated tissues. Sometimes called the "upper arm."

Articulation: The junction between two or more bones, typically held together by ligaments.

Artificial insemination: The introduction of semen into the female reproductive tract by artificial means.

Babbler: A hound that gives tongue when not on the trail.

Back: The dorsal surface (topline) of the dog extending (usually) from the withers to the croup, including the thoracic and lumbar vertebral regions; infrequently used to refer only to the thoracic region.

Bad mouth: Crooked or unaligned teeth; bite over or undershot in excess of standard specifications.

Balance: A condition wherein all proportions of a dog are in static and dynamic harmony.

Bandog: A dog tied by day, released at night. Tiedog.

Bandy legs: Having a bend of leg outward.

Barrel: A rib (thoracic) region that is circular in cross-section.

Barrel hock: Hocks that turn out, causing the feet to toe in. Also called wide "spread hocks."

Basewide: Wide footfall, resultant of "paddling" movement, causing body to rock from side to side. *See* Paddling.

Bat ear: An erect ear, rather broad at the base, rounded in outline at the top, and with orifice directed to the front (e.g., French Bulldog).

Bay: The prolonged bark or voice of the hunting hound.

Beady: Eyes that are small, round, and glittering, imparting an expression foreign to the breed.

Beard: Thick, long hair growth on the underjaw.

Beauty spot: A distinct spot, usually round, of colored hair, surrounded by the white of the blaze, on the topskull between the ears. (Blenheim Spaniel, Boston Terrier.)

Bee-sting tail: A tail relatively short, strong, straight, and tapering to a point.

Beefy: Overheavy development of the hindquarters.

Belly: The ventral (under) surface of the abdomen.

Belton: A color pattern in English Setters (named after a village in Northumberland) characterized by either light or dark ticking or roaning, and including blue belton (black and white), tricolor (blue belton with tan patches), orange belton (orange and white), lemon belton (lemon and white), and liver belton (liver and white).

Bench show: A dog show at which the dogs are kept on assigned benches when not being shown in competition, thus facilitating the viewing/discussion of the breeds by attendees, exhibitors, and breeders.

Best in show: A dog show award to the dog adjudged best of all breeds.

Bevy: A flock of birds.

Bilateral cryptorchid: *See* Cryptorchid.

Bird dog: A sporting dog bred and trained to hunt game birds.

Bird of prey eyes: Light yellowish eyes, usually harsh in outlook. Cited as a fault in German Shorthaired Pointer standard.

Bitch: A female canine.

Bite: The relative position of the upper and lower teeth when the jaws are closed, including scissors, level, undershot, or overshot.

Blanket: The color of the coat on the back and upper part of the sides, between the neck and the tail.

Blaze: A white stripe running up the center of the face and usually between the eyes.

Blinker: A dog that points a bird and then leaves it, or upon finding a bird, avoids making a definite point.

Blocky: Square or cubelike formation of the head.

Blooded: A dog of good breeding; pedigreed.

Bloom: The sheen of a coat in prime condition.

Blue: A dilution of black coat color, due to the recessive dilution (dd) color locus (i.e., BBdd or Bbdd dogs will be blue).

Blue merle: A color pattern involving black blotches or streaks on a blue-grey background. *See* Merle.

Bluies: Colored portions of the coat that have a distinct bluish or smoky cast. This coloring is associated with extremely light or blue eyes and liver or gray eye rims, nose and lip pigment. (Pembroke Welsh Corgi.)

Board: To feed, house, and care for a dog for a fee.

Bobtail: A naturally tailless dog or a dog with a tail docked very short. Often used as a name for the Old English Sheepdog.

Bodied up: Mature, well-developed.

Body length: Distance from the prosternum (anterior portion of the breastbone) to the posterior portion of the pelvic girdle, i.e., the ischial tuberosities.

Bone: A type of connective tissue that forms the canine skeleton. Informally used to suggest a quantitative characteristic of limb bones in proportion to overall size of a dog.

Bossy: Overdevelopment of the shoulder muscles.

Brace: Two specimens of the same breed presented as a pair; a couple.

Break: Term used to describe changing of coat color from puppies to adult stages.

Breastbone: *See* Sternum.

Breeching: Fringing of longish hair at the posterior borders of the thigh regions.

Breed: A domestic race of dogs (selected and maintained by man) with a common gene pool and a characterized appearance (phenotype) and function.

Breeder: A person who breeds dogs. Under AKC rules the breeder of a dog is the owner (or, if the dam was leased, the lessee) of the dam of the dog when the dam was bred.

Breeding particulars: Sire, dam, date of birth, sex, color, etc.

Brick-shaped: Rectangular.

Brindle: A color pattern specified by the e allele of the E (extension) locus, resulting in the layering of black pigment in regions of lighter color (usually tan) producing a tiger-striped pattern (e.g., Boxers).

Brisket: Usually refers to the sternum, but in some standards it refers to the entire thorax.

Brock: A badger.

Broken color: Self color broken by white or another color.

Broken-baited: A rough, wire coat.

Broken-up face: A receding nose, together with a deep stop, wrinkle, and undershot jaw (e.g., Bulldog, Pekingese).

Brood bitch: A female used for breeding. Brood matron.

Brows: The ridges formed above the eyes by frontal bone contours. Superciliary arches or supraorbital ridges.

Brush: A bushy tail; a tail heavy with hair.

Brushing: A gaiting fault, when parallel pasterns are so close that the legs "brush" in passing.

Bullbaiting: An ancient sport in which the dog baited or tormented the bull.

Bull neck: A heavy neck, well-muscled.

Burr: The inside of the ear; i.e., the irregular formation visible within the cup.

Butterfly: A partially unpigmented nose; i.e., dark, spotted with flesh color.

Buttocks: The rump or hips.

Button ear: The ear flap folding forward, the tip lying close to the skull so as to cover the orifice.

Bye: At field trials, an odd dog remaining after the dogs entered in a stake have been paired in braces by drawing.

Camel back: An arched back.

Canid: A family (Canidae) of carnivorous animals including dogs, wolves, coyotes, foxes, jackals.

Canines: The two upper and two lower large, conical pointed teeth lateral to the incisors and anterior to the premolars.

Canter: A gait with three beats to each stride, two legs moving separately and two as a diagonal pair. Slower than the gallop and not as tiring.

Cap: Darkly shaded color pattern on the skull of some breeds.

Cape: Profuse hair enveloping the shoulder region.

Carpals: Bones of the wrist.

Castrate: To remove the testicles of the male dog.

Cat foot: Round, compact foot, with well-arched toes, tightly bunched or close-cupped.

Caudal (coccygeal) vertebrae: The only regionally variable number of vertebrae among breeds in the axial skeleton, lying posterior to the sacrum and defining the tail region.

Cervical vertebrae: The seven vertebrae of the region of the neck, articulating anteriorly with the cranium and posteriorly with the thoracic vertebrae.

C.D. (Companion Dog): A suffix used with the name of a dog that has been recorded a Companion Dog by AKC as a result of having won certain minimum scores in Novice Classes at a specified number of AKC-licensed or member obedience trials.

C.D.X. (Companion Dog Excellent): A suffix used with the name of a dog that has been recorded a Companion Dog Excellent by AKC as a result of having won certain minimum scores in Open Classes at a specified number of AKC-licensed or member obedience trials.

Champion (Ch.): A prefix used with the name of a dog that has been recorded a Champion by AKC as a result of defeating a specified number of dogs in specified competition at a series of AKC-licensed or member dog shows.

Character: Expression, individuality, and general appearance and deportment as considered typical of a breed.

Cheeky: Cheeks prominently rounded; thick, protruding.

Chest: The part of the body or trunk that is enclosed by the ribs; the thoracic cavity.

China eye: A clear, flecked or spotted blue, light blue or whitish eye.

Chippendale front: Named after the Chippendale chair. Forelegs out at elbows, pasterns close, and feet turned out. *See* Fiddle front.

Ewe neck: A neck in which the topline is concave rather than convex.

Expression: The general appearance of all features of the head.

Eyeteeth: The upper canines.

Fall: Hair overhanging the face.

Fallow: Pale cream to light fawn color; pale, pale yellow; yellow-red.

Fancier: A person especially interested and usually active in some phase of the sport of purebred dogs.

Fangs: *See* Canines.

Fawn: A brown, red-yellow with hue of medium brilliance.

Feathering: Longer fringe of hair on ears, legs, tail, or body.

Femur: Thigh bone. Extends from hip to stifle.

Fetch: The retrieve of game by the dog; also the command to do so.

Fibula: One of the two bones of the leg (i.e., the "lower" thigh, second thigh, or lower leg).

Fiddle front: Forelegs out at elbows, pasterns close, and feet turned out. French front.

Field Champion (Field Ch.): A prefix used with the name of a dog that has been recorded a Field Champion by AKC as a result of defeating a specified number of dogs in specified competition at a series of AKC-licensed or member field trials.

Field trial: A competition for certain Hound or Sporting breeds in which dogs are judged on ability and style in finding or retrieving game or following a game trail.

Filled-up face: Smooth facial contours, free of excessive muscular development.

Flag: A long tail carried high. Feathering on tail.

Flank: The side of the body between the last rib and the hip. The coupling.

Flare: A blaze that widens as it approaches the topskull.

Flat bone: Refers to bladed or non-round limb bones.

Flat-sided: Ribs insufficiently rounded as they approach the sternum or breastbone.

Flews: Upper lip pendulous, particularly at their inner corners.

Floating rib: The last, or 13th rib, which is unattached to other ribs.

Fluffies: A coat of extreme length with exaggerated feathering on ears, chest, legs and feet, underparts and hindquarters. Trimming such a coat does not make it any more acceptable (e.g., Pembroke Welsh Corgi).

Flush: To drive birds from cover, to force them to take flight. To spring.

Flying ears: Any characteristic drop ears or semi-prick ears that stand or "fly."

Flying trot: A fast gait in which all four feet are off the ground for a brief second during each half stride. Because of the long reach, the oncoming hind feet step beyond the imprint left by the front. Also called suspension trot.

Foot: The digits or toes, each consisting of three bones (phalanges; sing. phalaynx) and a toenail or claw. The ventral surface is cushioned by pads of connective tissue.

Forearm: The portion of the forelimb between the arm (humerus) and the wrist (carpals), including the radius and the ulna.

Foreface: The anterior portion of the skull (head) that articulates with the cranium (braincase); i.e., the muzzle.

Forequarters: The combined front assembly from its uppermost component, the shoulder blade, down to the feet.

Foster mother: A bitch used to nurse whelps not her own.

Foul color: A color or marking not characteristic for the breed.

Fox: Sharp expression; pointed nose with short foreface.

French front: *See* Fiddle front.

Frill: *See* Apron.

Fringes: *See* Feathering.

Frogface: Extending nose accompanied by a receding jaw, usually overshot.

Front: The forepart of the body as viewed head on; i.e., forelegs, chest, brisket, and shoulder line.

Frontal bones: The anterior bones of the cranium forming the forehead.

Furnishings: The long hair on the extremities (including head and tail) of certain breeds.

Furrow: A slight indentation of median line down the center of the skull to the stop.

Futurity Stake: A class at dog shows or field trials for young dogs which have been nominated at or before birth.

Gait: The pattern of footsteps at various rates of speed, each pattern distinguished by a particular rhythm and footfall.

Gallop: Fastest of the dog gaits, has a four-beat rhythm and often an extra period of suspension during which the body is propelled through the air with all four feet off the ground.

Game: Hunted wild birds or animals.

Gaskin: The lower or second thigh.

Gay tail: A tail carried above the horizontal, several breed-specific applications.

Gazehound: Greyhound or other sight-hunting hound.

Genealogy: Recorded family descent. Pedigree.

Gestation: A period of 63 days in the dog, from fertilization to whelping, characterized by embryonic/fetal development.

Goose neck: An elongated, tubular-shaped neck. Also termed swan neck.

Goose rump: Too steep or sloping a croup.

Goose step: Accentuated lift of the forelimbs.

Grizzle: A mixture of black or red hairs with white hairs. Roan. Frequently, a bluish grey or iron-grey color.

Groom: To brush, comb, trim, or otherwise make a dog's coat neat.

Groups: The breed as grouped into seven divisions by the AKC to facilitate judging.

Guard hays: The longer, smoother, stiffer hairs which grow through and normally conceal the undercoat.

Gun dog: A dog trained to work with its master in finding live game and retrieving game that has been shot.

Gun-shy: When the dog fears the sight or sound of a gun.

Hackles: Hairs on neck and back raised involuntarily in fright or anger.

Hackney action: A high lifting of the front feet accompanied by flexing of the wrist like that of a hackney horse.

Hallmark: A distinguishing characteristic, such as the spectacles of the Keeshond.

Handler: A person who handles a dog in the show ring or at a field trial. Also see Professional handler.

Hard-mouthed: The dog that bites or marks with his teeth the game he retrieves.

Hare foot: Foot in which the two center digits are appreciably longer than the outside and inside toes of the foot, and the arching of the toes is less marked, making the foot appear longer overall.

Harlequin: Patched or pied coloration, usually black or grey on white (e.g., Great Danes).

Harness: A leather strap shaped around the shoulders and chest, with a ring at its top over the withers.

Haunch bones: The anterio-dorsal portion of the pelvic girdle (crest of the ilium); the "hip" bones.

Haw: A third eyelid or nictitating membrane on the medial (inside) corner of the eye.

Head: The anterior portion of the dog, including the muzzle and the cranium.

Head planes: Viewed in profile, the contours of the dorsal (top) portion of the skull from occiput to stop, and of the foreface from stop to tip of nose. Usually spoken of in relation to one another, i.e., parallel, diverging, converging.

Heat: Seasonal period of the female. Estrus.

Heel: See Hock; also a command to the dog to keep close beside its handler.

Height: Vertical measurement from the withers to the ground; referred to usually as shoulder height. See Withers.

Hie on: A command to urge the dog on; used in hunting or in field trials.

High standing: Tall and upstanding, with plenty of leg.

Hindquarters: Rear assembly of dog (pelvis, thighs, hocks and paws).

Hock: The tarsus or collection of bones of the hind leg forming the joint between the second thigh and the metatarsus; the dog's true heel.

Hocks well let down: Hock joints close to the ground.

Hocking out: Spread hocks.

Holt: The lair of the fox or other animal in tree roots, banks, drains or similar hideouts. Lodge.

Honorable scars: Scars from injuries suffered as a result of work.

Hound: A dog commonly used for hunting by scent or sight.

Hound–marked: A coloration composed of white, tan, and black. The ground color, usually white, may be marked with tan and/or black patches on the head, back, legs, and tail. The extent and the exact location of such markings, however, differ in breeds and individuals.

Hucklebones: The top of the hipbones.

Humerus: The bone of the arm (i.e., the "upper" arm).

Inbreeding: The mating of closely related dogs of the same breed.

Incisors: The six upper and six lower front teeth between the canines. Their point of contact forms the "bite."

Interbreeding: The breeding together of dogs of different breeds.

Iris: The colored membrane surrounding the pupil of the eye.

Isabella: Fawn or light bay color (e.g., Dobermans).

Jabot: The "apron" of the Schipperke, the part situated between the front legs.

Jowls: Flesh of lips and jaws.

Judge: Official approved by the AKC to judge dogs in conformation, obedience, and/or field trials.

Keel: The rounded outline of the lower chest, between the prosternum the posterior portion and of the sternum (breastbone).

Kennel: Building or enclosure where dogs are kept.

Kink tail: A deformity of caudal vertebrae producing a bent tail.

Kiss marks: Tan spots on the cheeks and over the eyes.

Kneecap: The stifle, with the bone known as the patella.

Knee: *See* Stifle.

Knee joint: Stifle joint.

Knuckling over: Faulty structure of carpus (wrist) joint allowing it to flex forward under the weight of the standing dog.

Landseer: The black and white Newfoundland dog, so-called from the name of the famous painter who used such dogs as models.

Lateral: Pertaining to the side.

Layback: The angle of the shoulder blade as compared with the vertical plane viewed from the side (laterally).

Layon: The angle of the shoulder blade as compared with the vertical plane viewed from the front (medially).

Lead: A strap, cord, or chain attached to the collar or harness for the purpose of restraining or leading the dog. Leash.

Leather: The flap of the ear; the outer ear supported by cartilage and surrounding tissue.

Level bite: When the front teeth (incisors) of the upper and lower jaws meet exactly edge to edge. Pincer bite.

Level gait: Dog moves without rise or fall of withers.

License: Formal permission granted by AKC to a non-member club to hold a dog show, obedience trial, or field trial.

Line breeding: The mating of related dogs of the same breed, within the line or family, to a common ancestor, as, for example, a dog to his granddam or a bitch to her grandsire.

Lion color: Tawny (e.g., Ibizan Hound).

Lippy: Pendulous lips or lips that do not fit tightly.

Litter: The puppy or puppies of one whelping.

Neck well set-on: Good neckline, merging gradually with withers, forming a pleasing transition into topline.

Liver: A color; i.e., deep, reddish brown, produced by recessive (bb) alleles of the B (black) locus.

Loaded shoulders: Excessive development of the muscles associated with the shoulder blades (scapulae).

Loin: The region of the body associated with the lumbar portion of the vertebrae column (i.e., posterior to the ribs and anterior to the pelvic girdle).

Loose slung: Construction in which the attachment of the muscles at the shoulders is looser than desirable.

Lower thigh: *See* Second thigh.

Lumbar vertebrae: The seven vertebrae of the loin region, articulating anteriorly with the thoracic vertebrae and posteriorly with the sacrum.

Lumbering: An awkward gait.

Lurcher: A crossbred hound.

Luxation: Dislocation of an anatomical structure, i.e., lens or patella.

Lymer: A hound of ancient times led by a liam.

Mad dog: A rabid dog.

Making a wheel: Term given the circling of the tail over the back that is characteristic of the Great Pyrenees when alerted.

Mandible: The bone of the lower jaw.

Mane: Long and profuse hair on top and sides of the neck.

Mantle: Dark-shaded portion of the coat on shoulders, back, and sides (e.g., St. Bernard).

Manubrium: The first sternabra of the chest. Prosternum.

Marcel effect: Regular continuous waves. Named for a French hairdresser.

(Specified in American Water Spaniel standard.)

Mask: Dark shading on the foreface (e.g., Mastiff, Boxer, Pekingese).

Match show: Usually an informal dog show at which no championship points are awarded.

Mate: To breed a dog and bitch.

Medial: Toward the mid-line of the dog.

Median line: *See* Furrow.

Merle: A color pattern involving a dominant gene (the M or Merling series) and characterized by dark blotches against a lighter background of the same pigment; e.g., blue merle in Collies and red "dapple" in Dachshunds.

Metatarsus: Rear pastern.

Milk teeth: First teeth.

Miscellaneous Class: A competitive class at dog shows for dogs of certain specified breeds for which no regular dog show classification is provided.

Mismarks: Self colors with any area of white on back between withers and tail, on sides between elbows and back of hindquarters, or on ears. Black with white markings and no tan present (e.g., Pembroke Welsh Corgi).

Molars: The posterior teeth of the dental arcade, with two on each side in the upper jaw and three on each side in the lower jaw in an adult with correct dentition (42 teeth).

Molera: Incomplete, imperfect, or abnormal ossification of the skull.

Mongrel: A dog whose parents are of two different breeds.

Monorchid: A unilateral cryptorchid. *See* Cryptorchid.

Mottled: Pattern of dark roundish blotches superimposed on a lighter background, e.g., the blue-mottled variety of the Australian Cattle Dog.

Moving close: When the hocks turn in and pasterns drop straight to the ground and move parallel to one another, the dog is "moving close" in the rear. Action places severe strain on ligaments and muscles.

Moving straight: Term descriptive of balanced gaiting in which angle of inclination begins at the shoulder, or hip joint, and limbs remain relatively straight from these points to the pads of the feet, even as the legs flex or extend in reaching or thrusting.

Multum in parvo: Latin phrase meaning "much in little," quoted in the Pug standard.

Music: The baying of the hounds.

Mute: To run mute, to be silent on the trail; i.e., to trail without baying or barking.

Muzzle: The head in front of the eyes–nasal bone, nostrils, and jaws. Foreface. Also, a strap or wire cage attached to the foreface to prevent the dog from biting or from picking up food.

Muzzle band: White marking around the muzzle (e.g., Boston Terrier).

Neck well set-on: Good neckline, merging gradually with withers, forming a pleasing transition into topline.

Nick: A breeding that produces desirable puppies.

Non-slip retriever: The dog that walks at heel, marks the fall, and retrieves game on command; not expected to find or flush.

Nose: Organ of olfaction; also, the ability to detect by means of scent.

Obedience trial (licensed): An event held under AKC rules at which a "leg" toward an obedience degree can be earned.

Obedience Trial Champion (O.T.Ch.): A prefix used with the name of a dog that has been recorded an Obedience Trial Champion by the AKC as the result of having won the number of points and first place wins specified in the current Obedience Regulations.

Obliquely placed eyes: Eyes with outer corners higher than their inner ones. Requested in Alaskan Malamute and Bull Terrier standards.

Oblique shoulders: Shoulders well laid back.

Occiput: Dorsal, posterior point of the skull.

Occipital protuberance: A prominently raised occiput characteristic of some sporting and hound breeds.

Open bitch: A bitch that can be bred.

Open Class: A class at dog shows in which all dogs of a breed, champions and imported dogs included, may compete.

Orange belton: *See* Belton.

Organized competition: Competition governed by the rules of a club or society, such as the AKC, organized to promote the interests of purebred dogs.

Otter tail: Thick at the root, round, and tapering, with the hair parted or divided on the underside.

Out at elbows: Elbows turning out from the body as opposed to being held close.

Out at shoulders: With shoulder blades loosely attached to the body, leaving the shoulders jutting out in relief and increasing the breadth of the front.

Outcrossing: The mating of unrelated individuals of the same breed.

Oval chest: Chest deeper than wide.

Overhang: A heavy or pronounced brow (e.g., Pekingese).

Overreaching: Fault in the trot caused by more angulation and drive from behind than in front, so that the rear feet are forced to step to one side of the forefeet to avoid interfering or clipping.

Overshot: The incisors of the upper jaw projecting beyond the incisors of the lower jaw, thus resulting in a space between the respective inner and outer surfaces.

Pace: A lateral gait which tends to promote a rolling motion of the body. The left foreleg and left hind leg advance in unison, then the right foreleg and right hind leg.

Pack: Several hounds kept together in one kennel. Mixed pack is composed of dogs and bitches.

Padding: A compensating action to offset constant concussion when a straight front is subjected to overdrive from the rear; the front feet flip upward in a split-second delaying action to coordinate stride of forelegs with longer stride from behind.

Paddling: A gaiting fault, so named for its similarity to the swing and dip of a canoeist's paddle. Pinching in at the elbows and shoulder joints causes the front legs to swing forward on a stiff outward arc. Also referred to as "tied at the elbows."

Pads: Tough, shock-absorbing projections on the underside of the feet. Soles.

Paper foot: A flat foot with thin pads.

Parent club: National club for the breed. Listing with name and address of secretary can be obtained from American Kennel Club, 51 Madison Avenue, New York, NY 10010.

Parti-color: Variegated in patches of two or more colors.

Pastern: Commonly recognized as the region of the foreleg between the carpus or wrist and the digits, i.e., the metacarpus.

Peak: See Occiput.

Pedigree: The written record of a dog's genealogy of three generations or more.

Pelvis: Hip bones, each consisting of three fused bones: an anterior ilium, a ventral pubis, and a posterior ischium, combined with sacrum forming the pelvic girdle.

Penciling: Black lines dividing the tan on the toes (e.g., Manchester Terriers).

Peppering: The admixture of white and black hairs, which in association with some entirely black and some entirely white hairs gives the "pepper and salt" appearance of some Schnauzer breeds.

Pied: Comparatively large patches of two or more colors. Piebald, parti-colored.

Pigeon-breast: A narrow chest with a protruding breastbone.

Pigeon-toed: Toes pointing in toward the mid-line.

Pig eyes: Eyes set too close. Specified as a fault in Miniature Pinscher standard.

Pig jaw: See Overshot.

Pile: Dense undercoat of soft hair.

Pincer bite: See Level bite.

Planes: See Head planes.

Plume: Either a long fringe of hair on the tail covering part of the tail only or involving the entire tail, or carried "plumed" over the back.

Poach: When hunting, to trespass on private property.

Point: The immovable stance of the hunting dog taken to indicate the presence and position of game.

Points: Color on face, ears, legs, and tail when correlated–usually white, black or tan. Alternatively, credits toward championship status.

Poke: To carry the neck stretched forward in an abnormally low, ungainly position, usually when moving.

Police dog: Any dog trained for police work.

Pompon: A rounded tuft of hair left on the end of the tail when the coat is clipped (e.g., Poodle).

Posterior: The portion of the dog carried hindmost (or toward the rear) during normal locomotion.

Pounding: Gaiting fault resultant of dog's stride being shorter in front than in the rear; forefeet strike the ground hard before the rear stride is expended.

Premium list: An advance-notice brochure sent to prospective exhibitors and containing details regarding a forthcoming show.

Prick ear: Carried erect and usually pointed at the tip.

Professional handler: A person who shows dogs for a fee.

Pump handle: Long tail, carried high.

Put down: To prepare a dog for the show ring; also used to denote a dog unplaced in competition.

Puppy: A dog under 12 months of age.

Purebred: A dog whose sire and dam belong to the same breed, and are themselves of unmixed descent since recognition of the breed.

Quality: Refinement, fineness, a degree of excellence.

Racy: Tall, of comparatively slight build.

Radius: One of the two bones of the forearm.

Ragged: Muscles appear ragged rather than smooth (e.g., English Foxhound).

Rangy: Tall, long in body, high on leg, often lightly framed.

Rat tail: The root thick and covered with soft curls; at the tip devoid of hair, or having the appearance of being clipped (e.g., Irish Water Spaniel).

Reach of front: Length of forward stride taken by forelegs.

Rear pastern: The metatarsus, the region of the hindquarters between the hock(tarsus) and the foot (digits).

Register: To record with the AKC a dog's breeding particulars.

Retrieve: A hunting term. The act of bringing back shot game to the handler.

Ribbed up: Long ribs that angle back from the spinal column. A reference to a long rib cage.

Rib cage: The collection of paired ribs, cartilage, sternum, and associated tissue that define the thoracic region. Among the ribs are pairs 1-9 wherein the cartilage articulates directly with the sternum ("true ribs"), 10-12 wherein the cartilage fuses with anterior cartilage ("false-ribs"), and 13 is not attached ventrally ("floating ribs").

Ringer: A substitute for; a dog closely resembling another dog.

Ring tail: Carried up and around almost in a circle.

Roach back: A convex curvature of the back involving thoracic and lumbar regions.

Roan: A fine mixture of colored hairs with white hairs; blue roan, orange roan, lemon roan, etc. (e.g., English Cocker Spaniel).

Rocking horse: Both front and rear legs extended out from body as in old-fashioned rocking horse.

Rolling gait: Swaying, ambling action of the hindquarters when moving.

Roman nose: A nose whose bridge is so comparatively high as to form a slightly convex line from forehead to nose tip. Ram's nose.

Rose ear: A small drop ear which folds over and back so as to reveal the burr.

Rounding: Cutting or trimming the ends of the ear leather (e.g., English Foxhounds).

Rudder: The tail or stern.

Ruff: Thick, longer hair growth around the neck.

Saber tail: Carried in a semi-circle.

Sable: A coat color produced by black-tipped hairs upon a background of silver, gold, grey, fawn, or brown, and determined by the Agouti or A series of multiple alleles.

Sacrum: The region of the vertebral column that consists of three fused vertebrae which articulate with the pelvic girdle.

Saddle: A black marking over the back, like a saddle.

Saddle back: Overlong back, with a dip behind the withers.

Scent: The odor left by an animal on the trail (groundscent), or wafted through the air (airborne scent).

Scissors bite: A bite in which the outer side (anterior portion) of the lower incisors touches the inner side (posterior portion) of the upper incisors.

Screw tail: A naturally short tail twisted in more or less spiral formation.

Second thigh: That part of the hindquarter from the stifle to the hock, corresponding to the human shin and calf. Lower thigh, including the tibia and fibula.

Self color: One color or whole color except for lighter shadings.

Seeing Eye dog: A dog trained as a guide for the blind.

Semi-prick ears: Ears carried erect with just the tips leaning forward.

Septum: The line extending vertically between the nostrils.

Set up: Posed so as to make the most of the dog's appearance for the show ring.

Shelly: A shallow, narrow body, lacking the correct amount of bone.

Short back: *See* Close coupled.

Sickle hocked: Inability to straighten the hock joint on the back reach of the hind leg.

Sickle tail: Carried out and up in a semicircle.

Sight hound: See Gazehound.

Single tracking: All footprints falling on a single line of travel. When a dog breaks into a trot, his body is supported by only two legs at a time, which move as alternating diagonal pairs. To achieve balance, his legs angle inward toward a center line beneath his body, and the greater the speed, the closer they come to tracking on a single line.

Sire: The male parent.

Skeleton: Descriptively divided into axial (skull, vertebrae column, chest) and appendicular (forequarters, hindquarters) portions.

Skully: Thick and coarse through skull.

Slab sided: Flat ribs with too little spring from spinal column.

Sled dogs: Dogs worked usually in teams to draw sleds.

Slew feet: Feet turned out.

Sloping shoulder: The shoulder blade set obliquely or "laid back."

Smooth coat: Short hair, close-lying.

Snatching hocks: A gaiting fault indicated by a quick outward snatching of the hock as it passes the supporting leg and twists the rear pastern far in beneath the body. The action causes noticeable rocking in the rear quarters.

Snipy: A pointed, weak muzzle, lacking breadth and depth.

Snow nose: Nose normally solid black, but acquires pink streak in winter.(Specified as acceptable in Siberian Husky standard.)

Soundness: The state of mental and physical health when all organs and faculties are complete and functioning normally, each in its rightful relation to the other.

Spay: To perform a surgical operation on the bitch's ovaries to prevent conception.

Speak: To bark.

Spectacles: Shadings or dark markings over or around the eyes or from eyes to ears.

Spike tail: Straight short tail that tapers rapidly along its length.

Splashed: Irregularly patched, color on white or white on color.

Splay foot: A flat foot with toes spreading. Open foot, open-toed.

Spread: Width between the forelegs when accentuated (e.g., Bulldog).

Spread hocks: Hocks pointing outward.

Spring: See Flush.

Spring of ribs: Curvature of ribs for heart and lung capacity.

Square body: A dog whose measurements from withers to the ground equals that from forechest to the buttocks.

Squirrel tail: Carried up and curving more or less forward.

Stacking: See Set up.

Stake: Designation of a class, used in field trial competition.

Stance: Manner of standing.

Standard: A description of the ideal dog of each recognized breed, to serve as a word pattern by which dogs are judged at shows.

Standoff coat: A long or heavy coat that stands off from the body.

Staring coat: The hair dry, harsh, and sometimes curling at the tips.

Station: Comparative height from the ground, as high-stationed, low-stationed.

Steep: Used to denote incorrect angles of articulation. For example, a steep front describes a more upright shoulder placement than is preferred.

Stern: Tail.

Sternum: Breastbone.

Stifle: The joint of the hind leg between the thigh and the second thigh. The dog's knee.

Stilted: The choppy, up-and-down gait of the straight-hocked dog (e.g., Chow Chow).

Stop: The step up from muzzle to back skull; indentation between the eyes where the nasal bones and cranium meet.

Straight-hocked: Lacking appreciable angulation at the hock joints.

Straight in pastern: Little or no bend at the wrist.

Straight shoulders: The shoulder blades rather straight up and down, as opposed to sloping or "well laid back."

Stud book: A record of the breeding particulars of dogs of recognized breeds.

Stud dog: A male dog used for breeding purposes.

Substance: Bone.

Superciliary arches: The ridge, projection, or prominence of the frontal bones of the skull over the eyes; the brow; supraorbital ridges.

Suspension trot: See Flying trot.

Swayback: Concave curvature of the vertebrae column between the withers and the hipbones.

Symmetry: Pleasing balance between all parts of the dog.

Tail set: How the base of the tail sets on the rump.

T.D. (Tracking Dog): A suffix used with the name of a dog that has been recorded a Tracking Dog as a result of having passed an AKC-licensed or member tracking test. The title may be combined with the U.D. title and shown as U.D.T.

T.D.X. (Tracking Dog Excellent): A suffix used with the name of a dog that has been recorded a Tracking Dog Excellent as a result of having passed an AKC-licensed or member tracking dog excellent test. The title may be combined with the U.D.T. title and shown as U.D.T.X.

Team: Usually four dogs exhibited by one handler.

Terrier: A group of dogs used originally for hunting vermin.

Terrier front: Straight front, as found on Fox Terriers.

Testicles: The male gonad which produces spermatozoa. AKC regulations specify that a male which does not have two normal testicles normally located in the scrotum may not compete at any show and will be disqualified, except that a castrated male may be entered in obedience trials, tracking tests, field trials (except Beagles) and as Stud Dog in a Stud Dog class.

Thigh: The hindquarter from hip to stifle.

Thoracic vertebrae: The thirteen vertebrae of the chest with which thirteen pairs of ribs articulate.

Throatiness: An excess of loose skin under the throat.

Thumb marks: Black spots on the region of the pastern.

Tibia: One of the two bones of the leg (i.e., the "lower" thigh, second thigh, or lower leg).

Ticked: Small, isolated areas of black or colored hairs on a white ground. Tied at the elbows: *See* Paddling.

Tongue: The barking or baying of hounds on the trail, as to give tongue, to open or speak.

Topknot: A tuft of longer hair on top of the head.

Topline: The dog's outline from just behind the withers to the tail set.

Toy dog: One of a group of dogs characterized by very small size.

Trace: A dark stripe down the back of the Pug.

Trail: To hunt by following ground scent.

Triangular eye: The eye set in surrounding tissue of triangular shape; three-cornered eye.

Tri-color: Three-color; white, black, and tan.

Trim: To groom the coat by plucking or clipping.

Triple Champion: A dog that has won bench show, field trial and obedience trial championships.

Trot: A rhythmic two-beat diagonal gait in which the feet at diagonally opposite ends of the body strike the ground together; i.e., right hind with left front and left hind with right front.

Trousers: Longish hair at the back of both upper and lower thighs of some breeds.

Trumpet: The slight depression or hollow on either side of the skull just behind the orbit or eye socket, the region comparable with the temple in man.

Truncated: Cut off. (Old English standard calls for jaw that is square and truncated.)

Tuck-up: Characterized by markedly shallower body depth at the loin. Small-waisted.

Tulip ear: An ear carried erect with edges curving forward and in.

Turn-up: An uptilted foreface.

Twisting hocks: A gaiting fault in which the hock joints twist both ways as they flex or bear weight. Also called "rubber hocks."

Type: The characteristic qualities dis-

441

tinguishing a breed; the embodiment of a standard's essentials.

Ulna: One of the two bones of the forearm.

U.D. (Utility Dog): A suffix used with the name of a dog that has been recorded a Utility Dog by AKC as a result of having won certain minimum scores in Utility Classes at a specified number of AKC-licensed or member obedience trials. The title may be combined with T.D. or T.D.X. title and shown as U.D.T. or U.D.T.X.

U.D.X. (Utility Dog Excellent): A suffix used with the name of a dog that has been recorded a Utility Dog Excellent by AKC as a result of having qualified in Open B and Utility B simultaneous, but not consecutively, in ten shows after being awarded its UD title.

Underline: The combined contours of the brisket and the abdominal floor.

Undershot: The front teeth (incisors) of the lower jaw overlapping or projecting beyond the front teeth of the upper jaw when the mouth is closed.

Unsound: A dog incapable of performing the functions for which it was bred.

Unilateral cryptorchid: See Cryptorchid.

Upper arm: The humerus or bone of the foreleg, between the shoulder blade and the forearm and associated tissues.

Varminty: A keen, very bright or piercing expression.

Veil: The portion of the dog's forelock hanging straight down over the eyes, or partially covering them.

Vent: The anal opening.

Vertebral column: The bones of the central axis of the dog posterior to the skull including cervical, thoracic, lumbar, sacral, and caudal vertebrae.

Walk: Gaiting pattern in which three legs are in support of the body at all times, each foot lifting from the ground one at a time in regular sequence.

Walleye: An eye with a whitish iris; a blue eye, fisheye, pearl eye.

Webbed: Connected by a membrane. Webbed feet are important for water-retrieving breeds.

Weedy: An insufficient amount of bone; light-boned.

Well let down: Having short hocks; refers to short metatarsals.

Wet neck: Loose or superfluous skin; with dewlap.

Wheaten: Pale yellow or fawn color.

Wheel back: A marked arch of the thoracic and lumbar vertebrae. Roached.

Whip tail: Carried out stiffly straight, and pointed.

Whiskers: Vibrissae or sensory organs (hairs) on the sides of the muzzle.

Whitelies: Body color white with red or dark markings (e.g., Pembroke Welsh Corgi).

Wind: To catch the scent of game.

Winging: A gaiting fault where one or both front feet twist outward as the limbs swing forward.

Winners: An award given at dog shows to the best dog (Winners Dog) and best bitch (Winners Bitch) competing in regular classes.

Wirehair: A coat of hard, crisp, wiry texture.

Withers: The region defined by the dorsal portions of the spinous processes of the first two thoracic vertebrae and flanked by the dorsal (uppermost) portions of the scapulae.

Wrinkle: Loose, folding skin on forehead and foreface.

Wry mouth: Asymmetrical alignment of upper and lower jaws; cross bite.

Xiphoid process: Cartilage process of the sternum.

Zygomatic arch: A bony ridge extending posteriorly (and laterally) from beneath the eye orbit (i.e., anatomically consists of two processes: zygomatic process of the maxilla and the maxillary process of the zygomatic bone).

INDEX

Page numbers in **boldface** *refer to illustrations.*
For the reader's convenience, all titles have been omitted from dogs' names.